De BRAHM'S REPORT

TRICENTENNIAL EDITION, NUMBER 3

This volume is part of a series of

Tricentennial Editions published by the

University of South Carolina Press,

Columbia, South Carolina,

on behalf of the South Carolina Tricentennial

Commission, to commemorate the founding of

South Carolina in 1670

De BRAHM'S REPORT
OF THE GENERAL SURVEY
IN THE SOUTHERN
DISTRICT OF
NORTH AMERICA

Edited and with an Introduction by
Louis De Vorsey, Jr.

To my wife, ROSALYN

... I have endeavored to trace all avenues possible,
which lead to the Wonders of Providence, wrote by the
Divine Finger with lively characters, and intelligible
Hieroglyphics in the great book of nature....

William Gerard De Brahm

Contents

Plates

Preface

In the preparation of this volume, it has been my intent to make William Gerard De Brahm's Report on the eighteenth-century Southeast both available and intelligible to the reader of the present day. To this end, an extended biographical essay is included as an introduction. Such an essay seems absolutely necessary in De Brahm's case. As the reader will see, he was a colorful but immensely enigmatic figure who frequently aroused strong reactions on the part of his contemporaries. Often these reactions were of a negative character and have strongly colored later scholarly interpretations of his abilities and contributions. Hopefully, this introduction will provide sufficient factual information to allow the reader personally to evaluate De Brahm's ambitious "Report of the General Survey in the Southern District of North America" and draw his own conclusions as to its author's ability and contribution to geographical knowledge. This is what De Brahm would have urged, had he been afforded an opportunity to do so.

In editing De Brahm's elegant manuscript for printing, I have endeavored to retain as much of the original as possible. Superior letters have been lowered to the line of the text, and omitted letters have been supplied when in the middle of the word and when clear as to meaning. The tilde (~) has been replaced by letters represented and diacritical marks have been rendered as appropriate letters. Also, De Brahm's degree, minute, and second symbols in geographic locations have been moved from their original position, directly above the numerals, to the accepted present-day position, which is just to the right-hand side. In abbreviations, periods have been substituted for colons, which were frequently employed. For example, De Brahm's S:E as the abbreviation for southeast has been changed to S. E., to conform with modern practice. In a very few instances obvious errors made by the scribe, who executed the manuscript under De Brahm's supervision, have been silently corrected. In most instances, however, capitalization, punctuation, and spelling have been retained as they appear in the original. Where misunderstanding seemed possible I have attempted to interpolate the correct spelling enclosed in square brackets [ ], or in informational footnotes.

What appears in this volume is what De Brahm prepared and presented to George III. The only material omitted consists of several pages of mathematical computations which seemed unnecessary for this edition. The location and extent of these computations is clearly indicated in the body of the Report as here printed. Finally, every care has been taken to collate this printed text with the original for accuracy. The reader may assume that what he reads here are De Brahm's words as his scribe recorded them two centuries ago.

Acknowledgments

I wish to acknowledge the considerable support which I have received from the University of Georgia Office of General Research and Department of Geography. This support made it possible for me to spend seven uninterrupted months working in British archives and another three months working in domestic archives. Without these opportunities to be completely free of teaching duties and to pursue my research uninterruptedly, this volume could not have been completed.

To my wife go special thanks for typing from De Brahm's manuscript pages and producing a legible and coherent typescript. More than an ordinary amount of effort and sacrifice was involved in her months of labor while we were in England. Thanks go, too, to Olive Pettit of Hersham, who helped with the typing when the pressure was the greatest.

Charles Lee, of the South Carolina Department of Archives and History, is deserving of special appreciation since it was he who first suggested that my interest in De Brahm's Report should be pursued in the form of a Tricentennial Edition. His support, as well as that of William L. McDowell and the assistant archivists at Columbia, has been of great value throughout my research and writing effort.

In Georgia, Mrs. Pat Bryant and her assistant, Mr. Marion Hemperley, at the Surveyor General's Department have been unstinting in their assistance and cooperation. So too, have John Bonner and the other librarians at the University of Georgia libraries in Athens. Mrs. Lilla Hawes of the Georgia Historical Society has also made a valuable contribution.

The trustees of the British Museum are due special thanks for making available the high-quality photographs of De Brahm's original maps and sketches which appear in this volume as Plates 1–29. Thanks are also extended to the many dedicated British archivists and librarians who assisted so willingly while I worked in their hospitable country. Among these, the staffs of the Public Record Office, British Museum, and Staffordshire County Record Office were particularly indulgent.

Many other individual and institutional contributions are acknowledged in notes which accompany the text of this volume.

To you all, named and anonymous, my sincerest thanks are extended.

De BRAHM'S REPORT

Introduction

The middle decades of the eighteenth century saw the world's three greatest powers—Britain, France, and Spain—joined in a contest for control of global empires. A series of military victories in the French and Indian War, as the American phase of the wider Seven Years' War was known, insured British control over the eastern half of the North American continent. This control was formalized and ratified by the terms of the "Definitive Treaty Concluded at Paris 10 February 1763," more familiarly known as the Peace of Paris. Spain, which had belatedly and ill-advisedly joined France in the later phases of the war, lost as a result the Spanish province of Florida, including most of what is today the state of Florida. In the Southeast only New Orleans, with a few other settlements along the eastern bank of the Mississippi south of the Iberville River, was denied to the British. This area was retained by the French, who secretly ceded it, with Louisiana, to Spain.

Thus Britain had title to the whole of the southeastern quarter of the continent from the Atlantic and Gulf coasts to the Mississippi River except for the strategic fragment enclosed by the Iberville River, lakes Maurepas and Pontchartrain, and the lower Mississippi River. To the north of the straggling New England colonies land was also gained for the British Crown. There, Nova Scotia, or as the French called it Acadia, and French Canada were added to the expanded British-American empire of 1763.

These vast domains had been only vaguely charted and superficially exploited by their original French and Spanish overlords. To the British they were *terrae incognitae* indeed. The official map, prepared to illustrate the new division of North America, serves to exemplify the geographical ignorance which rapidly became a major concern to George III and his chief ministers.[1] On this map the southern third of the Florida peninsula is erroneously depicted as a fragmented archipelago of large and small islands separated by elongated channels and large bays. A spur of mountains extends south from the Appalachian system to form a spine to the peninsula which is broken by a fanciful Saint Johns River flowing both to the north, in its normal course, and to the south to empty into the sea

3

via at least two nonexistent southern distributaries. Any British map showing
Florida in the 1760s and 1770s will reveal similarly gross distortions of Florida's
lineaments and geographic patterns. Just how, where, and why such geographic
misconceptions arose need not be a concern here, although they would provide
an interesting topic for study in their own right. One thing is certain, however:
the new British masters of the Spanish and French cessions in the New World
quickly felt the need for more accurate maps and geographic information as
they began to grapple with the problems of administering and developing their
vast new domain.

In a letter addressed to the Board of Trade on May 5, 1763, His Majesty's
principal secretary of state for the Southern Department, the earl of Egremont,
asked, "Can your Lordships furnish any Lights with regard to the Climate or
soil of the inland parts of Florida which tho hitherto neglected and useless are
said to be extremely fertile? Is there any reason to believe, that the mouth of the
Catahocke River is or might be easily made commodious for shipping? What
particular advantages might arise from such a harbour, or from that of Pensacola
or Mobile, or from any other on that part of the coast of North America, lately
ceded to His Majesty, which bounds the Gulph of Mexico to the North?"[2] The
Board of Trade found these, and a host of other queries concerning the new
American territories to the south as well as to the north, impossible to answer
with the information then available.

Such information became even more critically necessary as the British Crown
adopted its policy of limiting the continued westward expansion of the American
seaboard colonies. Colonists were urged to "emigrate to Nova Scotia or to the
provinces on the southern frontier where they would be useful to their mother
country instead of planting themselves in the heart of America out of the reach
of governments and where from the great difficulty of procuring European
commodities they would be compelled to commence manufactures to the infinite prejudice of Britain."[3] In a lengthy report dealing with its recommendations
for the organization and administration of the territories received by the terms
of the Peace of Paris, the Board of Trade observed that great advantage would
accrue to Britain through "the secure settling of the whole coast of North America . . . from the mouth of the Mississippi to the boundaries of the Hudsons Bay
settlements . . . by the industry of emigrants from Europe or from the overflowing of your Majesty's ancient colonies."[4]

In early 1763 and the months that followed, the British government began to
formulate a policy for the settlement of eastern North America which was to have
the most profound influence through the decade and a half which culminated
in the American Revolution. In its simplest outline, this policy involved the creation of a boundary line which would limit the growth of the seaboard colonies

toward the interior. This boundary was deemed essential because of Indian militancy and resentment concerning the accelerating European encroachment on tribal lands. Pressures on this boundary were to be lessened by the provision of stable colonial governments, ready economic opportunities, and easily available lands in the areas of the present-day Maritime Provinces of Canada to the north, and the colonies of Georgia, East Florida, and West Florida to the south. It was a policy which seemed to satisfy the needs and interests of many important groups. The Indians would once more be assured of the friendly intentions of the British, and the prodigious expense of fortifying and garrisoning the extended Indian frontier would be avoided or at least greatly lessened. The Indian trade would continue to flourish since hunting grounds could continue to provide their hirsute harvests to be profitably exchanged for goods of British manufacture. The growing colonial population as well as the European immigrants seeking a new life in the New World would, it was thought, find ample opportunities in Nova Scotia, Georgia, or the two Floridas. Here they would be within easy reach of British merchant and naval ships and perhaps less likely to "imbibe notions of independency of their Mother Kingdom" in the way that their fellows in the interiors of the older central colonies had.[5] Further, it was felt that the surest way of holding the expanded empire against present or future European threats was to populate it with a loyal landowning citizenry.

In attempting to cope with the myriad questions which arose as these grand designs were being worked out in London, the Board of Trade frequently felt a pressing need for more and better geographic information regarding the newly won areas of North America. In a representation to the king composed early in 1764 the board declared, "We find ourselves under the greatest difficulties arising from the want of exact surveys of these countries in America many parts of which have never been surveyed at all, and others so imperfectly that the Charts and Maps thereof are not to be depended upon, and in this situation we are reduced to the necessity of making Representations to Your Majesty, founded upon little or no Information, or of delaying the important Service of settling these Parts of Your Majesty's Dominions."[6] Such a condition was clearly intolerable. The board went on to recommend "in the strongest manner that no time should be lost in obtaining accurate Surveys of all Your Majesty's North American Dominions but more especially of such parts as from their natural advantages require our immediate attention."[7] Not surprisingly, these last-mentioned "parts" were to be eastern Canada and the province of East Florida.

To carry out these much-needed surveys the board suggested that "the continent of North America should be divided into a Northern and a Southern District with a Surveyor General of Lands to be appointed for each to act under such instructions as he shall receive from time to time from this Board." Captain

Samuel Holland, a well-recognized military surveyor and cartographer, "who has great knowledge of the northern parts of America," was suggested to fill the post of surveyor general for the Northern District.[8]

Holland had already won considerable praise for "the accurate map he has made of the settled parts of Your Majesty's Colony of Quebeck" and probably came to the Board of Trade's attention through a memorial he addressed to them in December 1763. In this memorial Holland proposed the creation of a northern surveyor generalship which he should be appointed to fill,[9] making several specific recommendations regarding the conduct of the survey which were later incorporated into the official program.[10] In fact, Holland's estimate of the costs of a general survey and a copy of his memorial to the Board of Trade concerning its conduct were annexed to the board's representation to the king. It is significant to note that Samuel Holland, a skillful and accomplished surveyor-cartographer with an abundance of experience in the American theater, played such a crucial role in the establishment of the office of the surveyor generals in colonial America. What he suggested was a thoroughgoing geographical reconnaissance illuminated with medium- and large-scale maps based on the best surveying techniques then available.[11] Contemporaries and later generations alike are much indebted to this extraordinary individual.

Royal assent to the Board of Trade's proposal was delivered on February 10, 1764,[12] the king ordering the Treasury and Admiralty to act in executing the recommendations of Holland and the Board of Trade regarding the establishment of the general survey. Holland was appointed surveyor general for the Northern Department and lost no time in recruiting assistants and obtaining the necessary equipage.[13] The Board of Trade's next task was to appoint a surveyor general for the Southern Department.

To fill this office they selected another accomplished surveyor-cartographer with a military background and considerable firsthand experience in the region concerned. He was William De Brahm, then serving with Henry Yonge as one of the two surveyor generals for the colony of Georgia. In June 1764, De Brahm's appointment as surveyor general in Georgia was terminated and he was appointed surveyor general of the new colony of East Florida and surveyor general for the newly created Southern Department.[14]

That De Brahm diligently pursued his duties as surveyor general of the Southern District is amply proved by his amazingly comprehensive manuscript "Report of the General Survey in the Southern District of North America," which is presented here in a published form for the first time. Before turning to De Brahm's Report, however, it is necessary to consider the life and qualifications of its author. No biographer has yet devoted his attention to this colorful figure of the eighteenth-century American scene, and the notices which appear in biographical dictionaries and other standard reference works are usually fragmentary and often factually incorrect.[15] To remedy this lack of biographical information the following sketch gleaned from official reports, letters, journals, newspapers, and other eighteenth-century sources is provided.

EARLY LIFE IN GERMANY, 1717–51

Although several authorities have identified De Brahm as having been a citizen of Holland, it is clear that he was a native of Germany.[16] There is no documentary support for fixing his birthplace in the Low Countries; rather, all the evidence available points to southern Germany.[17] De Brahm, born in 1717 and left fatherless at the age of six, later described his father as "an admirer of Natural philosophy," who was devoted to alchemy.[18] Though alchemy was then a more popular avocation than is now the case, it would appear that the elder De Brahm found it a less-than-profitable pastime since his son went on to report that he was "unfortunately too hasty and credulous loosing all his time with Metallurgians."[19] Although he concluded by observing that his unfortunate father had died without ever experiencing success in his efforts to turn base metal into gold, the younger De Brahm maintained an active interest in other branches of alchemy throughout his own long life. This engrossment was mentioned many times by De Brahm in his correspondence and other writings. Plowden C. J. Weston, the nineteenth-century editor and publisher of De Brahm's description of South Carolina, underscored De Brahm's alchemical interests when he wrote, "I know nothing of De Brahm's life; but he lived within the memory of persons now alive, much addicted to alchemy, and wearing a long beard."[20]

Precisely where William Gerard De Brahm grew up and received his education is not revealed in any of the materials extant in British or American archives. Perhaps future research in Germany will cast valuable light on this phase in the life of one of eighteenth-century America's most colorful and prolific polymaths. That he received an excellent education in languages (both classical and modern), mathematics, history, geography, literature, biblical studies, and the burgeoning experimental sciences of the day is amply proved by his later performances in colonial America. Charles L. Mowat recognized these attainments when he described De Brahm as "a man whose versatility of genius went beyond even that of the typical eighteenth-century dilettante: a surveyor, engineer, botanist, astronomer, meteorologist, student of ocean currents, alchemist, sociologist, historian and mystical philosopher."[21]

Like the details of his birth and childhood, De Brahm's social status in Europe is not entirely clear. It would seem that his family moved in circles close to or within the petty nobility of the day. Certainly De Brahm's marriage to an heiress in 1745 and his army commission indicate that he personally moved within these circles. It may even be that he held some tenuous claim to a title in his own right. On his first map of Georgia, drawn in 1752, he signed himself "William Noble of Brahm Late Captain Ingenier unter his Imperial Majesty Charles the VII."[22] In his wife's obituary it was stated that he "bore the title in Germany . . . of Lord John William Gerard de Brahm" and that he relinquished it along with his commission in the army upon emigrating to America.[23]

While the source of his own claim to a title is a matter of speculation, it is clear that his first wife was an heiress to a considerable estate in Germany. She was Wilhelmina, daughter of the Baroness de Gera. Baroness de Gera, in turn, was the niece of the wealthy and landed Baron William Ernest de Elz. Baron de Elz's estate, as described in 1774, included "the signory of Holzheimb containing a Castle, church and village of 30 now perhaps more famelys (all subjects) also a castle and mill in Calmunz [*Kallmunz*] situated N. N. W. 16 Engl. miles from Ratisbone [*Regensburg*], thirty years ago [*1744*] these estates were valued for £4,000 sterling now probably worth twice that sum."[24]

Baron de Elz, like De Brahm's father, would seem to have devoted himself to alchemy. De Brahm observed that he too had "lost many years and great costs with suchlike men as misled my Father."[25] The old baron's house in Kallmunz must have been of considerable interest to the young De Brahm. Going there after his wedding, he found it "filled with a crowd of sophistical aparatus, many manuscripts of Empiriks, and . . . but few books of genuine philosophers."[26] It is possible that much of this equipment and material became De Brahm's own property and may have accompanied him to Georgia as a part of the fifty-two chests of baggage which were brought by him and his group of immigrants to Ebenezer in Georgia, six years later.

De Brahm probably had more than one brother. In 1774, he mentioned "my eldest brother Peter Henry, Captain in the Treverian service and resident in Coblence [*Koblenz*] upon the Rhein [*Rhine*]."[27] It is clear that he kept in reasonably close touch with this relative, mentioning in a letter from Saint Augustine, April 29, 1770, that he had written to his "Eldest Brother, Captain in the Elector of Triers Service," and was expecting one of his nephews "a good ingeneer" to join him in Saint Augustine the following November.[28]

Always a deeply religious man, De Brahm decided, at some point during the late 1740s, to renounce the Roman Catholic faith. In 1748 he also resigned his commission as "Captain Ingeneer to the Emperor Charles VII."[29] According to his own account he had served in "eleven campaigns in Germany, Turkey, and France under Prince Eugene, Counts Wallis and Seckendorf."[30] As a result of his change of faith he found himself "persecuted and banished" from the Bavarian

Palatinate, a condition similar to thousands of other German Protestants in war-torn central Europe.

Like many other displaced southern German Protestants, De Brahm was befriended by the Bishop of Augsburg, Samuel Urlsperger. Urlsperger, one of two foreign members of the predominantly English "Board of Trustees for Establishing the Colony of Georgia in America," was actively promoting the colony by encouraging the emigration thither by displaced groups of German Protestants. Through Urlsperger's good offices De Brahm found himself, with his wife, in charge of a large group of "Families and Single Persons, who out of their own accord are resolved in the name of God, to go to and settle at Ebenezer in Georgia."[31] The thirty-four-year-old De Brahm made a most favorable impression on Reverend Urlsperger, who gave him "an excellent character as to his morals and abilities." The Augsburg prelate paid his passage and freight to Ebenezer "in hopes that he will be of service to the Colony in general, and to the settlement in particular."[32]

Prior to his departure, during the spring of 1751, De Brahm received from his last military commander, Count Seckendorf, a signed testimonial endorsing his claim to proficiency in the technical skills of military engineering and fortification as well as his qualities of character and leadership. This was a document which would play an important part in the young German engineer's rapid rise to prominence in southeastern North America in the next few years.[33]

LIFE AND CAREER IN GEORGIA AND SOUTH CAROLINA, 1751–65

De Brahm led his party of 156 emigrants to Georgia during the summer of 1751. The abilities and qualities which had earned him the backing of Count Seckendorf and Bishop Urlsperger were quickly perceived and appreciated by others in places of authority in the colony. Benjamin Martyn, the secretary to the Georgia Trust, recommended De Brahm as "a man of Parts and Spirit" in a letter to John Martin Bolzius, dated August 24 of that year.[34] Martyn also observed that De Brahm had been a captain in the Bavarian service and was "a very good engineer," whom Martyn had no doubt would be of "great service and comfort" to Bolzius, the leader of Georgia's large German community.

In his reply, Reverend Bolzius reported "the happy arrival of an Embarkaton of Germans under the prudent conduct of Mr. von Brahm," as De Brahm was known at that time, indicating also that the newly arrived De Brahm had lost no time in employing his technical skills. "The President and Assistants have employed Mr. von Brahm and other experienced Men to search good land for these New-Comers, first at Ogeechee River, and afterwards at Newport River near

Darien and this day Mr. von Brahm went up to survey Savannah River and to view the much praysed land at Bryar's Creek for a settlement either to himself and Mr. Von Munch, or to other of our countrymen who will come over soon upon invitation, if good land can be found for them."[35]

De Brahm's exertions on the frontiers of Georgia did not go without notice in official circles. James Habersham, the trustees' secretary and later an acting royal governor of the province, expressed his pleasure at the good health and general condition of De Brahm's party of immigrants. He noted that "the Trustees, I believe are not mistaken in Mr. von Brahm's abilities: He has been at a great deal of Pains to view the country to fix on a settlement and has taken plans of all the Places he has visited, and I look upon him to be one of the most intelligent men I ever met with, and will I doubt not make a very useful colonist."[36]

De Brahm's skill as a surveyor and cartographer was certainly quickly recognized and appreciated by his contemporaries. In more recent years workers in historical cartography and geography have come to share this appreciation of his talents.[37] He was not content merely to survey a plot of land and draw a rough sketch of the survey as was the common practice of most land surveyors. He betrayed the essential quality of a geographer in his approach to surveying, being interested in the larger whole of which the individual land parcel surveys were only fragments. De Brahm's mind was ever searching for broad patterns in nature. While he traveled about and conducted these early land measurements he was observing regional differences in such things as landform patterns, flora and fauna, soils, climate, and land use in the Southeast. As early as March 24, 1752, he presented the trustees with a "map of that part of Georgia, which I have had an opportunity of Surveying since my arrival here; and which I flatter myself will speak in my behalf, and be more satisfactory and agreeable than anything I could say in a long and tedious letter."[38] Like a true geographer De Brahm appreciated the eloquence of maps as graphic documents. Though he had earlier, on December 19, 1751, received 500 acres from the trustees,[39] he included in his letter of presentation a request that they "confer any office or employment, that they in their great wisdom may think me sufficiently qualified for." To emphasize his need of a public appointment he concluded by stating that "the schemes which I proposed to myself in Germany for my future happiness in Georgia have proved entirely abortive which makes the present situation of my affairs Dark and Disagreeable, unless kindly relieved by the Honble Trustees."[40] Exactly what these "schemes" had been is not revealed. It might be that they concerned De Brahm's hopes regarding some German inheritance or other. It seems even more likely, however, that he was referring to a scheme in which he would have acted as an overseer for several absentee German landholders.[41]

Governor Glen and the Fortification of Charleston

De Brahm's reputation soon carried beyond Georgia to attract the attention of South Carolina's energetic royal governor, James Glen.[42] During the spring of 1752 Glen was deeply concerned with efforts aimed at improving his province's badly neglected defenses. These efforts were to lead Glen into one of his many constitutional struggles with the colony's assembly.[43] Unfortunately, De Brahm soon found himself inadvertently in its midst.

Briefly, the controversy arose as Glen began to take steps toward the badly needed reconstruction of South Carolina's defenses. His commission as governor vested him with "full Power and Authority," with the consent of his council, to build, fortify, and maintain all forts and fortifications which were necessary.[44] The assembly, on the other hand, had empowered the province's commission of fortifications to operate in this area of responsibility several years before. Glen, however, told the assembly on May 5, 1752, that the commission on fortifications was "contrary to the Prerogative of the Crown."[45]

With this statement waving at the legislators like a red flag before a bull, Glen proceeded to outline an entirely reasonable program for renewing the colony's derelict fortifications. A central point in his argument was that a great deal of money had been spent in past piecemeal repair efforts which had added nothing to South Carolina's security. He bemoaned the fact that no "skillful Engineer" had ever been called upon to review the state of Fort Johnson before so much had been spent on it in the past. He called the walls of Fort Frederick no better than a garden fence. Glen concluded that "Forts and Fortifications, Batteries Bastions, Ramparts, and Revelings, all sound well; but if they are empty sounds, they will signify little. Let us, therefore, not amuse ourselves with words, but let us take the opinion of persons of experience, which of them are good and will prove a real defense in the day of danger; and let such be preserved; but let us not spend our money for what will not profit."[46] It would be hard to find fault in the governor's logic and rationality, but find fault the contentious assembly was bound to do.

Glen wanted his legislature to appropriate funds to support a thorough survey of the colony's defenses by a highly qualified expert. Being an excellent administrator, he had such a person already in mind, advising the assemblymen that "there is at present in this Province a Gentleman who has produced to me very honorable and ample testimonials of his skill and Experience as an Engineer."[47] This gentleman of engineering skill and experience was, of course, William Gerard De Brahm, who had earlier presented Count Seckendorf's testimonial and other cre-

dentials to Glen. It is interesting to note that it was at this point in his career that
the German surveyor-engineer dropped the prefix "von" from his surname and
adopted "De," which he retained until he died.

Glen urged that the South Carolinians "avail ourselves of his opinion and Advice with regard to all our Works in general." In more specific terms Glen proposed that De Brahm "in the first place make an exact Plan or Map of Charles
Town and the Present Works, as they now stand with his opinion which of them
are good for nothing, and what may be further necessary to be added for our defense and also an exact draught of the Harbour with the Soundings of the several
Channels from Sullivan's Island upwards."[48]

In conclusion, Glen recommended that the assembly provide funds to defray
the cost of such an inventory and survey. He observed that such a cost "cannot be
great and . . . may save us far greater expenses." However reasonable Glen's arguments may seem today, one must keep in mind the larger constitutional issues
which were involved. Certainly, the South Carolina assemblymen were strongly
moved by these issues as they deliberated on the governor's recommendations in
the spring of 1752. De Brahm was the central personality around whom the tide
of this constitutional debate was to flow.

The assemblymen refused to comply with Glen's wish that they endorse and
fund the proposed survey. Their refusal was based on the grounds that De Brahm
was a "Foreigner" and therefore not to be trusted with such vital military intelligence. They went on to observe that the endorsement attesting to De Brahm's
abilities and experience as an engineer was "not from any of His Majesty's Ministers; but is wrote in the French Language, and subscribed by Count Secendorff a
Foreigner also." The assembly's message to the governor took on an officious tone
and concluded by stating that "it is inconsistent with good policy to suffer foreigners, upon any occasion whatever to make Plans of our Works and sound our
Channels, and much more so would it be in us to employ them in a work that
might tend to the loss of our Country."[49] The assembly moved that it would not
defray any of the expense for "an Employment of so dangerous a Nature."

Faced with such a vigorous resistance from the assembly Glen decided to forward his scheme via another channel, the colony's upper house. Early in July he
acquainted the South Carolina council with the low state of the defenses. He recommended that the upper house employ De Brahm to inspect the fortifications
and prepare a report on what would be required to strengthen them. The council
unanimously agreed "that the said Engineer Brahm should forthwith be employed."[50] A letter to "Mr. Brahm Engineer" was sent on July 17, 1752, to inform
the addressee that he was "desired to repair to Charles Town with all convenient
Speed."[51]

De Brahm had meanwhile returned to Georgia from whence he replied to this summons. Perhaps exercising caution in view of the apparent political tension, he feigned a lack of interest. After protestations of an unconvincing modesty, however, the German engineer indicated that he would come to Charleston if the council would forward him a "convenient sum" in advance.[52]

During the month of September a natural disaster occurred which "totally demolish'd" South Carolina's already delapidated fortifications,[53] the destructive hurricane which followed the particularly hot and dry summer of 1752. According to one eyewitness, a violent northeast wind had

> stopped the Course of the Gulf Stream, which poured in upon us like a Torrent, filling the Harbour in a few minutes; before Eleven o'Clock A.M. all the Vessels in the Harbour were on shore, except the Hornet Man of War [*which*] rode it out by cutting away her masts; all the Wharfs and Bridges were ruined, and every House and Store etc. upon them beaten down, as were also many Houses in Town. . . . The town was likewise overflowed, the Water having risen ten Feet above High-Water Mark at Spring tides; and nothing was to be seen but Ruins of Houses, Canoes, Wrecks of Boats, Masts, Yards, Barrels, Stoves, etc. floating and driving with great violence through the Streets, and round about the Town . . . and many of the people being up to their Necks in Water in their Houses, began now to despair of life. . . . For about forty miles round Charles Town, there was hardly a plantation that did not lose every Out-house upon it, and the Roads, for years afterwards, were incumbered with Trees blown and broken down.[54]

Fortunately a rapid shift in wind direction caused the tempest to abate almost as quickly as it had struck.

Because of the calamitous state of the colony Governor Glen recalled the Commons House of Assembly, which was then in recess until November. In his address to the assemblymen, the governor reviewed the chaos wrought by the "dreadful Hurricane, which had proved fatal to the Lives of several of His Majesty's subjects, damaged a great number of houses, entirely demolished our Fortifications, ruined the high Roads, broke down bridges, and in a great number of places spoiled the crops."[55] Glen went on to urge that the fortifications be put in good repair with all possible speed to insure the security of the colony in its now-weakened state.

In their reply, the assemblymen were lavish in their praise of the governor's speedy response to the colony's needs during this time of crisis. However, they evinced no change of attitude regarding the manner in which the fortifications should be repaired. They requested instead that the governor fill existing vacancies in the ranks of the commissioners on fortifications so that body could get on with its job. Naturally Glen was not pleased with this request. In an address to the house on the topic of fortifications on October 5, 1752, a few weeks after the hurricane, he once more exhorted his legislators to avoid the past errors of a piece-meal approach to this important matter. Glen again urged that the colony "have a regular engineer, who has been bred to that business," undertake the supervision of construction, promising that such a person would "be under the Eye and Direction of the Governor and Council" while engaged in the work. Glen concluded by stating that he hoped "such works as we shall now raise will either by the reputation of their goodness deter an enemy from trying their strength, or that they will prove a real defense to the country should such tryal be made."[56]

De Brahm, in response to the call from the South Carolina council, repaired to Charleston, the colony's metropolis, and received Glen's instructions concerning a comprehensive plan for the city's defense. Losing no time, on November 24, 1752, he presented his report to the governor, accompanied by a meticulously drawn and colored manuscript "Plan of a Project to Fortifie Charlestown Done by Desire of his Excellency the Governour in Council by William De Brahm Captain Ingineer in the Service of his Late Imp: Maj: Charles VII."[57] Though this plan showed De Brahm's very elaborate original scheme to fortify Charleston, the works which were finally undertaken in early 1755 were greatly simplified and far more conventional. In his report De Brahm struck a note which could not have failed to impress and please Governor Glen when he mentioned that his proposals for Charleston's defenses were based on "the advises and schemes of the most famous Ingeneers Daniel Speokle and the Hanofereane, Georg Rumpler Leutenant Colonel and Ingeneer in the Service of his late Impereale Majesty Leopold the I."[58] Glen's colony in America would have a defensive system equal to the best in Europe if only the prodigious amount of £294,140 which De Brahm estimated as the cost could be found!

Although Glen felt De Brahm's plan to be both too expensive and too elaborate, he did not abandon his attitude concerning the need to have a skilled engineer oversee the construction of South Carolina's defenses. Nor did the Commons House of Assembly change its attitude concerning the role of its own commission on fortifications. The assembly voted against awarding De Brahm the £60 sterling which Glen requested to pay for the plan and report which had been received.[59] Once again De Brahm found himself in the midst of a bitter constitutional wrangle between the governor and the legislature which dragged on until 1755 when war with France seemed imminent.

Activities in Georgia and South Carolina

During 1753 and 1754 De Brahm was active on many fronts both in Georgia and South Carolina. In early February 1753, for example, he petitioned the government of Georgia for a grant of land on behalf of Mark Benz to adjoin his own land.[60] At the same time that this petition was being presented in Savannah he published a notice in the *South-Carolina Gazette*, soliciting subscriptions for a map of South Carolina and Georgia which he was planning to publish at a scale of three miles to one inch.[61] It was in Georgia, however, that De Brahm's fortunes were to rise most rapidly. During the summer of 1754, "Mr. Henry Yonge and Mr. William de Brahm" were appointed as "joint Surveyors of Land in Georgia at a Salary to each of 50 £ per ann."[62]

De Brahm and his colleague Henry Yonge lost no time in undertaking their important duties in the rapidly expanding colony. In February 1755 they addressed a petition to the governor and council of Georgia pertaining to their shared office, pointing out that the office of the surveyor general could not function properly until all land records and surveys of villages and townships could be brought together in one central place.[63] They indicated also that they were preparing a general map of Georgia and "particularly wanted" several items necessary in its compilation. Specifically, they mentioned their need of "the Town, Garden and Tything Lot" survey in Savannah, also the surveys of Frederica, Augusta, Ebenezer, and Darien, as well as the villages of Acton, Vernonburgh, Abercorn, Goshen, and the two "villages on Skidoway Island." Further, it was requested that all future surveys and land plats be lodged with them. The council ordered that all surveyors and others possessed of such material should deliver it to the surveyors general and also that the council's own collection of maps and plans be turned over to them.[64]

On March 4, 1755, the surveyors general addressed another petition to the council, noting that their considerable duties in the office would require their frequent attendance in Savannah where neither had land nor house. They pointed out that no house nor land was then available for rent in the town. The solution to this problem, which they suggested, was a simple one. They prayed to be granted one of the reserved town lots which they would divide equally. The council resolved that lot X would be divided between the two surveyors. De Brahm received the 60 by 90 foot portion "fronting on the Common" and Yonge the 60 by 90 foot portion "fronting the square in Anson's Ward."[65]

During this period, De Brahm was called upon by Georgia's ill-fated first royal governor, John Reynolds, to recommend a scheme of defense for the colony.[66] In this effort De Brahm made allowances for Georgia's small population and stressed the most economic use of both troops and resources. His scheme was based on the fortification of a small number of strategic sites which would have allowed the Georgians great flexibility in warding off Indian attacks from the interior. This scheme was clearly explained and illustrated in the "Representation of the Forts and Garrisons Necessary for the Defense of Georgia . . . ," which Governor Reynolds forwarded to London on January 5, 1756.[67] The "Representation" was

in De Brahm's usual style and included a detailed estimate of costs and labor required, similar to those which he had earlier provided in the case of Charleston.
Although De Brahm's signature was not placed on the "Representation," he did
sign both the colored manuscript map and sheet of plans for individual forts
which accompanied it.[68] It was probably through his close association with Governor Reynolds that De Brahm also became interested in the proposed town of
Hardwick. Reynolds was attempting to stimulate interest in the Hardwick development scheme and even attempted to move the government there from Savannah. De Brahm received a grant to town lot 260 in Hardwick but apparently
never developed it.[69]

This, however, did not signal the end of De Brahm's connection with the general problem of Georgia's fortification. In an act for "The Security and Defense
of the Province of Georgia by Erecting Forts . . . and Appointing Commissioners
to Carry the Same into execution," De Brahm was named a commissioner for
"Great Ogechee District," which included the Salzburger settlement Ebenezer.[70]
He continued to play a major role in the affairs of the colony until 1764 when he
was appointed surveyor general of the Southern District and moved to Saint
Augustine, East Florida.

De Brahm served the colony of Georgia as a military engineer, justice of the
peace, cartographer, tax collector, and commissioner for the repair and reconstruction of fortifications in addition to his primary role as joint surveyor general.[71] The chapter covering Georgia in his Report may be read in the knowledge
that De Brahm was a gentleman of considerable standing and responsibility
throughout the thirteen years of his residence there. He certainly was not fired
from his provincial post as some later authors have stated.

While he was pursuing his active public career and acquiring still more land in
Georgia, De Brahm kept close to affairs in neighboring South Carolina.[72] He resided in Charleston for prolonged periods while supervising the construction of
its fortifications. It was probably then that he succumbed to the charms of the
southern metropolis and its gracious citizens which he so eloquently describes
in his Report.

Fortifying Charleston, 1755

During the summer of 1755, as General Braddock struggled to lead his army
in an unsuccessful attempt to evict the French from the Ohio Valley, South Carolinians began to evince renewed concern about their lack of defensive fortifications. On June 3, 1755, Governor Glen informed the colony's commissioners for
fortifications that war with France was imminent. He suggested that it would be
proper to request De Brahm, who was then in Georgia, to come to Charleston immediately and begin the construction of the city's defenses. The engineer would

be instructed to first "construct and finish that part of the Fortifications between Granville and Broughton's Bastion which specimen would enable the Commissioners to form a judgement of Mr. De Brahme's abilities in executing of his plan and likewise of the whole expense of the intended Fortications."[73] In the face of the impending danger of an enemy attack, the longstanding feud over the constitutionality of the role of the commissioners for fortifications was laid to rest, a compromise solution emerging. Glen's engineer, De Brahm, would work under the direction of the assembly's commissioners. Governor Glen concluded his message to the commissioners by observing that "the List of utensils given in by Mr. De Brahme was so large that it would take the greatest part of £50,000 to Purchase them." Glen expressed the personal opinion that one-tenth part of everything on De Brahm's list would be adequate for the project.

The commissioners studied De Brahm's plan for fortifying Charleston before replying to the governor. They were very critical on several counts and urged that the plan be changed in advance rather than be undertaken as it was and fail.[74] The commissioners were particularly opposed to De Brahm's grandiose "Citadelle" which was to guard the city from a less-than-likely land attack, urging instead that the old line across the neck of the Charleston peninsula be strengthened with more bastions and a large moat. A compromise plan was agreed upon and De Brahm began directing the construction of a continuous line of "Ramparts, forming regular Bastions, detach'd or joined with Curtains," which he described in the South Carolina chapter of his Report.

Predictably, De Brahm was soon at odds with the commissioners on a number of matters concerning the project. The work went forward from July 1755, however, with the energetic German engineer in charge. On May 6, 1756, the editor of the *South-Carolina Gazette* indicated that the new fortifications were

begun some time last summer under the direction and conduct of William de Brahm Esq. (formerly a Captain Engineer in the Service of his late Imperial Majesty Charles VII) who was sent for from Georgia for that purpose, and are in much forwardness that at present the sea is damm'd out from Granville's Bastion to Broughton's Battery. Three Bastions erected on that front, capable of Mounting 130 pieces of Canon on the upper and lower batteries, and the work already raised above any high water Mark; From Broughton's Battery to Conselliers Creek, the Works are Continued and three more bastions erected; and in the same manner the whole Town is to be fortified, if this important design be encouraged with the same spirit in the continuation as in the beginning. The Fronts towards the River and Sea are faced with Fascines laid in, covered with mud and flak'd together, and the outside paved with Stones and oyster shells. This Facinage answers as well in boggy marsh as upon high ground; and last years experience hath taught us, that the sea rather brings ground to than washes away.

This newspaper report echoes several of the points which De Brahm mentions in his Report concerning the construction of Charleston's defenses and reflects also the general feeling of optimism which the fortifications seemed to inspire in Carolinians of the day.[75]

While De Brahm was supervising the construction of Charleston's defenses, the surveyor generalship of South Carolina fell vacant, due to the death of the incumbent George Hunter. On August 14, 1755, Governor Glen "appointed and commissioned William de Brahme, Esquire, To be Surveyor General for the admeasuring, surveying, and setting out of lands in our said province of South Carolina." De Brahm was also to act as the "Inspector and Controller of our Quit Rents and other rents and revenues arriving to us within our said province."[76] With characteristic alacrity De Brahm quickly assumed the duties of this important office while simultaneously supervising the construction of Charleston's defenses. Twice during August 1755 he published notices of his appointment as provincial surveyor general and his intention to open his office "at the House lately occupied by Capt. Hutchins, on White Point, where the needful attention will be given."[77] He also appointed several deputy surveyors during the next two months.[78]

De Brahm's appointment as surveyor general and inspector of quitrents was only an interim one. Egerton Leigh received a royal appointment to the position on November 3, 1755,[79] though there apparently was some delay before Leigh assumed the duties of this office. In the *South-Carolina Gazette* of April 22, 1756, De Brahm identified himself as the "Surveyor General" and gave notice that he had moved his office to "Mr. Hodsden's house, the South East corner of Church and Tradd Streets." Earlier in the same month he had acquired a lot in the new town of Beaufort, South Carolina.[80]

With the fortification of his colony's metropolis well underway, Governor Glen turned his energies toward the strengthening of South Carolina's interior frontiers. An essential element in this phase of Glen's program was the construction of a much-debated fort amidst the Overhill towns of the powerful Cherokee Indian Nation. In the terms of the treaty which he had signed with the Cherokee at Saluda Old Town in May 1755,[81] Glen had promised to build a fort in the area occupied by present-day Monroe County, Tennessee.

A Fort for the Overhill Cherokee

In February 1756, Glen informed Attakullakulla, one of the most influential Cherokee chiefs, that he was preparing to begin the promised fort in the very near future. Glen outlined the role and functions of the proposed Overhill fort,[82] stressing that it was to serve primarily as a defense against attack on the Cherokees by the French and their Indian allies. To serve this purpose Glen felt that the fort should be located along the Little Tennessee River "near the place where enemies are most frequently discovered." It was also to serve as a refuge "to receive your women and children" in the event of surprise attacks by undetected bands of marauders. On this score Glen observed, "It must not therefore be at a great distance from [*the*] towns which it is to protect." For the benefit of the garrison which would man the fort when it was completed, Glen desired that a site be chosen "in a good air and near good water not very near any Eminence and not far from good corn land or from a convenient range for their cattle."

Glen himself led the party of over three hundred regular and provincial troops who were to build and man the Overhill fort. They left Charleston for the Indian country on May 19, 1756. In Glen's party was William De Brahm, who was charged with the design and construction of the proposed fort. While still on the trail Glen learned that his replacement, William Henry Lyttelton, had arrived in Charleston to take over the governorship of South Carolina. The expedition was disbanded on Lyttelton's order and Glen reluctantly returned to Charleston.[83]

After a brief flurry of domestic political housecleaning, Lyttelton turned his attention to the pressing problems of frontier defense and Indian relations. In his first address to the council, Lyttelton informed the members of his plan to halt Glen's progress. He also stated that he intended "to write to Mr. De Brahm desiring to see him in Charles Town concerning measures which had been taken for the building of the fort, and to lay before him any plan he had prepared for the same."[84] On the advice of the council, Lyttelton dispatched a message to the Overhill Cherokee leader, Old Hop, informing him of the change in plans and reassuring the Indians of Carolina's intention to complete an Overhill fort without undue delay.[85]

Fort Loudoun and the Feud with Captain Raymond Demere

On July 29, 1756, Lyttelton informed the council that all necessary steps preparatory to the construction of the Overhill fort were complete except for "a survey or exact description of the nature of the ground where it is proposed the said fort shall be built."[86] After reviewing in De Brahm's presence the several fort plans which were at hand, the council felt that they all lacked provisions "for the logement, Security, and protection of the women and children of the Cherokees in time of War which was the principal desyne and intention of the said fort." De Brahm was charged with making proper provisions for this need in the fort he was to build and to use "low works" rather than the plan for a high tower which he had apparently originally proposed. In the absence of an accurate map of the Overhill area, the council observed that they were entrusting De Brahm with a wide latitude of discretionary power in choosing a site for the fort. The council concluded, "Therefore it was expected for the sake of his own character as well as the Public interest he would construct such a Fort as would most effectually answer the ends proposed."[87]

Ironically it was as a result of his involvement in the construction of ill-fated Fort Loudoun, as the Overhill outpost was later named, that De Brahm's character became the subject of violent criticism by his contemporaries and more recent scholars alike. At that moment, however, during the summer of 1756, De Brahm's fortunes were running high. He enjoyed the confidence of the colony and was in charge of its most important public works. In addition to his public successes, his personal life was enriched by the birth of a son, George Charles De Brahm, who was baptised by Reverend William Hutson in Charleston on August 4, 1756.[88]

Late in the same month, De Brahm joined two companies of Carolina Provincials under the command of Captain John Stuart and Lieutenant John Postell, who were then making their way toward the Indian country. On the evening of August 24, the engineer presented himself to Captain Raymond Demere, the military commander of the force assigned to proceed through the Appalachian mountains and build the Carolina fort amidst the Overhill Cherokee towns. During this meeting De Brahm presented the letter of instructions which he had received from Governor Lyttelton.

Demere later expressed concern over certain concessions which had been extended to De Brahm in this document. He also felt that the German engineer's proposed labor requirements for the fort's construction were excessive in view of the size of the force assigned.[89] In a postscript to his letter reporting this initial contact with De Brahm, Demere observed that "Mr. De Brahm is a little indisposed with a fever." Demere's health was also in a fragile state during this period. His first official letter to Governor Lyttelton included a request to be relieved of his command. He wrote that "when I set out from Charles Town, I was sickly and infirm, and continue so still. My staying here long will be of great prejudice to me."[90] It is possible that the rancorous differences of opinion which soon arose between these two might have been accentuated by their mutual indispositions. Whether for this or other reasons, Demere and De Brahm were shortly to become engaged in a personal feud which at times threatened British relations with the strongest branch of the allied Cherokee Nation.

Differences between De Brahm and Demere became acute when they arrived on the banks of the Little Tennessee River, with the Cherokee leaders Old Hop and Attakullakulla, to choose a site for the fort. Demere records that

> Mr. De Brahm did not approve of the place chose by Mr. Pearson, it was more for
> Contradiction's sake than anything else. He went on a mile further and pitched

upon a place where the river made a kind of a fork but a very dismal place and a kind of a desert, and where there was no planting land for the men. The Indians told him that if he should build the fort there the men would starve; 1st, because they had no planting ground. Secondly, it was a very dangerous Place for them to come to, that the Enemy was always lurking thereabouts. Thirdly, that the Fort if built there, would be of no service to them, that they should never come near it nor their women should never be permitted to bring us any necessarys. Mr. De Brahm still insisted the fort should be built there on account of the River. Mr. De Brahm thereupon took one his pistols from his holster, and offering it to me, told me to shoot him through the head. This he spoke with such passion and fury that the like was never seen. I told him he might blow up his own brains if he would.

When Old Hop and the Little Carpenter saw this, they said that the fort should not be built there, and after great argument he came back to the first ground, which is a fine spot, pleasant and agreeable, there being seven hundred acres of land, beautifully situated, belonging to it, which I was put in possession of.[91]

As might be anticipated, De Brahm's account of this episode, which appears in his Report, is quite different.[92] It seems clear from his own account and his conduct during the construction of Fort Loudoun that De Brahm felt himself to be in charge of the project. Thus a clash between Demere and De Brahm, both men of considerable talent and ability, was almost inevitable. If blame is to be fixed for the controversial state of affairs which persisted at Fort Loudoun until De Brahm departed in late December 1756, it should rest on Governor Lyttelton, who had failed to establish a clear chain of command.[93]

This clash of personalities may have contributed in an important manner to the growing Cherokee disaffection with the British cause. This disaffection matured and culminated in the surrender of Fort Loudoun and the massacre of its garrison during the summer of 1760. The Indians, it will be recalled, were chiefly concerned with the provision of fortified refuges for their people in the event of an attack by the French or their hostile Indian allies. To fill this need, Old Hop requested that three forts be built. Two of these were to be refuges, one built near Chote and the other near the Indian town of Tomately. A third fort could be located by the Carolinians for strategic reasons wherever they chose. The old Indian "Emperor" further specified that the Carolina fort should be located within the sound of a gunshot from the other two.[94] De Brahm, however, was charged with the construction of a single fort, and a single fort he commenced in a European manner with elaborate earthworks and "a full command of the River." Late in October, however, Old Hop visited the works to report his fears concerning the danger of an imminent attack and the perilously exposed state of the Carolinians. He urged the Carolinians to take immediate steps to defend themselves.

Demere informed De Brahm of the old Indian's intelligence and in his account of the interview noted that "all animosities are laid aside at least on my part and Mr. De Brahm has dined with me and appears better natured."[95]

Faced with the imminent threat of attack, De Brahm temporarily abandoned his elaborate earthworks in favor of the more common frontier expedient of wooden pallisades. On November 7, 1756, Demere reported:

> We are now pallasadoed round, but it is not sufficient for we are too much exposed. The Fort is commanded at present from the Top of a Hill and I believe will be the same when the Works are finished but Mr. De Brahm depends very much on a Bastion that takes in Part of the same Hill. Mr. De Brahm is now setting up another row of Pallasadoes with traverses of the inside of the Fort twelve feet distance from the first and a great deal higher. We are now nothing but Pallasadoes. It's to be wished that Mr. De Brahm had built the Fort on the same spot that Mr. Pearson had pitched upon, it being a fine levell and even spot of ground which would have answered much better than to be a blowing rocks out of this hill which he is obliged to have done to make trenches for the Pallasadoes. It would have answered much better the intended purpose for quick Dispatch, and would have saved a great deal of money to the Province.[96]

Demere's criticism of De Brahm's original design grew even sharper in the weeks that followed. In one letter to Governor Lyttelton, Demere observed that De Brahm had built his fort "as if the River was navigable for Men of War."[97]

Relations between Demere and De Brahm steadily deteriorated as the autumn of 1756 wore on. According to the former, De Brahm was beginning to sow "seeds of Mutiny and Desertion" among the troops. At a "Council of War Held By Captain Rayd. Demere" on December 16, 1756, it was decided that Captain Stuart should read his commission and instructions to the troops in formation. They were further "admonished not to give ear to any seditious insinuations tending to promote mutiney and Desertion by Mr. De Brahm or any other person whatever."[98] Demere concluded by informing the men that only he, and not De Brahm, had the power to dismiss them from their duty.

Tempers were near the boiling point and a breakdown in discipline seemed imminent when one of the troopers was overheard making a mildly threatening comment. This was Henry Hammon, a member of John Postell's company. Postell was sympathetic to De Brahm and thus out of favor with Demere, Stuart, and the other officers. When Postell was threatened with confinement should he accept a discharge for his men from De Brahm, the loyal Hammon was heard to say, "By God if they confine my captain there will be bloody noses." For this indiscreet comment, Hammon was court-martialed on December 16, 1756. The court found, however, that "the Greatness of Crime which is proved against the

Prisoner is much alleviated by his being ignorant of Martial Law, and by having such notions instilled into him and the rest of them by the frequent insinuations of Mr. De Brahm." Since some example needed to be made, Hammon received 200 lashes from "a Catt with nine tails."[99]

After several threats to return to Charleston, De Brahm sent Demere a communication which included his "Final directions for accomplishing the works, which should take about three days." On December 26, 1756, Demere informed his officers that "Mr. De Brahm is clandestinely gone away and left this Fort unfinished."[100] A council of war decided that all the Carolinians should immediately move into the fort and prepare for any eventuality. Demere continued to strengthen his position by building a pallisade around the whole fort projecting eight feet above the earthen breastworks which De Brahm had left.

After a surprisingly mild rebuke from the South Carolina council, De Brahm put his affairs in order and gave public notice of his intent to return to Georgia.[101] The question of his culpability in the Fort Loudoun affair, however, remains to be answered. Clearly, Demere's condemnation ranged from charges of professional incompetence to virtual treason. Demere's correspondence to Governor Lyttelton during the late autumn and winter of 1756–57 is an almost unbroken series of vitriolic attacks on De Brahm. As a result, De Brahm has frequently suffered in the hands of scholars of the present age. John P. Brown, for example, after a study of the Demere letters, found De Brahm to be "a stubborn, conceited and somewhat cowardly man," as well as "a pompous strutting fellow."[102] Nor did John Richard Alden treat De Brahm very kindly in his own authoritative study devoted to John Stuart.[103]

While the purpose of this discussion of the German's role in the construction of Fort Loudoun is not meant to attempt any judgment, some final observation seems necessary before the matter is concluded. It seems obvious that both De Brahm and Demere were occupying exceedingly difficult positions during this period. Added to the problem of an unclear chain of command, their relationship suffered also from the general climate of uncertainty which prevailed amid a group of whites who found themselves in the midst of the little-known and unpredictable Cherokees, hundreds of miles from the nearest secure British settlements. This uneasiness reached the level of near-hysteria as the danger of a French attack seemed to become imminent.

Further, though the Indians desired refuge against attack, it was actually Glen who, a decade earlier, had managed to convince them to "request" a fort to protect their Overhill towns. The massive effort which the South Carolinians poured into the conception and construction of Fort Loudoun seems to indicate, however, that their motives went beyond a simple concern for the safety of their Indian allies and neighbors. Fort Loudoun was conceived and built as an outpost of empire in the struggle with the French for the control of the eastern half of North America. Perhaps De Brahm perceived his role in these larger international terms while Demere, the practical soldier, reacted more locally and immediately. Their controversy would thus become more understandable, as would the fact that De Brahm was so little criticized by Lyttelton or any other officer in either the provincial or imperial hierarchy. Demere realized the need for a modest and conventional frontier fortification while De Brahm, like his superiors, perceived the necessity of a much stronger base for British ambitions in the transmontane west.

The Indians soon realized that their needs were being only incidentally considered at Fort Loudoun. In Old Hop's words, "The place pitched upon by your beloved man [*De Brahm*] is too remote; our people may be killed before you come to our assistance."[104] To an influential element of the Cherokee tribe, Fort Loudoun, almost from the first days of its construction, came to represent one more despised British encroachment.

While constructing Fort Loudoun in the Cherokee heartland, De Brahm availed himself of the excellent opportunity to study the Indians and their way of life firsthand. Ethnologists, linguists, and others will profit from such observations in the Report. Of particular value and interest is the Cherokee-English dictionary which he compiled and appended to the South Carolina section.

There is no doubt that De Brahm maintained a continuing interest in the Indians throughout his long life.[105] It would also appear that he may have maintained more or less continuous contacts among the Cherokees through the years. Two German missionaries who traveled into the Cherokee country in 1799 left an account which mentions De Brahm's influence among the Cherokees at that date. The missionaries told of their visit to an old German "Seventh Day Baptist" who resided with the Indians in the village of Hiwasee. The old German mystic, named Frederici, claimed to have had a revelation that the Indians of America had originally come from Germany and that their true name was not "Indians" but *hutten*. In support of his belief, old Frederici told the visiting missionaries that "De Brahm, also, knew this very well. O De Brahm has a very fine understanding."[106]

Following this encounter the missionaries were invited to visit the home of an influential Indian named Kulsathee. While being entertained there they reported that "he gave us to read a small printed work, that dealt with three great days and published by De Brahm." They continued, "Kulsathee then began to question: what had we brought? He was under the impression that we had something to say about De Brahm's letter—referring to the little printed work."[107] Doubtlessly Kulsathee was disappointed when he learned that his guests carried no news of his admired author.

Plans for the Defense of Georgia

The February 10, 1757, edition of the *South-Carolina Gazette* carried an advertisement in which De Brahm announced his intention to depart Charleston for Georgia during the following week. All persons indebted to him were urged to contact Mr. John Edwards, his attorney. In the same ad he mentions his loss of two bay horses at Ninety Six while on his way to Upper Cherokees during August of the preceding summer. A "pistole" reward was offered for each.

Since De Brahm continued to play a significant part in Georgia's affairs while he was functioning as South Carolina's interim surveyor general and chief fortifications engineer, it is likely that he made frequent trips to Savannah and Ebenezer while he was engaged in the construction of Charleston's fortifications. In his letter to the Board of Trade, dated January 5, 1756, Georgia's Governor John Reynolds mentioned that he had "consulted with Mr. De Brahm, one of the Surveyors (who is a very able Engineer, and who is now fortifying Charles Town) about what will be necessary to be done to put this Colony into a proper State of Defence, and making an Estimate of the Expence."[108] The governor, obviously very favorably disposed toward De Brahm, stressed "the necessity of a good Engineer to Superintend the Whole; and I beg leave to recommend Mr. William De Brahm, who is a German Gentleman of Great Honour and Ingenuity."[109]

Nothing came of the Reynolds–De Brahm defense scheme, however. Charles C. Jones, Jr., the respected chronicler of early Georgia, notes that the costly plan was not accepted by the Board of Trade and Georgia's defenses "were suffered to remain in a deplorable condition."[110]

Henry Ellis replaced Reynolds as governor early in 1757. In his first report to the Board of Trade, he devoted a great deal of space to a review of the colony's weak defenses. He observed that "the Representation of the defenceless state of this Province that has been transmitted to your Lordships by Mr. Reynolds is true as far as I can judge, and the plan proposed by Mr. Debrahme of fortifying the Province is judiciously concerted but so expensive that I despair of seeing it suddenly carried into execution."[111] The new governor prefaced this observation by noting that "at present we enjoy a sort of Calm—We hear of no settled plan among the Indians to attack us, altho we are convinced they are not entirely satisfied with us."[112]

Ellis wrote that he planned to defend Savannah by "raising a little fort out of the wretched materials we have."[113] According to De Brahm, the governor requested his advice and assistance at about this time. De Brahm then proposed the "well pallisadoed Intrenchment to envelope the City, so as to make it a Receptacle and Shelter for all the Planters, their Families, Slaves, Etc.," which he describes in the third chapter of the Georgia section of his Report.[114] It would appear that Ellis accepted De Brahm's advice concerning the desirability of encompassing the whole town within a defensive wall. On August 1, 1757, he reported that he was overseeing the "fortifying of this whole town," rather than the "little fort" which he had mentioned earlier. His description of Savannah's defenses closely accords with the one provided by De Brahm in his Report. As De Brahm states, Ellis improved Savannah's defenses during the next three years.[115] An analysis of both the Ellis and De Brahm descriptions makes it clear that the "Plan of the City Savannah and Fortification" which De Brahm included in his Report is incomplete, showing only a small portion of the elaborate network of defenses which protected Savannah in 1760 as the French and Indian War drew toward a close. In the light of this fact, there is a need to reappraise earlier studies which relied heavily on the De Brahm plan and description in attempting to recreate the eighteenth-century defenses of Savannah.[116]

De Brahm's plan has had an exceedingly wide currency because it was engraved and included in his *History of the Province of Georgia: With Maps of the Original Surveys*, published by George Wymberly-Jones in 1849. However, it was only a plan which De Brahm suggested to Ellis and not in fact a map of the defenses of Savannah as they evolved under Ellis's direction during his three-year tenure as Georgia's governor. It should be concluded that De Brahm played a significant role in helping Ellis to protect the Georgia settlements with a system of fortifications which the governor described as rendering the colony "more respectable in the eyes of the Indians than we were." Ellis wrote also that the defenses had "served to abate considerably the apprehensions of our own people."[117]

On March 16, 1763, a letter from De Brahm was read in the Commons House of Assembly. In this communication he expressed his gratitude for the reward of twenty guineas which he had received "for his Services as Engineer."[118] He was, however, disappointed to find "that nothing appeared in the House of my Employment in Laying out the Circum Vallations of Savannah and conducting the same for which an equal sum had been promised but till now delayed."[119] De Brahm mentioned that he had also "been employed about the projection of a new church" and "an exact map of Georgia wherefore I would humbly beg that the same may also be taken into your wise consideration."[120]

This request went unanswered until December, when De Brahm again petitioned Georgia's legislature for compensation. On this occasion he again pressed his claim for the twenty guineas due him for his work on the "Circumvallation" of Savannah. He also mentioned that he had, in December 1762, presented the house with a map of Georgia from latitude 29° to latitude 33°. He wrote that the map was "the product of the Memorialists own Industry and Labour which was lost out of this House to the great detriment of the memorialist, who is deprived of those benefits he expected to reap from the publication of that his industrious performance."[121] This second petition for compensation was favorably received, and on February 2, 1764, the provincial treasurer was ordered to issue "to William De Brahm Esqr. for raising Lines of Circumvallation round the Town of Savannah in the year 1757, and for all his other publick services forty two pounds."[122]

Landholdings in Georgia

While engaged in his varied provincial activities and services during the decade of the 1750s De Brahm was diligently acquiring land in the rapidly developing colony of Georgia. The 500 acres of land which he received upon his arrival in the colony with a large contingent of German emigrants in 1751 may have been the tract which De Brahm called "Bethabram" and showed on his printed map of 1757.[123] Bethabram, on the head springs of the Little Ogeechee River to the west of Savannah, was sold to Benjamin Farley on May 11, 1756.[124]

In June 1757, the following year, De Brahm sold another tract of 457 acres in the District of Savannah to Bartholomew Zauberbuhler.[125] It would seem that De Brahm had become somewhat disenchanted with the region west of Savannah and had moved north to be within Georgia's German-speaking community centered at Ebenezer. In a petition dated June 7, 1757, he described himself as being settled at Ebenezer and desirous of improving lands in the area.[126] He formally requested that he be permitted to purchase 100 acres "part on the island opposite Ebenezer and other part sundry vacant lots in the town of Ebenezer." Permission for this acquisition was granted subject to the usual conditions.

It would seem that De Brahm's surveying activities in the neighborhood of Ebenezer caused some discontent on the part of established residents. On February 7, 1758, Christopher Cremer and other settlers complained of De Brahm's altering property lines on the southeast side of the town.[127] In their words, garden lots located there were "rendered less commodious and beneficial" by the new survey. The petitioners were called, with De Brahm, to discuss the problem with Georgia's governor and council. De Brahm's plat of the survey was examined in the course of the hearing. It was found that no real injury was suffered by the petitioners and the survey was allowed to stand as valid,[128] an event which has significance because it represents an important contemporary endorsement of De Brahm's skill as a surveyor and cartographer. It also would seem to add a considerable degree of authenticity to the three large-scale maps of the Ebenezer area found in the Georgia portion of his Report. These are "The Salzburger's Settlement in Georgia," "Plan of the Town Ebenezer and its Fort," and "The Bethanian Settlement in Georgia."

During the autumn of 1758, De Brahm petitioned for another grant of land. In this petition he described his family as consisting of himself, his wife Wilhelmina, and two children. Just when and where his second child was born has not been discovered. It seems certain, however, that this second heir was his daughter, who accompanied De Brahm to Saint Augustine in 1764. In addition to his wife and children De Brahm mentions that he then owned four Negroes and had agreed to purchase four more who were expected daily. The land which De Brahm was requesting is described as 500 acres on an island "northeast of Ebenezer opposite to his dwelling."[129]

Action on this petition was postponed temporarily and reconsidered on August 7, 1759, at which time De Brahm presented an affidavit attesting that he had two children and five Negroes for whom he had not yet obtained land. He was granted 300 acres subject to the usual stipulations,[130] probably the 300-acre tract which De Brahm shows as his own on his large-scale maps in the Georgia portion of his Report.

De Brahm's other holdings in the vicinity of Ebenezer were registered in the official "Register of Grants" on April 28, 1759.[131] According to this source, he owned: 1) town lot # 5 of the first row in the first division in the town of Ebenezer, which measured 60' x 90'; 2) all of the garden lot containing 2 acres, bounded by his own land on the northeast and southwest and by the town of Ebenezer on the northwest; 3) a 14-acre island in the mouth of Ebenezer Creek to the northwest of the town of Ebenezer; and 4) an 86-acre tract adjacent to the southeast side of Ebenezer's garden lots.

Early in 1761, De Brahm petitioned for a further grant, on purchase, of 500 acres of land "lying on Great Ogeechee." In this petition he mentioned the land already granted to him in family right, stating that this land had now been settled and improved. His petition was granted on January 6, 1761.[132] He was disappointed, however, to find the land which he desired already occupied and on March 3, 1761, petitioned for land in another locale.[133] His alternate choice was on an island in the Altamaha River at a place known as Spell's Bluff. The Altamaha was then the southernmost boundary of the colony and to a large extent debatable ground, which probably contributed to the governor and council's decision to postpone any action on De Brahm's request.

De Brahm was recognized as a community leader of considerable stature. In an act designed to raise a large amount of money for the province's courts of oyer and terminer, dated March 27, 1759, he was named as a collector in the town of Ebenezer and parish of Saint Matthew.[134] In June of the same year the governor and council promulgated a new "Commission of the Peace" and a list of the commissioners of the peace for the province.[135] The list was headed by the names of the council members. Following the councilors came a group identified as "Esquires," an honorary title of considerable significance during the eighteenth century. It was in this group that "William De Brahm Esqr.," was named as the commissioner of the peace for the District of Ebenezer. In an act for repairing and rebuilding the colony's fortifications, dated April 24, 1760, he was named as a commissioner for Saint Matthews Parish.[136]

While the exact location of De Brahm's Ebenezer homeplace is difficult to fix, it would appear that he referred to it as "Anaugasta" or "Anaugusta." The first spelling is found in a brief letter which he wrote to Thomas Rasberry, the well-known Savannah merchant, on September 3, 1759.[137] The second spelling is found in the manuscript "Register of Grants Book C" located in the Georgia surveyor general's department. Anaugusta probably served as the De Brahm family home until 1760, when the Savannah house, described in the Report, was built.

Cartographic and Engineering Activities

James Wright, Georgia's longest-serving chief executive,[138] arrived in that colony in 1760. Governor Wright, like his predecessor Ellis, had a keen appreciation of the need to keep Georgia well defended against surprise attack by both Indian and European hostiles. When a French privateer was sighted in the Savannah River during the summer of 1761 he responded by taking vigorous steps toward having a fort built to defend the river below Savannah town.[139] Rumors that Spain was on the verge of joining France in the war then still in progress against Britain were a subject of concern and alarm among the Georgians of the day. To many, Spanish fleets and forces at Havana and Saint Augustine seemed an ominous threat to Georgia's existence. To insure the security of the sea approach to the colony's metropolis, Wright proposed the construction of a small fort on Cockspur Island where land had earlier been set aside for this purpose.

In the defensive scheme which De Brahm had devised for Governor Reynolds in 1755 (mentioned above on p. 25), Cockspur Island was designated as a site for the construction of "a Blockhouse in a Redoubt." On July 28, 1761, Governor Wright and his council "ordered that Mr. De Brahm do make a sketch of a Battery and Buildings . . . and report the same, that an Advertisement may be published for Persons willing to undertake the work to give in their proposals."[140] In a letter to the Board of Trade dated June 10, 1762, Governor Wright enclosed a sketch "of the Fort now Erecting at Cockspur Island."[141] This manuscript sketch includes both a large-scale map of Cockspur Island and the Savannah River channels adjacent as well as a detailed sketch of the "redoubted Caponiere." The manuscript page is marked "projected and directed by W. G. De Brahm Late Captn. Engeneer."[142] This fort was known as Fort George and is

clearly shown by De Brahm on sketches which he includes in the Georgia portion
of his Report. His "Plan and Profile of Fort George, on Coxpur Island," Plate
12, should be consulted for details regarding Fort George's site and appearance.

Georgia, while frequently preoccupied with the threat of attack during the
period of the French and Indian War, was fortunate in averting any large-scale
hostility. The colony's leaders had succeeded in maintaining a peaceful relationship with the neighboring Indian tribes while South Carolina had suffered the
ravages of the Cherokee War at the opening of the 1760s. This fact goes a long
way toward explaining Georgia's rapid economic progress and population growth
which De Brahm describes so glowingly in his Report. Concomitant with this
period of growth and expansion in Georgia was a change in the whole political
power balance in the New World. In 1763, with the signing of the "Definitive
Treaty of Peace" in Paris, the Spanish surrendered their colony of Florida to
the British. Georgia was thus freed of the Damoclean threat from the south
which had influenced its development since its inception under Oglethorpe's
guidance thirty years before. A decision reached by the British Crown in the
same year made Saint Mary's River the colony's southern boundary and formally
permitted Georgians to extend their settlements to the region south of the Altamaha River. In 1764, a commission to the governor of Georgia further defined
the colony's bounds and made the Mississippi River the westernmost boundary.

Thus it seemed that Georgia, under a vigorous royal administration and relieved
of external threat from rival European powers, was free at last to expand and
provide a haven for unlimited numbers of immigrants from the northern colonies,
the British Isles, and Protestant Europe. This might have been the case, except
for one all-important factor—the American Indians who vigorously claimed most
of the Southeast at the time. Eighteenth-century Georgia was an arena containing
the people of two dissimilar cultures in competition for the possession of the most
fundamental of resources—land. Land was demanded in ever-increasing amounts
to provide opportunities for cultivation and exploitation by those of the growing
European culture group in Georgia. On the other hand, this same land represented the vast wooded "hunting grounds" which were deemed absolutely essential by the Indians who claimed them and who passionately felt that these vast
tracts were vital to the way of life they loved and frequently fought to maintain.
The British Crown undertook a program which was aimed at placating the tribes
by convincing them that their hunting grounds would be protected from encroachment by the whites. An essential element in this policy was the establishment of a boundary line which would separate the colonies from the tribal
hunting grounds.[143]

Significantly, the first formal attempt to implement this policy and negotiate
with the Indians over a boundary took place in Georgia. This was the southern

Indian congress which brought the governors of the four southern colonies face to face with large numbers of the Indians and their leaders at Augusta during the autumn of 1763.[144] One of the chief concerns of this prestigious gathering at Georgia's wilderness outpost was the task of fixing the location of a boundary which would be surveyed and marked. In his preparations for this conference, Governor Wright called upon his joint surveyors general, De Brahm and Yonge, to compile a map of Georgia which could be used during the negotiations. It would appear that two maps were drawn, one by De Brahm and the other by Yonge. De Brahm's version is now found in William L. Clements Library and Yonge's is located in the British Museum.[145] The maps are similar but not identical and are drawn at slightly different scales. Shown on both are the original limits of Oglethorpe's 1739 cession from the Indians as well as the large additional area which Governor Wright hoped to obtain for his colony during negotiations. These two manuscript maps are extremely important and valuable cartographic sources showing what was known of the geography of Georgia during this crucial period.

With his letter informing the Board of Trade of the successful outcome of the congress, Governor Wright included a copy of the treaty signed, as well as "a map of Part of the Province of Georgia, shewing what lands were formerly ceded by the Indians to the Trustees, and what Part was Ceded at the Late Congress."[146] Wright went on to state that "I have been much indebted to the Surveyors General for their assistance in Furnishing me with this map which was in a great measure taken from Private draughts and Materials Collected by Mr. De Brahm."[147] On February 2, 1764, the Commons House of Assembly issued a list of disbursements to be paid by the provincial treasurer. Among the items listed was "a gratuity to the Surveyors General for preparing two maps of part of the province necessary to be had at the late Congress; each ten pounds ten shillings."[148]

It can be seen that De Brahm's cartographic expertise was as highly regarded in Georgia as it was in South Carolina. Governors of both colonies had alluded to his considerable abilities in this sphere in numerous communications to the Board of Trade and other high-level offices in London. These endorsements were reinforced in a most important way in 1757 when De Brahm's detailed printed map of South Carolina and Georgia appeared from the plates of Thomas Jefferys, the highly regarded royal geographer and mapmaker. This was "A Map Of South Carolina And A Part Of Georgia. Containing the Whole Sea-Coast; all the Islands, Inlets, Rivers, Creeks, Parishes, Townships, Boroughs, Roads and Bridges: As Also, Several Plantations, with their proper Boundary-Lines, their Names and the Names of their Proprietors. Composed From Surveys taken by the Hon. William Bull Esq. Lieutenant Governor, Captain Gascoign, Hugh

Bryan, Esq: And the Author William De Brahm, Surveyor General to the Province of South Carolina, one of the Surveyors of Georgia, And late Captain Engineer under his Imperial Majesty Charles VII. Engrav'd By Thomas Jefferys, Geographer to his Royal Highness the Prince of Wales."[149] To insure that his map achieved recognition in the most influential branch of the British government, De Brahm dedicated it "To the Right Honourable George Dunk, Earl of Halifax First Lord Commissioner and to the rest of the Right Honourable the Lords Commissioners of Trade and Plantations. This Map is most humbly Inscribed to their Lordships By their Lordships most Obedient and most devoted Humble Servt. William de Brahm."

Present-day scholars have been generous in their praise of this attractive and valuable map. Louis C. Karpinski wrote, "De Brahm is the first strictly scientific cartographical expert to practice his art in the Carolinas. For his activity in America after 1751 and involved work in Georgia and East Florida, the title of Surveyor General of the Southern District of North America was well deserved."[150] William P. Cumming described De Brahm's 1757 map as "far superior to any cartographical work for the southern district that had gone before." Cumming added that "with De Brahm we turn from the amateur to the professional, from the general outlines of the region to topographical accuracy. However much De Brahm must have owed to the other surveyors whom he mentions, Bull, Bryan, and especially Captain Gascoign, he was the author and to him should go the credit."[151] This map went through a number of editions in both English and French and appeared in widely circulated atlases by both Jefferys and his successor William Faden.

It seems very likely that this famous map, published in 1757, included information which De Brahm had gathered during his surveying expeditions of 1751 and 1752. On February 5, 1753, he had the following announcement inserted in the *South-Carolina Gazette*: "William De Brahm—To be printed by Subscription, A Map of South Carolina and Georgia, Containing the whole sea-coast, all the Islands, Inlets, Rivers, Creeks, Parishes, Roads, Bridges, Townships, Boroughs; as also the Several Plantations with their proper Boundary Lines, their names and the names of their Proprietors: Composed of the Surveys made by the Hon. William Bull, Esq. Lieut. Governor, Capt. Gascoign, Hugh Bryan, Esq. the subscriber himself and others. The whole will be divided into four parts, each Three Feet Square, laid down by a Scale of three miles in an inch. By William De Brahm, late Captain-Engineer under his Imperial Majesty Charles VII."[152] While not identical, this lengthy title includes all of the elements of the title applied to the 1757 map. Since there is no record of a map printed in the colonies by De Brahm prior to the appearance of the Jefferys edition it may be assumed that sufficient support in the form of subscriptions to finance this project was not locally forthcoming. It does indicate, however, that De Brahm was interested in publishing a map of his newly adopted homeland less than two years after his arrival there from Germany. It does not seem unreasonable to suggest that the 1757 Jefferys–De Brahm map of Georgia and South Carolina was the final fruit of the proposal which was announced in the *South-Carolina Gazette* late in the winter of 1752–53.[153] This excellent map could not have failed to attract favorable attention in London where geographical information regarding the American colonies was eagerly sought. It is safe to assume that it, like Samuel Holland's map of "Quebeck" (see p. 6), played some role in the decision to appoint De Brahm to the surveyor generalship of the Southern District in 1764.

APPOINTMENT AS SURVEYOR GENERAL AND REMOVAL TO EAST FLORIDA

The British Crown moved vigorously during the winter of 1763–64 toward the establishment of the two new offices of surveyor general for the American colonies (see pp. 5–6). Exactly when De Brahm was selected to fill the southern office is difficult to determine. It would seem, however, to have been during this winter period, since, as early as May 26, 1764, Governor Wright alluded to De Brahm's appointment in a letter to the Board of Trade written on that date.[154] The warrant appointing De Brahm as surveyor general of the new colony of East Florida was dated June 13, while another appointing him as surveyor general of the Southern District was dated on the 26th of the same month.[155] At the same time Henry Yonge was named as the sole surveyor general of lands for Georgia.

De Brahm received the official letter enclosing his commission and instructions for the execution of his new office on November 3, 1764.[156] The lengthy letter acquainted him with the nature and scope of his new duties. De Brahm was to have cognizance over the surveying and mapping of "all His Majesty's territories on the Continent of North America, which lye to the south of Potomac River, and of a line drawn due west from the Head of the main branch of that River as far as His Majesty's Dominions extend."[157] Within this huge area, however, the Board of Trade placed first priority on "that part of the Province of East Florida, which lyes to the south of St. Augustine, as far as the Cape of Florida, particularly of the lands lying near the sea Coast of the great promontory [*which*] appears to their Lordships to be of the most pressing expediency, in order to accelerate the different Establishments which have been proposed to be made in that part of the country." Here, De Brahm was told to concentrate his efforts. His survey was "to be in great measure the guide, by which His Majesty and his servants are to form their judgements upon the different proposals that shall be offered for making settlements upon these coasts."

Precision and exactness would, of course, be "required and expected." Latitudes and longitudes of the most important places were to be determined "by just astronomical observations." The coasts and channels were to be sounded and depths of water recorded along with any other information which could add to the safety of navigation. De Brahm was further instructed to forward his observations and remarks which could "tend to convey a clear and precise knowledge of the actual state of the country contained in the survey, its limits, extent, quantity of acres, principal rivers and harbours, the nature of its soil and produce, and in what points capable of improvement." And, to cover anything which might have been left out of this comprehensive list, he was to add "every information" that he thought might help in forming "a true judgement of the state of this important part of his Majesty's dominions." As complete and detailed as these instructions seemed, their Lordships desired that De Brahm consider them "as a rude sketch or outline only." Clearly, De Brahm's task was much more than an exercise in coastal charting. He was charged with the conduct of a comprehensive geographical reconnaissance in a distant and little-known region for which only the crudest maps were available. De Brahm was instructed to be "very punctual and exact" in reporting to the Board of Trade and to forward "the most full and particular account of all your proceedings, together with copies of such maps and charts as you are able from time to time to render complete and correct." Obediently, he forwarded many lengthy letters and several maps to London during the six years when he was actively pursuing the general survey from his base in Saint Augustine.[158]

To finance this ambitious undertaking, De Brahm was annually allotted £700-17-0 of which £100 was appropriated to a salary for a deputy surveyor who would carry on De Brahm's functions as provincial surveyor of lands in East Florida. The remaining £600-17 was to provide assistants and equipment and cover the expense of conducting the general survey. The surveyor general was sternly admonished that his "plan of expense should be strictly confined to this sum . . . no demand beyond this sum will or can be allowed."[159] From the very outset, however, De Brahm felt that this allowance was inadequate for the task at hand and regularly informed his superiors of this fact. In addition to the annual allowance which De Brahm was to draw upon for the conduct of the general survey, he was to receive a salary of £120-0-0 annually as provincial surveyor of lands for East Florida. It would seem that the tacit understanding was that De Brahm's position as provincial surveyor of lands with its salary and perquisites would provide his main income while the allotment made for the general survey would go primarily for the actual expenses incurred in that service.

De Brahm moved rapidly during the autumn of 1764 to prepare for the start of the first expedition of the general survey. Writing to the Board of Trade during December of that year, he informed that body that he was sparing no effort in his preparations and was seeking the best advice "in a business so foreign to these parts."[160] He proposed to proceed south along the Florida coast with a schooner, a bark, and a small boat in addition to the schooner's own boat. The small boat would be under the direction of a deputy and would be nearest the shore observing and sounding. A second deputy would command the bark, marking observations and soundings in the middle ground while De Brahm, on board the schooner, would sound the deepest water and direct their advance, making both land and sea observations. The party would move directly south toward the cape without stopping at the inlets. On the return journey it would explore and map all inlets along the coast. As the survey progressed, De Brahm modified this scheme and managed without the bark in the middle ground.

According to his original plan, sixteen people were to participate in the survey, including two "geometers," as De Brahm termed his deputies, a master, mate, crew, and attendants, in addition to De Brahm himself. All of this, with the charter of the schooner, provisions, and expensive surveying equipment "would leave but a small share of emolument to recompense the endeavours of the Chief Conductor of this expedition." Even before getting underway De Brahm was gently acquainting his superiors with the inadequacies of the allotment available for the general survey. This theme was to run throughout his voluminous correspondence with his superiors in the years to come.

In order to comply with the requirement concerning the recording of the latitude and longitude of important places determined "by just astronomical observations," De Brahm sought to acquire equipment that was, for its day, extremely sophisticated. He mentioned "three quadrants of uncommon size, two of equal dimensions vizt. of 57 1/3 inches diameter for the use of the boats and one 114 2/3 inches diameter to be worked by small pulleys for the altitude observations on the sea coast, by whose means I will be able to observe the meridian altitude to the very second."[161] These instruments he reckoned as indispensible for the survey. Unfortunately he felt it would be tedious to include "a catalogue of other instruments, books, paper and advertisements, powers of Attorney agreements, and of articles as yet not occurred," which would necessarily add to the expense of the survey. Such a detailed list would be most welcome to present-day students of the history of surveying and historical cartography.

To better inform his fellow Georgians about his new undertaking De Brahm published the following announcement in the December 6, 1764, issue of the *Georgia Gazette*:

The subscriber being appointed surveyor-general for the southern district of His Majesty's dominions in North-America, gives notice, that he will in a very short time set out to make general surveys both of coast and main, will engage in said employ by the month, at least for a quarter of a year, a good convenient schooner, with one four rowing and two smaller boats, properly fitted out and manned with ten sailors, under command of a master and mate, all well experienced mariners; also two surveyors well versed in trigonometry. Such as may be willing to enter the said service are desired to be expeditious in sending their proposals to Joseph Ottolenghe, Esq. in Savannah, or to the surveyor-general's office in Augustine.

De Brahm left Georgia to begin his new life in East Florida on January 22, 1765, only 2 1/2 months after his commissioning as surveyor general. When viewed in the context of the usually leisurely eighteenth century, this was alacrity. His entrance into Saint Augustine was delayed at the harbor bar, however, by adverse winds from the 25th until the 29th, a foretaste of the contrary Florida weather which often vexed and sometimes imperilled him on his surveys. He quickly "settled the office and set in motion the land business for this province," losing no time in beginning a survey of Saint Augustine. He observed the latitude of East Florida's metropolis at "29°37′25″ with three degrees east variation" and sounded the depth of water over the bar, all during his first week of residence there.[162] He again noted how difficult his work was in the absence of "all necessary instruments." He especially required "a quadrant with a telescop fixed on its diopters, and a micrometer sufficient to take an observation of Jupiter's moons; instruments unknown in this part of the world more less to be met with."[163]

In describing the sea approach to Saint Augustine De Brahm first mentions the influence of the Gulf Stream, an oceanic phenomenon which he describes at great length in his Report and published in his *Atlantic Pilot*. Both his maps and descriptions of the Gulf Stream have attracted scholarly interest in recent years.[164]

The General Survey Begins

Before leaving Savannah De Brahm entered into an agreement to charter the schooner *Augustine Packet* which was then "lying at anchor in Savannah River." Francis Goffe, her master, agreed to "fit out the said Schooner in the best manner by fresh Sheathing, Painting and repairing her so that she may hold out upon occasion an Eighteen Weeks Voyage."[165] Several specialized items of equipment and furniture were to be provided by the terms of the charter agreement. For example, it was specified that the schooner's cabin should contain "a Table sufficient for three Persons to write and draw Plans and do other Business upon." The quarterdeck was also to have "a Table Seat and an awning for three Persons upon occasion." Double sets of "sails, anchors, and cables," as well as "a Jury-mast, two dozen poles, two flags, and two Jacks of different colours for signals" were to be provided by the schooner's master.

Goffe agreed to "steer and sail such courses both on the coast, in the Inlets, Bays, Creeks, Rivers, Arms, Keys, Islands, Lakes, and Lagoons, as he shall from time to time be directed by, and follow all such orders as he shall for that purpose receive from the said William Gerard De Brahm and shall also send out a Boat or Boats sufficiently manned and provided when and where he the said William Gerard De Brahm shall order the same." In addition to the schooner's regular boat Goffe was to "find and provide one rowing Boat with four Oars a Mast and Sail, one other rowing Boat with two Oars a Mast and Sail." Each of the boats was to be fitted with "a compass" and "a set of half minute and quarter minute glasses." In order to determine soundings and bottom conditions the *Augustine Packet* was also to provide the surveyors with "two six pound Leads, two four pound Leads, two three pound Leads, and four two pound Leads, also Six Lines of fifty Fathom each, four Lines of thirty Fathom each, three Lines of twenty Fathom each, and four Lines of twelve Fathom each." The strength of the lines was to be "proportioned to their different Lengths." For all of this plus an impressive list of provisions to be consumed on the survey, Master Goffe was to receive "the full Sum of Three Hundred Pounds lawfull Money of the said Province (being equal in value to the like Sum Sterling Money of Great Britain)."

The general survey of the Southern District of North America began on February 11, 1765, when De Brahm sailed out from Saint Augustine aboard the well-equipped *Augustine Packet* with Francis Goffe at the con. In addition to the ship's company and his own attendants, he was accompanied by his two deputies, Mr. Charles Yonge and Mr. Spark. The party sailed due east, sounding and sampling the bottom for sixteen miles, finding "between 60 & 72 feet water in a variety of white, grey, & black sandy bottom sometimes mixed with shells." At about one in the afternoon they turned south to parallel the coast and make further soundings. The bottom remained sandy "accept when near the coast where I fell in with a green muddy bottom in 34 feet water, a mile & half from the shore. The anchor was dropped after 6-O'clock in 51 feet water."[166]

On the next day De Brahm sent his deputy Charles Yonge "in the barge with four sailors to make for the shore." The barge was to proceed at a quarter of a mile from shore abreast the schooner. Signals were agreed upon so that Yonge knew "when to proceed, when to come to anchor, when to make land marks, and when to come on board." They proceeded southward, sighting landmarks, sounding the bottom, and charting the coastline in this fashion until reaching "Musketo Inlet" or, as it is known today, Ponce de Leon Inlet, on February 13. Here De Brahm recalled Yonge and ordered him to take the barge and "reconoiter the channel, being suspended in my judgement by the great appearance of Breakers." A safe entry was made by following the barge and "keeping the south shore in a S/2 W. Course as near as possible with a table like figured mangrove tree . . . in direction." Within the channel they anchored in "11 feet water hard sandy bottom with mud underneath in the middle of the Bay."

The party remained in Musketo, or as De Brahm later referred to it on his map, Plate 22 of the Report, Mukoso Inlet, for three weeks, conducting detailed explorations and surveys of the surrounding area, of which De Brahm gives detailed description in the Report. It was here a short time later that Dr. Andrew Turnbull was to plant his ambitious colony of fourteen hundred Greek, Italian, and Minorcan indentured servants. The settlement, which became known as New Smyrna, formed, with Saint Augustine, one of the colony's two largest population clusters at the outbreak of the American Revolution.

The thoroughness of De Brahm's survey and description of the environs of Ponce de Leon Inlet is impressive and may be taken as typical of his assiduity through the six years of his tenure in East Florida. Having entered the inlet in the early afternoon, he noted "the very same day I began my survey of the inlet and bay." On the following day he dispatched his deputies, Yonge and Spark, in two canoes, each with crews of three sailors; "the former to reconoiter and survey to south called Hillsborough River, & the latter the north called Hallifax River, with precise orders & directions not to exceed four days absence, unless, they or one of both had a prospect of discovering a communication with St. Johns or any other river, myself continuing the same forenoon the survey of the Inlet." Thirteen closely written manuscript pages in his letter to the Board of Trade dated April 4, 1765, are devoted to the observations made in the region around this one inlet along the extensive Florida coast.[167] Such diverse topics as tides and currents, bottom irregularities, oyster banks, mangrove trees, barilla (with instructions for reducing it to potash), wildlife including "fine oysters, turtles, & fish, as trouts, mullets, sheep heads, drums, bass & porgies," amber, Indian shell mounds, wild oranges, as well as lengthy comments on the soils and climate of the area are included in the surveyor general's commentary. At every opportunity he advised on how the natural bounty of the area might be profitably utilized by industrious settlers.

After leaving the inlet on March 4, De Brahm "proceeded successfully until March 13th when I separated from the barge & cast off the coast through the Gulph Stream about the ocean, till the 20th March, when with the divine hand, was brought into St. Augustine Bay & met there my people who happened to arrive a few hours before me." The barge had been abandoned and the party had "come by land suffering these many days all miseries next to that of perishing." De Brahm's own progress home to Saint Augustine had included the weathering of a hurricane which overtook the schooner at midnight on March 17. On March 24 he headed a letter to the Board of Trade "Floating in Distress in the Ocean in Latitude 30°57′35″, March 24th 1765."[168] He held this letter with a map ready in a cask "to commit to the waves & winds under devine Conduct & blessing in Case I should become exposed to another danger of my life." He described the schooner as a "vessel being without a keel & not so fit for the sea, as calculated for the shore and inland passages," hardly the ark to ride out a hurricane in comfort and security.

Undaunted by these harrowing experiences and near disasters De Brahm refitted and continued his survey of Florida's east coast during the early summer of 1765. Space does not permit a review of his subsequent sea, river, and landborne surveys around and into the Florida peninsula during the following five years. Such a review might well comprise a book in its own right. Hopefully, however, this brief review of his first expedition in the role of surveyor general clearly identifies De Brahm as the dedicated explorer and geographer that he was. Later charges arising out of his controversy with East Florida's royal governor, James Grant, as well as De Brahm's own penchant for mystical writing, have attracted considerable attention through the past two centuries and may have obscured his contributions as surveyor general.[169] His careful attention to detail provides some measure against which the reader may judge the statements and descriptions included in his Report.

LIFE IN EAST FLORIDA AND CONTROVERSY WITH GOVERNOR GRANT

East Florida was one of the newly created British colonies which evolved in the aftermath of the Peace of Paris. The governor of this infant colony was James Grant, the imperious hero of the recent Cherokee War that had ravaged the Carolina frontier a few years before. Though his attitude toward the governing of his province was frequently more that of a military commander accustomed to being obeyed than that of a politician sensitive to the will of the majority,[170] Grant was, above all else, dedicated to the creation of a viable British colony in East Florida and spared no energy toward this end. De Brahm, as the colony's surveyor of lands, occupied a particularly strategic and sensitive position in Grant's administration, though he was not Grant's appointee. Between these two peculiarly strong-willed and gifted individuals friction and controversy seems almost predictable.

It appears that De Brahm brought his wife and daughter to Saint Augustine in 1765, but there is no mention of his young son, who presumably had died earlier in Georgia. The new surveyor general set to work with his characteristic alacrity to acquire a home and property in his new base of operations. On June 22, 1765, the council of East Florida issued De Brahm the necessary warrants of survey allowing him to acquire "Town Lots in St. Augustine."[171] Later in the same year he was also issued a warrant for a five-acre garden lot adjoining the town. Several years later De Brahm's property in Saint Augustine was described as

> One Lot of Land in the Town of St. Augustine Governors Quarter by Grant to him dated 17th February 1766 containing nearly half an Acre—on which premises was a large Stone House Containing eight Rooms with a Piazza to the North and South, Kitchen, Outhouses & a large garden and late in the Tenure of the Hnbl Jess. Hume his Majesty's Chief Justice of the said Province and which said Lot is valued at . . . £800-0-0 One Lot of Land on the Bay in the said Town of St. Augustine No. 5 Society Quarter by Grant to him dated 31st December 1766 Containing nearly one quarter of an Acre, on which was a large Stone House, Kitchen, and a large garden late in the Tenure of Steward & valued at . . . £320-0-0.[172]

With the first spring and summer expeditions of the general survey completed, death again struck when, on September 1, 1765, De Brahm's wife died.[173]

At about this time the controversy with Governor Grant, which was to eventuate in De Brahm's suspension from office, began to occupy the surveyor general. Grant appears to have employed the engineer James Moncrief to conduct surveys and prepare maps prior to De Brahm's arrival in East Florida.[174] De Brahm writes that "it was publickly said, the Governor intended to get Mr. Moncrief appointed in the Surveyor General's place."[175] As time passed the rift between De Brahm and Grant grew wider and their differences became increasingly complex.

Shortly after De Brahm's harrowing arrival at Saint Augustine, Governor Grant had sent him a very specific set of instructions concerning his duties as East Florida's surveyor general of lands.[176] However, De Brahm's royal commission to his provincial post, almost identical to his commission as surveyor general of the Southern District, seemed to place him under the authority of the Crown, Treasury, and Board of Trade, rather than the royal governor.[177] De Brahm found himself in a position similar to the one he had occupied vis-à-vis Captain Demere at Fort Loudoun.

As East Florida's surveyor general of lands, De Brahm was charged with the responsibility of appointing deputy surveyors who in turn would survey the tracts of land desired by the holders of provincial warrants of survey. Warrants were issued by the governor and council to qualified grantees. Upon the completion of a survey, the warrant and surveyor's sketch or "plat" of the property were returned to the council for final ratification of the grant. De Brahm could, of course, make surveys personally and thus increase his income by fees which might otherwise go to a deputy surveyor. Evidently the surveyor general frequently augmented his income in this manner to the annoyance of Governor Grant. The latter complained bitterly in a letter to Lord Hillsborough that De Brahm "from a covetous disposition . . . has always been troublesome & irregular." The governor continued, "But the love of money which seems to grow upon him has lately carried him such lengths that it is impossible in justice to the Publick to overlook the Impropriety of his Conduct any longer."[178]

Other arguments marked De Brahm's relationship with Grant. When De Brahm decided to go to Charleston to purchase a schooner for use on the general survey rather than allow one of Grant's "particular Favorites" named Branton to build one under contract, the governor, according to De Brahm, "flew in a vehement passion and with menaces hindered the Surveyor General from going that time to Charlestown to purchase said Vessel."[179] As the rancor of their arguments increased, De Brahm went so far as to allege that the governor had suggested that Mrs. De Brahm might do well to "prove her Husband a Mad-Man."[180]

In June 1767, De Brahm refused to issue an order, or as it was termed "precept," to empower two deputy surveyors to undertake the survey of a 5,000-acre grant for Thomas Wooldridge. According to Grant, De Brahm insisted on issuing the precept to "Seton Wedderburn Row his Brother in Law, a Boy unacquainted with the Country, who had never surveyed an acre of land in the province and who had only been admitted as Deputy Surveyor two days before."[181] Wooldridge, who was the provost of East Florida, complained to the governor. Grant sent David Yeats, the colony's deputy clerk of the council, to inform De Brahm "that he was in the wrong to Mr. Wooldridge."[182] It would seem that De Brahm refused to admit any error in his action and stoutly maintained his right to name whomsoever he chose in a precept. To Grant, however, it seemed that De Brahm was engaging in nepotism by directing the surveying precepts to the Rows, his father- and brother-in-law.

After Yeats informed Grant of De Brahm's reply, the governor invited the surveyor, who was his next door neighbor, to his chambers to discuss the matter. De Brahm recounted precedents for his behavior based on his South Carolina and Georgia experience. Grant retorted that he seriously doubted whether the precedent existed for allowing the surveyor general to name a particular deputy for a particular survey, "but if it was the custom in every Province in America, I will not allow such an abuse in the Province put under my care." Grant went on to stress just how much De Brahm was profiting from land grants in the colony. Grant observed that "Mr. De Brahm seemed convinced and agreed to everything that was proposed, but expressed a wish of throwing something in the way of his family—he was told that nothing was more reasonable when the Boy, his Brother in Law, became master of his business and had by his Diligence recommended himself to the good opinion of the Publick, but that no partiality must be shewn on his part to the Detriment or Inconvenience of Settlers, and the business must go on as formerly."[183]

Any illusions which Grant may have had concerning De Brahm's retreat from his earlier stand on the Wooldridge survey were shattered two days later. Wooldridge returned, reporting that De Brahm still insisted on naming his brother-in-law, Row, in the precept, albeit in association with James Delaire, one of the surveyors originally desired by Wooldridge. Yeats once again went to "expostulate with Mr. De Brahm to convince him of his error if possible & to shew him his danger if he persisted." De Brahm reacted with a great show of obstinacy and moved to suspend both Delaire and John Funk, the other deputy surveyor originally requested by Wooldridge. Angrily De Brahm wrote Grant that he, De Brahm, would "do the Field Business himself." Grant objected because "there are at least Forty Warrants of Survey in force for Lands in different parts of the Province," and De Brahm "from his age & infirmities . . . is not in a situation to undergo the Fatigue." Even were De Brahm in good health, "tis impossible to make His Majesty's Subjects wait 'til one man can wander over the Face of the Country to mark their several settlements, every body, knows that the Settlers who come here are impatient of the least delay."[184]

After being warned by the colony's attorney general, De Brahm continued to insist that he was in the right, writing to Grant to reaffirm that by the terms of his commission he was "only to receive his orders from England." A very uneasy peace was achieved between the governor and his surveyor general, but Grant was far from happy with the state of affairs. On January 4, 1768, he and his council addressed a set of regulations concerning the conduct of the surveyor general's department to De Brahm. In the terms of the council's journal, these were designated to "facilitate the business of the province and to prevent future disputes in the Surveyor General's Department."[185]

Following this, De Brahm recounts the details of one particularly bitter row which he and Grant had in the presence of Frederick Haldimand, commander of the brigade stationed in Saint Augustine from April 1769 to April 1770. De Brahm protested that the governor had exceeded his authority by imposing regulations on him in the conduct of his office. He told Grant "that the Governor exceeded his power by assuming diametrically in Opposition to His Majesty's Commissions to enforce upon him [*De Brahm*] his verbal and written order, only suiting the Governor's private interest; thereupon producing His Majesty's Commission, begged His Excellency to read them with Moderation." In a rage, Grant "indecently stroke with his hand His Majesty's Commission from him and almost out of the Surveyor General's Hand."[186]

Matters came to a head during the spring of 1770, when Grant wrote to Lord Hillsborough, presenting a lengthy statement of De Brahm's malpractices and abuses of office.[187] Grant's charges and specifications were well documented and clearly aimed at having De Brahm suspended. In his letter to Hillsborough, the governor proceeded to "recommend Frederick George Mulcaster (who is married to Mr. De Brahm's Daughter an only child)," as successor to the office of provincial surveyor of lands for East Florida.[188] This was nothing short of rubbing salt into an open wound since his daughter had married Mulcaster in spite of De Brahm's vigorous opposition to the match. The governor added that "Mr. Mulcaster served at the Reduction of Goree and Martinique, is Godson to the late Prince of Wales, was brought into the army, under the immediate protection of the Royal Family, and has the honor to be known to the King, His Majesty will recollect him if your Lordship is pleased to mention his name."

Grant was leaving no stone unturned in his campaign to unseat East Florida's testy and argumentative surveyor of lands. Grant officially suspended De Brahm on October 4, 1770, "til His Majesty's Pleasure is known."[189] On the same day Mulcaster was appointed to act in his father-in-law's place. Grant's action later met with the approbation of Hillsborough, who ordered De Brahm to return to England to answer Grant's charges during the summer of 1771.[190]

ORDERED TO LONDON TO ANSWER CHARGES

De Brahm, who had been ordered to proceed to England forthwith, "was obliged to dispose of all he had left by disadvantageous over hurryed sales in order to keep up his reputation and credit by satisfying his honorable Carolina Creditors, and support the voyage expences of himself and wife, only without attendance from America to Europe."[191] After his arrival in London, he complained bitterly in a letter, dated October 8, 1771, to John Pownall, secretary to the Board of Trade, about having suffered "a suspension proving in effect a discharge before I am heard tryed and sentenced." De Brahm emphasized his chagrin by stating, "I can only bewail the lowness of my spirits and my incapacity of putting my hand to anything whatsoever especially to that plow, which afforded me bread and I left it out of obedience this eight years to searve two of the greatest Monarchs in the Universe to both of which Grand Father and Son I have acted with all the honor and diligence and faithfulness becoming a true servant. . . ."[192]

In December, De Brahm received the substance of Governor Grant's charges against him. He was instructed to prepare a "justification" of his conduct, "in the several instances wherein Mr. Grant states you have been blameable," a task to which he addressed himself with his usual energy. In his efforts toward clearing his name, De Brahm sought legal aid and advice in preparing the comprehensive "Abridgement of Governor Grant's Deportment against the Surveyor General William Gerard De Brahm" which he presented to the "Right Honorable the Lords Commissioners of His Majesty's Treasury," early in 1773.[193] During that summer he appeared in person before the Treasury Board at least once and presented memorials to that body on at least two occasions.[194] It would appear that his representations were well received since his memorial praying payment of the £700-17-0 due for the expenses of the general survey for 1773 was favorably acted upon.

To his great relief the Treasury's action indicated clearly that his tenure in the office of surveyor general of the Southern Department was secure. Doubt regarding his provincial post in East Florida lingered until the following summer, however. On July 28, 1774, De Brahm was heard by the Board of Treasury in the matter of Governor Grant's charges. That Grant had never come forward to press his case against De Brahm in person though in London weighed heavily in the surveyor general's favor. The Treasury decided that De Brahm should be reinstated in his post as provincial surveyor in East Florida.[195]

Preparation of the "Report of the General Survey in the Southern District of North America"

As early as 1769, De Brahm had begun a correspondence with Lord Dartmouth which was to flower during the period of his London residence.[196] Dartmouth, who succeeded Hillsborough to the office of secretary of state for the Southern Department in 1772, had a deep interest in American affairs, particularly in Florida land and colonization schemes.[197] Added to these mundane interests was Dartmouth's devotion to scientific and metaphysic studies. When all things are considered it is not surprising to find that De Brahm became closely associated with Dartmouth or, indeed, that he looked upon this influential peer and minister of government as his patron and protector.[198] The present reader has good reason to appreciate Dartmouth's patronage since it was under his enlightened guidance that De Brahm completed his "Report of the General Survey in the Southern District of North America," published for the first time in this Tricentennial Edition.

Just when De Brahm began to compile a general and comprehensive description of his surveys and discoveries is difficult to determine. It is possible that he had intended such a work from the beginning of his tenure as surveyor general. One thing is certain, however: his return to London to defend himself against Governor Grant's charges provided both the strong incentive and opportunity to undertake such a demanding task.

In 1769, Lord Hillsborough had requested De Brahm to collect all of his many surveys and incorporate them into a general map, "the drawing to be made with the greatest care and exactness and not copied upon such thin slight paper as those you have already sent—which being in detached pieces and upon different scales cannot be made use of without great difficulty and inconvenience."[199] De Brahm set to work on such a general map of Florida which he reported would be drawn "by a scale of two & half miles per inch."[200] His original instructions from the Board of Trade, dated August 15, 1764, specified that he should include a detailed regional description with each map he forwarded. It may be that the effort to produce a general map of his district was paralleled by a similar effort to produce a general and comprehensive written description of it. In commenting on "the General Map of the Northernmost part of East Florida containing 2,560,000 acres of land," forwarded on January 6, 1771, De Brahm observed that "this map my Lord may depend is an exact representation of what I personally and faithfully examined on the spot of what is surveyed by my deputies and that I shall never attempt to make any return or insertment in General Maps of any other characteristick."[201] An inspection of De Brahm's large manuscript maps now in the Public Record Office reveals that broad areas of the Florida interior are blank, indicating that the surveyor general remained true to his word.

De Brahm's suspension in 1771 concerned only his provincial position in East Florida, so that he continued to function and draw his allowance as surveyor general for the Southern District throughout his stay in London. To justify this income and ensure his continuation in the post, De Brahm devoted considerable time and energy to the preparation of both general maps and his Report. On August 12, 1772, in a letter to Dartmouth, he mentioned having completed "my general map, joined its sections and delivered it with my report to Mr. Pownall."[202] In the Report, De Brahm's dedicatory statements to both Dartmouth and King George III state that this map was delivered during June 1772. In what appears to be another reference to the map, De Brahm, in an undated memorial to Dartmouth, prayed "that his Reports and General Map of East Florida 25 foot in length, which he has delivered last Summer may be laid before the Board of the Right Honble the Lords of Trade and Plantation, and have their Lordships aprobation of both his Conduct and Services as also the Customary certificate to receive the Salary as Surveyor General for the Southern District with £700-17- due since last mid Summer 1772 in order that he may be able to produce the same when ordred to appear at the Board of His Majesty's Treasury."[203] It may be assumed that the general maps and Report aided De Brahm in his successful petitions for reinstatement and restitution before the board.

In his work with the Cape Florida Society De Brahm reports utilizing his general survey materials in the preparation of a large-scale map to show Dartmouth's Florida landholdings in their proper location, "with the extremity in Latitude 25°30'00" and in the first degree and fortyth minute of the fourth climate...."[204]

It would seem that at some point during early 1773 Dartmouth decided to have De Brahm attend the king and personally present him with a copy of the first portion of the Report, covering the provinces of South Carolina, Georgia, and East Florida. This is not altogether surprising in view of the king's lively interest in American geography, nor was De Brahm's name unknown to Britain's monarch. Several of the surveyor general's letters, reports, and maps dealing with the general survey had been laid before the king during the preceding years. On March 19, 1773, in a letter to Dartmouth chiefly concerning the Cape Florida Society, De Brahm queried "whether fryday next is the day convenient for introducing me to His Majesty?"[205] On Friday "The 2d of April 1773," De Brahm reports, "I had the distinguished honour to present to Your Majesty my first report...."[206] This was the first bound manuscript folio volume which, in the course of time, has devolved to the British Museum where it is now cataloged in the Department of Manuscripts as Kings Ms. 210.

De Brahm continued working on the second volume or "Tome" of his Report during the summer of 1773. On August 31, 1773, he informed Dartmouth, "I am almost ready with the continuation of my report consisting of hundred pages more, a precise description of my surveys in twenty six Tables and Several plans, of the different soils and natural productions, manufacturys, possible improvements, and directions for navigating all inlets and the Florida Stream near the Martiers, Cape Florida and the Coast, by which I endeavour to prove authentically, that I have really employed all my days in America in His Majesty's Service and am inhumanely injured by Colonel Grant's Deportment and accusations."[207] It should be noted that one of Grant's chief charges against De Brahm had been that the latter engaged in jobbery by neglecting the general survey in favor of his more lucrative provincial post. Grant had claimed that De Brahm "remains in his office in Town & trusts the General Survey to the Provincial Deputies, who are very unequal to such a task, tho they may be fit enough to measure and locate particular tracts of land in the province."[208]

On September 24, 1773, De Brahm forwarded the second tome of his Report to Lord Dartmouth, who was then "in the country" and could be expected to have more leisure in which to peruse it.[209] De Brahm pointed out that "the subjects of the 5th and 7th Chapters I have in a great measure, but not fully nor properly anticipated to Your Lordship; those of the 4th and 6th Chapter are entirely new, and [*I*] flatter myself, they will increase Your Lordships favorable opinion of that country." De Brahm added, "I am about the copy (which if Your Lordship approve) I will present to Her Majesty," though he would not be able to complete the copy until he had Dartmouth's decision on whether it should contain the "Apendix" or not. Dartmouth seems to have decided that Tome Two, like its companion volume, should go to the king and that the "Apendix" should be omitted, since it is clearly dedicated to Queen Charlotte's husband and lacks the colorful appendix found in the version located in the Harvard Library.[210] De Brahm acknowledged on October 23, 1773, that "The Report is finishing under my hands with all speed agreeable to the received directions."[211]

Tome Two was shortly completed and laid in the king's hands during the autumn of 1773. It joined its handsome companion volume in George III's personal collection of original manuscript materials on American geography, and, also in the course of time, became Kings Ms. 211 in the British Museum. Together, these two tomes form the complete "Report of the General Survey in the Southern District of North America." De Brahm's text, sketches, and maps comprising this comprehensive report form a unique and valuable source, rich in firsthand knowledge of the Southeast during the quarter century preceding the American Revolution. It is here made available in a published form for general readers as well as scholars for the first time. This is not to say, however, that De Brahm and his work has heretofore been unknown in print. On the contrary, important portions of his Harvard manuscript have been published at different times. Regrettably these have been abbreviated offerings available in very limited editions and so only found in the larger research libraries.[212] It is unfortunate indeed that this colorful and factually rich source has remained so long in obscurity and disuse.[213]

SCIENTIFIC WRITING AND PUBLISHING IN LONDON

During his time in London De Brahm engaged in a number of publication efforts. His first published book, titled *The Atlantic Pilot*, appeared in 1772.[214] This now rare work was printed for De Brahm by "T. Spilsbury, in Cook's-Court, Carey Street; and sold by L. Leacroft, Opposite Spring-Gardens, Charing Cross." It includes much of the material found in "Chapr. 7th" of his Report covering East Florida (see pp. 241–51 of the Report), including the maps and "Tables of the Hydrometrie from Charleston in South Carolina to London. . . ." Omitted is De Brahm's ambitious plan for two huge lighthouses or "Pharuses" which he suggested be constructed to safeguard navigation "through that dangerous and inevitable Passage between the Island of Cuba, and the Promontory of

East Florida." Significantly the book was dedicated to Lord Hillsborough, indicating that the project was underway before Hillsborough was succeeded by Dartmouth in the office of secretary of state for the Southern Department. *The Atlantic Pilot* was a thoroughly practical book, "calculated for the safe conduct of ships in their navigation from the Gulph of Mexico along Cuba and the Martieres, through the New Bahama Channel to the Northern Parts of His Majesty's Dominions on the continent of America, and from thence to Europe." As such it was well received, one reviewer noting that De Brahm "seems to have executed his commission [*as surveyor general*] with great Fidelity, accuracy, and diligence."[215] Although Bernard Romans, one of De Brahm's ex-deputies with whom he was at odds, launched a strident attack on *The Atlantic Pilot* in his own book on the Floridas published a few years later, it would seem that the appearance of this book in 1772 helped De Brahm regain his threatened positions in the colonial administration of America.[216] Proof that it had a continuing influence is found in the fact that a French translation was published in Paris sixteen years later.[217]

Through his relationship with Lord Dartmouth De Brahm was exposed to the scientific avant-garde of eighteenth-century London. Dartmouth, possessed of a most active and questing mentality, was a member of the Royal Society. One of the new areas of research and discovery being reported to that body during 1774 concerned the use of the mercurial barometer in the determination of terrestrial elevations. The results of experiments conducted by J. A. De Luc had been published in Geneva in 1772. De Luc provided detailed instructions for the construction of height-finding barometers and rules for their accurate use. His formulae for relating pressure with elevation by compensating for temperature and meteorlogical effects were to enable surveyors to obtain heights rapidly by releasing them from a reliance on laborious trigonometrical methods.[218] Nevil Maskelyne, the Astronomer Royal, and Samuel Horsley, a clergyman astronomer, both published papers which made De Luc's findings and techniques available in the English language during 1774.[219] In view of De Brahm's ability with languages it is probable that he was able to work directly from De Luc's publication without awaiting these English translations. On April 24, 1774, and before either translation had appeared, De Brahm wrote Dartmouth, mentioning that he had already forwarded his "Physical System of the Variation in the Mercury in the Barometer." He requested that Dartmouth present his "twenty-two paragraphs" to the Royal Society so "that their opinion may accelerate the establishing of those laws now preparing under the hand of Mr. Horsley in Crosby Row Newington."[220]

De Brahm carried forward his work with the barometer during the summer of 1774, on August 4 sending Dartmouth a copy of his "Atmospherical Tables" which had just been printed.[221] Concerning their publication, De Brahm observed that "considering the precariousness which I have too often experienced by setting out on extensive surveys with a single set of mathematical aparatus, I concluded it equaly as dangerous to depend on a manuscript of Tables, which I have calculated with unwearied and uninterrupted application, I have therefore thought it prudent to have of so tedious elaborations [*a*] few copys made in print of my Atmospherical Tables." These "Atmospherical Tables" formed De Brahm's second publication, produced in London by T. Spilsbury, the printer of *The Atlantic Pilot*.[222] An inscribed copy of *The Levelling Balance and Counterbalance* . . . , as this rare book is titled, was presented to the Royal Society by De Brahm and is now found in the library of that venerable scientific body.[223]

In his August 4 letter to Dartmouth, De Brahm mentioned still another project that was then in preparation for the printer. This was his "Calculations for the Northern and Southern 25 climates consisting of 804 meridians and as many parallels each laid down with all its degrees, minutes, and seconds in 68 Tables." These tables appeared from T. Spilsbury's busy press in 1774, under the title of *De Brahm's Zonical Tables, For the Twenty-five Northern and Southern Climates*. Like *The Levelling Balance and Counterbalance* . . . , this work was probably printed in limited numbers and is now quite rare. It is valuable, however, in clarifying De Brahm's scheme of climatic classification which he employs in his Report.

At least these three works were published by De Brahm during the same productive period of four years which saw him completing his large general maps and Report. This was also a time of petitioning and litigation in connection with Grant's accusations as well as considerable efforts with the Cape Florida Society in behalf of Dartmouth. Not content to rest on the deserved laurels of such a productive outpouring, De Brahm's main concern became the mounting of a new survey expedition to the southern colonies of North America.

RETURN TO AMERICA

In his official correspondence, De Brahm occasionally drew attention to the fact that his opposite number in the Northern District, Samuel Holland, had a larger budget and the use of an Admiralty vessel to support his surveying efforts. While in London, De Brahm dedicated himself to obtaining similar provisions for his own efforts in the South. In a letter to Dartmouth written in 1772, he again mentioned Holland's favored position and bemoaned his own. He pointed out that he was Holland's senior in terms of royal service and that Holland had no accomplishment in his record to approach De Brahm's own establishment of

Bethany in Georgia. He concluded that he should be recommissioned to continue the southern surveys and given an allowance and support equal to Holland's.[224] Early in the following year he again requested that Dartmouth "grant me only the aides of a vessel and tender, thereby to enable me to be eight months in America expedying the General Surveys and four months vid. elicit. June, July, August, and September in London to make out my Reports and plans and be at hand when Governor Grant is willing to give me a chance to justifie myself against his Assertions."[225]

Dartmouth espoused the surveyor general's cause in several important quarters during this period. It is not surprising, therefore, to find De Brahm early in 1774 presenting an official memorial to the Board of Trade which included the request for a survey vessel as well as an allowance for the purchase of surveying instruments. Nor is it surprising to find that the board, after making inquiries into the arrangements of the northern survey, ordered that a recommendation endorsing De Brahm's scheme be forwarded to the king.[226]

During the spring of 1774, De Brahm busied himself with inspecting Admiralty sloops to find one suitable for use on the survey.[227] On March 10, 1774, a presentation, signed by Dartmouth and three members of the Board of Trade endorsing De Brahm's request for such a vessel, was delivered to the king.[228] With such a strong endorsement De Brahm's new survey was assured of support and backing similar to that enjoyed by Holland. The armed ship *Cherokee* was assigned for his use and, on December 1, 1774, De Brahm wrote Dartmouth to report that only the want of a commander and crew to man her was then delaying his return to America and the general survey.[229] On December 21, 1774, he requested that his allowance for the purchase of "astronomical and surveying instruments" be increased from £200 to £500, observing that "nothing detains me in Europe but the not commissioning of the Vessel, which had been reported fit to receive men sometime ago." In the meantime, however, he was "setting about the General Map of the Southern District for your Lordship's Department, which Mr. Pownall has ordered."[230]

De Brahm had only to wait until January 17, 1775, when, according to an entry in the "Masters Journal for the Cherokee from the 17th day of Jany. 1775 to the 13th of March following," "This day lieut. Ferguson took command of his Majesty's Arm'd ship Cherokee, artificer's Emp. on Board."[231] Finally, on June 19, 1775, De Brahm, his wife (née Row), brother-in-law, and nephew Ferdinand sailed from Guernsey bound for Charleston. The voyage was not to be a simple passage of return. To the contrary, the surveyor general utilized the ten weeks of the *Cherokee*'s slow voyage to conduct an oceanographic survey. In his own words, "Setting out on my voyage from England to America I had two objects in view both equally interesting for Navigation and the learned world. The one was to discover the Bread[*th*] and directions of the constant currents upon the coast of Europe and Africa, and whether [*they cross*] the Atlantic from Africa to America, as I always supposed. The other object was the preciseness of fixing the Line of No Variation."[232] His success in these major objectives is confirmed by his lengthy manuscript volume, "Continuation of the Atlantic Pilot," completed after the voyage.[233]

In addition to tracing "a current if not a stream . . . sweeping the coast of France, Spain, Portugal, and Africa," and past the Canary and Cape Verde Islands to a course between the Equator and Tropic of Cancer, "through the Carribbee Islands into the Gulf of Mexico," and fixing the position of the agonic line, De Brahm continued his experiments with the barometer on the voyage. He utilized "Nairnes Marine Barometer and a Thermometer," which supplied him "with new materials of an object not inferior to the two originally in my view and for the same benefit." He observed that "my daily observations of the Barometer and Thermometer have furnished me with the disposition of phenomena in the Atmosphere." De Brahm was relating the migration of low-pressure centers to storms at sea and noting the generally lower atmospheric pressure of the tropics. He went on to relate that "it was by their change, that I the 31 of August foretold a Hurricane was approaching, and we had scarce time to dismast the ship of her two Top Gallons, all sails were expeditiously furrld; the missen main Sail rift for Ballast, the Healm lashed, the Boats extra secured by stays the shrouts Stranghtned by rolling Brasses, for fore yard let down, the dead lights put in, and all Scuttles and Hatchways (except the main) cross laid over."[234] While the master of the *Cherokee* did not use the term "Hurricane" nor go into such an elaboration on storm readiness as De Brahm, he did note in his log entry for Saturday, September 2, 1775, that "at 7 ship'd a great sea w:ch wash'd away the Binical and Steerage Companion broke two brass compasses and glasses and stove in the Larboard Quarter lodge Wash'd the spare pumps overboard."[235] De Brahm compared this Hurricane to the one which he had weathered while surveying the coast of Florida in March 1765, generously noting that the *Cherokee* "otherwise a very dull sailor behaved extremely well."

ARRIVAL IN CHARLESTON

Land was sighted to the north of Charleston early on the morning of September 7, 1775. Just before reaching the city the ailing Mrs. De Brahm died while still on the *Cherokee*.[236] De Brahm himself, sick with "a violent fever," waited until September 9 before going ashore to see his wife buried in South Carolina's capital, now a hotbed of insurrection. The *Cherokee* was taken from his service and her commander, Lieutenant Ferguson, and a detachment of sailors ordered ashore to dismount the cannons in Fort Johnson in an effort to deny their possible use by the rebels. As the wind of rebellion intensified in Charleston, the *Cherokee* was more and more involved in the military maneuvering which served as a prelude to the Revolutionary War in the South. Writing from Charleston on September 18, 1775, De Brahm decried the impressment of the *Cherokee* for military duties. He lamented "that a ship so positively disqualified for military purposes should be detailed for doing what it cannot, and perhaps fall a sacrifice, when it may as soon as the equinoctials are over, bring me to the Bahama Islands or the Gulf of Mexico, having in both places many Surveys to make, where the present unhappy disturbances do not, nor will reach to interrupt me."[237]

Unfortunately the "unhappy disturbances" then clouding the Charleston skies did not abate and De Brahm was permanently denied the use of the *Cherokee*. At first he busied himself by completing the report of his observations made during the voyage from England, described as comprising "160 pages in folio containing all my Astronomical and physical observations made between Greenwich and America, laid down in 88 Tables to be submitted to the best Judges."[238] He moved into a house "at the west end of town" where he could hear "at a distance . . . the sounds of drums and fifes [*and*] some times of canons." At this address, which he referred to somewhat grandly as the "Royal Observatory in Charleston," he missed no opportunity to "increase the number of my observations by day and night." He planned "to draw from the mean of many the exact longitude of this place from Greenwich."[239] In 1777, after his return to Europe, De Brahm reported the precise location of Charleston as latitude 32°47′ North and longitude 79°52′54″7‴ West from Greenwich.[240]

De Brahm remained in Charleston until June 27, 1777, when he sailed for France aboard the American ship *Hancock and Adams*, having become persona non grata in the eyes of the South Carolinians when he refused to abjure his allegiance to the king. Ever the surveyor general, he reported that "I concluded to make on this Traject a third survey of the Atlantic in order to increase the number of observations for better establishing the system of the current, counter currents, variations of the compass, their bearings and how far parallel with the line of No Variation, which on a distance of 900 miles bearing N. 54°17′20″ W. I have passed and repassed six times."[241]

While he was still in Charleston an event took place which was to cause De Brahm considerable embarrassment and anxiety during the next few years and to trouble historians ever since. The event concerned the British attack on Charleston during the spring of 1776, when Sir Peter Parker and Sir Henry Clinton, in command of the British sea and land forces respectively, conducted an abortive attack which was considered a victory for the rebellious Americans. It is clear from the "Proceedings of the South Carolina Provincial Congress" and other sources that a military engineer named De Brahm was employed in the construction of fortifications built to defend Charleston against the British attack. Unfortunately, these records and pay entries refer only to a "Mr. De Brahm" or to a "Capt. De Brahm (Engineer)," at no point including a Christian name. Certainly the best-known holder of this uncommon surname during the eighteenth century was the surveyor general.

It is not surprising to find that questions were raised concerning his loyalty when later he had occasion to plead for compensation from the royal government in London.[242] Nor is it surprising to find that historians of the present era have continued to assume that William Gerard De Brahm's loyalty to the king lapsed during 1776.[243] Indeed one widely quoted authority would even put the surveyor general in the pantheon of American heroes, stating that De Brahm's fortification on Sullivan's Island was "an achievement that aided materially to the victory of the Americans over the British."[244]

What then was his role in the American defense of Charleston? De Brahm himself provided the best answer to this question two years later when he returned to London seeking redress and compensation. In a memorial to the Board of Trade dated March 3, 1778, he wrote that "Your Memorialist is very unfortunate in having been deceived by a Nephew, of his Name, who has taken part with the Rebels, but for so base an action has been deserted by Your Memorialist."[245] Included with this memorial was a letter from the respected ex-royal governor of South Carolina, William Bull,[246] who testified that De Brahm had been forced to leave America along with other "servants of the Crown" for "refusing the oath of abjuration." He added that he too had heard rumors of De Brahm's contribution to the American cause, but "they be owing to Yr. Nephew De Brahm, relative to you, who was employed by those in Power as an engineer." Regarding Sullivan's Island, Bull went on to observe that "further I have been credibly told that you were in Mr. Fenwick's house in Charleston on the day His Majestys ships made the attack on Sullivan's Island and believe you had not been on that Island after Lord William Campbell left Charleston."[247]

The solution to the mystery resides in the person of Ferdinand De Brahm, the son of the surveyor general's eldest brother. Ferdinand had immigrated to America to serve his uncle as an assistant on the general survey. There is no doubt that by 1776 he was a skillful engineer and cartographer, well schooled by his uncle. The map collection of the William L. Clements Library contains two manuscript maps of the New York military campaigns of 1776, drawn by Ferdinand Joseph Sebastian De Brahm, which were included in the papers of Sir Henry Clinton.[248] The younger De Brahm went on to distinguish himself in the service of the new American nation. On February 11, 1778, he received a commission as "Major Engineer" in the Continental Army. He was taken prisoner at Charleston on May 12, 1780, and exchanged on April 22, 1781. On February 6, 1784, he received a promotion to "brevet Lieutenant-Colonel" and was retired from the service.[249] How long he remained in his adopted homeland is uncertain, but by 1787, he appears to have returned to his home in Germany, being included in a list of foreign dignitaries elected to membership in the American Philosophical Society who received letters of announcement from Thomas Jefferson in that year.[250] In correspondence with Jefferson concerning his pension, Ferdinand stressed the length of his past services by stating "I have served the whole war in America."[251] In view of the available evidence bearing on the Charleston defense of 1776 it seems probable that it was he who contributed to the American cause rather than the surveyor general.[252] It might even be said that one of William Gerard De Brahm's most consistant traits through nearly half a century following his emigration to Georgia until his death was his outspoken devotion to his adopted British monarch. If he did cooperate with the Americans in 1776 it was a temporary lapse of allegiance only and quite out of character. Certainly there is no indication to show that De Brahm was ever seriously considered as disloyal. In fact, the "Estimate of the Expense Attending General Surveys of His Majesty's Dominions in North America for the year 1777" included the following item, "To Mr. De Brahm for his support in Georgia [*this was incorrect, it should have read "South Carolina"*] being under imprisonment by the Rebels, at 10s p.d. 182-10."[253]

On February 18, 1776, "William Gerard De Brahm Esq." married "Mrs. Mary Fenwick, widow of the late Hon. Edward Fenwicke Esq. deceased."[254] Mrs. De Brahm, née Mary Drayton, had married Edward Fenwick, a member of the royal council of South Carolina in 1753. Fenwick had died during July 1775, leaving his widow with several children and an endowment.[255] The third Mrs. De Brahm survived her husband.[256]

RETURN TO ENGLAND VIA FRANCE

Upon his return to London by way of France in the autumn of 1777, De Brahm successfully petitioned for the salary due him as provincial surveyor general.[257] On April 2, 1778, he signed a receipt for £77-7-0 "in full for my salary as Surveyor General of East Florida from the 24th day of June last."[258] His other affairs were not, however, going so smoothly. His wife's annual annuity of £243 and the educational allowance of £160 yearly for his two stepchildren, provided by Edward Fenwick's estate, were not being received from Charleston because of the war. Another and far more significant concern was his loss of the surveyor general's income. In the "Estimate of the Expence attending General Surveys of His Majesty's Dominions in North America for the year 1778," De Brahm was allotted only £182-10-0 for himself and £91-5-0 for his deputy.[259] This was to be his last income as surveyor general of the Southern District. In his sixtieth year, De Brahm found himself left with only his provincial office in East Florida.

From 1778 until 1784 De Brahm was, in his own words, "for the most part an invalid . . ." in Topsham near Exeter in Devon.[260] Apparently he was officially on a leave of absence for the year 1779, blaming his poor health on the exertions required by the general survey.[261] On July 22, 1782, he wrote his old patron Dartmouth to say that he was recovered enough to take advantage of the summer weather for a journey to London. The purpose of his visit was to present himself to the "minister, and learn whether I continue or have been discharged from His Majesty's service." He went on to state that he had received no income or support from the government since 1779, "yea even without an answer to my many letters and memorial presented these three years passed during which my bills upon the Agent for my salary have been protested."[262] Broken in health and in serious financial straits, the aging De Brahm observed that he realized the present time was not propitious for Dartmouth to forward his name for the pension list but that he dreaded the thought of attempting to resume his office in Saint Augustine. De Brahm "found it impossible to support the common necessarys in house keeping with £150 per annum . . . in peaceful time what must it be in these melancholy confusions for an old sickly man to struggle with."[263] Of course, even the hope of the meager salary for his East Florida position was dashed when in 1783 Britain retroceded the colony to Spain.

During the period of De Brahm's convalescence in Topsham, the tide of international politics had swept Florida once more into Spanish hands after twenty years of British control. British subjects were, of course, to be compensated for genuine losses suffered through the retrocession, and a Commission for East Florida Loyalist Claims was established. On December 2, 1786, De Brahm submitted a claim to this board containing a list of his properties still located in the province.[264] Although De Brahm put the value of these at £3,000, he received only £1,448-10-0 in compensation.

In 1784 De Brahm traveled to Germany in an effort to "claim my right to the Signory of Holzheim in the Bavarian Palatinate, the country whence in 1751, [I] was banished."[265] He wrote that he had done this "for my grandchildren to Major Mulcaster at Portsmouth."[266] In the same year he returned to London but received no attention to his requests to the government for compensation.

Leaving his wife in England, De Brahm returned to Charleston to restore his family's American fortunes. On February 18, 1784, the "Petition of Sundry Persons in behalf of William Gerard De Brahm and Mary his wife late widow of Edward Fenwick deceased" was read by a committee of South Carolina's senate.[267] After succeeding in having his name removed from the state's confiscation list, De Brahm found it necessary to institute legal action in an attempt to recover his wife's estates.[268] After what he described as "three years of painfull applications," De Brahm reported collecting "but a pittance of £200 in lieu of £5,000."[269] Nearly reduced to penury, he returned to London during July 1788.

While in Charleston De Brahm addressed a letter to the king, enclosing a lengthy essay titled "Natural Astronomy," illustrated with a diagram of the "Natural Solar System." In a covering letter, De Brahm recounted his long period of service and unbroken loyalty, concluding, "Witness my surveys of East Florida, Georgia, and South Carolina, which I was indulged personally to delivery in thy Royal Hands." Then he provided a cryptic passage which served as a portent of the direction in which his career was to turn. He wrote, "My loyalty and faithfulness is now of a Spiritual Nature and not Subject to change or even to be dissolved by Eternity. I cannot resist but am disposed cheerfully to obey its impulse in Submitting this manuscript to thy Royal contemplation with my prior manuscript and pray thou will condescend to believe I continue thy loyal and faithful friend John De Brahm."[270]

It would seem that De Brahm had become a Quaker either during his three years in Charleston (1785–88) or earlier. Certainly from 1785 onward he exhibited a strongly religious turn of mind and tended to sign himself as "John" rather than "William." In a statement taken and affirmed by Phineas Bond in Philadelphia on November 2, 1787, De Brahm stated that he was "one of the People called Quakers."[271] Though he had always exhibited a strongly religious facet to his many-sided character, from 1785 onward religion seemed to dominate his life to the exclusion of practically all else. All of his publications from this period onward were devoted to religio-philosophical themes.

Residing in the less-than-fashionable London suburb of Hackney during 1788 and 1789, De Brahm addressed memorials to the Board of Commissioners for the American Loyalists and letters to persons of influence in government requesting a pension or some sort of provision for himself and his family, who were now in a seriously limited financial position.[272] In this correspondence there is a copy of a letter which De Brahm sent to Queen Charlotte,[273] a fascinating document in which De Brahm refers to his continuing interest in physico-alchemical research. He comments on George's illness, which De Brahm felt had its origins in an "excess of mental and corporeal motions." As a remedy he offered to provide an "admirable salt" with which he had been experimenting. There is no record of the queen's complying with his request to "command my appearance in thy presence," so it is doubtful that he ever ministered to the ailing king. In keeping with his newly adopted style of address he signed this letter, "thy True Friend—John William Gerard De Brahm."

The indications are that De Brahm's prayers for financial aid and a pension were no more favorably received by the government in 1788 than they had been earlier. In the records of the Loyalist Claims Commission, meeting in New Castle House, Lincoln Fields, during the summer of 1788, there is a memorial from De Brahm endorsed "July 20—Mr. De Brahm informed the Board Can do nothing in it."[274] He tried again in the autumn with no greater success than before.[275] In quiet desperation he wrote to Prime Minister William Pitt from his lodgings in "Mutton Lane, Hackney" on April 30, 1789, to make a last plea for recognition and compensation. He must have presented a pathetic figure. In his seventy-second year he was so infirm that he was able "but seldom to foot it from Hackney to London." Before signing this, his last letter found in British government archives, he concluded, "My head is with honour grown hoar in the King's Service: do it Justice I pray! to bring it in honour to its grave."[276] Shortly after this final plaintive appeal, De Brahm and his wife set sail for Charleston. After tarrying in Mrs. De Brahm's home city for a period, they then turned their faces toward Philadelphia, perhaps the most attractive refuge for an aged German Quaker Loyalist in the post-Revolutionary era.

FINAL RETURN TO AMERICA

It would seem that De Brahm and his wife Mary settled in the Philadelphia area sometime during 1791. Clement Biddle's *Directory* of that year lists a John W. I. De Brahm then residing at 254 High Street.[277] In his account of the Tattnall and Fenwick families, D. E. Huger Smith mentions a conveyance of July 29, 1791, in which the De Brahms were described as "of Philadelphia, late of Charleston."[278] The same year also saw the beginning of De Brahm's association with the Philadelphia printer, Zachariah Poulson, Jr., Poulson's press issuing *Time An Apparition of Eternity*. This was De Brahm's first of several books devoted to mystical themes well larded with biblical references. During the next several years, he continued to write mystical works, including his *Apocalyptic Gnomon Points Out Eternity's Divisibility Rated with Time, Pointed at By Gnomon Siderealis*. This last effort was referred to by one anonymous biblio-biographer as a "very curious and madly mystical book."[279]

De Brahm is reported to have resided for a period in one of the historic buildings listed in *Historic Germantown from the Founding to the Early Part of the Nineteenth Century*, a photograph being included in this ambitious volume.[280] In 1796, De Brahm purchased an estate of just under forty acres in Bristol Township,

Philadelphia County, from the well-known Quaker, Henry Drinker.[281] It was here, at the home known variously as "Bellair," "Clearfield," or "Fairfield," that De Brahm spent the last three years of his long life. According to the account of one local chronicler he lived in a genteel and colorful manner there.[282] Anne D. Mears, writing in 1890, reported that "from what I have heard my grandparents say of d'Brahmes, they were social and kind persons, given to much hospitality, like all Frenchmen with education and refinement." She went on to recount how "D'Brahme kept his coach and livery, and on the doors of the carriage were silver locks, when the guests entered these were closed and the key carried by the footman until the house was reached, when d'Brahme was there to receive his guests and unlock the door. He was very fond of the society of young people, and never let the opportunity pass by when he could have them at their house." The Charleston-bred Mrs. De Brahm was described as "a most agreeable and refined woman." Mrs. Mears ended her account of the De Brahms by reporting that Mrs. De Brahm returned to Charleston after her husband died following a short illness in 1799.[283]

While it is difficult to authenticate Mrs. Mears's account, she is accurate concerning the facts of his purchase of land from Henry Drinker as well as the time of his death and Mrs. De Brahm's return to Charleston. If Mrs. Mears has correctly reported her grandparents' knowledge of De Brahm's character and activities in his last years, it would seem that his metaphysical and religious preoccupations had succeeded in leading him to a greater degree of contentment and peace of mind than he had enjoyed earlier.

De Brahm's will was written on July 11, 1796, after he had purchased Bellair from Henry Drinker.[284] He died sometime during the early summer of 1799, since that document was affirmed and recorded on July 3 of that year. In his will De Brahm described himself, in 1796, as being "late of the City of Philadelphia but now of Bristol Township in the County of Philadelphia in the Commonwealth of Pennsylvania, being in a weak state of bodily health, but of sound mind, Memory and Understanding. . . ." He left his complete estate including Bellair to his widow.

After selling Bellair to the apothecary, John Hart, Mary De Brahm returned to her family and friends in Charleston.[285] The widow of the surveyor general followed her husband to the ultimate reward in 1806. In her own will Mary De Brahm mentioned several of her "late beloved husband's" relatives abroad.[286] To Frederick William Mulcaster, his grandson, she gave the sum of twenty guineas, "which I request him to accept for a memento of his late venerable grandfather John William Gerard de Brahm." She also mentioned De Brahm's relatives in Germany, "who having lost their whole property by the ravages of the war are entitled to my consideration, in preference to his grandson who is in affluence.

. . ." Four of De Brahm's surviving nieces were mentioned and awarded a total of " £500 (British sterling money)."

The March 28, 1806, edition of the *Savannah Republican* carried a lengthy notice of Mrs. De Brahm's demise, reporting that "She died at Charleston in the bosom of her affectionate children who in compliance with her desires, sent her remains to Philadelphia, in order to be conveyed to Germantown and buried by her late husband. The interment was solemn, attended with a comfortable evidence that she had exchanged a scene of trial in this probationary state of being for eternal peace and rest. . . ."[287]

Unfortunately, the records of the burials at the Friends Burying Ground which would cover the period of William and Mary De Brahm's interments are not extant,[288] nor is there any headstone marker which would indicate the exact site of their last resting place.[289] It is ironic that De Brahm, who contributed so much to the geographical discovery and accurate mapping of the colonial Southeast, rests today obscure and anonymous in an unmarked grave surrounded by the urban sprawl of metropolitan Philadelphia. Hopefully, this book, coupled with a growing interest in the historical geography of the United States, will lead to a fuller discovery and appreciation of William Gerard De Brahm, His Majesty's surveyor general for the Southern District of North America.

South Carolina

To the King's most Excellent Majesty,
Sire!

By your Majesty's Commission, dated the 26th, of June 1764 I had the Honour to be appointed Surveyor for the Southern District of North America, and was ordered to make General Surveys both of the Inlands and Sea Coasts, with the Soundings, as well on the Coast, as within the Harbours, to obtain their Latitudes and Longitudes, and make such Remarks, as might conduce to the Security and Information of Your Majesty's Subjects, who may navigate those Seas. These Observations and Remarks as well as every other which can tend to convey a precise Knowlege of the Actual State and Limits of the Country, the Quantity of Acres, the principal Rivers and Harbours, the Nature and Produce of the Soil, and in what Points capable of Improvement, I was ordered to report in Maps and seperate Descriptions. I have accordingly begun the General Surveys from the Southernmost Extremity of the District, vide, from East Florida; and in June 1772 returned to your Majesty's principal Secretary of State for the Colonies, and the Right Honourable the Lords Commissioners for Trade and Plantations the Surveys and Soundings of the Western Atlantic Coast, from Lattitude 24°20′ to 30°26′49″ (which makes a Meridian of 423 3/4 miles) and from Cape Florida West 103 1,243/8,000 miles to the Indian Boundary Line, which is a Parallel of 1°41′41 1/2″. And although I have not at present accomplished the Surveys of the more Northern Parts, yet the different Mathematical and other Operations, in which I have been concerned in South Carolina and Georgia have furnished me with a compleat Knowlege of these Provinces; and since the History of Georgia takes its Origin from that of South Carolina, [2] and that of East Florida has Affinity with the History both of South Carolina and Georgia; I could not make my Reports to your Majesty with Precision were I by beginning with East Florida to reverse the Materials, of which the Roots are in those ancient Provinces, and the Branches only reach to East Florida.

I therefore most humbly beg Leave to commence my Historical Report from South Carolina, of which Province, in these Presents, is not only a full Description, but also the Pattern by which I am framing all future Reports; most humbly praying, that Your Majesty will graciously order such Amendments and Additions, as may appear necessary, in order, that I may be able to discharge compleatly that Trust, which Your Majesty has most graciously been pleased to repose in me, who am, with the most perfect Submission, Obedience and Humility,

Your Majesty's
Most faithful and
Most dutiful Subject
William Gerard de Brahm.

Report
of the
General Survey
in the Southern District
of
NORTH AMERICA:

Delivered to the Board of Trade and Plantations in three seperate Returns, and Sections entering with the History of South Carolina and Georgia; then proceeding to the History of East Florida, and Surveys, containing in general of said Provinces, the Climates, Beginnings, Boundaries, Figures, Contents, Cultures, Soils, Natural Products, Improvements, Navigable Streams, Rivers, Cities, Towns, Villages, Vapours, their Effect, and Remedies, burning of Forrests, Winds, how to preserve Health, Pathology, Materia Medica, Diet, and Regimen, Ports, Bars, Number of Inhabitants, and Negroes, Exportation, Riches, Number of Trading Vessels, Cattle, Governments, Forces, Fortifications, of Fort Loudoun in particular; Indians and Apalachian Mountains, their Soil, Natural Produce, Air and Communications compiled from the Surveys, Voyages, Astronomical, Philosophical, and Chymical Observations and Experiments, Sea and Land Surveys of

William Gerard de Brahm,

His Majesty's Surveyor General for the Southern District of

North America.

4

Advertisement.

The Historical Report of South Carolina, Georgia, and East Florida is con-created from the Abstracts of Journies, Astronomical Observations, Actual Surveys and Voyages performed by the Author, from the year 1751 to the year 1771; during the Course of which time he has been acting in the several Capacities, and bearing Commissions of Engineer and Surveyor of the Southern District of North America; and hereby endeavours first, to account to His most Gracious Sovereign for the Industry and Zeal, which he has during the Series of twenty years cultivated for His Majesty's Service and Interest; and next to deliver unto Posterity from his Hands, what may facilitate others Industry of adding and improving, when and where in the Course of Time, Nature and Art will introduce a Change of present Existence.

The Author begins his Remarks in the year 1751, when, with a Number of 160 German Colonists, reinforced in eleven Months after, by a like Number (the Relations and Acquaintances of the former) he established the flourishing Settlement of Bethany in Georgia, during the Reign of His Majesty of most glorious Memory King George the Second; and he made a General Survey of the Frontiere, or Eastern Part of that Province, to which, joining the Surveys of William Bull Esqr., Lieutenant Governor of South Carolina, he delivered to the Public in 1757 the first Map of South Carolina and Georgia. In the year 1755 he fortified Charles Town in South Carolina. In 1756 erected Fort Loudoun on the west Side of the Apalachian Mountains on Tanassee, one of the Mississippi Branches. In 1757 he fortified Savannah and erected a Fort at Ebenezer in Georgia. In 1761 he directed the Construction of Fort George on Coxpur Island, in the Sound of Savannah River. From 1765 to the present time he is employed in measuring the western Atlantic Coast, the Marteers at Cape Florida, and the Eastern Coast of the Gulph of Mexico. He took all Soundings, and surveyed great part of the Inland Situation. In the Whole all what is situated between the Latitudes of 24°20′ and 30°26′49″ North, upon the Atlantic Ocean on a Parallel of 103 1,243/8,000 miles long, which make 1°41′31 1/2″ difference of Longitude from Cape Florida, West to the Indian Boundary Line.

5

South Carolina

CHAPTER 1ST

General Description of South Carolina, its Boundaries, Figure, its Contents, and Culture, and a particular Description of Flour, Hemp, Wine, Indigo, natural Products, and Improvements.

The Province of South Carolina is situated in the middle of the 5th Climate, where 14 hours and 15 minutes determine the longest Day, and the Summer Heat rises the quick Silver up to 108 Degrees in the Sun on a Termoscope, who, by its Graduation marks temperate with 55 Degrees, and in well built Houses rises up to 95 Degrees; and where in the Winter the Quick Silver seldom falls under 25 Degrees.[1]

This Province is fully calculated for Plantation, Trade and Navigation. Its Settlement begun in 1663 in the Reign of King Charles the Second, is divided, besides four Counties, into nineteen Parishes, and distinguished from its Neighbouring Provinces by the following Boundaries.[2]

To the South-East by the Atlantic Ocean, that is, from the Mouth of Little River on a S. W. 1/2 deg. W. Course of 180 common English Miles to Savannah River.

To the North East by an artificial Line marked on Trees from Little River across great Woakamaw [*Waccamaw*] Stream, and Jadkin [*Yadkin*] River, on a N. W. Course of 128 miles, as far North as Latitude 35°.

To the North, by above Line, continuing west 209 miles as far until stopped by the River Savannah, ten miles below Keowee and Fort Prince George; these artificial Lines divide the Province of South from North Carolina.

To the South West by the Stream Savannah 268 miles on a S. E. Course straight Line, which Stream is the Boundary between South Carolina and Georgia.[3]

By the aforesaid Boundaries, the Province receives the Figure of a Trapezoide, and contains 33,760 square miles, or 21,606,400 Acres; most of it good plantable Land, on which is [6] cultivated Rice, Indigo, Provisions of all kinds, and all manner of Garden Herbs, Shrubs, and Fruit Trees.

The unplantable Land produces good Pine Timber and Cattle Range. The Land proper for the Cultivation of Rice spreads very near parallel with the Sea Coasts, as far back in the Country as the Trees are hanged with a kind of Moss, which grows to the Length of three yards, and when baked in Ovens or hangs long on the Trees, assumes the Likeness and almost the Nature of long black

Horse Hairs, is used in Saddles and Mattasses [*mattresses*] by the common Inhabitants. As long as it is fresh on the Trees in the Winter, Horses and Cattle seem fond to feed upon it. This Moss is no longer met with in the Woods, than where the Air ceases to be impregnated with the Sea Exhalations, and is a true Mark of (what is called) a fresh Air. From this quasi Division Line, the Land is considerably higher, and more particularly calculated for the Culture of all European Grains, as also Hemp, Silk, and Grape Vine.

The Experience, obtained by Practice, is a full Demonstration of its Truth, for the back Settlers, chiefly consisting of German Protestants, have these many years furnished the Charles Town Market with their Flour, and they actually cultivate more Hemp than is wanted to supply their own Vessels with Cordage; which proves superior in Goodness to what is imported from England; for it can be had new and fresh, while the other has approached the first degree of Decay at its Arrival in America. The Author had the Experience of both European and American Cordage, when rigging his Vessels employed in the General Surveys with both kinds, found the Preference to be due to the American, which would be without Fault, if the Carolina Manufacturers would use less Tar.

At New Bourdeaux, upon Long Cane River, a Colony of French Protestants under the Care of Mr. Lewis Gervais,[4] have, through six years Industry (spent in the Vine Culture) experienced that the Grape Vine needs no Support, neither of Sticks or Frames, but prospers by being winded on the Ground, and piled up in a manner, that the Vine itself forms a kind of a close Bower, (or as the French call it a Chapele) where, under it shades its own Ground to retain all Moisture, which also covers and preserves the Blossom of the Grapes against vernal Frost, and the Grapes themselves against the violent scorching Summer heat, which by former Methods, when the Vine winded on Sticks or Frames, deprived the Soil of its Moisture (the Vehiculum of Nourishment) So that the Stocks of the Grapes withered, and consequently shut up the Channels of the Sap, which, after the next Rain rising, found no Passage into the Wine Berries, they [7] of Course seperated from their Stocks and dropped off, for which Disorder of the Vine no Remedy could be prescribed in former times, so that New Bourdeaux is justly intitled to that Merit; which must be allowed a great Acquisition in the Culture of Vine upon that extensive Continent of America, when a sixty years experimental Inquiry has met with no more Discovery than to condemn America as not possessed with the Faculty to produce Wine; notwithstanding of the good success which yearly crowns the Settlement of California between the Latitude 25° and 30′ [30°?] North, established by the Manilla Jesuits to give to the Manilla Gallions in their way to Aquapulca [*Acapulco*] all manner of Refreshments besides Wine of their own Product, made yearly equal in Perfection to the lesser kind of Madeira; not only the Truth of this, but so unjust a Decision is offended, but also

Nature itself, which, without human Assistance, of its own Virtue, covers America all over with three Sorts of Vine Plants. The first is the Vine, common to all Europe, producing Cluster Grapes; the second is only peculiar to America; commonly called the Fox Grape-Vine, produces single Berries, much the Size of a middling Cherry. The third kind is a perfect Tree, and only met with in the Southern Regions, vide, to the Southward of the middle of the 4th Climate, which is a Latitude of 27°5′ and is in East Florida, in the Description of which Province, a full Account shall be given of this Grape Tree.

What is peculiar to South Carolina, and the more Southern Provinces, is, that although Vines are met with on high and in low Lands, yet the Vines on high Places produces none or very few, while the Vines in low Grounds are always full of that pleasant Fruit, and the more so, the nearer they are to a running Water, which seem to contradict the general Observation and Experience in Europe, where only the high Lands are recommended for the Vine Culture, which Insinuation of Nature in America being postponed to European Experience has probably contributed much to the bad Success of the Industrious unto the Ara [area?] of New Bourdeaux. As for the Goodness of the Wine itself, its Decovery may, without Doubt be very shortly expected, and prove the Merit of those, who in the first place are Masters of Zimotechnie(a) and in the second place find out an appartment, to which all Degrees, from temperate downwards can be given, to govern the outward Phlogistic Motion through the Bung in a manner, that thereby an Attritus (motus fermentations) be effected; and when this [8] Motion has brought up (sublimed) all heterogenea, which may be judged by the Quietness of the Motion and Cleaness of the Yest [yeast], than by bunging the Cask to exclude the Phlogistic, and leave the Wine to its own intestine secretory Motion, and preserve him in it, so that the Wine may disengage itself from, and precipitate its terrea, and afterwards by a motus digestious, disengage, volatilize and combine itself with the fix Phlogiston of its precipitate Earth, for which the Wine needs a less Degree of Warmth, than he required at the time of Fermentation. Without such Apartment, all Pains bestowed upon the Vine Culture will be lost, and cannot be well obtained otherwise, than in a Brig [brick] or stone Building of about 50 feet square, from 5 feet under to 5 feet above Ground in all 10 feet high with 3 Windows (3 feet square) on each side; its Position should be as near North and South as possible; a 40 feet square Apartment for a Cellar is to be partitioned from the Building by two Walls, so that this Apartment has two Halls, on the East is one, and on the South another; the Partition on the East is without any opening, the Door is on the South Partition; a Piaza six feet wide and 5 feet high from the Horizon is to be conducted all round the Building; a Dwelling House may be

(a) that is the Art of Fermentation.

raised upon it, to which the Piaza will serve as a private Communication to all the Rooms, without taking off from the Rooms what is necessary for a Passage through the House by the North and West Windows in the Cellar, as well, than by the East & South Windows in the Halls, the different warm or cold Airs may be let in, to ventilate the Cellar, so as to make thereby the Quick Silver on a Termoscope rise or fall in it at Liberty; Experiments of which must be made previously, in order to obtain a full Knowlege of this Management. The Author has raised such a Building in Savannah, and now existing, where he ventilated cooled Air in his Cellar, when an intense heat was without the House.

At the time, when the Wine is in the Casks, the Termoscope is to be brought down or raised a little above temperate; and then hanged in the Bung of one Cask, so that the Ball only is in the Wine, and by rising or falling of the Termoscope, and by the Violence or Slowness of the Fermentation, the Air may be modified in the Cellar either by Cold, or warm Ventilation.

The Culture of Indigo is as well calculated for the Settlers upon the Sea Coast, as those in the remotest back Country; this Produce is actually brought to its Perfection, and proves little Inferior to that manufactured by [9] The Spaniards of Guatimala in New Spain in Latitude $14°25'$. In some years, has been obtained of one Field in South Carolina three full Crops of that Culture.

The great Tracts, which formerly have been granted by Royal Patents, and the great Number of Inhabitants increased by five generations, with the great Number of Emigrants from Great Britain, France, and Germany have occupied the Land of the Province in a manner, that only a small Portion remains King's Property, to be granted to New Settlers, near and about the artificial Lines, and in that Triangle formed by the Long Cane River; Savannah Stream and the westernmost Extremity of aforesaid Line; all Lands upon, and along the Sea Coast, upon and between Navigable Streams and Rivers are occupied, and at this time become private Property.

The Land near the Sea Coast is in general of a very sandy Soil, bears Pine, Palm (Vulgo Cabbage) Trees, Palmeta Royal, Opuntia, Kali (barilla) Casina Tea and a Variety of Shrubs.

Where this sandy Land is mixed with a little Mould, it produces large live Oaks, and Myrtle Bushes; also an indifferent kind of Grass not fit for Pasture. This Soil along the Coast has as yet not been able to invite the industrious to reap Benefit of its Capacity, for the common Opinion of Man (who claim Experience in the Nature of Vegitation) is diametrically opposite in its Prejudice, so that as yet no Experiment has been made on it, but stands condemned as a barren Land unfit for any Cultivation; but the general Opinion as yet is grounded on bad Philosophy; for there is no Land ever so sandy, rocky, stiff, or boggy, but what can be rendered useful for Cultivation to the Ingenious and industrious, especially in Climates near the Tropicks, where plastic Nature is abundantly provided with Phlogistic, (Electric) Matter to operate, provided the necessary Vehiculum (Moisture) can be unintermittedly administred by the reserving Dew and Rain from above; or below from the general Water Source under the Quick Sand, which in the low Lands in general lays very near the Surface of the Earth, in the latter Case the Industrious needs little Labour, but reaps the Multiplication of his Seeds, provided they are sowen in the Vallies and between, but not upon the Beds, in which his Field is to be laid out; this Phlogistic, if mixes with sulphureous matter, is in its nature (without being sufficiently diluted with Moisture) a Fire, which consumes Plants and Animals, and Calcines Stones & Metals.

On higher Land, where Dew and Rain is to be prevented from filtering and sinking below the Reach of the Roots through the great Interstices [*10*] of the sandy Soil, it is necessary to dissolve the Sand about an Inch deep into a Marl, which plowed under the Sand below, will in a great Measure fill up those Interstitia, and keep Moisture from sinking too deep; this Solution of the Sand into Marl can be effected by covering the Ground with any Opaque Matter nearest at hand, be it Stones or Shells gathered, and piled in heaps or Ridges, which are to be moved every year, and thereby become a perpetual Manure; by this Method the Sun is prevented for twelve months from rarifying and exhaling the Moisture ascending from the Quick Sand, whereby the Phlogistic Matter will not be moved by Winds or Sun, but left undisturbed with the Moisture to combine itself therewith, and constitute the Othereal Acid of Niter; which Acid, eager for a Basis to rest on, will always be busy and corrode the Sand into Atoms, which filling up closely the Interstices in the sandy Soil, stop Moisture from sinking, and that Acid itself is carried by the Vehiculum of Moisture as a Nourishment into the Roots of the Vegitables.

By these Means (only with greater Patience and in longer time) Rocks can be made pregnant. Stiff Soil can be made tractable by covering it with Sand, and plowing it among the Clay, and boggy Soil can be drained from its superfluous Moisture by Intersections of Trenches, and raising the Beds with the Soil dug out.

However, without this Experiment of dissolving the sandy Soil into Marl, this Land in its present Condition, may be cultivated with the Opuntia for the Propogation of the Cocheneal Worm, which is a small tender Buck [*bug*] filled with the Tinchure of that Plant, and is covered against the Inclemency of Weather, by a Web of white Silk; is only found on those Leaves which lay flat on the Ground; this Buck on its Web exposed to the scorching Sun, will die and dry, and thus bottled up, is the whole Process.[5]

If the Opuntia is planted very close, suffered to spread all over the Ground, and its rising Leaves half cut, so as to sink and lay them flat on the Ground, and thus left for five or six years, the Land will thereby be covered against the Sun etc. and improve its Soil, and the constant Collection of the Cocheneal Buck will richly reward the Pains and Patience of the Undertaker.

Besides the Opuntia, it may also be sowed or planted with Kali (Barilla)[6] a Plant very common near the American Sea Coasts, especially in those places which Spring Tides will cover with salt Water, of which the famous Barilla (commonly called Pearl) Ash, or more properly an Alkalin Salt is manufactured; the common Method to obtain it by Incineration, Elixivation, Evaporation, and Calcination is so well known, that it needs not to be mentioned here, but to reduce the whole process [11] only to Calcination (by which great Labour is saved, and more than twice the common Quantity of Salt is obtained) Shall be mentioned at another time.

The Myrtle Bushes may also be cultivated on this sandy Soil, whose Berries bruised and boiled, and while hot, strained through a coarse Cloth, will yield an aromatic Wax swimming on the Top of the Water, when cold, this Wax (altho' naturally green) will be more so, if the Berries are boiled in a copper Kettle, and after they are strained, the hot Water and Wax together poured back in the copper Kettle again, to cool in it.

Young live Oaks may be transplanted in Places where the Sands seems to have partaken of some Mould. These Oaks furnish a suitable Lumber fit for Ships-knees and Beams etc. also for Wheels in Mills and other Machines, and its Acorns (being very sweet and not much inferior to Walnuts) are a fine food for Hogs.

The Casina Tea Shrub[7] may also be propogated, and its young Leaves made useful in Equality to those from the East Indies, by filling earthen or glass Vessels therewith, and placing them in boiling Water as long until the Moisture is evaporated out of the Leaves, and they well secured in Bottles corked and pitch'd[8] are put by for a Season.

The Cabbage Tree,[9] which grows on this Soil, makes good Posts in Salt Water, to secure Dams, etc., which thereby are not liable to become useless in Consequence of their Posts being eaten by the Sea Worms.

Deep Places near the Sea Coast are filled at Spring Tides and rainy Weather, with a Mixture of Salt and fresh Water; these Places go by the Name of Ponds, in which nothing grows but a salt water marsh Grass; this (while green) is a tolerable Food for Horses and Cattle, only it makes their Milk disagreeable, nor have these Places as yet been thought useful, altho' they with a little daming, and Sluces could be turned into Salins, to secure at every overflowing Spring Tide, the rich Treasures of Sea Salt by Evaporation, Cristallisation, and Decantation in the hot Seasons.

The Lands upon the Rivers and Streams etc. if low (commonly called Swamp or Marsh Land) they both are of a very rich black Mould with a Fundation of blue Clay (a).

[*12*]
The Swamp Land produces

Arum. bot.	Hickory swamp Tree	⎧Spruce
Bays ... (dif. Sps. Tree)	Locust Tree Pine	⎱ Tree
Beech Tree	Magnolia (Laurs. regs.)	⎩Swamp
Birch Tree	Maple Tree	Poplar (tulip tree)
Calamus aroms. ... bot.	Myrtle Tree	Sasafras tree
Canes	Willow Tree	Serpentinaria ... bot.
Cardomon ... bot.	⎧Chesnut	Siccamor Tree
Cedar Tree	⎪Green	Tupelo Tree
China Root ... bot. Oak	⎨ Tree	Umbella tree (Spes.
Cypress Tree ...	⎪Holm	magnolia)
deciduous	⎩Spanish	Vine Cluster Grape
Elm Tree Palm	Shrub (palmetoe)	Wahoo tree
Gum Tree	Persimon tree	Walnut (swamp) Tree
		Whortleberry Shrub

In the Marsh Land grows no Tree or Shrub, but fresh Water Marsh Grass and wild Oats; besides that the Pasturage of both these Swamp and marsh Lands, vide, Canes, fresh water marsh Grass and wild Oats is an exceeding good Food for Horses and Cattle, and most of the Trees above are fit for Timber of different Uses, which when cut down, the Swamp Land, as also the Marshes are the only Lands capable for the Culture of Rice.

If the Land is high, 'tis either rich Mould, or sandy Soil, both supported by a red Clay (a) Foundation.

The rich Land bears

Agnus castus ... bot.	Ginsem ... bot.	Pink Indian ... bot.
Angelica ... bot.	Hickory Tree	Rhaponticum-bot. (b)
⎧prickly	Holley Tree	Sanguinaria ... bot.
Ash ... ⎨ tree	Hippo ... bot.	Santomicum (Jerum.
⎩smooth	Jalap ... bot.	Oak) bot.
Aspin	Mind, wild-bot.	Sasafras tree
Bay, red (laurus tree)	Cardus benedictus	Scamimonium ... bot.

(a) which on account of its fine Sand and easy to vitrify in the Fire, is very fit to be manufactured into earthern Vessels for keeping all manner of Spirits and Oils.

(a) of which good Brigs [*bricks*] are daily manufactured

(b) Lapathem, or Rhabarbarum monachorum

Cherry (wild) Tree

Chinquopin Tree

Cicuta ... bot.

Cyclamen agreste. bot.

Datura (Sps. Solaminis)

Dogfennel ... bot.

Dogwood tree

Ebulus (vul powke) bot.

Mulberry wild tree

Oak { Live / Red Tree / White }

Palm bushes (palmetoe)

Passion flower, frugiser

Patience-bot. (b)

Persimon tree

Silk grass Shrub ... (c)

Snake Root { Heart (asarum) / Simpson / Virginia }

Verbascum ... bot.

Vine, fox grape

Walnut Tree

[*13*]

As well the abovesaid Trees answer different Uses in Building, and Oeconomy, as also the aforesaid different botanical Herbs are useful in Medicines as faint Succedaneous, when chymical Preperations cannot be had; faint they are indeed, in comparing the Effects of both Chymics and Botanics, the Preference must be given to the Chymics, both as to Effect, than Dependence of Operation; either because the Botanics have lost their ancient Virtue, or human Diseases are become more desperate. The Soil of this Land is well calculated for the Culture of Indigo, Corn, Peas, Melons, Potatoes, both sweet and Irish; also all manner of European Granes and Garden Products.

The sandy Soil produces

Chinquopin Shrub

Esula, various Sps. bot.

Ellebore ... bot.

Hoarhunt ... bot.

Grass { Buffelow / Bunch / Wire }

Indigo, wild

Lillies americ ... various kinds.

Myrtle Bushes

Oak { Black / Shrub / Poison ... bot. }

pine { Pitch / Tree / Yellow }

Snakeroot ... bot.

Whortle bushes.

Altho' This Soil is equally rejected with that of the Sea Coast as unfit for Cultivation, yet on account of its Grass, the Land is chosen for Pasturage, both for Horses and Cattle; the yellow Pine is esteemed the best for Boards, both used in the building of Houses and Vessels; and the Pitch-Pine furnishes Turpentine, Tar and Pitch, as also good Posts for Garden Fence and Cottages.

(c) The Shrub of the Palmeto Royal, its Roots when 24 hours soaked in Water is a good Succedancum to use it in lieu of Soap water for washing coarse Cloth, and its Leaves, when broiled may be used as Strings, and made up into extemporaneous ropes.

CHAPTER 2D

Of navigable Streams and Rivers, Towns, inland Communications, Industry, whence Vapours, their Effect, Remedy, burning of Forrests, Observations on Winds, how to preserve Health.[10]

In South Carolina are

4 Streams			*And 22 Rivers*	
Wackamaw	Yatkins	Tyger	Cooper	Cambahee
Santee	Black	Linwells	Ashly	Pocotalego
Port Royal	Catabaw	Little	North Edisto	Chilifini
Savannah	Congaree	Great Saludee	South Edisto	Coosahatchee
	Broad	Little Saludee	Ashipoo	May
	Pakolet			Long Cane

[*14*]
Besides the Metropolis of Charles Town

Are two Sea Port Towns
{ Beauford [*Beaufort*], on Port Royal Island, and
George Town, on Wackamaw Stream

Seven inland Towns
upon
Navigable Streams
and Rivers
{ Orange-burg, upon North Edisto
Dorchester, upon Ashly River
Amilia Town, upon Santee Stream
Saxegotha, upon Congaree River
New Bourdeaux, upon Long Cane River
New Windsor }
Purisburg } upon Savannah Stream

The abovementioned Streams and Rivers washing these Towns, take their Courses in the following manner:

Yatkin River and Wackamaw Stream (after crossing the artificial Boundary Line) meet each other at George Town, and stream together north of Cape Carteret into the Atlantic Ocean; the Head of Yatkin River is in North Carolina, near the Source of Konhaway, otherwise New River.

Santee Stream empties itself in the Ocean at the south side of Cape Carteret, is supplied by Catabaw River at Amilia Town, this Catabaw River forkes into a

North and South Branch, the latter is the longest, and springs between the Heads of Yatkin and Konhaway.

Santee is also supplied by the River Congaree at aforesaid Amilia Town, which latter River receives eight miles N. W. of Saxegotha Town, the Waters of the following Rivers, vide, Broad, Pacolet, Tyger, Linwells, Little, Great Saludee, and Little Saludee. The general Course of Santee is N. W. by W. westerly, which with Savanah (whose Course is S. E. nearest) are the greatest Streams in this Province. These aforesaid are fresh Water Rivers and Streams.

The navigable salt Water Rivers are vide, Cooper and Ashly, which at their Meeting, empty themselves in the Charles Town Port, on the Confluence of these two Rivers is built the Metropolis of this Province called Charles Town.

Item, the two Rivers, North and South Edisto, the latter with the River Ashipoo, Cambahee and Coosaw Creek form the Saint Helena Sound; the Rivers Pocotalego, Chulifinee, Coosahatchee and Port Royal Rivers form Port Royal, alias Calaboge Sound.

The Province is conveniently traversed with public Roads 33 feet wide, well causwayed in low and boggy places, and the Rivers are made passable with well constructed wooden Bridges, as well for the Conveniency of [15] Travellers from North Carolina to Georgia, as also from Charles Town, to the interior Settlement for the Benefit of Carriages etc. coming to Market.

Private Roads (which are in nothing than in Breadth inferior to the Public) are as many as private Settlements.

The Hospitality of this Province makes travelling through this Country very agreeable, pleasant and easy; for most of the Inhabitants keep a Negroe at their Gate near the public Roads, to invite Travellers to Refreshments, Dinners, After-Noon Tea, Suppers and Lodgings: yea they will forward them with Chairs, Horses, and Attendance, even in bad Weather, when Roads are become impracticable, they accompany Travellers over high Land with their Negroes to cut down small Trees in the Way of the Carriages, to forward and guide through unfrequented Forrests, assist with their Boats and Hands to set them over Streams, Rivers, and Creeks, provided there is no Ferry established. Thus Hospitality and Industry join in Concert for the Good and Convenience of Man in general; but here are not as yet the Bounds and Limits of Industry, for it extends farther, and produces also many ingenuous Stamp Machines, or rather Rice Mills, and has erected innumerable Dams for the Use of reserving Water to inundate the Rice Fields, after the first hewing or weeding, in order to hinder the Roots of Grass and Weeds from sprouting again, and this by the same principal Reason as aforementioned in the 1st Chapter, vide, the Phlogiston finding a Superfluity of aqueos particuls in motu fluiditatis without local motion, suitable to corporifie itself by its own intestin Motion, being promoted per motum fluiditatis from particul to particul in the Interstices of the water Globules to an Acid, (which as long as it is not confined by any Alkalin, Calearic, or Metallic Basis) is in a perpetual Agitation, causing a Friction and Attritus upon all Materials in his way, until it finds a suitable Habitation or Basis; in its Progression it destroys whatever cannot combine itself with this Acid; hiding therefore upon Plants used to the Air (which are in general of open pores in a thin Texture) this Acid makes his way very soon through the Barks, occupies the Passages for the Sap, coagulates and prevents the Sap from rising, of course, the Plants for want of Nourishment must perish. Water Plants being well fortified with a close and solid Texture, are defended against the Consequences of that Friction.

The Author in his planting-time, has observed, that the Air Plants, as well as the Water Plants, will thrive in Water, provided it is not in motu fluiditatis stagnant, but always in local motions a runing, [16] whereby the Phlogiston is deprived of that Quiet and Time it requires for a digestive Motion (composed of the Motions of Fluidity and intestin) of course prevented from generating any Acid.

As much those Constructions of Dams (made to reserve Water) testify of the great Skill, Industry and Improvement of this Province, and as much they contribute to their Opulence, so much the corrosive Vapours of these Stagnant Waters evaporating and mixing with the Air become prejudicial to Health by cloaking the Stomachs of the Inhabitants with Slime, and corrupt their Blood; from whence different Disorders, as Agues, Fevers and Relaxations are brought, as well upon the European, as the African Descendants, unless they moderate their imbibed corrosive Vapours by a prudent and moderate Use of Spirits, which dulcify (obtund) all corroding matters, otherwise apt to coagulate the Humidities, relax the Tonum, and cause Putrefaction, which to prevent, ardent Spirits always prove themselves the most convenient Speciffica antiseptica; but it is only to be understood from pure wholesome Spirits, for if they are otherwise, that is, when in their Distillation the Acidity remaining in the Alembick is not prevented from following the pure and wholesome Spirit; this Acidity will corrode the Copper, concenter itself in the Acid of that Metal, and distill together into the Spirit, who by the many aqueous parts is hindred from obtunding with its oily Quality, as well the Arsenical Particuls of the Copper, as the concentrated Acid of course inflames the massam Sanguinis, whence Consumption; it coagulates the Humidities, renders the pancreatic succus viscous, and consequently unfit to dilute the Bile; whence all colerique Disorders, it constitutes and conveys a Salin aquosite in the sinus cerebri, to the Prejudice of the Nerves, whence nervous Disorders take their Cause etc.

The Wholesomeness and Purity of any Spirit can easily be tryed by setting flame to five spoon fulls of Spirit, if more than one Spoonfull of Aquosity remains after the Spirit is burnt, it will not prove medicinal (a) but since these carefully alkolised Spirits would not fetch a greater market Price than those carelessly distilled, this wholesome Spiritous Medicine therefore can only be wished for, but not obtained, unless by those who take the Trouble to cohabate (redestill) them; which Operation requiring some Skill and Trouble, will not be undertaken by many; so that the preventing the Evil, proceeding from the corrosive Vapours, for the Generality must be committed to Futurity, when the Province will be more open and cleared from its Woods to give greater and unobstructed Passages to the ranging Winds, which will extenuate and scatter these Vapours in the Air, that only an inoffensive small Share can be imbibed by those, who breath upon it.[11]

[*17*] Although the burning of the Woods is not at all times a Remedy to purifie the Air, when filled (besides Vapours) with Phlogistic matters, which by the Sulphur disengaged from its Adherent matter thro' Combustion is augmented, and thereby enraged; this will be the Case, if so that the burning of the Wood (Forrest) is applied as a Remedy in high Summer Seasons, when the Sun is near, or in perigeo; but when the Sun is between its perigeo and apogeo in the foggy Seasons, which are in Spring and Fall, when the Forrests are set aburning, the Fire and Heat will rarify and dispose the Fogs to ascend, settle and mix with the lightest Air above the heavy Atmosphere, and the Inhabitants are greatly releaved from the morbifical Proximity of these Vapours. In these Seasons Grass and Bushes are dry, and inclining to take and spread Fire all over the high, and also low Lands, in case the latter has been without Water on it for a long Season. Persons who are not acquainted with the Nature of burning the Woods in America, may be apt to suppose, that the Trees are liable to be set a burning, which if one did intend ever so much, would find himself disappointed, for if this was practicable, all the Trees in America would have been burnt down, before any European came there.

The burning of the Grass and Underwoods in the Forrests is an ancient Custom of the Indians; they practised it, in order to alure the Deers upon the new Grass, as also to discover the Impressions of their Enemies Tracts [*tracks*] in the new burnt Ground distinguishable to their Women and Children in Case the Raven (a) should be sick or out of the way, who, as well as any other Indian (as they all apply themselves to hunting) are by Practice so keen and precise, that they can distinguish and follow all Tracts, be it of a white Man, Negroe, Indian; or be it of a Bear, Wolf, or Deer, Horse, or Cow, even on hard bottom, not admitting of Impression, so as on soft Ground, altho' covered all over with Leaves, so that the Ground itself is not visible, and even bare of any Grass or Bushes which by

(a) or five penny weight of Spirit burnt on a pair of Scales, if more phlegma remains than one penny weight, the Spirit is not medicinal.

(a) this they call the Lookout, whose Business is to recognize the Avenues of their Towns.

their irregular Bend may indicate a Creature (human or animal) having trod upon or brushed by it.

The Author has frequently observed the Tops of young pine Trees burnt by the Fire, which nevertheless he met in few months after, quite recovered, sprouted and green; if an old dying or dead Tree is in the Way of the Fire, it will indeed flame and burn down; but seldom with the first Fire; likewise if hurricane Trees lay long on [*18*] the Ground, and their Branches become Fewel to the Fire, it will of course continue on that Spot to consume Branch and Body; as also the young by-standing Saplins, especially in a high Wind; in which Cases they are utterly destroyed, but a green full grown Tree never takes Fire, unless at the Bottom, with no more Effect, than to have his Bark a little sindged.

The Fire of the burning old Grass, Leaves and Underwoods consumes a Number of Serpants, Lizards, Scorpians, Spiders and their Eggs, as also Bucks [*bugs*], Ticks, Petilies [*reptiles*], Muskitoes, with other Vermins, and Insects in general very offensive, and some very poisonous, whose Increase would, without this Expedient cover the Land, and make America disinhabitable.[12]

Many Objections are made against certain Winds, as if at all times coming from a certain Quarter was prejudicing the State of Health of the Inhabitants; but it is difficult to determine with Propriety and Preciseness, which and when a Wind is really a wholesome or an unwholesome Wind, as long as the Wind's Quality depends from Circumstances, and these Subjects to Alterations and the Disposition of Matters with which the Interstitia of the Wind is filled up, as for Instance: If the Wind comes from the west in Summer, which is over the Apalachian Mountains, he is pregnant with sulphuric and arsenical Exhalations, and in the Winter its Globules sealed with Frost are hard; if the Wind blows East from the Sea, he conveys a Cargo of amonical Salt more in the Summer than in the Winter; if the Wind brushes through the Woods from the North, especially in Spring and Fall, it carries the corrosive Effluvia from Savannahs (Meadows) Marshes and Swamps etc. But not always the same Quantity; If the Wind in Summer rolls from the South it is a Point or focus formed (near north Latitude 30°) by the Contract of the two Winds, one leaping from the Pacific Sea over New Spain: (the Isthmus which joins Mexico to Peru) And the other traversing the Atlantic Ocean, and meet in the Gulph of Mexico. These Winds jointly take their Direction North, and sweep before them all Vapours and Effluvia in their Way; great part of which they loose, combing the great Forrest, which contains the Provinces of Florida and Georgia.

The Meeting of these Winds in Mexico is generally at 9 a.m.—arrives at Savannah in Georgia at 11, and at Charles Town in this Province at 12; so that in a Minute of an hour these combined Winds travel a Minute of a Degree (a) From

(a) a minute of a Degree on a Meridian is a Distance of 6,116 feet.

the Premises appears the necessary Consequence, that Winds are more or less wholesome, as they are [*19*] more or less pregnant with sound volatile Salts, sulphureous Aromatics, or pernicious corrosive Effluvia and Vapours, and that in a measure, as they are more or less in Quantity, and in a Degree as they approach gradually or surprize suddenly, now from a hot then from a cold Quarter, or vice versa; these sudden Changes are very common and more pernicious than the corroding Vapours (with which these Winds are sometimes charged) especially when they surprize the human Frame without being prepared at its Arrival.

A Person otherwise of a healthy Disposition may preserve his Health by frequent bathing in salt water, in warm and hot Seasons; by wearing suitable Apparel, rather of Wool than Silk, Cotton or Linnen; by keeping his Feet warm, and bearing few Hairs on his Crown; by chusing his House of Retirement from Business, without the House at the hours when the Termoscope rises to the Degree of Blood-heat, by mixing always the best Spirits with his drinks-Water, to drink frequently but small Draughts, especially at meals; by chusing the best Wine, and to use it very moderately after Meal (a) by abstaining in Summer from Tea, Coffee, and Chocolate, from hot meals, and N. B., Spices of all kinds, unless when the Bile is too much diluted by the pancreatic Succus (b); also to abstain from salted and dryed Provisions, in which is no Nourishment, and parboiled fresh meat or Fish which lays too long in the Stomach and causes Putrefaction; or half boiled Vegitables, which will ferment and raise Flatulence and Acidity; by never overcharging the Stomach with Liquids, more less with Victuals, which unproportionably dilates the Vessels; finally by taking moderate Exercise without exposing himself to Morning and Evening Dews, nor Rains, which shuts the Pores and prevents Perspiration; but in case of having transgressed in the Premises, to dissolve immediately the slimy Humidity, and procure them easy Passages through the different Emunetoria by Diaphoretics, v. g. Purgatives, Diapnoiks and Diureticks before any Disease has fixed and particularized itself.

(a) in the Spring and Fall, Port, or rather adstringet, but in the Winter Madeira, or other spirituous Wines, the same in Summer; altho' good Spirits mixed with Water is preferable to any Wine in Summer.

(b) In which case the Deficiency of the Bile requires a substituent succedaneum, which is of the same Effect, as the Bile vide, Spices.

[20]

CHAPTER 3D

Of Pathology, Materia Medica, Diet, and Regimen

As Diseases, Remedies and Regimens have transiently & superficially passed under the Recognizance of the Author, he apprehends that a more precise Account of what is so universally interesting, will be expected from the Title of his Report; in Conformity to which He will philosophically communicate his Experiments and Observations. To enter upon this Subject with Propriety, a Hypothesis, accompanied with a short allegorical Speculation, supported with an Experiment, will not be thought an unnecessary Digression, in Order to display both Pathology and materiam medicam.

All Disorders (whatever their Denominations may be) proceed only from two principal Causes vide, Inflamation and Relaxation.

The Construction of the human Body with all its Vessels contained therein, can reasonably be compared with a chymical Athanor and its different Circulotaria, Sublimatoria, Colatoria, Alembicks, etc., which are all governed by a Calneum Vaporio, by whose Regimen the whole Digestion, Secretion, and Excretion is performed every 24 hours, altho' not at all times with the same Order and Effect, nor to have the same Benefit, which clearly can be demonstrated from the different Excretions of the many Secretions greatly altering in Proportion at the various Seasons of the year in this Climate, as appear from the statical Experiments made in Charles Town, and laid down in the following Table.[13]

Proportion of the Excretions in every Season				
Seasons	by Urine	by Perspiration	by Dejection	Sum
	Parts	Parts	Parts	
Spring	53	33	26	112
Summer	36	51	29	116
Autumn	37	48	40	125
Winter	53	31	26	110
Sum	179	163	121	463

By this Experiment the Adept does prove, that Man, through the Course of the whole year discharges most through the Emuntorium urinale, less through the Cuticularia, and least through the Dejectorium; and that the [21] Excretion

increases from the Winter to the Autumn in the following Progression, 0/110
2/110 3/110 7½/110; from whence all at once it diminishes again from 7½/110 to
0/110 which sudden Alteration cannot but cause Inconveniencies unto delicate,
and Diseases (if not Death) unto worn Constitutions.

The human Frame is above compared to an Athanor (a) and its Fire to a
Balneum Vaporis, caused by the several Motus, mentis, Toni, Secretionis, Ex-
cretionis, and progressions Sanguinis; the Vapours excited by these Motions; are
confined, or let out profusely by the Pores of the Skin, either too closely shut by
their inflamed, or left open, by their relaxed Glandules, both are an Excess; but
when these Glandules are neither inflamed or relaxed, they have a regular tonic
Motion, and ventilate the Body by opening and shutting without ceasing.

By the different Proportions of the Dejections in the foregoing Table, it is
remarkable, that the Digestion in the Winter and Spring only is moderate, and
regular, for at that time the outward Coolness neither inflames nor relaxes, but
braces the Glandules of the Pores, through which the inward Vapours are properly ventilated, and circulate in a regular manner from Vessel to Vessel; at last
perspire, and give room to new Ones arising in the Balneum by Virtue of the
several Motions: Mind, Tonic, Secretory, Excretory, and progressive Sanguin
(as before mentioned) causing a Balneum, and being strengthened by the same
Balneum (so that causa and effectus support each other) constitute a perpetuum
Mobile, by which all individual Particuls of Victuals passing the Vessels are
wonderfully enalyzed, disengaged and adapted for the different Passages or
Colatoria of the Glanduloze Parts, as per Instance, the Liver and Reins, etc. So
that in those two Seasons only, the human Body has its proper tonic and other
Motions, as also its Chylification, Nourishment and Increase.

In Summer the Power of the increasing Phlogistic Motion, (outward heat)
relaxes the Glandules so, that they are not able to open, and to shut the Pores
regularly, but leave them longer open, than they are able to shut them; thus
give vent to the Vapours to perspire so immoderately, as they are generated by
the different Motions, which are hurried by the outward motus phlogisticus, and
the Balneum is forced above its proper Degree, so that the Digestion is changed
into an attritum, whence a motus fermentatious is brought on, which subtilizes
the Particuls of Nourishment into Vapours, from which Man receives no Chylus;
of course no [22] Lympha, consequently no Blood, Nourishment or Increase, or
at least not in Proportion, whereby the tonic, and other Motions are not only
overdriven, but also receives not their Share of Nourishment.

These Irregularities through that Season draw the fatal Consequence, that in
Autumn all Motions are reduced, of course, Relaxations take place; the whole

(a) is a particular Construction of a chymical Oven, which preserves a regular Degree of
Heat for several Days, Weeks, or Months.

human Athanor lays open to the outward Phlogistic Motion, which storming in
through all the Openings, generates only by its own Virtue the inward Vapours,
and expels them also; so that they have not time to supply sufficiently the succus
pancreaticus; this Succus in such Condition is scarcely able, half to dilute the
Bile, so that the Victuals at such times, in lieu of being dissolved by the Bile, are
preserved by the same, and the Excretions through the three principal Emunctoria
(for want of a proper and regular Secretory Motion) are near of equal Proportion, in lieu, that a regular Secretion would have divided and proportioned them
as one 3d Urine is to a 5th Perspiration, and a 6th Dejection; by the improportion-
ate autumnal Dejection, the Body decreases, its Vessels are uncommonly dilated
and relaxed; as also the Pores stand open even at the time when cold and hot
Winds are suddenly exchanging and re-exchanging Possession, to which this
Country is so very subject, the Consequences must be fatal.

From these Changes of the Seasons, working so strangely upon the human
Frame, one should be obliged to determine the different mortificial Effects, as
depending principally from the Glandules irregular Ventilations of the Body,
which passive under the outward phlogistic Motion, lays open to expire the
necessary Proportion of its indispensable Vapours, and also apt to every sudden
Obstruction of the phlogistic Motion by cold Winds, to have its Humidities
coagulated in a sour Slime, or rendered diaphan, replinished with congealed salin
Particuls; at the same time to have the Tonus suddenly restored to the Glandules
of the Pores, which no sooner recover their Motion, than that they are inflamed
and deprived of their Activity, by the salin Particuls filling the Pores, which
thereby are entirely stopped up, and the Body suffers a Dissolution or Stagnation
of both Lympha and Blood.

This Irregularity is a Check to Nature, which knowing only to go on in a
regular Procession, finds her Passages inconvenient, [23] either by an Atonic
or Baricadoe, is rendered confuse in its processus and Operations; from which
Confusion proceeds,

Abortus	Erysipelas	Mania
Angina	Epilepsia	Melancholia
Asthma, all manner	Fevers, all kind	Nephritis
Atrophia	Hemorrhoides Caco	Palpitatis cordis
Calculus	Gout, all kind	Partus difficilis
Cardialgia	Hepatitis	Pestilence
Cephalagia	Hypochondriacu malu	Peripneumonia
Colera morbus	Histerica	Pleuritis
Colicks, all manner	Intermittents, all kind	Singultus
Contractura	Lipyria	Variola

All which belong to the inflamatory Class, and take their primary Cause from the Pores being stopped by inflamed Glandules:

But when they are relaxed, and the Pores stand open, the Disorders caused thereby belong to the relaxant Class, and are,

Anorexia	Debilitas-ventriculi	Obstructis alvi
Cruditas ventriculi	Flatus	Vermes
Acida, and nidorosa	Nausea	

These Disorders above mentioned take Cause from the lesser Degree of Relaxation: But a higher Degree brings about the following, vide:

Coriza	Hæmopthysis	Sudor nimius
Decolaratis mens	Hæmorrhagia narium	Tussis pectoralis
Diarhea	Icterus	Vomitus Communis
Dysenteria	Lienteria	Vomitus orientus
Fluor albus	Mictus cruentus	
(Hepaticus	Passio Cæliaca	
Fluxus{ Menstruns	Scabics	
(Hæmorrhoidalis	Scorbutus	

Disorders caused by a Relaxation of the last Degree are,

Apoplexia	Incontinentia Urina	Prolapsusuteri
Cachexia	Lethargus	Syncope
Carus	Lipothymia	Tremor
Catarrhus suffocatious	Paralysis	Vertigo
Hydrops & its Species	Procidentia ani	

The Remedies to assist Nature in the Defects of most of the inflamatory Class are immediate Bleeding, and every hour or half hour in Coffee, Tea, or Water, twenty Grains of the following artificial [24] Bozoardic. Rx. Tartar Vitriol, Antimon: Diaphor: Depurá Niter: Conchæ prepa. ā ā 4 1/2 dram; Camphor, Zinab: Antim, or Natio ā ā 1 dram fiat pulvis (a)

(a) The Operation of the Bozoardic is nearly thus: the tartar Vitriol dissolves the Phleme concreted from Acids, sulphurics and Water; the Conchæ absorbe the Acid, and constitute a sal cathardic, which leads the retained Secretion to Excretion. The tartar Vitriol likewise as a diuretic proceeds in the Lymphe and massam sanguinis, where it dissolves what is coagulated and promotes Secretion, the Niter as an antinephritium cools and lays itself in the Rain to give easy Passage to the secreted Salts. Antim, diaphor by gentle friction on the Stomach causes a perspiration the Zinabarum is sublimed by the volatil sal comphori in the sinus cerebi, where its terra sulphurea contracts & strengthens their Dilatation.

If the Patient complains not of Pains in his Head, the Camphor and Zinab Antim can be omitted. The Patient is to be kept in a temperate Room with sufficient Drink of Water clarified by boiling and a little duperated Niter dissolved in it; in case the Disorder does not abate in 24 hours, then the following Pills to be given. Rx. Sweet Mercury (which is without the least Taste upon the Tongue) salt Tartar, or any alkalin Salt, ā ā 2 drams; Gum of the aloe Succotrin, Balsam Locatelli; Sapovenet, ā ā 3 drams, fiant pillulæ 120. Of these Pills the Patient takes every three hours beginning with two, and adding every time one more, until they operate; if thereby any Salivation should be brought about, greatly inconvenient to the Patient; then 10 grains of Gum Aloes Succotrin (b) may be given to procure by Stool a Cessation of the Ptyalism, which however will cease of its own accord in one or two days, if no more of the Pills are administered; but in case the sweet Mercury should not be approved by every Physician, as some are still apprehensive that it dissolves the Blood as well as any other coagulated matter; without entering in any Controversy, and without setting forth the Practices followed ever since seventy years, and so many happy and successful Experiments in cold and hot Climates, even with Children in the Preperation of the small Pox, in Worms and different other Diseases; the Author would recommend to substitute the following Obstruction and martial Pills once in 24 hours for two or three Days, until a Passage is obtained, or to accelerate their Operation by Enemata, and then the next alterant Pills: vide, Rx: Gum Aloes Succot: 1 Ounce: extract: panchimag: 1/2 ounce; Limatura martis pulverisata 2 drams, mix [25] fiant Pill, from 4 to 6 grains for a Dose. When a Passage is obtained, then for five or six days every Evening the following Pills.

Rx — Extract: abin: exti: Cardui benedic: extr: Cochle: extr: fumary ā, ā 1/2 dram, Gum Benz; Gum Junip; Gum hederae, Gum Mastick: salei terebin: Venet: ā, ā 1 1/2 dram; Gum aloes Succol: Myrhae rubrae ā, ā 1 Ounce, mix fiant Pill 20 grains for a Dose. These Pills being only alterantes, the following antispasmotic to be given every 3, 4, or 6 hours, 20 grains for a Dose.

Rx — Tartar Vitriol: deput: niter ā, ā 9 drams, Zinabar, antimon, or Natic Camphor ā, ā 1 dram, mix fial pulvis. In Case any feverish Disposition, or even the paroxismus itself should happen at the hour of taking either of the Powders (Bozoardic or antispasmotic) they are so safe Medicines that by no means their Administration must be omitted, in as much at that time they are beneficial in opening the Pores, by dissolving the Salt Particuls congealed in them through Perspiration, consequently taking away the Inflamation of their Glandules, of

---

(b) The Gum of the Aloes is obtained by pounding it into a Powder and infuse it with distilled cold water, its extractum is decanted, and fresh water cohabited in the Aloe as often until the water extracts no more; these Extractions are evaporated by the Sun or gentle Fire. The Residum is the Gum or Earth of the Aloe, which only possesses the stimulating Faculty.

course appeasing the febrile Effects by this gentle Diaphorism; these Powders may be taken in all kinds of Liquids, they prove most effectual in Wine, but when Wine is not proper to be given, Water, Tea, Coffee, Milk, Broth, or any other liquid Vehiculum will do; for the Effect of these Powders cannot be altered in the least by any Vehiculum whatever. Should in this course some Patients still incline to Obstruction, Enemata are to be suggested. In Cases where the Patient labours under no Obstruction, the martial (obstruction) Pills may be omitted, and the alterant Pills administered only along with the antispasmotic Powder.

The Remedies to assist Nature in the Diseases belonging to the Class of Relaxation, they being of different Degrees, require different Attention, the first however, is general, for they all require an Opening in primis viis, vide:

1st. To purify the Stomach with the following Vomit, Rx. Tarter Emet: 3 grains, dissolve them well in a Quart of Water: of which the Patient takes one third part; if that operates not in half an hour, he takes half of the Remainder, if after the second Draught does not follow four or five Operations, he must take in half an hour (after the second Draught) what remains of the Emetic Solution, which certainly [26] will do its Effect; (a) after the Operation a little muld Wine is given to pacify and revert the motum peristalticum.

2dly. After this Vomit next day the Patient takes the following: Rx. Salglauberi manna selee ā, ā 7 1/2 drams: niter Depur, 1 Seruple, dissolve and strain it; when taken it is to be worked off with two Tea Cups full of Water-Gruel after every Passage.

3dly. Every day a Doze of Bitters an hour before Dinner, and one or two Glasses of good strong wine (such as Madeira) after Dinner is to be recommended, and that the Patient takes great care by no means to overcharge the Stomach with any kind of Nourishment.

Persons subject to the Disorders of the next degree of Relaxation where Nature forces an Evacuation of the massam sanguinis, they,

1st. are to avoid hard Exercise, which excites great Motions, as also Anger, strong Drink, high Seasoned Victuals, and

2dly. chuse such Regimen and Remedies by which they may prevent Obstructions abdominis, which in these Cases are very dangerous.

3dly. Use frequently foot Baths before Bed, and Baths to be made warm, of different aromatic Herbs or salt Water.

4thly. Keep their Legs and Feet always very warm, so that they are in a constant Perspiration.

5thly. Bleed once or twice a year, but in case by all these Cares they should have an attaque (if male) they are to use the Obstruction Pills, as prescribed; but if female the alterant Pills for 5 or 7 days running; and besides the Pills, every two or three hours a Doze of the pulvis antispasmotic, continuing the above Regimen of bathing and keeping their Feet warm and by no means to lay in hot Rooms, or to use more than moderate Coverts on the upper part of the Body, least they excite Perspiration, which on that part of the Body is very precarious for sick Patients.

Where Phlem, Bile or aquosite requires to be evacuated, the above mercurial Pills are the most proper, and the Vessels may be reborated with Bitters in an Extract of Bark made of red Wine, to be taken 3 times a day, especially before Dinner; to this is to be observed, that in bileous Disorders the Patient is by no means to lay on his right side, as thereby the Bile will be compressed and increase her Effusion into the Stomach and intestins to the greater Stimulation of the motus peristalticus.

As to the Disorders proceeding from the last Degree of Relaxation, they are deeply rooted and obstinate, may justly be called Herculeans, the best Physician can only bewail his Patient in these Cases, and lament the want of proper Medicines to support and encourage Nature, which [27] in these Cases requires effective Assistance of Aperients, alterants, Roborants and Sedatives, to which the above Bozoardicum, Mercurial and alterant Pills approaches very near and are effectual in the Beginning of these Disorders, when they may make a Cure, and give Relief, but will be ineffectual, when radicated.

The World has reason to bemoan the Fate of Valerius Cordus,[14] an eminent Italian Physician and Chymist, who was accidentally killed by his Horse in the 30th year of his Age anno 1544, he was the last Possessor (some say the Inventor) of a sweet Oil of Vitriol, or rather the Quintessence of the Vitriol Oil (summum sedativum) the Process of which was found among his Papers.

Frederic Hoffman,[15] the famous Prussian Chymico-Physican has the Merit to have nearly restored that Secret again to the World, which is now called Liquor-Anodyn-mineral-Hoffmanni; but the Conveniency of the Chymists has reduced the genuine Mineral-anodyn Liquor into a common dulcified Spirit of Vitriol.

This Oleum dulce Cordi is properly the Sulphur martis maturatum in Vitriolo cum oleo vini Volatilisatum, and is a Sedativum leniter adstringens in Opposition to the sedative Opiatic, which is leniter, and sometimes vehemently relaxent; these two Medicines, masterly prepared, one to relax the tonum in Inflamations, the other to brace it in Relaxations, may be called the two Hands of a Physician, who, for want of the former must go through many herculean Labors (as it were) only one handed with little Comfort. Thus Physicians will continue to their Grief, until proper Encouragements are given to Chymists for the Product of this Treasure, hidden in the common Vitriol and Wine. The Neglect of which is the more deplorable, as daily great Cares are taken for the Productions and Improvements for the Support of Luxury, and cannot be properly enjoyed, when they are obtained.

The Author, among other of his chymical Experiments some years passed, elaborated the Anodyne mineral Hoffmanni in a new way with great Success, at which time He, by a certain Phænomenon had an Indication of the secret manner, how to obtain the Oleum dulce or Sulphur martis maturatum Vitrioli, thus encouraged, he made all Preperations, but it happened that Royal Orders obliged him to proceed upon Business of Importance, which drew him off from this Expirement; a Retorde is to this day filled with the Materials among the Author's Chymical Relics in America.

[*28*]

CHAPTER 4TH

Of Charles Town, its Ports, Road, Bar, the Number of Inhabitants, of both City and Country, Number of Negroes, in what and how they are employed, Exportation, Riches, Number of trading Vessels and Cattle.

The City of Charles Town is in every respect the most convenient and by far the richest City in the Southern District of North America; contains about 1,500, and most of them, brick Houses, arrayed by straight, broad, and regular Streets; the principal of them is 72 feet wide, called Broad Street, is decorated besides many fine Houses with a State House near in the Center of said Street, constructed to contain two Rooms, one for the Governor & Council, the other for the Representatives of the People, the Secretary's Office and a Court Room. Opposite the State House is the Armory-house, item, Saint Michael's Church, whose Steeple is 192 feet high, and seen by Vessels at Sea before they make any Land; also with a new Exchange on the east end of said Street upon the Bay. All four Buildings have been raised since the year 1752, and no Expence spared to make them solid, convenient and elegant.

The City is inhabited by above 12,000 Souls, more than half are Negroes and Mulattoes; the City is divided in two Parishes, has two Churches, Saint Michael's, and Saint Philip's, and six Meeting Houses, vide, an Independent; a Presbyterian, a french, a German and two Baptists; there is also an assembly for Quakers, and another for Jews, all which are composed of several Nations, altho' differing in

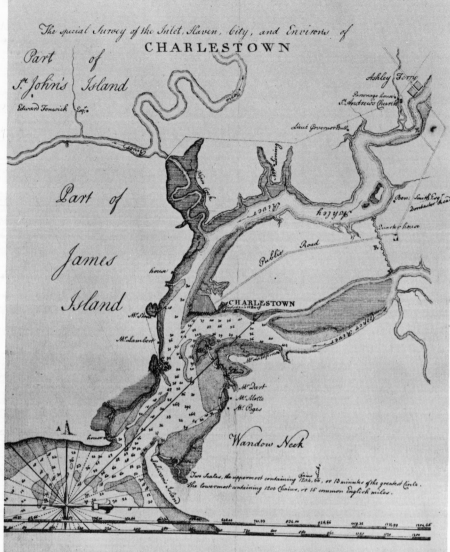

The special Survey of the Inlet, Haven, City, and Environs of

CHARLESTOWN

Part of St. John's Island

Edward Fenwich Esqr.

Part of James Island

Ashley Ferry

Parsonage house St. Andrew's Church

Lieut Governor's

Ben: Smith Esqr Dorchester Road

Quaker house

Public Road

CHARLESTOWN

Wando Neck

Two Scales, the uppermost containing 1204, 56, or 13 minutes of the greatest Circle. The lowermost containing 1200 Chains, or 15 common English miles.

EXPLANATION

A. the Light house

B. the principal Channel thro' the Bar

C. Fort Johnson

D. the detached Bastion projected

All Soundings are at high Water

E. the fortified Canal projected 6 miles from the City

F. the Eagle's Marsh, thus called from the Surveyor General's Schooner the Eagle being cast away on it.

G. A Marsh, called Skutts Folly

H. Place intended for a Bridge

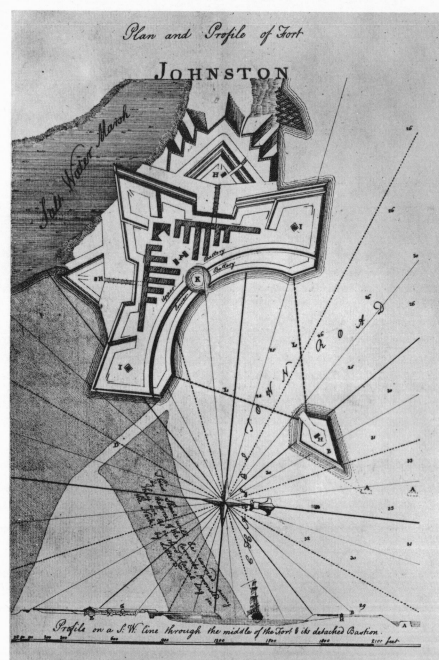

Plan and Profile of Fort

JOHNSTON

Profile on a S.W. line through the middle of the Fort & its detached Bastion.

EXPLANATION

A. Artificial Breakers, sunk across the Channel to bring the best Water between the Fort and detached Bastion.
B. the detached Bastion, built in the Channel, for which the Foundation is raised by sinking artificial Breakers.
C. An Epéron to lead the Force of the Current off from the N.W. Bastion. D. a Canal to be made through the Shoal's Neck, for the Water to wash the Channel thro' d. E. the Commander's house. F. the main Guard. G. Barracks, both which contain upon one floor 72600 square feet, 1200 for a Captain, 450 for a Lieutenant, 360 for an Ensign, 4800 for one hundred Men, does 6510 sq.ft. & Company. thus the 2 Barracks will accommodate 11 Companies, and there yet remains a Room 33 by 30 for a Hospital. H. Guard houses.
I. Powder Magazines. K. small Haven for an armed Sloop, and the Garrison's Barge. L. the two Booms to bar the Passage thro' the Channel in time of War. N.B. the two land Poligons contain each 1200, but the two water Poligons 1500 feet. the Booms form the Curtains to join the detached Bastion to the N.W. and S.E. Bastions.

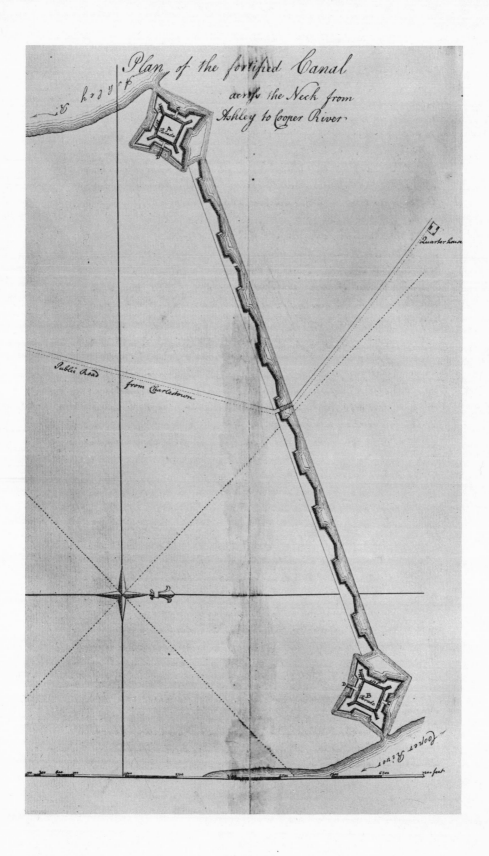

Plan of the fortified Canal acrofs the Neck from Ashley to Cooper River

religious Principles, and in the Knowlege of Salvation; yet are far from being encouraged or even inclining to that Disorder which is so common among Men of contrary religious Sentiments in many other parts of the World, where that pernicious Spirit of Controversy has laid Foundation to Hatred, Persecution and cruel Inquisition, in lieu of ascertaining thereby how to live a Godly Life. A Society of Men (which in Religion, Government, and Negociation avoids whatever can disturb Peace and Quietness) will always grow and prosper, so will this City and Province, whose Inhabitants were, from its Beginning renowned for Concord, Complaisance, Courteousness & Tenderness towards each other, and more so towards Forreigners, without Regard or Respect of Nation or Religion.

The Port of Charles Town is shut up by a Bar stretching from North to South 6 miles, which has 6 Channels, the best of the six is that, which bears E. by S. 2 1/2 miles from the Light House lately erected in Latitude 32°40′00″ on James Island here the Variation continued E. 1°52′ anno 1770.

[29]

This Port is very extensive, contains within the Bar to the west end of the City in both Rivers, Cooper and Ashly, sixteen square miles, Sounds all over (the Bar's Channel included) from 19 to 60 feet at high water. N.B. The Bar itself and Shoals excepted, for on the Bar, especially on the Shoals, the Soundings run so shallow as not to give 3 feet at high Water: But the main Channel has no less than 26 1/2 feet Depth at high water mark.

At a Distance of 2 1/2 miles S. E. by E., has formerly been erected a Fort, by Governor Johnston,[16] from whom it bears its Name, has a Barrack to accommodate 50 Men. The Fort's Commander is a King's Officer, and at present Colonel Howard; this Fort lays on a high Bluf, commands the Channel, which is here only 3/4 of a mile wide, but the Construction and Age of this Place cannot afford much Defence, unless from a new Battery, which is lately erected at its Foot, mounting fifteen 18 pounders and five 9 pounders, in all twenty Cannons, rather too weak a Battery to stop a Vessel from passing.

The Author proposed Anno 1755 to Governor Glen a Project of a new Fort at the same place, with two (vide, a high and low) Batteries of 200 Cannons together, and a Bastion detachee in the Channel to mount 50 Cannons more, and a Boom to barricade the Channel between the Fort and its detached Bastion.[17]

He proposed also to make the City (which by Nature is a Peninsula) six miles to the west of it, by a fortified Canal from Ashley to Cooper Rivers, to an Island,[18] in order to secure the City by the Fort against a sudden Surprize from the Sea, as also against an Insurrection of the Negroes or Indian War by the fortified Canal; in the first case, the Citizens would have time to send in the Country their Wives, Children and Treasures, and prepare themselves for a Defence of the City. In the second Case, Planters may resort their Families,

Effects and Provisions from the Country within the Fortification of the Canal; this Project is even now the only Expedient to secure their Wealth, Families & Negroes, which at this time by the nearest Computation, consist in City and Country together in 35,000 Freemen, Women and Children; and of 80,000 Slaves, 68,000 of which may be counted to be employed in planting Rice, Indigo, Tobacco, & Provisions; in sawing of Boards and scantling, in splitting of Rails, Staves, and Shingles; also in clearing of Land.

One Slave cultivates five Acres of Land (one Acre of Corn, Peas and Potatoes, and four of Rice or Indigo). The Culture of either is estimated equal Labour; this is their Task both in newly cleared, or old [*30*] worn Ground without altering the Denomination of an Acre, only with this difference, that the same Measure of 220 feet (by which Overseers lay out an Acre of Ground) is diminished by Degrees every year, until its Reduction comes down to 200 feet; the first measure of 220 feet makes an acre of new Land 1/9 too big, and the last measure of 200 feet in old Land better than 1/12 too little; this they do, because new Land produces scarce any Grass, and once hewing [*hoeing*] will do for the whole Season; but the Grass comes and increases yearly in a manner that sometimes three hewings are scarce sufficient in one Season; and

EXPLANATION

The Canal extends 11,600 feet across from River to River, is defended by ten Bastions, from one Bastion's Point to another measures 950 feet; each end of the Canal is defended by a Citadel, both intended for 2,000 Men.

The Citadels contain their Barracks, each Barrick measures 450 feet on a side, and each Wing measures 125 feet, each Barrick contains with their four Wings 65,100 square feet on a floor, to accommodate ten Captains with 1,200, ten Lieutenants with 450, ten Ensigns with 360, and 100 private Men with 45 square feet each.

A Parade in the Center, sally Ports C, outwards, and Communication Gates D, with Bridges to the City.

Citadel A guards and defends half the Canal and Ashley River.

Citadel B defends and guards the other half of the Canal with Cooper River; this Canal cuts off from the Main a Tract of Land containing 17 1/2 square miles, or 11,200 Acres of Land.

Five square miles are sufficient for an Encampment of 280 Batallions of 500 Men each, and 252 Squadrons of 160 [per] Squadron, in all 180,320 Men, allowing for two Batallions or 4 Squadrons 396 feet front, and 990 feet depth: A Tract of Land containing 392,040 square feet, exactly nine acres of Land; so there yet remains 9,573 Acres for Intervals, a Park of Artillery and Magazines, without incumbering the City, although comprehended in the 17 1/2 square miles.

The Canal will serve also for the Convenience of Boats and small Craft coming down Ashley River to Charlestown, in order to avoid White Point, a Place very tedious and at times dangerous on account of easterly Gales.

when this comes to be the Case, the Planters relinquish those Fields for Pasture, and clear new Ground of its Woods. An Acre of which is a day's Task for eight Slaves, but they do no more than cutting down the Trees; the lopping and burning of the Limbs and Underwoods is performed without tasking the Negroes.

The Planters set their weak Hands, (Women and Boys) to cut down the Bushes and Shrubs with Hoes and Hatchets, before the Tasks are laid out and marked, and after this, the Trees are all cut down; this is daywork; but the lopping and burning is nightwork vide, at Sun-set all Slaves leave the Fields and retire to their Cottages to rest an hour; then all hands are turned out to lopping and firing, which they continue until 9 o'Clock at night. The Fires are made but small, and in many Places, in order not to burn the Soil, yet to destroy all Branches, Shrubs and Bushes, whereby they scatter the Salt in the Ashes all over the Ground; the Bodies of the Trees remain on the Land, and as many as are fit for Rails and other Timber are manufactured to those Purposes, as they have Leasure, the rest are by Degrees split for Fire Wood, and with the remaining Limbs (not consumed by the Fire) brought to the Planters and Negroe Houses for Fire Wood, which is not moved by tasking the Slaves, but they dare never return from their Fields without bring[ing] a Load of fire wood on their Shoulders.

This is the Practice, except of those Planters who have an immediate Market for their Fire Wood and Timber; they set about sawing, splitting, cutting and piling immediately after cutting and lopping the Trees without firing new Land, except with the Shrubs and Bushes.

Although most new Fields remain for a long time lumbered with the Bodies of Trees for one or two years, this however does not hinder Planters from cultivating the clear Spots; mean while the Places thus covered with the Bodies of Trees, improve in Goodness of Soil. The weekly Task of a pair of Sawyers is 600 feet of Pine, or 780 feet of Cypress, Cedar, Red-bay, or poplar Boards, provided the Trees are cut, squared and pitted to their Hands, or else, if they must cut, square, and pit, their Task is 500 feet Pine, [*31*] and 650 of other Trees. A Slave splits 100 Rails a-day. The tasking of a Negroe and providing Employ, for such hours (when the Weather will not admit them to be turned out) is one of a Planters principal Studies, since the preventing of Idleness is the Art, from which depends the whole Discipline of the Negroes and the Planters Success.

The Carolina staple Commodities are

Bacon	Indigo		Rice	
Beef, salt or barrd.	Cedar		Rum	
Butter	Cypress	live	Skins	
Cheese	Lumber { Oak..... { red	Snake root, Virginia	
Cotton	Pine	white	Sugar	
Cordage	Red bay		Tobacco	
Corn	Peas		Tallow	common
Flour	Pink root		Tar......	green
			Turpentine	bees
Hides	Pitch		Wax.....	myrtle
Hemp	Pork, salt and barrd.			

Of these Commodities Rice is the Principal, which is brought there to the highest Perfection, and as such known in all the European and America Markets.

The annual Export of Carolina Rice amounts to above 100,000 Barrels, of which two contain 1,100 Weight, so that the whole makes out above 55 millions Weight of neat Rice, worth in Carolina £275,000 Sterling: Next to which is Indigo, whose Exportation comprehends no less than 600,000 Weight, worth in Carolina £150,000 Sterling, and the whole annual Exportation may be valued at £637,000 Sterling.

Above 300 top-sails, besides small Vessels do yearly enter, and clear out of this Port, charged with the Products and Manufactories of the Province for the North American and West Indian Markets, but chiefly for Holland, the Mediterranean and Portugal.

The Cattle in this Province are thus increased, that all Pains would prove in vain to number them, yea the Province is rather over stocked, and in order to make room for the yearly immense Increase, great Herds, from 3 to 1,500 Heads have been driven from this into the Neighbouring Province of Georgia, there spread between Savannah and Hogetohee [*Ogeechee*] Streams, ever since 1757, and kept in Gangs under the Auspicie of Cowpen Keepers which move (like unto the ancient Patriarchs, or the modern Bodewins in Arabia) from Forrest to Forrest in a measure as the Grass wears out, or the Planters approach them, [*32*] whose small Stock of Cattle are prejudicial to the great Stocks, from among which, the former draw the Bulls, and sometimes the Calves, (the latter, if not marked are apt to become the Planters Property) and as the Cows follow the Bulls also, great Gangs are apt to be misled to the Pasturage near the Plantations, which not affording sufficient Range for a great Stock, the Cattle are in Danger to grow poor and sick, for which reason the Cowpen Keepers prefer their Solitude to the Neighbourhood of Planters.

The Cow Pen-keepers determine the Number of their Stocks by the Number of Calves, which they mark every Spring and Fall; if one marks 300 Calves per annum, he reckons his Stock to consist of 400 Heifers, 500 Cows and 300 Steers, in all 1,500 Heads besides Horses; this proves that not even a Cowpen-keeper knows the true Number of his own Cattle.

If they sell a Stock of 300 Heads, they allow 124 Cows, 80 Steers, including the Bulls, 90 Heifers, and 6 Horses, which Stock they sell for £300 Sterling, and deliver them gratis on the other side of one, two, or three navigable Rivers, according as the Cowpenkeepers are in want of selling.[19]

CHAPTER 5TH

Of Government and Forces.

The Government is composed of a Governor and His Council; of a Speaker, House of Representatives and a Treasurer; of a Chief Justice, with two assistant Judges; an Attorney General; Attornies at Law; Clerk of the Crown and Common Pleas; a Grand and Petty Jury; Justices quorum anus; and Justices of Peace.

Of Colonels, Captains, Subalterns, Militia, a Troop of Horse, and Artillery Company.

A compleat Council consists of the Governor, or in his Absence of the President and four; and in particular Cases, if four cannot be conveniently met with two Counsellors will do.

To make a full House of Representatives, the Speaker must have the Assistance of at least twelve Members, but that Number may be multiplied.

To make a Grand Jury requires absolutely twelve; they may be double that Number.

To make a Petty Jury cannot be less, or admitted more than twelve, inclusive of the Foreman.

[33] By the King, are appointed the Governor, all Counsellors, the Chief Justice, Attorney General, Clerk of the Crown, and Clerk of Common Pleas.

By the Governor, are appointed the Treasurer, Assistant Judges, Attorneys at Law, Justices quorum anus, Justices of the Peace, Colonels, Captains and Subalterns.

By the Peoples Election, are appointed their Representatives, out of which the Speaker is chosen by the Members, and approved of by the Governor.

Jurors, both for the Grand and Petty Jury, are chosen by Ballot, and their respective Freeman by the Jurors.

The Governor's principal Duty and Attention is, to preserve the Prerogatives of the Crown; next to promote the Welfare of the People and Province; lastly to defend his Province in Absence of King's Forces, as a General, at the Head of the Provincial Army by Land; or as their Admiral at the Head of a Fleet by Sea.

Although the latter Character has not as yet appeared in that Station and Authority, yet would Need's take Place, should an Enemy make himself Master of the Province, when Expeditiousness would require to save the Archives and Treasure to a Neighbouring Province on board of a Fleet formed of pressed Vessels in the Harbour, and manned with the Provincial Army in order to return reinforced with the Neighbouring Militia to disposses the Usurpers of His Province; as otherwise a Governor cannot leave his Province and continue Governor and Commander without the Limits of his Province; which Character he maintains with all force at the Head of his Army, altho' absent from the Metropolis, where he may send his Directions to His Council.

The Militia in Carolina consists of about 8,000 Men properly regimented; each Regiment under a Colonel; these Regiments, one of which is Cavalry, are several times in the year excercised by their Commanders; besides these Regiments, there is also a very respectable Corps of Artillery, which by frequent exercising has obtained great Skill in Gunnery.

The General Assembly of Representatives meet upon any extraordinary Case, when the Governor needs their Concurrence, besides this they meet once a year to regulate the Tax Bills for the Support of the Provincial Expences and Sums demanded by the King; also to make such Laws as they find salutary for the Welfare of the Province.

[34] These Laws (as well as any other) Bills are three times read in the House of Representatives; also three times in Council, after which six Readings, the Governor gives his Assent to the Bill, from which Date the Bill is lawfull; if it is a Law, that Law is in force as long until repealed by the King.

The Chief Justice holds annually the several Courts appointed by Law; vide, General Courts of Oyer and Terminer or Gaol Delivery; and the Courts of Common Pleas.

In the General Courts of Oyer and Terminer the King is Plaintiff, and [in] this Court are determined all criminal Causes. The Attorney General files the Bills of different Crimes in Number of the Offenders in Prison, for on this day all Prisoners must be delivered up, and brought at the Bar to be arraigned, and their Cause determined, if they, or any of them are indicted of more than one Crime, in case they are cleared of the first, they must stand the next Trial either in the same or next following Court; for no more than one Trial can be brought on a time against a Person in either of the Courts.

The Provost Marshal or Sherif opens the Prison and brings the Prisoners to the Bar of the Court.

The grand Jurors are sworn by the Clerk of the Crown; their Foreman who has previously been chosen by them, is the first qualified with the [oath].

The Attorney General calls for the Foreman of the Grand Jury, & delivers him all the Bills he has filed against the Prisoners at the Bar.

The Foreman, with the Grand Jury, retire into a private apartment, in order to examine the Bills, if they find any Exception against any or all the Bills, they have Power to declare and indorse them, not a good Bill, upon which the Prisoner or Prisoners cannot be tryed, but must be put at Liberty, and in case they find the Bill good, and indorse it as such, they deliver all Bills indorsed to the Clerk of the Court, who reads the Indorsments publicly in Court.

The Petty Jurors appoint their Foreman, and are all sworn by the Clerk of the Court, who delivers all Bills indorsed as good Ones to the Foreman, who also receives his Instructions from the Chief Justice upon the Bench: but before they proceed upon Business, they, one after another, place themselves before the Criminal, whose Action is to be arraigned, (every Criminal having Liberty to except against 20 Petty Jurors) if the Criminal excepts him who presents himself, that Juror is to retire, if not excepted, he proceeds upon Business; the petty Jurors must all agree in the Verdict, either clear or bring the Prisoner guilty; determining the Crime [35] in its Class subject to a bodily Punishment, pecuniary Mulct, Imprisonment, Transportation or Death. Sometimes they recommend the Criminal to the Mercy of the Court, sometimes they declare him not guilty.

The Chief Justice pronounces and mitigates the Punishment, but if he gives a Sentence of Death, that Sentence cannot be executed until he himself has brought the Sentence, and layed it before the Governor.

The Governor, altho' he signs the Sentence of Death, may hinder the Execution of it by reprieving the Criminal; but if that Reprieve is not granted, the Criminal is executed accordingly, and within the time appointed by that Sentence; as the time of executing the Sentence elapses by any Reprieve, a great Controversy lately did arise, and with good Ground of Reasons demonstrated, that the Provost Marshal has no Authority and Power to execute that Sentence, which by the Expiration of its limited Term lost its Force.

In the Court of Common Pleas, all manner of Controversies concerning Heritages, Debts, Possessions etc., are determined by a Jury, which are generally

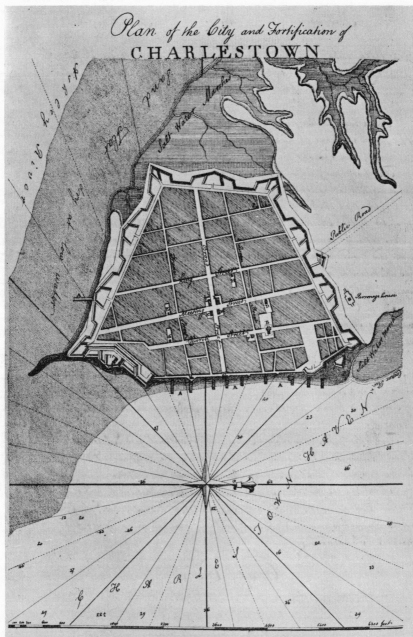

Plan of the City and Fortification of

CHARLESTOWN

EXPLANATION

A. Wharfs   B. St Philip's Church   C. St Michael's Church   D. Independent Meeting house

E. Scotch Meeting house   F. French Meeting house   G. Baptist Meeting house   H. Quaker Meeting house

I. House of Correction   K. State house, or Basilica   L. Armory house   M. Beef Market

N. New Exchange   O. Old Exchange

The south side has 3 Poligons, each of 1150 f. the west side has 2 Poligons, each of 1088 f. and the north side has 3 Poligons, each of 1050 feet.
A Poligon of 1000 f. with a detached Bastion joins the Bay from the north. Another Poligon of 1425 f. with a detached Bastion joins
the Bay from the South, which and part of the south side has been executed.

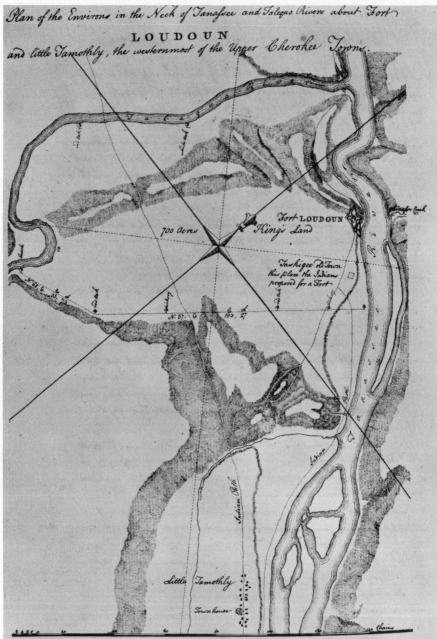

Plan of the Environs in the Neck of Tanassee and Taleque Rivers about Fort

LOUDOUN

and little Tamothly, the westernmost of the Upper Cherokee Towns.

Above is the Representation of the 700 Acres of Land which the Cherokee Nation anno 1755 has ceded to the King, for the Use of a Fort, bounding N. Ewardly upon Tanassee River, W. and S.W.wardly upon Taleque River; & S.Ewardly on the Indian Land, distinguished by an artificial Line drawn from Tanassee across the Neck to Taleque River. Surveyed in the year as above pursuant to an Order from His Excellency James Glen Esqr, Governer in chief over His Majesty's Province of South Carolina

By William Gerard de Brahm
Surveyor General

picked out and consist of the best Men, known to be conversed in those particular Matters, but Controversies under the Value of 29 Shillings Sterling are settled by the Justices of the Peace, assisted by two or more Freeholds.

For Grand Jurors, are chosen Men of good Estate, Reputation and Judgment.

For Petty Jurors, are chosen Men with or without good Estates, but of good Principles; Surgeons, and Butchers are the only excepted; because they are thought less compassionate than other Men.

Such are the Privileges and humane Constitution of the British Government, that no Man can loose his Life or Effects, nor be brought to any Punishment, without the Generality agrees and declares Sentence against him.

CHAPTER 6TH

Of the Fortification of Charles Town, the Building of Fort Loudoun, & its Fate, of the Cherokee Indians, and the Apalachian Mountains.

In the year 1755 James Glen Esqr. being Governor of this Province,[20] the Author was then employed as Engineer to fortify Charles Town[21] with Ramparts, forming regular Bastions, detach'd or joined [36] with Curtains, to which he allowed 84 feet Basis, whose Scarps he gave a Slope of 30 Degrees on the Water side, and raised their Platform four feet above the high water mark, which was observed after the Hurricane that happened on the 15th of September 1752, these heavy works were unavoidably to be carried across boggy marshes, under which no hard Foundation was attainable even with a Rod of 17 feet long. An Experiment was made by Colonel Beal,[22] one of the Members of His Majesty's Council (a Gentleman of great Ingenuity and Judgment) he run down the 17 foot Rod without any other Force, than his own Hands, and he might have run another with the same Ease of 34 feet down without meeting any hard Bottom, as the boggy Marshes chiefly (especially where the Experiment was tryed) have no other Foundation than the Quick Sand. Such Places the Author secured with a kind of Grillees[23] made of Cedar Pots [*posts*] covered with two inch Cypress Planks, and well secured thereupon with Iron Spikes; on this he directed a Stratum of Fascins,[24] some six feet long, to be layed across the Ramparts, and some of twelve feet long to be layed the long way, well fastened with Staves drove through them at every three feet distance, to secure the Ends of the short Fascins, which afterwards was covered with a Stratum of Earth; with such Stratis He erected these Ramparts, the Foundation of this Construction he only could lay at Ebb Tides, for the Flood covered his Work for near seven Weeks, after which time he gained the Advantage of the Flood.

The Earth, for this immense and heavy work the Author chose to be dug between three quarter Ebb and low Water mark, by forming Ditches parallel with the Ramparts; these Ditches, by every Flood Tide (especially when set in with easterly Winds) was filled up from the Channel, in a Manner, that none of the Ditches appeared any more at Ebb Tides; thus the Earth was successively supplied by the Sea, without the least Expence to the Public, which without this Expedient would have found this Article intolerably expensive, as there was no Earth to be had unless what must be brought in Flats or Vessels from a Marsh in the Mouth of Cooper River to the East of the City, and from the opposite Shore of Ashly River on the South Side of Charles Town.

In ten Months, with 300 Men, all the Ramparts were raised, which (especially those on the East, most exposed to the open Ocean) have resisted the Violence and washing of the Sea to this day.[25] The Works on the South side of the City are now, by the Proprietors of the Lands (over which said Ramparts were conducted) laid level, and with great Cost filled [37] up within, to gain the Level of the City; by this Industry she is considerably enlarged and encroaches upon the Channel of Ashly River, which may be expected will in time make its Bed considerably deeper.

In 1756 the Author was desired by Governor Glen, to build a Fort upon Tanessee River,[26] in the Country of the Upper Cherokee Indians, where He previously sent a good Geometer, one Captain Hamilton, whom he gave Instructions to pitch upon a Fork of Tanessee, a Place, which was as little as possible commanded by an Eminence, and then lay out the 700 Acres of Land, which the Indians had obliged themselves to cede to the King for ever. To which Tract, Tanessee River should be one, and its Branch another Boundary; also to keep a Journal of his Observations in going and coming, in order that in his Report may appear a full Account of the Roads, Passages and Distance.

At his Return the Author learned, that the Spot intended for a Fort had been chosen by the Indians before Hamilton's Arrival in a fine Plane, but commanded from the opposite Mountain,[27] which is a long Ridge on the North side of Tanessee; that the Apalachian Mountains are near 200 miles in breadth from East to West, and divides the Tract of Land ceded to the King from the Settlements in the Province; that these Mountains had many difficult Passages, some of which, from the Information of the Report, appeared, that ten Men with Ease may defend them against 100 and frustrate their Passage.

The Author, after sufficient Deliberation, concluded, it was prudent and necessary, that he should make a Remonstration of the Difficulty in sending Amunition, Stores, Relief, and Reinforcement to a Fort at so great a Distance through impregnable Defilee's and a savage People, easily offended and revengeful, among which a Garrison cannot but be accounted a Hostage, and Sacrifice to a formidable Savage Nation consisting at that time of 10,000 Souls, among whom are 2,000 Warriors and Gunmen, less to be depended on than a civilized Nation, to which never a small Garrison would be trusted on any terms whatsoever.

He therefore did not advise to the Construction of the Fort, but the Indians having solicited (as appeared from the Correspondence of the Governor with the Lords of Trade and Plantations, which the Governor then produced) ever since ten years without ceasing;[28] that a Fort should be built and garrisoned with King's Troops, to defend their westernmost Settlement against their Enemies, when all Warriors and Gun Men are out a hunting or at War, that their old Men, Women and young children in time of Danger may have a Place to resort to for Protection; therefore [38] his Remonstration and Advice could not be attended to; He then undertook that Service, was allowed 300 Men and £5,000 Sterling to support all Expences of maintaining and marching these Men, Provisions and Stores over the Apalachian Mountains, to build the Fort, afterwards called Loudoun, upon Tanessee and near Talequo Rivers[29] in Latitude 36°1'15" & Longitude 5°0'45" N. W. 1/2 W. 372 miles in a straight Line, but by the common Road 450 miles from Charles Town.⊙

When the Author arrived with the 300 Men at little Tomathly,[30] on the west side of the Apalachian Mountains, he went recognizing [reconnoitering] the Place intended for a Fort; was accompanied by the Captains Raymond Demere, John Stuart, and John Postel;[31] also by the Indian Emperor (old hope); the great Conjuror (Attakulla-kulla; or little Carpenter), and young Beamer, a Mustee, who served as Interpreter; when the Author saw the Place, he observed not only that a Ridge of Mountains at the N. E. side of the River, but also, that two Eminences, on to the N. W., and another to the S. E. commanded the Place, so that he could not agree to fix upon that Spot seemingly a favourite Place of the Indians, wherefore he had much ado to convince Them of the Impropriety to build a Fort between three commanding Eminences; His Arguments would have required less Force, had the other Officers (who seemingly inclined out of Complisance to the Indians to favour their Choice) joined the Author, who at last shewed the Indians that the Men's very Shoe Buckles were seen from either of these three Mountains, could therefore not serve for a Fort to protect their old Men, Women, and Chil-

⊙ this Long is west from the Meridian of Charles Town, obtained by a travelling Survey's observations made by the Author at the time when leading the Troops for the Fort Loudoun Construction.

dren, what could not protect its own Garrison. They then consented He should choose the Northwestern Mount, being a narrow Ridge on which he laid only a Poligon with two Bastions, not finding sufficient Plane on its Top for the whole Fort. He therefore layed another Poligon with two Bastions below at the South side of the Mountain's Feet, which he joined to the Westward with a Poligon to that on the top, and secured it with Traverses against enfilading, and on the East upon the River with another Poligon, on which he formed a hornwork, Cavalier & Lunettes before the Courtain, thereby to have a full Command of the River, and make the most of the Territory, which descended towards the River in several Steps. A Rhombus with two obtuse and two accute angular Bastions was the Figure which the Fort could receive from the Bearings of the River and Mountain, who with a rocky Precipice 41 feet high from the Waters Superfices terminates upon the Rivers edge, each Poligon extended 300 feet in Length, with a Breast-Work of 21 feet thick.[32] In the Ditches he directed a Hedge to be planted of young Locust Trees (a), which in less than twelve [39] Months time filled the Ditch from the centre Scarpe to the Scarpe, so that there was no possibility to come to its feet with Intent to cut or burn it down. The Locust Trees are full of Thorns, which are three and some four Inches long, and out of each Thorn projects four other Thorns more, perpendicularly forming a Cross, in the manner of a cheval de frees, so that the medling with this Hedge is in every respect impracticable, and renders the Fort impregnable, at least against Indians, who always engage naked; each Bastion mounts three Cannons, each Cannon is of 16 ounces caliber, or bore. These small Cannons were brought with the greatest Difficulty, and great Expences over the Apalachian Mountains; the Indian Trader (one Ellis) undertooke to bring them from Fort Prince George opposite Keowee, on the east side of the Apalachian Mountains; Ellis contrived to poise on each Horse a Cannon crossways over the Pack Saddle, and lashed them round the Horses Body with Belts (a); but as these Horses had to cross a Country full of high Mountains, and these covered with Forrests, it would happen, that sometimes one End of a Cannon did catch a tree, twist upon the Saddle and drew the Horse down, some of which had by these Accidents their Backs broken under the Weight, and lost their Lives; the longest Journey these Horses could make was six miles in a day.[33]

In 1759, when William Henry Lyttleton Esqr., was Governor of South Carolina, War broke out between the Cherokees and the Carolinians. The Garrison in Fort Loudoun consisted then of 100 Men, King's Troops, commanded by Captain Paul, the Brother of Raymond Demere, and 100 Provincials commanded by Captain John Stuart, the Indians not judging themselves a Match for that Garri-

(a) A Locust tree or old shrub is full of very long and elastick Thorns.
(a) These Belts are called Wantons by the traders and Pack horse-men.

son (resolute and well fortified) guarded all the Avenues of Fort Loudoun, by a Blocadoe from February 1760 to the end of July the same year, during which time the Garrison determined to keep Possession of their Ground, made the best Shift they could with their Provisions, to which they added their own Horses early. The Plumbs growing on some Bushes of the Hedge in the Ditch, made also an additional Meal; these Plumb-Bushes (when young) resembles those of Locust, and was by a lucky Chance and Mistake planted in the Hedge.[34]

Attakulla-kulla, a true Friend to the English, from time to time secretly supplied the Garrison with few Bushels of Corn etc.; but a Stop was put to this friendly Supply, as soon as the other Indians made a Discovery of it, the Garrison conceived no Doubt, but that they should be succoured [40] either from Virginia, North Carolina, Georgia, their own Province, or from all the Provinces together.

Colonel Bird, with a Regiment of Virginia Provincials, was ordered from the Governor of that Province to relieve the Garrison at Fort Loudoun;[35] He, in Consequence of those Orders to him, marched his Regiment as far as Hudson's River,[36] and made a Halt, sending threatning Messages to the Cherokee Indians, but they had no Effect upon a Nation, which was not unacquainted with the Difficulties an Army had to conquer by entering their Country.

At the Request of the Governor of this Province, General Amherst sent by Sea 1,200 Men, King's Troops, from New York under Command of Colonel Montgomery, which arrived in April; they marched towards the Apalachian Mountains the first of June in the Night, after a March of 60 miles without any halt; they arrived in the Indian Settlements Northwestward of Keowee, burnt the Town Kanasechee Toxoway and Walaze; to which the Colonel marched his Troops in the Night, and took between 30 and 40 Prisoners; some Indians were burnt in their Houses, and the rest flew in the Mountains.

The Colonel (after his Men had rested a short time at Fort-Prince George) he went in quest after the fugitive Indians, and came, within the Reach of four days easy March of Fort Loudoun, in the middle of the Apalachian Mountains, where the Indians have a large Settlement of several Towns, from which they assembled themselves in a great Body, attacked the King's Troops and killed 100 Men. The Colonel had many wounded, and no Convenience to form an Intrenchment, nor a sure Communication to be supplied with Provisions etc.

The Colonel thought it therefore necessary to gain by moderate Marches with his wounded Men, the Shelter of Fort Prince George. In July he received Orders from General Amherst to return to New York, where he set out from Carolina in August.[37] This unhappy turn of the Colonel's Success in July dissolved all hopes of the Fort Loudoun Garrison to have any Relief, therefore found itself obliged to submit under the disagreeable Necessity of capitulating with Savages.

They surrendered the Fort with the twelve Cannons, Amunition, and Stores, with Condition, that the Indians should accompany & provide the Troops with Venison, until they reach the Settlements of the Province.

The 9th of August 1760, the Garrison marched out, the Savages, who had no Notion to be punctual to their Agreement by Capitulation-[*41*]Articles, conveyed the Garrison only to the first Incampment, between Chotee and great Talequo, after Sun-set they absconded by one after another, so that at Midnight the Camp was deserted by all the Indians.

The Troops were paraded before day of next morning. At Day-brake several Discharges from the Indian Fire-Arms out of their several Ambuscadoes, were poured upon the Parade, after which about twenty seven Men, and (what is peculiar) all Officers fell, Captain Stuart excepted, who, besides the rest of the Men (which all laid down their Arms) were made Prisoners.[38]

Among the killed Officers were Captain Paul Demere, Commander in Chief, and Commander of the King's Troops, Lieutenant Adamson, and Ensign Anderson, Officers of the Provincials, and Captain Stuart Subaltern.

This unhappy Catastrophe might have been prevented, had the Troops been marched all Night, and reposed under an armed Party, relieved every four hours in open Places, or advantageous Ambuscadoes during the day time, because the Indians, altho' very cunning in distressing their Enemies from behind Ambuscadoes, are not as yet expert to attack them, more less when defended by regular Troops, nor do they study engaging in open Fields unless they are forced to it in Extremities; but as to make any Assault upon their Enemies in the Night is what they as yet have never attempted.

In the year 1742 Captain Don Fabricio de Bartoli, with his Lieutenant Pedro D'Escobar, commanded a Garrison of 92 Regulars in Fort Quimiri, in the Kingdom of Perou; this Garrison was blocaded by the Chunckas Indians until all their Provisions were spent; de Bartoli nailed his Cannons, of which he had only four; burnt his Ammunition, Stores and the Fort; he marched his hungry Troops through the Indians to the Balcedere (Ferry) (a) of the rapid River Tapo; finding the Ferry destroyed by the Indians, and the River being no where formidable [*fordable*], he fronted his closely pursuing Enemies, when 3,000 Men in Number fell upon him, and he died with his Lieutenant and 90 Men fighting their Arms in-hand, two only surrendered themselves as Prisoners, which were the Messengers afterwards that brought the true Account to Lyma, where, doubtless de Bartoli and D'Escobar would have brought the greatest part of their half starved Troops, had the River Tapo not been in their way.

[*42*] The Cherokee or Apalachian Mountains, altho' very rocky and gravelly, yet they are well stocked with Forests chiefly producing

(a) Balcedere is a Raft covered with Planks, navigated with a Rudder and square Sail.

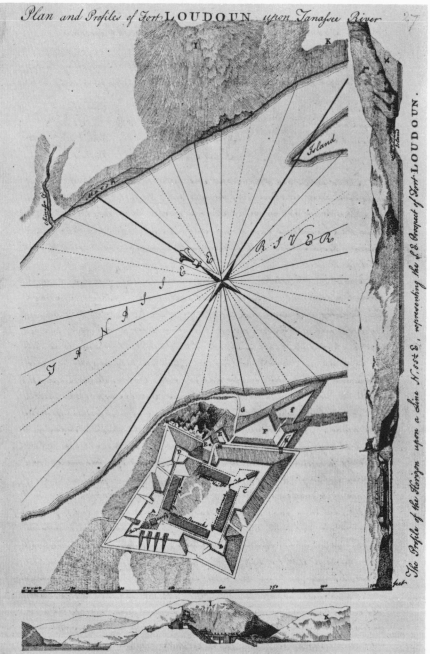

The Profile of the Horizon upon a Line N. 65° E, representing the S.E. Prospect of Fort LOUDOUN.

The Profile of Fort LOUDOUN, upon a S. 14. W. Line, drawn through the Center.
A. the King's Bastion. B. Duke of Cumberland's Bastion. C the Queen's Bastion. D. Prince of Wales's Bastion, is on a level with the King's Bastion, and 28 feet higher than Cumberland's and Queen's. E. horn work, Lyttleton, its Cavalier Ee is on a level with Cumberland and Queen, and its lower part is 37 ft lower than Wales's, the upper part of the Lunette Glen F is 37 ft lower than Wales's, and its lower part f is 40 ft lower than Wales's. G. the Communication to the River. H. the two Bridges over the Ditch between the Fort and the hornwork, also the Passage in the Fort. I.K. part of the Ridges on the N.E. side of the River. The ground commanding the Fort.

Bay Tree	Cypress, not decidious	Oak Tree
Cedar Tree	Ginsem .... bot.	Plumb Tree
Chesnut Tree	Hickory Tree	Vine ... { cluster grapes / fox grapes
Chinquopin Shrub	Locust Tree	Walnut

Their Vallies are of the richest Soil equal to Manure itself, almost impossible in Appearance ever to wear out; the putrified matters from the Mountains are in rainy Seasons washed down into the Vallies, and leave the Mountains bare of good Soil; the Land in the Vallies by this Means (besides being well watered with Rivulets) is become a real Matrix to receive.

From the Phlogiston, the Impregnation of Niter, so that there is at present a perpetual Renewal of what encourages Vegitation. Should this Country once come into the Hands of the Europeans, they may with Propriety call it the American Canaan; for it will fully answer their Industry, and all Methods of European Culture, and do as well for European as American Produce (the Rice only excepted) For Provisions of all kinds, as also Indigo, Silk, Cotton, Hemp, Flax, Oil, and Wine; be it for raising Stocks of Horses, Cattle, Sheep, Goats, and Hogs; be it for Metals, Minerals, Fossils and Stones; or be it for Manufactories of all kinds. This Country seems longing for the Hands of Industry to receive its Beginning ready to deliver them up; and altho' She has left no Difficulty to receive, yet it must also be observed, that She has made no Communication fit to export them; for many Passages from one Ridge of Mountains to another, are Ridges of half and three quarters of a mile in Length, both sides near perpendicular, between 4 and 500 feet high, and not above six feet wide at the top, which properly may be called natural Bridges, on which two Horses, when meeting cannot pass by each other, unless their Burthen, Saddles and Bridles are taken off, and carried behind them, so that they only meet each other quite bare; when these Creatures, apprehensive of the Danger, sometimes will brush against each other so close, that they rub off their Hairs. These natural Bridges may be artificially widened by Wall Parapets on both sides, or crossways the Bridges Beams layed, on the Beams Slippers, and on the latter Planks secured with Posts and Rails on both sides. But there are still worse Places on which one descends, or ascends, which Places form prominent Ridges not much unlike a Pair of Stairs, whose Steps are two and three feet high, about four [43] Feet wide, and not above five feet long, with both sides Precipices; on these Stairs is not so much Room as to admit the Leader to go on one side of his Horse, but must either go a-head, ride, or follow the Beast. To go a-head is dangerous, for should the Horse stumble forward, it will infallibly send the Leader before it down either of the Precipices to both their Destruction; to ride the Horse is as bad, if not worse, for when the Horse descends from one Step to another, (which it must perform with both feet together, and is with a kind of a Fall), at that time the Rider must lay himself back upon the Horses Rump (which in this Case is near three feet higher than its Shoulders) if the Gird and Crupper should give way, the Rider will, without Remedy slip over the Horses Head, and run the Risque of his Life.

The Author made once this Experiment, but had so compleat a Prospect of his eminent Danger, that he never after attempted a second Tryal of that kind; consequently to follow the Horse is the only sure Method, as the Beast will be the sole perishing in case of Accident; but the Difficulty remains, that few Horses are willing to go-ahead.

The ascending on these Steps is likewise dangerous, for the Author mounting moderately and leading his Horse, at times the Animal would set his Hoof upon his Spur and embarrass him from disengaging his Foot otherwise than by slipping his Spur again when he ascended briskly, and with a mis-step made a Fall; the Horse in a Hurry to follow, had liked to have stepped upon him; and this would be the case whether he held the end of the Bridle, or drew it over the Horses Neck, for Horses seem to have a Notion of less Danger, the nearer they can be to their Rider.

To make these Ascents or Descents (a) practicable, and render them safe, can only be effected by one gradual Descent returned on the side of the Mountain from the Top to the Bottom, in a manner that the Basis of the Descent be at least thrice the Length of the Perpendicular-Heighth of the Mountain; in case the Slope of the Mountain has 38 feet Basis, allowing 12 feet for the Breadth of [44] the Descent, it will admit of a Return from the Middle of the Mountains-heighth, so as to land with the return perpendicularly under the Beginning of the Descent at the top; if the Slope has 48 feet, it will allow two returns, and if 60 feet, it will allow three Returns, and so on.

Although these Mountains transpire through their Tops sulphureous and arsenical Sublimations, yet they are too light, as to precipitate so near their Sublimatories, but are carried away by the Winds to distant Regions. In a heavy Atmosphere, the nitrous Vapours are swallowed up through the Spiraculs of the Mountains, and thus the Country is cleared from their Corrosion; when the Atmosphere is light, these nitrous Vapours rise up to the arsenical and sulphureous (subliming through the Expiraculs of the Mountains), and when they meet with each other in Contact, the Niter inflames, vulgurates and detonates, whence the

---

(a) when the Indians come to a high Bluf or Mountain, they do not as Europeans, take their Passage obliquely on the side, but go down or up straight before them on Blufs or Hills or rich Soil or Clay, 'tis with the greatest Difficulty for a Horse to go up or down, the Creature having no other Method than to sit upon his hind Heels and slide down, at the End of which Slope both Horse & Rider overset, tho' without Danger.

frequent Thunders, in which a most votalized Spirit of Niter ascends to purify and inspire the upper Air, and a phlogiston Regeneratum (the metallic Seed) descends to impregnate the Bowels of the Earth; and as all these Mountains form so many warm Athanors which draw and absorb, especially in foggy Seasons, all corrisive Effluvia along with the heavy Air through their Registers (Spiracles) and thus cease not from that Perpetual Circulation of the Air, corroding Vapours are no sooner raised, than that they are also immediately disposed of, consequently the Air in the Apalachian Mountains is extreamly pure and healthy.

The Indians are Strangers to epidemical and contagious Disorders, they never remember such Incident. They are very skilful in dressing and curing of Wounds, Veneral Disorders, Bites of Rattle and other Snakes; they preserve themselves against Fevers, nervous and rheumatical Disorders by a regular and moderate Diet, bodily Exercise, by bathing both Winter and Summer.

When in 1759 the Small Pox was brought among the Cherokees and Catabaws, both these Nations discovered not only their great Ignorance of the Disorder, but also of any Remedy to cure it, they in their greatest Distress took Recourse to Bathing, by which fatal Experiment all were carried off, which took Relief that way. This Disorder would have extinguished both Nations, had they not left off bathing; this either by their own Notion, or by the Advice of the Europeans, being at that time among the Cherokees, as Garrison, and among the Catabaws as Traders, the latter who always live within the Indian Nations, and are licenced by the Governor, that they may encourage the [45] Indians, in employing themselves to hunting for the Sake of the Skins, which are a considerable Branch of the Carolina Trade; for these Skins the Traders exchange European Manufactures vide:

Belts, (Leather with Buckles)	Guns (very slight)	Razors
Blankets	Hatchets	Ribbans (silk)
Bracelets (silver and brass)	Kettle brass	Salt
Bullets	Knives	Scizzars
Callicoes	Linsy-woolsey.	Shirts
Combs	Looking Glasses, (small)	Strouts [*strouds*]
Earbobs	Needles	Thimbles
Flints	Pots, (tin)	Vermillion
Garters	Powder (gun)	Wire, (brass & Iron)

The first and principal Exercise of the Indians is bathing and swiming, in which they are very dextrous. Every Morning, immediately after rising, both in Summer and N. B. in Winter, coming out of their hot Houses, they take their Babes under their Arms, and lead their Children to the Rivers, in which they enter be it ever so cold. The Mothers learn their Babes swiming before they can walk, which greatly encreases their Strength, and of Course their Growth.

The Author, who had an Opportunity to see many Nations, as Creeks, Cherokees, Chicasaws, Chactaws, Catabaws, Utchees and Jamasees, never met with an Indian who was born a Cripple, but observed them to be all well made, tall and robust, neither very lean, nor inclining to Fatness, of the latter, he saw in all, only three, two Men and one Woman, all three Creeks, who were corpulent. They all walk very straight, upright, and rather with stiff Knees, which they scarcely bend. They are very dextrous and nimble in their next Exercise, which is wrestling, jumping, throwing and running; as also in their third Exercise, hunting and shooting, both with Arrow and Guns. An Indian once kept up, runing a-foot, for three hours, with the Author, who kept his Horse in a constant Gallop, from Keowe to Estetowe, and never left him.

The Indians never eat without Inclination, and then only very little, and that with much Regularity and Temperature; therefore they keep no regular time for Meal, but they love strong Liquors, especially Rum or Brandy, at all times, which they prefer to anything in the World, and this is the only Commodity, for which they exchange [46] their Horses; but great Care must be taken that, after they have consumed the Liquor, they dont steal and carry off the Horse; this is the only Theft they are known to be guilty of, which, besides the Crime of the Lie, Knavery and Drunkenness were not known to them, before the Europeans Arrival in America. The Indians have clear Ideas, which for want of sufficient Words they can only communicate by paraphrasing, and thereby they deliver their Intentions and Sentiments very plain.

They endure Pain with great Fortitude; are Strangers to Care and Affliction; are never cast down or elevated, therefore not hindered to exercise and improve their Minds with Politics, of which they have a great Share, as well as of a strong Memory, which they express by all occasions with their Resentments; when the same thing is repeated to them, they are very apt to be offended, and say, we need not hear that overagain, you have told us the same thing before.

The Indians exercise Hospitality in time of Peace with as much Generosity to their Guests, as they inflict Punishment in time of War, with Cruelty, upon their Enemies, whom, when they can bring as Prisoners to their Towns they make a great Rejoicing by larding their Skins with bits of Lightwood, to which they set Fire, dance round them, and encourage them also to sing and dance in the Middle by themselves; in case they faint under these Torments, the Indians endeavour to refresh them by throwing water over them, and (when recovered) set fire to another side: thus they continue until they die, which lasts at times upwards of 20 hours: But in case they cannot conveniently drive their Prisoners before them, they strike a Tomahawk (Hatchet) anywhere in the Body, wherewith they leave him, after having taken off his Scalp, which they spread on a small Hoop, and carry it in Victory as a Token of their Exploit to their Town Houses, where all the Scalps are publickly exposed during several Weeks, until every body has examined and declared them not to have been taken unwarrantably from their Friends; but bravely from their Enemies.

A certain Number of Scalps are required from the Hands of a young Indian before he can be honoured with the first military Title, which is a Slave-Catcher; and a certain Number more for the next higher Title, which is a Raven. The next higher Title to this is a Man-killer (as much as a Colonel); their highest Military Rank is that of a Warrior, (as much as a General). They receive at every Promotion, certain Marks on their Necks, Cheeks, and Breast printed in the Skin, [47] with Scratchings of a Pin and Gun Powder or Coal Dust; before they have any Title given them, they are only called Gun-Men or Boys, which in time of hunting and War attend their Chiefs as Servants, bringing them Water, Wood, Fire and Venison; a Gang or Troop take only one Woman to War with them. She is to take care of the Camp, Fire, Provisions etc. This Woman, after some Campaigns is raised to the Dignity of War Woman, to which all Prisoners must be delivered alive (without any Punishment) as her Slave, if she requires it, which is a Privilege no Man can enjoy, not even their Emperor, Kings, or Warriors; there are but few Towns in which is a War Woman; and if she can come near enough to the Prisoner as to put her hand upon him, and say, this is my Slave, the Warriors (tho' with the greatest Reluctancy) must deliver him up to Her, which to prevent they in a great hurry drive a Hatchet in the Prisoner's Head, before the War-Woman can reach him; therefore the War Women use that Stratagem to disguise themselves as Traders, and come in Company with them, as if out of Curiosity to see the Spectacle of the cruel War-dance.

The Indians have no Distinction of Dress among themselves, or do they seem to have a Fancy for it, except it be in Painting their Faces with red in time of expressing their peaceful Friendship, and with black in time when they intend to indicate their warlike Inclinations, and ornamenting their Hair, Ears and Necks with Feathers, Garters, and Beads; as also their Arms with Bracelets: If they have a Blanket or Piece of Strout [*stroud*] (by them called a Watch-Coat) to hang about them as a Mantle in the day time, and to roll themselves in it at Night, they are satisfied, as they use very little else to cover their Body or Head; for which they seem to take no manner of Care, unless their Legs and Feet, which they always keep rapt up in leather Socks (Mockasins) and woollen Leggings. The Men pull out their Hairs vide, Eye-Brows and Beard, so that they appear as being born without the former, and grown Men without the latter, and thereby misled many Europeans to observe in their Journals that the Indians have neither Eye Brows or Beards, and that by Nature, whilst they might have seen the Women to have all very strong Eyebrows.

The Indians have as yet no Notion of shutting themselves in Forts, nor to fight without the greatest Necessity in open Fields; They lay in Ambuscadoes and from behind the [48] Trees fight their Enemy, and surprise them in their Camps or Houses early in the Morning, taking the greatest Care not to expose themselves to any kind of Danger if possible to avoid it.

The Indians build their Houses of Posts, on which they lash in-and- out-side Canes, and plaster them over with a white Clay mixed with small Pieces of Talck (itchy-ocolla), which in a sun-shiny day gives to these Houses or rather Cottages a Splendor of unpolished Silver; they are about 12 feet wide, and 20 or more long, covered with a clapboard Roof, have no Windows, but two Doors on the opposite sides, sometimes only one Door; the Fire Place is at one End of the House, with two Bedsteads on both sides of the Fire; the Bedsteads are made of Canes, raised from the Ground about two feet, and covered with Bears Skin; their Corn Houses are built in the same manner, but raised upon four Posts, four and some five feet high from the Ground; its Floor is made of round Poles, on which the Corn-worms cannot lodge, but fall through, and thus the Indians preserve their Corn from being destroyed by the Weevils a whole year.

Two or more Families join together in building a hot-house, about 30 feet Diameter, and 15 feet high, in form of a Cone, with Poles and thatched, without any Air-hole, except a small Door about 3 feet high and 18 Inches wide. In the Center of the hot-house they burn fire of well seasoned dry-wood; round the inside are Bedsteads fixed to the Studs, which support the Middle of each Post; these Houses they resort to with their Children in the Winter Nights. Upon the same plan of these Houses (only on a greater Diameter and perpendicular) their Town Houses are built, in which the Head Men assemble to consult in War, Peace or other Concerns, and every Evening during Summer all Families of the Town meet to dance and divert themselves.

The Indians have a Notion of Immortality, and of a future State, wherein they expect to enjoy Wives, Guns, and large hunting Grounds well stocked with Deers (a). They have an Apprehension of Spirits; [49] this they prove in such

(a) This seems rather influenced to them out of Ridicule by the ignorant, or rather perverted Traders and their Pack-horse-men; for the Indians could have no such Tradition from their Ancestors, who knew nothing of Guns, nor were the hunting Grounds so interesting to them 200 years ago, when they only killed the Deers with Bows and Arrows, and no more than in Proportion as they wanted Meat, and Skins for Mokasins and Leggings, having no Strouts [*strouds*], Blankets, Shirts, Beads, Vermillion etc. to exchange: for these things are now in Comparison with their former Simplicity to be accounted Luxury, for which sake they make a great Carnage among the Deers, kill them for the sake of their Skins, and leave

times, when the Warriors return from the Wars with their Scalps, and (as above mentioned) expose them for several weeks on the Squares before their Town Houses, no Woman, Girl, or Boy can be prevailed upon to go near the Town House at Night, they say, among the Scalps wander the Spirits of the killed, these Spirits the Cherokees call Skina.

The Indians have also but a very scant Knowlege of a divine Being, which Knowlege, or rather Notion, extends no further, than that they believe he is good. The Cherokees call him (Hianequs) the great Man, whom the Catabaws call (Rivil) Overseer; but they pay no Manner of Adoration to him, or any thing existing; or have they any Ceremony at all, more than to extinguish all their Fires once a year in July at the time, when the Indian Corn (May's) is in its Milk, which they squeeze out by beating & straining then boil that Milk by a Fire, new caught from Electrisation, which they perform with two green Sticks rubbed with great Velocity across each other, until they are lighted; when this Milk is boiled to a Consistency, they let it cool, then form it into little Cakes, which they fry in Bears Fat, and are (while warm) a delicious Eating (a) with them they keep feasting three day's. To this Season they postpone all Elections, Promotions, and their King's Coronation.

[50] The Author has been present at the Installation of the King of Estatowee, which (as common) lasted three days; during which time the King lives without eating, only by chewing the Ginsem Root, given to him by two Physicians (by them called Conjurors) who are always with the King and take Seat one to his right and the other to his left, before and after the Installation Ceremony on his Throne, which is a Plank hewed out of a solid Tree with Hatchets; this Throne is planted all round and covered over with Bushes, so that the Sun may be kept off, on which the King sits naked, and is fanned with two large Fans made of Turkies Tails by two naked Indians standing before him at both Corners of his Royal Seat. The Physicians perform the Ceremony of the Installation, and begin with putting on his Feet a pair of Socks (Mokasins) made of white dressed Deer

---

their Carcasses in the Forrests. This critical Observation makes room for a reasonable Conclusion that the first Spaniards arriving in Mexico and Perou (at a time when the Ignorance of the Indians could easily be prevailed on, so as to make them believe their new Guests to be more than Men) used the Stratagem to captivate the Indians with romantic Notions, the best Bait for Ignorance, and led the History of their Yncas farther than the Indians could be conducted by their own Traditions, which could tell them no more than Yupan Qui, the Ancestor of Tupac Yupan Qui and their last Ynca Inticuti hualpa; these three no doubt were known by genuine Tradition, to which a Romancer may readily add two Yupan Quis more, make of Tupac a few Capacs, and by way of change some Rocas, and conclude with a Manco capac, the first of Yncas. This was inspired in the oldest and by them handed to the youngest, they unacquainted with Criticism, and pleased with the Tale, soon lost the Spring of its Issue, took all for real Tradition, purely handed down from their first Ynca Manco capac.

(a) the same may be made out of any Grain or Seed before it is ripe.

Skin; next they tie a white dressed Deer Skin round his Waist to hang behind half way down to his Heels; thirdly they offer him two fur Sleeves made of whole Rattoons [*raccoons*] Skins, in which he slips his Arms; fourthly they sling another white Skin over his left Shoulder and under his right Arm by way of a Mantle; the fifth are two Strings of Deer Claws, which they fasten round his Ancles; the sixth is a Diadem of a Roll of Fur pieced together of Rattoon [*raccoon*] Skins, some dyed yellow, and some crimson, (a) this they tye on his Head, and let two long ends hang down his Back, two Pieces of the same kind are fixed to the Diadem to go across his Head to keep the Diadem from slipping on his Neck in dancing. The seventh and eighth is a Swan's Wing and a white Leather Tobacco Pouch. The former he receives in his right, and the latter in his left Hand; but none of all these Robes and Regalia must touch his Body, before he has, by spitting upon each in particular, sacrated it to his Use. During his Installation, which always is performed in Public on the Square before the Town House, the Band of Musicians, consisting of Singers, (or rather howlers) concerted with Rattles and Drums set in the Center of the Square under two May Poles, and all the Sex in a very modest Dress, and grave Look, without gazing to the right or left, dance two and two, File after File, whom the King, when installed in his Royal Robes, follows a dancing; this Savage Monarch, much resembling a Hercules, in his Skins, is followed by all the Warriors and Gun Men with different Arms in Batallion; altho' savage as the Music and their Dance appears, yet there is the nicest Regularity kept up, so that all right and left Feet are lifted up and put down on the Ground in Conformity with the times observed by the Music.

[*51*] The King is obliged to dance three times round the Square, every Step which he performs is a leap [*which*] in his first round [*is*] a foot from the Earth; in the next round 18 Inches, and in the last is 2 feet. This Ceremony is performed every day a fresh, during the three days of that Feast, which they call the green Corn Feast.

Although the Cherokees have an Emperor, some Kings, Warriors, Men killers, Ravens, and Slave Catchers (all honorable Titles and Preferments, suitable to the Excellency of Principles conceaved by unrefined Ideas) bestowed on their head-Men; yet they are without any Legislator, of Course without Law or Government, nor do they pay any Obedience unto their head-Men, unless when they go out upon a warlike Expedition, then The Conjuror prepares the whole Troop with medicinal Decoctions of Roots, and reduces them by fasting, so that a leather Zone (Belt) with 15 or 18 Inches will incompass their Waste, after this Preperation they follow their Head-men with the greatest Observance, they neither drink more handfuls of Water, (a) or eat a Morsel more than their head-Men,

(a) The Indians are very expert in dying those two Colours.
(a) their way of drinking is, by throwing the Water with their Hands into their Mouth.

copying in every respect after his Example and obeying his Command, in case even accidentally any Fault should be omitted, they account it a bad Omen of fatal Consequences.

When the Author erected Fort Loudoun, the oftementioned Atakulla kulla, the great Conjuror proposed with his Warrior and Gang to go upon an Expedition against the French in Fort Charles upon Mississipi River, in order to divert their Notions, if they should entertain any, to disturb the Builders of Fort Loudoun, as Atakulla kulla passed the Fort with his Troops, he made a short Stop in order to give the Garrison time to prepare for a military Salute with the great Guns, which he in Consequence of his Departure did receive, during his Halt at the Fort, his Warrior came to take leave from the Author, who, according to the Ceremonies with which he always received the Indian Warriors, complimented him with a Bowl of Punch, the Warrior (who was a better Judge of the Sacredness to his martial Religion than the Author had a right to be) drank very freely, either not being so superstitious as Attakulla-kulla, or designedly.

In six weeks the Indians came back, Attakulla-kulla complained that since he left Fort Loudoun all things were ominous & dreadfull, [52] that when near Mississipi he discovered, that his Warrior had disqualified himself by drinking Punch with Skajegunsta Dutchee[39] this was the Apellation of the Author by which he was known among the Cherokees wherefore, sure of bad Success, he had been obliged to return without attempting any Hostility against the French; but the whole resembled a political Artifice of Attukulla-kulla, who probably suffered, with Consent, that his Warrior should defile himself with Skajegunsta Dutchee's Punch, in order to have a plausible Excuse for not performing what perhaps he did not intend when he proposed it; thus far the Obedience of the Savages to their Superiors.

As to breaking or making Peace, the Advice of their Emperor, Kings and Warriors etc. are necessary, and they consult in their Town-Houses sometimes several Months before they agree to break the Peace; a bold Indian, who has some military Merits, may with a menacing Speech put them all in Confusion, and prevent the War, altho' it be already agreed upon by all the rest, not much unlike a Polish Slack Shiz (a) (petty Nobleman); by this it appears, that all the Power of the Indian head-Men consists in no more than their Advice, or rather Force of persuading.

As the Cherokees, like unto the rest of all northern Indians, are expert in and

(a) Who at an Election Day may enter the Circle of the Polish Diet, when they have actually agreed upon the Person for their Kind, this Desperado crying out, Nieposvolum, (I wont) then makes his Escape as fast as he can, to prevent being cut in Pieces by the Horsemen of the Crown Army, who will follow him immediately; but should he escape, the Election must go overagain, by which the opposing party obtains an Interval to gain more to their Interest.

fit for nothing but hunting, one should conjecture, that they came from Japhet, the Son of Noah; this Japhet had seven Sons, and of five vide, the 2, 3, 5, 6 and 7th, called Magog, Madai, Tubal, Mesech, and Tiras, no mention is made by the Pentateuch, what is become of them and their Generations, and as Hunters making no Settlements, (pursuing their Fathers favourite Passion) were led in the remotest part of the Earth, from whence no History nor the least Information could be obtained by those who remained in Assiria; these Hunters probably were seperated from the European Continent in the time of Peleg the Son of Noah's great grand Son, when the world (according to sacred History) was seperated, supposing it to have been a civil and physical Seperation of America from Europe and Africa, in nothing absurd, as long as the Map of America with all its Bays and Capes will fit the Capes and Bays of Europe and Africa, in case the Atlantic Ocean is cut out of the Map.[40]

[53] As to the Southern Indians, they are evidently the Descendents of the ancient Cartaginians, who in their Days, as the greatest Merchants in the Universe, discovered by their Trading Vessels many Islands, and sent Colonies to the Cultivation and Improvement of them; probably some of their Vessels in the Pursuit of their Discoveries recognized the more southern Shore, fell in with the Trade Winds, not experienced in Sailing upon the Wind, were blown over into the Gulph of Mexico, which Cartaginian Navigators carried with them the Knowlege of conveying their Histories to Posterity by Hieroglyphics, from which the northern Indians have learned to leave their particular Adventures and martial Exploits with red and black on Trees nearest by, as Evidences of the Truth; many of these Hieroglyphics the Author has met with in the American Forrests, especially in the Apalachian Mountains, representing Figures executed with so much Art, as those, which appear on the Coffins of the Egyptian Mummies.[41]

It is much to be lamented, that no Pains have been taken to instruct these People in the Knowlege of God and Christ, which they could be the easier influenced with, as they are not possessed with Prejudices and wrong Notions of Idolatry, a Charity the Carolinian's should not owe to the Cherokees or Catabaws, who have not only sacrificed many of their Nation's Lives to assist the Carolinians against their Enemies, but have also very generously resigned their own Territories to them, and they reap the Riches thereof, with which the Carolina Treasures at this time are abounding; of course have a just Claim to a Share of Divine Knowlege from their Guests and adopted Brethren, who, preferably to all other Southern Provinces (a) but also with real Piety in their Conversations and Family Devotions, and by all their Actions shewing that Christianity consists not only in out- but also in in-ward Piety.

(a) have been abundantly blessed not only with a knowlege and Zeal in Religion

Compendium

Of the Cherokee Indian Tongue in English[42]

A

Acilaw .... Fire	Anaketóg .... Brother, it Sister
Acilaheste .... Burn	Anihagkókaw .... He lies, a Liar
Aggeté .... Back	Anógsci .... Snow
Ahiga I	Antlaw .... No, I dont know
Ahigeléste .... Knife	Antlaw
Ahika .... My	kawanhatíga .. I cannot talk with you
Ahika aquo cheri	Antlaw nukáhes .... None at all
kalistchota .... Within my house	Anukáw .... A Pond
Akikigenári .. My mate, you are my mate	Anuwóke .... Shirt
Ahosetaw .... Too much	Anuwóke squalóhe .... Jacket
Ahówe ....⎫	Anuwóke utennaw .. Match coat, mantle
Ahowikaw ....⎬Deer, item Venison	Aque losti .. low. Cher.
⎰thus Children call each	.... Hair line, silk Ribn.
Akenáthle ....⎱other, born of one Fa-	Aquocheri .... Within
ther and Mother	
Aki .... I am	Aquonatow .... Never
Akikula .... I am busy	Askowaskówe .... Hundred
Akitatatéki .... I am dry	Askowaskokówe .... Thousand
Akinulahaskaw........... I am not able	Askówe .... Ten
Alhe .... Sweet, your drink is sweet	Asnogi .... Petticoat
Allschiki .... To dance	Asquetuóki .... Hat
Alstahita .. low. Cher. .... Eat	Ashi .... Stop
Amma .... Water	Asthi .. up. Cher. .... Thread
Amahi .... River	Asulógi .... Breeches
Ammahi equo .... Sea	Asulokila .... Pull off the Breeches
Ammahi nukahes	Ata .... Firewood
kejusti .... Island, water all round	Atarikále .... Ginsem Root
Ammahi tahe	Atela .... Beads, Lace
wilohee .... By water let us go	Atelihaliloglohe
Ammaketita .... Soup	.... Arm band, brass or silver

Ammó . . . . Salt   Atloki . . . . Handkerchief
Annakate . . . . Alltogether

C

Chelikó . . . . Walk   Chizówa . . . . Fort, Fence, Palisadoe
Chemhé . . . . Pack horse man   Chizówa hawína . . . . In the Fort
Chenaleki . . . . What you please   Chizówa tohitla . . . . . . Outside the Fort
Chestó . . . . Let alone   Chikatáw . . . . Do you know

[55]

Chonetá . . . . Eight   Chowaskówe . . . . Thirty
Chonetaskówe . . . . Eighty   Chowatú . . . . Thirteen
Chonetatu . . . . Eighteen   Chowatú netaw . . . . . . 13 months, a year
Chotalaskowe . . . . Sixty   Chowé . . . . Three
Chotaluta . . . . Sixteen   Chulekosti . . . . You are troublesome
Chotále . . . . Six   Chumekoheste . . . . . . your Drink is sour
    Chicha . . . . A Boy

D

Dajesandénsti . . . . Fingers   Dikasdé . . . . Bladder
Dehalihadokáhe . . lo. Ch. . . . . . Earbobs   Diskastikatóg . . . Crow, Dig in the Earth
Dekachuri . . . . wash your hand   Dukasinsti . . . . Smoke
Dikatolí . . . . Buttons   Dukasinsti stequo . . . . . Too much Smoke
Didlia dokahe . . up. Ch. . . . . Earbobs

E

Echesti . . . . Laugh   Equó . . . . Great
    waháko echesti . . . . why do you laugh   Eschkaw . . . . Do you dance
Ekahike . . . . Kettle   Eskili . . . . Ghost
Elika . . . . Enough   Eskina . . . . Devil
Enatitaw . . . . I drink to you   Etchiú . . . . Boat–Canoe

G

Gázo	Where	Geniza	Many
Gazowahí	Where are you going	Gláglehanutché	Shew me the way

H

Hadlé	Warm	Híga	Canes
Halstahiá	To eat	Higáneka	White Man, European
Halstahiti kaskalogi	Table	Higanequo	Got
Halstahito	Do eat	Hihi	He
Hána	Come	Hikicho	I pray, beseech you
Hána halsthahia up. C.	Come and eat	Hinassoka	Tye the Garters
Hánakeháka	Come set down	Hinskénke	Elbow
Hankóre	Let see	Hiskaskówe	Fifty
Hatananaw	Go away	Hiski	Five
Hátawóda	Go dress, clean, wash	Hiskikatú	Fifteen
Hatíga	Speak	Higskiansi	Bring
Hawequo	Elk	Hohiga	Farewell, 'tis very well
Hawina	In	Hohigénthla	Cold
Hichénne	Neck	Hontchánka	Lay down
Higánke	Fork	Hutelokiski—low. Ch.	Brass or Iron Screws
Higanto-qualoski	Thunder		

[56]

I

Iánki	A Needle	Ina	A great way
Igohówi	To kill	Iohunó	Time passed
Igóno	A Bear	Ithi . . low. Ch.	Thread
Igónokaneki	Bear Skin	Itlaw	Hair
Igónohówi	Bears Fat	Iunelisko kanhéhe	Shot
Iká	Day	Iwokonékaw	A Negroe
Ilikóko	It is right		

K

Kaduki	Town	Kanetléntaw	Pompion
Kahigútiha	Girl	Kanetli .. up. Ch.	Bed .. Cabin
Kakaheske	Face	Kannéche	Ball
Kakaheskuwodá	Dress, clean, wash your face	Kanokówe	Tooth
		Kanowíno	Mortar, of wood or stone
Kakisté	Water Melons	Kanukéne	Foot
Kakohihi	Who is he	Kappa Léna	Coat
Kalagogé	Seven	Kaskaw	Rain
Kalaguaskowé	Seventy	Kaskáw noquo ukanna	It rains now no more
Kalaguatú	Seventeen		
Kaláleti	Heaven	Kalihadókee	{ hang on the Earbob, properly ear'in.
Kalinaw	Ears		
Kalenstówe	Cutting Trees	Káto	What, which
Kahíge	Goose	Katohátiga	What you say
Kalistehótaw	House	Katoli	Eyes
Kallakohoska	Tree	Katotilo	What you call that
Kalogesté equó	Ax	Katówe kenakaw	Burning Ground
Kalogésti	Hatchet	Katóg	Earth
Kaloquákanehíta	Gun	Kátokatúki	From what Town are you
Kaloquá skóla	Pistol	Katú	may's [*maize*] Bread
Kanahéhe	Chin	Katú delíko	Wheat Bread
Kanahóho	Shoulder	Katú kanath lénta	Pompion Bread
Kananówa	Pipe	Katú nunáw	Potatoe Bread
Kanasetchi	Sugar	Katúki	Mountains
Kanaté	Woman's Breast	Kawán	Will
Kanatíhe	Brother German	aki-kawan	I will
Kanéki	Skin with hair	Kazo	Where
Kanekíwosi	I am hungry	Kegakosta	Brother-in-law
Kanekoléhe	Pin	Kegusti	Round
Kanesáhe	Small Trunk	Kehákaw	Set down
Kanétchi . lower Che.	Bed, Cabin	Kekekehe	Red
Kanekadi	Conjuror, or Physician	Kelaghígu	Forget

[57]

Kelaghiguaki, autláw	Forget I will never	Kilhikina	Cold
Keloslégo	A Bridge	Kistahé	Lock
Kena–low. Cher.	Come	Kochelíko	To send
Kenhaw	Turkey	Koggessóle	Nose
Kenáli	Friend	Koheli .. up. Ch.	{ Paper, Book
Kenató Kannáw	Come Friend	Koheraki .. low. Ch.	
Ketotá	Father	Kohíge	By and by

Kikáw .... Blood
Kilágu .... More
Kilhahiko-cheliko . { my horse shall come for you, Ill send you my horse
Kilhi .... Horse
Kilhikehehé .... Mare

Koklánnow .... I make
Kóre .... See
aki Kore .... I see
Kówe .... Fat, Butter
Kukú .... { all manner of drinking Vessels

L

Lako nukákes .... { how many, how you count these
Lesusto .... Thimble
Lukáhe .... Must come

Sig lukahe .... You must come
Lukahedlaucenná ... from whence come you

N

Ná .... I give
Nahihí .... I give you
Nahahú .... Take
Skinahé .... You give, give me
Nahanehátaw .... This, there
Nahiguraw .... All times
Nakaskówe .... Forty
Nakatú .... Fourteen
Nakí .... Four
Nannéska .... To work
Naski .... Yea, I will
Nastatléste .... Love
Aki nastatléste nihi .... I love you
Nataletné .... Remember
Neskaw .... Speech
Netaw .... Moon
Nihikehéhe .... Woman
Nitali .... Sun
Noggohorénaw .... Hunter

Nogsci .... Lightwood
Nohóra .... Quickly
Higlukáke nohóra .... { you must come quickly
Nohoté .... Rum
Nohoté kikekehésta ... Wine (red Rum)
Noquo .... Now, directly
Noquóhakíchukegúhaw .... Ill pay for it directly
Noquó akí luschaw .... Now I come
Noquó elika .... Now enough
Noquó nukáhe .... 'tis now all
Noquó stilúke .... Now he comes
Noquo uleségka ... Now rest, good night
Noquo unwahé .... Now I go
Nukahes ....All
Nukahes itchonasesti ..... { none of them would go
Nunaw .... Potatoes

[*58*]

O

Okadaríhe	Husband	Osígo hi néskaw ...	Good is your Speech
Ouhi	After	Otassite	Mankiller
Oquojénne	Hand	Owassaw	Alone, by himself
Osígo	{ yes 'tis very well, how do you do, farewell		

Q

Quelóste .... Hair Line, silk Ribbon

S

Sanóha	Last Night	Steguo	Much, (too much)
Sanohí	Night	Stikigú	Little
Seráw	To tell	Stikigú titáska	You drink little
Aki. seraw	I told you	Stukisti . up. Ch.	Brass or Iron Screw
Scenstóte	Candle	Stuté	Door
Scélu .... May's [*maize*] (Indian corn)		Stutestáke	Door Lock
Scitalúska	Clapboard	Sunále	Soon
Sikqúa	Hog	Sunalukáke	Come sooner
Sirnágle	Sleep	Szelschki	Have you danced
Skóli	Head	Szichísqua	A Bird
Sogné	Nine	Szisto	Rabbit
Sognécatu	Nineteen	Szoláw	Tobacco
Sognehaskówe	Ninety	Szúflow	Fox
Sohíga	Weather	Szuláleti	Striped, Cloth or linnen
Sohíga osígo	Fair, good Weather	Szuskonáne	Blanket
Sohóko	We, both	Szuwétchi	Eggs
Squáhaw	Spouse	Szuwétchi kátog	Eggs broken, or on the Earth
Skaigúnsta	Warrior		
Squohehe	Smoke, smoak a Pipe	Skaigústa	War Woman

T

Tahetó	Time to come		Talúcha	Basket
Táku	Flies		Talukíski	Candlestick
Taketi	Looking Glass		Tankícho	I hear, understand
Takenalihatíga	a Talk		Tankiska	I hear not, understand not
Talaskówe	Twenty		Taqualélu	Riding chair
Talátu	Twelve		Tallósti	Garters
Tále	Two		Tenóki	Take, accept
Taletó equó	Great Plate		Tilesulóki	Shoes
Talequisco up. Ch.	Tin Pot		Titaleto	Plate
Talschki	Do you dance		Tiquezo	Indian Garters

[59]

Tilihetlówe	Bracelets		Titawtí	Spoon
Tilihóki	Stockings		Titinása tínsti	Wart
Toliofí	To write		Tiquétchi	Babes
Tilláw	Pole-Cat Skin		Tlestikálena	I cannot hang on it
Tilstohíti	Scissars		Tohitaw	Outside
Titá	Drink		Tolóste	Pistol
Titatáki	Dry I am		Tutelokiski	Dish
Titatówa—low. Ch.	Tin Pot			

U

Uhichéni	Whips		Unestálaw	Ice
Uká	Emperor, Governor		Unquétchi	Grown Children
Ukalókaw	Leaves		Unogkatú. azate	Fish catching
Uka nastóta	Hereditary Emperor, Emperor to come		Uskówa	Scalp
			Usquanahataw	Busy
Ukchénne	Back-Seat		Usquelati—low. Cher.	Pin
Ukoma	Broth		Usquolege	Body
Ulienki	Prisoner, Slave		Usquóte. up. Cher.	Pin
Ullo Killa	Clouds		Utchí	Way
Unahu	Heart		Utchiníthla	I go a long way
Ulaschéte	Heels		Utchilaka—up. Ch.	Lightning
Ulesegka	Rest		Utchistarka—low. Ch.	Lightning
Unéka	White		Utchiwílohe	Go out of the way
Unekátaw	Angelic Root		Utuhésti	Cheek
Unelsqualetaw	Wampum (Indian Beads) made of the purple spot in the oyster shells		Uzo	Raw Skin
			Uzowóda	A dressed Skin

W

Wágga	Cow	Wodá	{ to dress, clean, wash.
Wággahígan	Bull		
Wagga kanágti	Cow Milk		
Wagga kína	Calf	Wodikéhe	Indian, painted Man
Wagga kówe	Butter	Wohahýga	Wolf
Watoli	Corn house	Wohodé	Paint, Dress
Woakó	Why	Wohiki	Take, accept

Compendium

Of English in the Cherokee Tongue.

A

After .... onhí	All times .... Nahigúraw
All .... Nukatga, or nukahés	Altogether .... Anakáte
It is all .... Noquonukahés	Angelic Root .... Unekataw
Alone .... Owássaw	Arm Band of silver .... Ateli aliloglóhe
Let me alone .... Chésto	Ax .... Kalogéste equo
All round .... Nukáhes kejusti	

B

Babes .... Tiquétchi	Buttons .... Dikatóli
Back ....Aggeti	Boy .... Chúza
Back-seat .... Ukschénhe	Bracelets .... Tilihétlowe
Balls .... Kannéhe	Bread, european .... Katú deliko
Bands on Arms .... Ateli aliloglóhe	Bread of May's (Indian Corn) .... Katú
Basket .... Talúcha	Bread made of Pompions .... Katú
Beads ....Atela	kanatléntha
Bear .... Igóno	Breast of a Woman .... Kanáte
Beaten .... Tilihenika	Breeches ....Asulogi
Bears Fat .... Igonokówe	Bridge .... Keloslégo
Bears Skin .... Igonokanéki	Bring .... Hiskiansi
Bed...............{ Kanechi . low. Ch.	Broth .... Ukómaw
kanetli . up. Ch.	Brother .... Anaketáw
Bird .... Szihisquá	Brother-in-law .... Kegakósta
Back .... Kanekéhe	Bufelow .... Ignóso
Bladder .... Dikasdé	Bull .... Wágga hígan
Blanket .... Szuskonáne	Buring Ground ...... Katowi kenakáw

123

Blood .... Kikáw
Board .... Sitalúka
Bobs in Ears .... { dekalihadokáhe up.
                      { dekalenokáhe—low.
Body .... Usquolege
Book .... { Kohéli—up. Ch.
               { Koheraki ... low. Ch.
Butter of a Cow .... Wágga kówe

Burn .... Asciláeste
It burns until } .... Asciláeste sunalego
  tomorrow   }
Busy, I am busy .... akiula, or
                             akiusquanekáta
By and by .... Kohíge
By myself .... Owássaw

[*61*]

C

Cabin .... { kanéchi low. Ch.
                   { kanétli up. Ch.
Calf .... Wággakina
Call, what you call that .... Kátotí
Can .... Haskáw
  I can, I cannot .... Akihaskaw, akimu-
                       lahaskaw ......
Candle .... Scentóte
Candle Stik .... Talukiski
Canes .... Higaw
Canoe .... Etchin
Chair to sit on .... Kaskalóga
Chair, riding Chair .... Taqualelu
Chin .... Kanahéhe
Cheek .... Utuésti
Check Shirt .... Utuesti anuwóki
Children growing .... Unquétchi
Children of one Father } .. Akenáthle
& Mother call themselves }
Clapboard .... Scitaluka
Cloth striped .... Szuláleti
Clouds .... Ullokilla

Coat .... Kappaléna
Cold .... Hohigénthla
Colt .... Hilki kína
Come and eat .... { hanahalstahiga up.
                     {   Ch.
                     { Kena alstahita low.
  He comes now ...... Noquo stilúgche
  I come now .... Noquo akilukáhe
Come in .... Haná
From where are } Lukahed lakucenna
  you coming ..... }
Come and sit down ... { kana keháka up.
                      {   Ch.
                      { kena kehaka low.
Come sooner .... Sunalukahe
Come quickly .... Siglukahenohára
Corn, May's .... Sielú
Corn House .... Watoli
Cow .... Wággaw
Crow, Iron Crow .... Diskostikatóg
Cutting Trees .... Kalenstówe
Conjuror, or Physician .... Kanekadi

D

Dance, to dance	Allschkí	Door Lock	Stukistáke
do you dance	Tallschki, or eschkáw	Dry, or thirsty	Titatéki
have you danced	Szelschki	Dry, I am dry	Akititatéki
Day	Ikáw	Dressed Skin	Uzowóda
Deer	Ahowíha, or akówi	Dress yourself	Wodá
Devil	Eskina	Drink Brother, or Sister	Anaketawtitáw
Directly	Noquó	Drink Brother German	Titakanatihí
Dish	Tutelokiski, or taletóequó	Drink a little	Stihékotitáska
Do, or I pray you	Hikícho	I drink to you	Ena titáw
Dog	Sisqua	Drink Friend	Kenalititáw
Door	Stuté	Drink Vessel any kind	Kukú

E

Ears ... { Kalihado low. Ch. / kalenaw up. }

Earbobs

Earth

Eat, to eat ......

Come and eat .... Hána

Do eat .... Halstahíta

European (white Man) ...... Hijanéka

Eggs .... Szuwétchi

[62]

Broken Eggs	Szuwetchikátog	Emperor to come	Ukáwnastótaw
Elbow	Hiaskénnhe	Enough	Noquo, or noquó elíka
Elk	Hawequo	European Bread	Katudelíko
Emperor	Ukáw	Eyes	Katoli

F

Face	Kakathés	Fish catching	Unogkátu aszate
Face, wash. dress	Kakathes wóda	Flies	Táka
Fair Weather	Sohiga o'sigó	Foot	Kanuskéne
Far off	Ináw	Forget, I shall never / forget you }	Kelaghigú aki antláw
Farewell	O'sigó, or hohíga		
Father	Ketóta	Fork	Híganke
Fence	Chizówe	Fort	Chizowi
Fat	Kówe	in the Fort	Chízowa hawína
Fingers	Dagesadensti	outside the Fort	Chizowa tohitlaw
Fire	Ascíla	Friend come	Kinnatókannáw
take fire	Nahagi ascilá	Fox	Szúflow

G

Garters . . . . Tatlósti	let us go by water . . . Amahitake wílohe
tie the Garters . . . . Hinussóka	where are you going . . . . . . gazó wáke
Ghost . . . . Eskili	Go wash yourself, dress . . . . Hatawóda
Ginsem Root . . . . Atarikále	God . . . . Higanequó
Girl . . . . Kahigutcha	God be with & look after you . . Hijanequo
Give, I give it you . . . . Ná	Kalalé, Tegká keká tita
Give me, you give . . . . Skináhe	Good Night, (now rest) . . . . Noquó ules
Great way . . . . Ináw	Goose . . . . Kahíge
Go away . . . . Hatananáw	Governor . . . . Ukáw
I am going a long way } . . . . . . Utchí níthla	Governor to come . . . . . Ukáw nastótaw
Now I am going . . . . Noquo unkwahé	Gun . . . . Kaloquá kaneheta
Go out of the way . . . . Utchiwílohe	

H

Hand . . . . Oquo jénne	I cannot hang 'em on (properly I cannot ear'in) } . . Tlestikalénaw
Hand washing . . . . Deka shúri	
Hang on the Earbobs (properly ear'in) } . . . . . Kalihadoke	Hair . . . . Itlaw
	Hair Line . . . . { quelosti up. Ch. / aquelosti—low. Ch.

[63]

Haste, make haste . . . . . Sighoquá nohóra	Heaven . . . . Kaláleti
Hat . . . . Asque tuóke	Heels . . . . Ulaschéte
Hatchet . . . . Kajoléste	Handkerchief . . . . Alóki
How do you call that . . . . Káto titó	Hog . . . . Sikqua
How do you do . . . . O'sigó hohíga	Horse . . . . Kilhé
How many Men . . . . Lako nukáhes	Horse Whip . . . . Uhichéni
He . . . . Hihi	House . . . . Kalistchótáw
Head . . . . Skoli	in my house . . . . Aika aquaschéri
Hear, I hear you . . . . Tankícho	kalis thótáw
I do not hear you . . . . Tankíska	Hungry, I am hungry . . . . Kanekioli
Heart . . . . Unahú	Hunter . . . . Nogghorénaw
we are both one Heart and Friend . . . . } Sohoko unahú Kinilí	Husband . . . . Okadarihe

I

I	Ahíga	In	Hawína
I am	Akíki	Indian	Wodikehe
Jacket	Anuwóko squalóhe	Indian Garters	Tiquezo
I can	Akiháskaw	Island	Ammohi Nukáhes kejusti
I cannot	Akinula háskáw	yes, I will, tis	
Ice	Unestálaw	very well }	Naski

K

Kettle	Ekahíhé	Knife	Ageleste
Kill, to kill	Igohóhi	Know, do you know	Chikataw
Knee	Kanekoléhe	I dont know	Autlaw

L

Lace	Atéla	Lightning {	Utiláka up. Ch. Utchistaska low.
Last Night	Sanoka		
Laugh	Echestí	Lightwood	Nógsci
what you laugh?	Woáko ochestí	Linnen, striped	Chuláleti
Lay down	Honchanka	Little	Stikin
why dont you lay down	Woako antla ikatli heganka	Lock	Kistáhe
		Looking Glass	Taketú
Leaf, or Leaves	Ukalókaw	Love, I love	Nastatleste akínastat léste
Let alone	Hatananáw	I love you	Akinastatleste nihi
Let see	Hantkóre	Lye	Aniagkokequo
		he lies (is a Liar)	Aniagkoka

[64]

M

Man-killer	Otássite	Melons, Water Melons	Kakíste
Make, to make	Koklannaw	Milk of a Cow	Waggá kanágti
Make haste	Sigluhá, nohoro	Moon	Netaú

Many ....Genira
   how many Men?..Cakogenira niskagau
Mare ....Kilhi kehéhe
Mate ....Enari
   you are my mate ....Ahiki enári
Match Coat or mantle........Anewoki
               utennaw
Matter, what is the matter ....Kató

More ....Kilagú
   no more, ('tis all) ....Noquo nukáhe
Morrow, tomorrow ....Sunalégo
   tomorrow morning ....Sunaléste
Mortar of stone or brass.......Kanoino
Mountain ....Katúsi
Much ....Stequo
   Too much ....Ahole'taw

N

Neck ....Hichenne
Negroe ....Iwokonéka
Never (now, never) ....Aquónataw
Needle ....Janki
Night ....Sanóki
   last Night ....Sanóha

No ....Antlaw
None at all ....Antlá nukáhes
None of them would do ......Nukáhes
              ichena sesti
Nose ....Kojessóle

P

Pack horse Man ....Chemhé
Paint, Colour ....Wohóde
Pallisadoes ....Chizowi
Paper.............. { koheli up. Ch.
              { Koheraki . low.
Pay, I will pay you } Noquo ahichuko-
   instantly for it   }   juháw
Pestle of brass, Iron or Wood .. Tolóste
Petticoat ....Asnogi
Pin................... { usquote. up.
                  { Ch.
               { usquelati low.
Pipe ....Kananówa
Pistol ....Kaloqua skóla

Physician or Conjuror........Kanekadi
Place, the whole Place ....Anakati
Plate ....Talalétó
Please, what you please ......Chenaléki
Pole Cat Skin ....Tilláro
Pompion ....Kanathlénta
Pond ....Anukáw
Pot, tin Pot............ { talequisko up.
                { Cher.
              { tetatowa low.
Potatoes ....Núnaw
Pray, I pray you ....Hikíhi
Prisoner, or Captive ....Ulíenki
Pull, pull of your Breeches.....Asulokisa

Q

Quickly ....Nohara

[65]

R

Rabbit	Szistó	Rest	Uleségka
Rails	Chizówi	I rest	Ahigulesegka
Rain	Káskaw	Ribbans, of silk	Quelesti
the rain is over	Kaskaw noquo ukánnaw	Right, it is right	Illikokó
		River	Amóhe
Red	Kikekéhe	Round	Kagúste
Remember	Natalétne	Rum	Nohóte

S

Salt	Ammó	Silk Ribbans	Queléste
Savannah–Meadow	Anukáw	Sister	Anakétaw
Say, what says he	Káto hiki hatiga	Skin with hair on	Kaneki
Scissars	Tilstóhiti	Skin, raw	Uzo
Slave	Uliénki	Sleep	Simágle
Scalp	Uskáwa	Smoke	Dukasinsti
Screws, brass or iron	{ stukisti . up. Ch. hute lokiski low.	it smokes too much	Dukasinsti stéquo
		Smoke a Pipe	Squokéhe
Sea	Amahi equó	Snow	Anógzi
See	Koré	Sooner, come sooner	Sunnalukáhe
I see	Akikoré	Soup	Amoketíta
Send, Ill send you my horse, my horse shall come	{ Kilhakiko- cheliko	Sour, your drink is too sour	Chune kohéste
Set	Keháwkaw	Spouse	Squaháw
Set upon the Chair	Kashadó kehekáw	Spoon	Titawtí
Shirt	Anuwóki	Stockings	Tilihóki
Check Shirt	Utuésti anúwoke	Stop	Ashi
White Ditto	Uneka anúwoke	Striped Linen or Cloth	Chuláleti
Shot	junes líko kanhéhe	Sun	Nitali
Shew me the way	glaghehán utchi	Sugar	Kanasétchi
Shoes	Tilesuloki	Sweet, your drink is sweet	Alhé
Shoulder	Kanahóhó		
Sick, I am sick	{ utlenta . up. Ch. uzanka . low.		

T

Tobacco	Szólaw	Talk, or do talk, speak	Hatígaw
Table	Halstahitckas-kalóge	what you talk?	Káto hatígaw
Take, do take it	Tenoki, wohiki'nahahu	I will talk with you	Akikawanhatígaw
Take fire	Acila nahahe	a Talk	Takenalihatígaw
Take Tobacco	Szoláw Tenoki	your Talk is good	O'sígo heneskaw

[66]

Tell, I told you	Aki séraw	time ago	johúno
Thank, I thank you	Wohúto	Town	Kaduki
There	Nahahehatáw	from what town are you	Káto kaduki
Thimble	Lesústo	Tree	Kalla kohosku
This	Nahanehátaw	Troublesome you are	chulekosti
Thunder	Hiantoqualóski	Trunk, small ⎱ Trunk ⎰	Kanesahi
Thread	⎧ asthi . up. ⎨ Ch. ⎩ ithi . . low.	Tongue	Kanohówe
		Tooth	Kajukówe
Time, all times	Nahiuraw	Turkey	Kenhaw
time to come	tahetó	Tye, tye your Garters	⎱ Hinasokaw

U

Understand	tankicho	I understand you not ⎱	tankiskaw
Venison	ahowiga, or ahowi		

W

Walk	Cheliko	What do you call that	Katotitó
Wash, dress your face	Kakáes stiwoda	When	Laggihúra
your hand	dekasúri	Whence	Ucennáw
yourself, dress yourself	hadawoda	Where	gázo
Wompom (Indian Beads)	Unelsqualetaw	Where are you going	gázo máhi
Warm	Hadle	Whip	Uhizeni
Wart	Titinasatinsti	White	Uneka
Water	Ammá	Who is he	kakohihi
Water Melon	Kakisté	Whole Town or Place	Anakati
Way	Ulché	Why	Woakó
		Will you	Kawatchi

I am going a long way .... Ulchiníthla

shew me the way .... glaglehán utchi

go out of the way ...... utchi wílohe

Well, farewell .... Osígo, or hohíga

'tis very well .... osígo, or hohíga

Weather, fair Weather ...... Sohi, osígo

What .... Káto

What will you   } .... Kato

What is the matter } .... Kato

Warrior .... Skaigunsta

I will .... Kawán

I will speak with you .. Akikawanhatigá

Wine .... Nohote, kikekéhesta

Wolf .... Wohahiga

Wood for fire .... Atáw

Woman .... Nihikehehe

Written .... tiliofi

Worker .... Nanneska

War Woman............... Skaigusta

[67]

Y

Yea .... naski, or ohiga   Year (13 months) ...... chowatu netáw

---

NUMBERING,

One .... shohé	Eleven .... shohatu	Thirty ..... choweskówe
Two .... talé	Twelve .... Talatu	Forty ...... nakaskowé
Three .... chowé	Thirteen .... chowatú	Sixty ...... chotelaskowe
Four .... naki	Fourteen .... nakatú	Seventy ... kalaguaskowe
Five .... hiskí	Fifteen .... hiskikatu	Eighty .... chonetaskowé
Six .... chotalé	Sixteen .... cholatú	Ninety .... sognehaskowé
Seven .... kalagogé	Seventeen ..... kalaguatú	Hundred .. askowaskowé
Eight .... choneataw	Eighteen ...... chonetatú	Thousand ....
Nine .... sagné	Nineteen ...... sogneratú	askowaskokówe
Ten .... askowé	Twenty ...... talaskowé	

N. B. Although the Upper and lower Cherokees speak the same Language, yet there are some Words, in which they differ as appears in the foregoing Compendio.

Georgia

To the Right Honorable the Lords
Commissioners of Trade and Plantations.
My Lords,

When I set out on His Majesty's General Service to make Surveys of Seas and Lands, I had before me your Lordships Orders in a Letter, in which, altho' your Lordships condescended to mention your Intention was, that I should consider these Orders as a rude Sketch or out Lines only, yet they (as I thought) contained this precise, that I should add (insert in my Report) every Information that I think may tend to the forming a true Judgment of the State of that important part of His Majesty's Dominions; that your Lordships may be enabled to lay before His Majesty such Propositions as may be most conducive to His Majesty's Interest and the Public Service; this was not the only Preciseness I observed in your Lordships Orders, for I was by them also confined by Civil Limits, determining the Boundaries of the District, which I am to represent in the Execution of exact Maps and Charts; but no physical Bounds, beyond which I should not extend my Historical Report was fixed by these Orders, the Omission of which I could by no Means adjudge as a Want, when, by the Tenor of your Lordships Letter I had it insinuated, that your favourable Opinion of my Faithfulness reposed a full trust in me, and therefore intentionally set no bounds to my Historical Report, which I always shall endeavour to answer in the best manner and utmost Degree my imperfect Abilities afford; which to improve, I studied, by copying after the best I knew, who went before me upon similar Expedition vide, Charlevoix,[1] don George Juan,[2] don Antoine de Ulloa,[3] and Bougainville;[4] also by embracing those hints exofficio, to make my Returns of a Composition with Subjects worth the attention of such, who are Lovers of Botany, a Branch of Philosophy; animated also by the Thanks for few Specimens of Vegitables etc. sent with my Reports and Plans to the Secretary of State; I therefore hope, that my inserting several Branches of Philosophy favouring my Province will not be thought useless or superfluous, but rather suitable Companions to the Principal Object in my Report, the more so as my Office I am charged with would be imperfectly executed if not philosophically, or rather by the near infallible Rules of Philosophy, which is unlimited in her Province, and excludes nothing; She is as [70] one who gives an Entertainment to all Men, supplying his Table with a Variety of all Things in several Courses, that each at the Table may meet with what he likes best, well knowing, that one Dish, ever so large and ever so excellent dressed would not find general Approbation, and perhaps some would not eat at all, because they do not meet with what suits their Palate, and altho' his Table may be adjudged Profusion in the Eyes of many, they however cannot but agree with the Generality in the Conclusion, that the procuring and Performance were difficult and expensive, the more so, if the Articles have been procured by a Man interrupted with so various Dilemmata as would have rendered unactive many, although ever so honest Men; therefore as he by persevering in the Execution of the Principal Object, has endeavoured to delude all Impediments, he cannot but hope to draw the general Attention also in his Favour and be esteemed an honest Man by all.

I know it bears the Blame of many to do more than one is obliged, and that it is condemned as criminal by all to neglect Duty, or to do less than one is ordered; but to sail between these two Rocks over a shallow rocky Bar (a) is easier for a Vessel only in Ballast (b) than one which is heavy loaden (c); the latter must think herself very happy, if she has Wind enough to loof up altho' She runs foul upon the former, provided She can bear away sufficiently so as to sail clear of the latter Rock.

I humbly beg your Lordships Permission to go on upon the present Plan, to make out what I shall hereafter transmit from my Office to your Lordships Board, until your Lordships will think proper to set to my Historical Report, Bounds similar to those minuted for the Execution of my Maps and Charts, agreeable to which Bounds is laid down my general Map of the Western Atlantic Coast between Latitude 24°30′ and 30°26′49″ delivered to your Lordships Office June last 1772.

I beg leave to recommend myself to your Lordships Protection, and am most respectfully,

My Lords,

Your Lordships

Most obedient and

Most humble Servant

William Gerard de Brahm

1772

(a) a Service, whose Difficulties few men have experienced.
(b) a Person who only depends on his Friends and his own Flattery.
(c) a Man who has nothing to depend on than his Honour and Merit.

*Province
of
Georgia*

Georgia

CHAPTER 1st

General Description of the Province, its Climate; when settled under the Trustees; when it became a King's Government; Boundaries, Figure, Contents, Culture of Silk in particular, and a particular Description of the two Colonies, Ebenezer and Bethany; with an Observation on the American Natives.

As the Province of Georgia extends from Latitude 30°26′49″, to 35°30′, it takes, in very near the whole 5th Climate, which begins in and ends in 36°28′, in the beginning of which Climate, 14 and its end 14 1/2 hour determine the longest day, and the Termoscope, whose temperate is marked with 55 Degrees, when exposed in the Sun, in Summer commonly rises the Quick Silver up to 116 degrees, but in well built Houses, that is in the Shade to 93 and seldom falls to 25 degrees in Winter.

Its Settlement begun, 59 years after that of South Carolina, in 1732, under the Auspices of General Oglethorp, during the Reign of His Majesty, of most glorious Memory, George the Second, by a Grant to Trustees, for a term of [21] years, which expired in the year [1752], when it became a King's Government,[5] under the first Governor, John Reynold's Esqr., after him, was Governor, Henry Ellis Esqr., who arrived in 1757; and was succeeded in the year 1760 by James Wright Esqr., by whom the Province is governed to this day.[6]

Under Governor Wright, the Province was divided into twelve Parishes,[7] and in the year 1763 (Saint Augustin and Pensacola, with all the Spanish Dominions on the Continent of North America being ceded to the Crown of England by the Treaty of Peace between England and Spain) the Boundaries of Georgia were thus fixed.[8]

To the East upon the Atlantic Ocean by the Sea Coast, beginning at the Mouth of Savannah Stream 127 1/2 mile on a S. W. by W. Course to the Mouth of Saint Mary's, thus called by the Spaniards, and by the Indians Thlathlothlaguphka Stream.[9] (a)

[73] To the South by the said Saint Mary's Stream, running with its general Course S. 73°, 45 W. 29 31/80 miles, then 35 miles more S. by W. to the great Swamp Oekanphanoko[10] (a), from thence by a supposed Line to the Fork of

(a) Thlathlothlaguphka, is a Creek-Indian Appelation, and signifies a rotten Fish.

(a) signifies unpassable, the Indians pretend to have a Tradition that this Swamp is inhabited by an immortal Race, which in the Creek Indian Tongue are called Fatchasika this Race could neither be conquered by the Spaniards or Indians, and that they have their Habi-

Chatahuchee[11] and Flint Rivers, bounding therewith upon the Province of East Florida, further continuing on the River Chatahuchee, as far North as Latitude 32° and from thence by a due west Line home to Mississipi Stream so far bounding upon the Province of West Florida.

To the west, by said Mississipi Stream as far North as Latd. 35° 30', which Stream forms the Boundary between the English and French Dominions.

To the North by a Line from Mississipi River due East across the Apalachian Mountains, ten miles to the Southward of Hughnakahe Mount (b), home to the northernmost Spring of Savannah Stream, following the same 10 miles below Fort Prince George and Keowee[12] vide, to Latd. 35°, which is the Boundary between this Province and North Carolina and from Latitude 35° continuing with the Stream and including all Islands in said Stream as far as the Mouth of Savannah, which Stream's general Course from its Spring to its Mouth is S. E. nearest 290 miles, by which Stream Georgia is bounded upon the Province of South Carolina.

Georgia assumes no mathematical Figure, unless its South and North Boundaries are continued from Latitudes 30°26'49" and 35°30' West & East, then it will be a Romboides. It contains 145,600 square miles, or 93,124,000 Acres of Land (in Soil and natural Products similar to that in South Carolina) on which is cultivated, without Exception, to [74] the same Perfection, and in every respect equal to South Carolina: Rice, Indigo, Provisions of all kinds, all manner of Garden Herbs, Shrubs, and Fruit Trees.

The unplantable Land produces the same Timber, and affords the same Pasturage as South Carolina, and the Limits of the Sea or Salt Air has its natural Marks by long Moss hanging on the Trees (only of plantable Lands) and chiefly are parellel with the Sea Coast making a Zone of Land generally 140 miles in breadth from the Sea Coast to the interior part of the Country which continues so through the whole Front of the Province, in every respect conformable with

---

tations in the middle of said Swamp, that they are sometimes seen without, but their Avenues are undiscoverable.

(b) Hughnaky is the highest of the Apalachian Mountains, on the foot of which vide, S. E. from the top of the Mountain, springs beaver Dam Rivulet, a Branch of Hiwassee River after crossing that Rivulet the Author measured on a N. N. W. and N. W. course 4 miles to the top, from whence he could overlook the Apalachian Moutains all round, and from his Elevation they all appeared not bigger than mole hilloks, and the Trees on them like young Cabage Plants.[13] He could plainly see the Valley Tanessee Tehotee and Tehutaco on Tanessee River 29 miles north,[14] from the top of this mount on its N. E. issues Talequo River, passing by Talequo and Tehahekee, two contiguous Indian Towns;[15] and after passing by the Camp, in which the Fort Loudoun Garrison, after surrendering the Fort was attaked, some killed and the rest made Prisoners.[16] Talequo runs in general with a N. 1/2 W. course and empties itself a mile north of Fort Loudoun into the Tanassee River, which takes its Origin 29 miles due west from Keowee.

that in South Carolina. The Land is rising gradually from the Sea Coast in general 37 miles to the inner part of the Province and then it begins to form in Hills; from among which, down to the Sea Coast, and as far as the Zone reaches, the Land proves by Experience to be calculated for the Culture of all European Granes, for Flax, Hemp, Grape Vine, Tobacco and Silk; as also for Mays, [maize], Potatoes, Pompions, Melons, Rice and Indigo; for the Culture of Mulberry Trees, both spanish and Portugal, for Apples, Peaches, Necterons, Plumbs, Pears, and Apple Quinces; also for all manner of European Garden Products, the annual Cultivation and successful Productions of the Premisses fully evidence this part of the History, the Improvement of the Vine is the only Object as yet neglected. The Lands between this and the Sea Coast is inhabited generally by the English and best Planters, but from the Hills westward the Zone is chiefly inhabited by Germans.[17]

The Aboriginals of the Germans in Georgia are Protestants and Natives of the Bishoprick of Salzburg in Austria, from whence they were expelled by the Roman Clergy out of a Catholic Zeal and were sent over by the Reverend Mr. Samuel Urlsperger,[18] Bishop of Augspurg [Augsburg] in Suabia [Swabia] and Mr. Christian de Munch, Banker of the same Place,[19] both Deputy Trustees for the Colony of Georgia; these Salzburghers were settled upon Savannah Stream 41 miles N. W. from the Sea, where they have built a Town called Ebenezer.

To the Northwestward of which Settlement the Author Anno 1751, planted the Colony of Bethany with 160 Germans, [and] joined through his means 160 more the Relations and Acquaintance of the former, in eleven months after, exclusive of the Salzburghers, which consist of about 1,500 Souls.

From the Settlement of Bethany, the Province of Georgia begins its Era of Prosperity, for it was at the Arrival of the Author so lowly reduced that, had it not been for the few English in the Governments Employ, and the Salzburgers, the Author, at his Arrival would have found this [75] Province intirely deserted of Inhabitants, [a] few days before he arrived, a Lot with a tolerable House on it in the City of Savannah, had been sold for [a] few shillings; the Author might have bought at that time with twenty Pounds Sterling near half the City. His arrival soon spread over the Neighbouring Province of South Carolina, and whilst the Author was recogniting [reconnoitering] the Province, and making a general Survey of its Eastern Parts, a Deputation was sent from the Beach Hill Congregation in South Carolina, which he met in Savannah, and disposed them to make a Settlement upon the Branches of the two Newport Rivers; the Draught of which he then had executed and was able to give Weight to his Advice by the Situation of that Country, represented in his Map, which he afterwards delivered to the Trustees and a Copy thereof to his Friends in Germany, in order to encourage by his Draught several more to become British Subjects; and he did thereby a considerable Service in the Promotion of the Province of Georgia, at that time.[20]

The Beach Hill Congregation settled upon the Heads of the two Newport Rivers early in the year 1752 when they left Carolina in a great Body,[21] they continued drawing their Effects and Cattle after, settling all other Concerns in their Native Province until 1755, many rich Carolina Planters followed the Example of that Congregation, and came with all their Families and Negroes to settle in Georgia in 1752; the Spirit of Emigration out of South Carolina into Georgia became so universal that year, that this and the following year near one thousand Negroes were brought in Georgia, where in 1751 were scarce above three dozen.[22]

The German Settlements have since stretched eastwardly, about 32 miles Northwestward from the Sea upon Savannah Stream, from whence they extend up the same Stream through the whole Salt Air Zona;[23] they cultivate European and American Grains to Perfection as Wheat, Rye, Barley, Oats; also Flax, Hemp, Tobacco and Rice, Indigo, May's [*maize*], Peas, Pompions, Melons; they plant Mulberry, Apple, Peach, Nectorins, Plumbs, and Quince Trees; besides all manner of European Garden Herbs, but in particular, they choose the Culture of Silk their principal Object; in which Culture they made such a Progress, that the Filature, which is erected in the City of Savannah could afford to send in 1768 to London 1,084 Pounds of raw Silk, equal in Goodness to that manufactured in Piedmont; but the Bounties to encourage that Manufactory being taken off, they discouraged, dropt their Hands from that Culture from year to year in a manner, that [76] in 1771 its Product was only 290 Pounds in lieu of 1,464, which must have been that years Produce, had this Manufactory been encouraged to increase at a 16 years rate.[24] In lieu of Silk, they have taken under more Consideration the Culture of May's [*maize*], Rice, Indigo, Hemp, and Tobacco: But Vines have not as yet become an Object of their Attention, altho' in the Country, especially over the German Settlements, Nature makes all the Promises, yea gives yearly full Assurances of her Assistance by her own Endeavours, producing Cluster Grapes in Abundance on its uncultivated Vines; yet there is no Person who will listen to her Addresses and give her the least Assistance, notwithstanding many of the Inhabitants are refreshed from the Sweetness of her wild Productions.

The Culture of Indigo is brought to the same Perfection here as in South Carolina, and is manufactured through all the Settlements from the Sea Coast, to the Extent of the interior Country.

The Author has made a peculiar Observation of those Germans, with whom he made the Settlement of Bethany, among which were very few well built At-

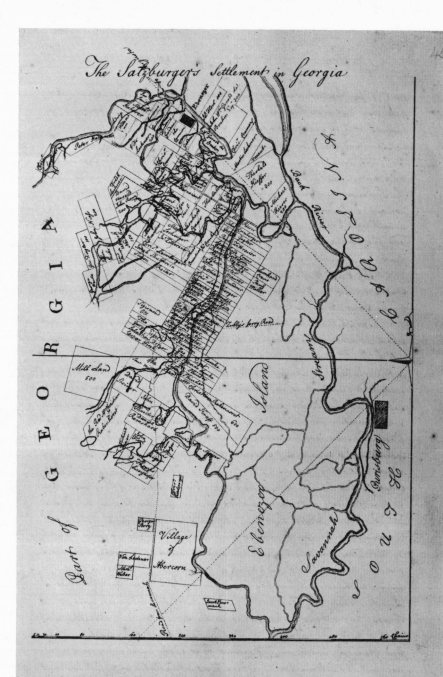

The Salzburger's Settlement in Georgia

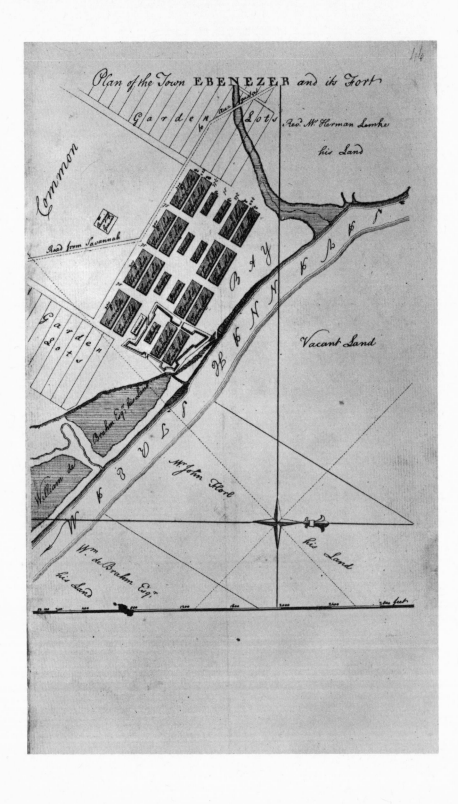

Plan of the Town EBENEZER and its Fort

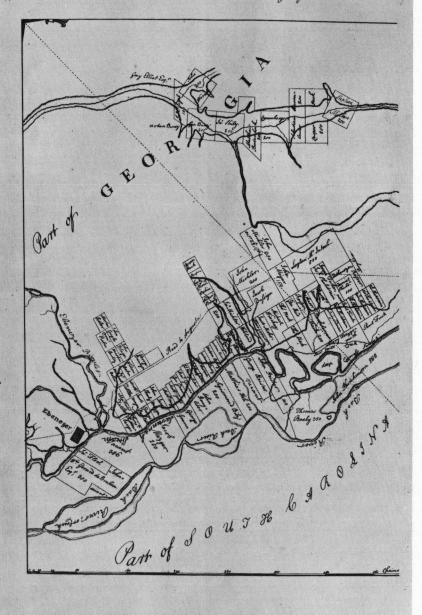

titudes, and much less likely Faces, and very few of them has to this day learned as much English, as to make themselves tolerably understood, nor is there any English Family settled among them, and their Schools, as also Divine Services are all in the German Language:[25] this, notwithstanding the Children born there, are all of a genteel Attitude, of likely and some very handsome Countenances; and what is as peculiar, all speaking English as easy as the German Language; for which the Author allows the following Causes: that the Parents, when in Germany, their native Country, they laboured under hard Oppressions in time of War, more than in time of Peace; also under great Cares and Anxieties to raise their Taxes and Quit Rents, which kept their Minds always pressed with a gloomy Downcast, to which they became so familiar that they even printed them on their Features, where they served as Characters or Hieroglyphics to indicate the Condition of their Minds to those, as are Connoisseurs; but coming to America where they enjoy the Sweets of Peace, and the Bounties of Liberty, where they have all Things in Abundance surrounding their Houses, and but small Taxes to pay to the Legislator, and a smaller Quit Rent to their Humane King, their Minds are raised and elevated with Joy and Gladness, which, altho' it cannot be so lively imbossed on their own worn out and callous Countenances; yet it is printed with full and sweet Characters on the delicate Features of their Babes, which, as they are growing without being compelled by their Parents (as they were by their Ancestors) to submit their tender Shoulders to a share of hard domestic Burdens, in order to help acquiring what must pay the peremptory Demands of their [77] Princes, Lords and Nobles; they therefore have an uninterrupted and undepressed Procession in their Growth; and as their Minds are not perplexed, consequently not weakened in their liquid Spring, as those of their Parents have been; their Memories, like soft Wax take and retain all the Impressions of Sounds and Words they receive from those English, which peradventure pass through the Settlements, and are necessitated to enter one or two hours Conversation, now in one, then in another Family.

The Author has made a general Observation among all Natives in America; they are in general of very elevated Spirits, and most of them with very little Education; yea some by reading good Authors only, acquire real Knowlege and great Wisdom (a). He was often surprised at the good Judgments and Argumentations of Men whom he knew had been brought up intirely to Mechanism without any more Education, than reading and writing, they, after acquiring Estates, being in easy Circumstances of Life, and in a Country not as yet debauched by

(a) But as they have no Opportunities to improve their Wisdom for want of Employment in matters of State, of course they have no Encouragement to increase their Knowlege by applying themselves to a close Study, therefore are satisfied with that share of Wisdom they have acquired at an easy and cheap Rate, being sufficient to shine in their Politics.

European Luxuries, such as Balls, Masquerades, Operas, Plays, etc., they applied themselves to reading good Authors, of which (yea the best) America has no reason to complain of a Want. There is scarcely a House in the Cities, Towns, or Plantations, but what have some Choice Authors, if not Libraries of Religious, Phylosophical, and Political Writers. Booksellers endeavour to import the newest Editions, and take Care to commission the best, well knowing they will not incumber their Shops long, but soon find Admirers and Purchasers; besides that, many of their Books they write for are commissioned by the Inhabitants. This Province was scarce thirty years settled, before it had three fine Libraries in the City of Savannah; the fourth at Ebenezer, and a fifth 96 3/4 miles from the Sea upon the Stream of Savannah. In these Libraries could be had books wrote in the Caldaic, Hebrew, Arabic, Siriac, Coptic, Malabar, Greek, Latin, French, German, Dutch, Spanish, besides the English, vide, in thirteen Languages.

[*78*]

Chapter 2d

Of Towns, navigable Streams and Rivers, their Springs, Latitudes, and Longitudes, Courses, Lengths, and Outlets, the Indian Boundary Line.

Besides the Metropolis of Savannah, upon Savannah Stream, 17 miles from the Sea,

are 4 Sea Port Towns	Hardwick, upon great Ogetchee Stream
	Sunbury, upon Midway Stream
	Darian
	Frederica } upon Alatamaha Stream
and 4 Towns upon navigable fresh water Rivers	Brandon (a) upon little River; navigable only to the Cataract above Augusta
	Augusta, upon Savannah Stream, 150 miles from the Sea
	Queensburry, in the Fork of Lambert's River and great Ogetchee Stream, 120 miles from the Sea. (b)
	Ebenezer, upon Savannah Stream, 57 miles from the Sea.

(a) Since Governor Wright's Administration (this Place being deserted in Governor Reynold's time by Edmond Grey) revived again under the name of Wrightsborough, in-

There are several Villages laid out and inhabited v. g. Hampstead, Highgate, Acton, and Vernonburg, situated west of the City of Savannah upon Vernon River and its Head.[26]

In Georgia are

12 Streams

Savannah,	fresh water	Sapelo	salt water
Little Ogetchee	salt Ditto	Alatamaha	fresh Ditto
Great Ogetchee	fresh Ditto	Turtois	salt Ditto
Midway	salt Ditto	Little satilla	salt Ditto
North Newport	salt Ditto	Great satilla	fresh Ditto
South Newport	salt Ditto	Saint Mary's	fresh Ditto

15 Rivers, all fresh

Toogelo	Lamberts	Oakmulgee
Broad	Buckhead	Ohoopee
Little	Cowannochee	Phennohaloway
Briar	Wilustee	Flint
Vernon	Oconee	Chatahutchee

Savannah Stream begins in the Apalachian Mountains, in the middle Settlements of the Cherokee Nation, from whence the Stream takes a S. E. Course nearest for a Distance of 290 miles, and mixes with the Ocean in Latitude 31°57′; and the Savannah Stream chiefly is bordered with scarce any other than exceeding rich Lands, which in many Places extends for several miles into the Country. This Stream is navigable up to Augusta, which is 150 miles, it ebbs and floods 60 miles upon a straight Line from the Sea. Its Rivers are in Number 4, vide, Toogelo, Broad, Little, and Briar. Toogelo springs ten miles N. W. of Augusta. Little River takes its Beginning W. by N. off Augusta and breaks into Savannah Stream 25 miles N. W. of Augusta.[29] The above Rivers would be navigable to the Sea, were

---

habited by above 60 families, and its Township contains above 200 families all Quakers; they are indulged by the Governor that no person but such as they approve of shall be permitted to settle among them.[27]

(b) Queensburry is inhabited by about 70 and its Environs by above 200 families, most Irish, from which it is generally called the Irish Settlement.[28]

it not for the Cataract in Savannah Stream 10 miles N. W. of Augusta. This Cataract might be made navigable by a Batardeau raised at the Foot of the Cataract; which Batardeau to be raised in Heighth 6 feet higher than the Superfices of the Stream above the Cataract, from the Sides of the Batardeau two strong Walls to be carried back as Wings on both sides the Cataract as far as will be necessary to keep the Stream within Bounds of its Shores. In the middle of the Baterdeau to be a Sluce of 9 feet wide by 5 or more high, measuring from the Superfices of the Stream below the Cataract; this Sluce is shut, to fill the Baterdeau within its Wings for admitting and sinking Boats (which come down the Stream) to the Level of the Water below; as well for raising Boats (which are going up the Stream) to the Level with the Water above. Briar River begins near west of Augusta, and falls into Savannah Stream 30 miles N. N. W. from Ebenezer. Great Tracts of plantable Land are bordering upon the aforesaid Rivers of Savannah Stream.

Little Ogetchee is a short salt Water Stream, takes its Origin 8 1/4 miles west of the City in the Tract called Bethabram, formerly the Property of the Author.[30] It mixes his Waters with those of great Ogetchee near the Ocean, and makes a rich, plentiful and well situated Country, both for Land Carriage to the City, and Water Carriage to the Town of Hardwik. This Stream is well settled and inhabited by some of the best Planters in this Province.

Great Ogetchee Stream takes its principal Spring near Horse Cheek Mount situated to the westward of the Place, where broad River enters Savannah Stream, which is described above among the Rivers of said Stream. Its general Course is S. E. easterly, on a Distance of 245 miles, and disembogues in the Ocean, joined with [80] Little Ogetchee, in Latitude 31°40′ and 10 Minutes west of Savannah Inlet. The Lands upon this Stream are in Quality nothing [*inferior*], but in Quantity inferior to that upon Savannah Stream. Great Ogetchee is navigable up to Irish Town, which lays on a general Course of the Stream S. E. by S. southerly 116 miles from the Sea. The Rivers of great Ogetchee are the four following vide, Lamberts, Buckhead, Cowanoochee and Wilustee (a). The Head of Lamberts, called Chevers Rivulet is W. by N. of the Mouth of Briar (the fourth of the Savannah Rivers) and empties itself in great Ogetchee Stream at Irish Town. Buckhead issues east of, and near Chevers; its Entrance into great Ogetchee is 25 miles E. by S. from Irish Town. Cowanoochee springs S. by E. from Irish Town, and falls into great Ogetchee, ten miles N. W. of Hardwik.

Wilustee takes its Beginning due west from Hardwik, and joins Cowanoochee about 25 miles W. by N. from Hardwik. No richer Lands can exist, than what

(a) Wilustee is a Creek Indian Name, signifies: black.

is traversed by these four Rivers of Great Ogetchee Streams, which are all fresh Water. Between the Mouths of Great Ogetchee and Savannah Streams are the three Islands, vide, great Tibe, little Tibe and Wilmington, seperated from the Main by Saint Augustin and Wassaw Creeks. Skedoway and Wassaw Creeks, with great Ogetchee Stream and the Ocean incompass great and little Wassaw, Skedoway and Green, in all four Islands.

Midway is a short salt water Stream, springing near Hardwik: it forms a rich, well settled Country, as far as Sunburry, then tiding thro' an open Marsh Country into the Ocean, in Latitude 31°33', and 19 Minutes of Savannah Inlet. Great Ogetchee Stream, Saint Catharine's Creek, with Midway and the Ocean, make the Boundaries of Hasobaw Island.

North and South Newports are two short salt water Streams, each of them issues due west of its own Outlet, into the Ocean, but they both bend in their Middle vide, the North Stream bends south, and the south Stream bends north in an open marshy Country, in which they come so near to each other, that they at high-water, by several short Creeks in the Marsh enter from one into the other. The Country, between North Newport and Midway (being a Continuation of open marsh) communicates with each other at high water by two Creeks, and include the Island Bermudas. North Newport streams into the Ocean at the same Place with Midway: But the South Newport discharges its water in the Ocean in Latitude 31°23' and from Savannah Inlet W. 21 Min. called Sapelo Sound, the Heads of these Streams form a fruitful Country, and is settled by the Beach Hill Congregation, which began to leave South Carolina in 1752. Between the Mouth of Midway or North Newport, and the Mouth [81] of South Newport, as also between the Ocean and the Eastermost Creek communing with the two Newports, is situated Saint Catherine's Island. Out of South Newport makes a Creek into the next salt water Stream (called Sapelo), which Creek is bordered to the West by an open Marsh Country, in which lays Demetrius Island; on this Island the Author found in 1753 the Vestigia of an Intrenchment of a mile and a quarter in Length; as also many Ruins of ancient Houses, by all Appearance proving a Settlement made there before, or in the Beginning of the 17th Century.[31] For no Carolinian, much less Georgian can give any Account of it, so that by the Author's Opinion, it has been a Settlement, which was neither favoured by the Spaniards nor left quiet by the Indians, and was at last extirpated or its Inhabitants forced to leave the Place. The Length of the Intrenchment indicates that it had many Hands for its Constructors, and Defenders: By its Situation it does not appear to have been a Spanish Out-Post, stationed there to be guarded by a Detachment from Saint Augustin, in order to discover and intercept Surprises and Hostilities from the English settled in Virginia; as the high

Land on the east side of the Mouth of black Beard's Creek on Blackbeard's Island, would have suited much better for an Intrenchment, and a good Battery 1 1/2 mile due west of the Intrenchment on a Point of Sapelo Island (a) Passage, and from the Intrenchment, to discover whatever passes along Shore: of course no other Conclusion remains, but that this Settlement consisted either of a Nation neither English or Spanish, or of a Body of dissenting and disgusted Spaniards, which in this remote and secret place intended to be a Republic or independent Settlement, much like that which was formed by one Edmond Grey, a pretending Quaker, who left Virginia with a Number of those Inhabitants, and settled Brandon upon little River in this Province. He again left Brandon (in the time when John Reynolds Esqr., was Governor) and settled on those Lands between Alatamaha and Saint Juan's Streams; a Country of one Degree in Latitude, esteemed neutral Lands, which were not to be settled either by the English or Spaniards. All Persons incapable or unwilling to satisfy their Creditors; as also Men guilty of criminal Actions would resort both from the English, and Spaniards to said Edmond Grey, who, when ordered away by the Spaniards, he moved to the River Alatamaha, and when ordered away by the English, he did pretend to go and settle on the south side of Saint Mary's; thus deluding both English and Spaniards, increased daily, and became very formidable, no doubt would have very soon been ungovernable, had not [*82*] this neutral Land been added to the Government of Georgia by the Cession from the Crown of Spain to the Crown of England, which was one of the Articles stipulated in the Treaty of Peace between these two Crowns, made in 1763.

Sapelo is the shortest salt water Stream, it heads near the Spring of South New Port, and joins its Water with that of South Newport in Sight of the open Ocean. Several good Settlements are made at the Head of this Stream.

Alatamaha is the longest Stream in the three Provinces, its Head forks at the now deserted Cherokee Town called Oconee 23 miles due west from Keowee,[32] in Latitude 35° 10'. This Stream takes a S. E. by S. course for 373 miles; excentres into three Streams at Fort Barrington 30 miles W. N. W. from the Sea, and enters the Ocean by three Outlets, the northernmost is in Latitude 31°15' at the South End of an Island (which is formed by Sapelo Sound, Sapelo Creek, this Outlet, and the Ocean) called Sapelo Island. The next Stream lets out in Latitude 31°10', both aforesaid Outlets are West of Savannah Inlet, 0°26'0'', the Southernmost Outlet is in Latitude 31°05' and West of Savannah Inlet 29', is called Jekyl Sound; Alatamaha does not only divide in three Streams, but breaks also by several Creeks from one into another, so that thereby twelve Islands are formed, the principal, and easternmost of them are great and little Saint Simons. Alatamaha

---

(a) Comanding Sapelo Creek, from the latter to Dispute the Inland passage.

has four Rivers vide, the main Stream, (bearing its Name from the Oconee old Town), Oak Mulgee, Ohoope, and Phennohaloway (a). The Source of Oconee is mentioned at the Head of this Chapter. Oak Mulgee takes its Origin between the Latid. 34° and 35°; and falls with Oconee into Alatamaha Stream, near due west of the City Savannah, 87 miles from the Sea, by the general Course of the Stream. Oconee is watered by many Rivulets, four of which are known and called Crooked, Little, Town and Buffelow; and Oak Mulgee is supplied by the seven following Rivulets vide, Town, Tauvalagaw,[33] James, Muddy, Commissioners, Great and Little Tobosophskee.[34] The Stream, with all its Rivers and Rivulets as far as 39 miles on a N. W. Course from the Sea lay in the Land, which is reserved by the Creek Indians for their Hunting Ground by a temporary Line marked since 1763, of which a more precise account shall be given below. Ohoope River heads due west from Ebenezer about 60 miles, and discharges itself into Alatamaha about 80 miles from the Sea, of course is also within the reserved Indian hunting Ground. Phennehaloway River is watered from a great Swamp situated due west 17 miles from Jekyl Sound. Phennehaloway River and its [83] Stream overflow the Country, situated between them for eleven or twelve miles distance, East and West, whereby the whole is made a Swamp; this River meets with its Water, that of the Stream in its regular Channel about 28 miles due west from Sapelo Sound.

Turtois is the greatest of the salt water Streams, takes its Spring 16 miles due west from Frederica, and discharges itself into Jekyl Sound. Ten miles up this Stream; on its north side is a fine half-moon Bluff, seemingly calculated for a Town (a). The Land from the Sound, a good way up, is bothsides Marsh, which ends also on both sides on Pine Land, but the good plantable Land lays about the Head, known to the Inhabitants by the Name of Buffelow Swamp.

Little Satilla is scarce superior in Largeness to Sapelo Stream, it heads near 16 miles due west of Jekyl, and falls into Cumberland Sound, is entirely surrounded by an open Marsh Country; this is the last salt water Stream on the Coast of Georgia.

Great Satilla Stream takes its Origin due west about 100 miles from Jekyl Sound; its general Course is W. by N., northerly on a distance of about 105 miles, and disembogues in Latitude 30°57'; and W. of Savannah Inlet, 29' nearest in Cumberland Sound, which, and a Creek from this into Turtois Stream with Jekyl Sound and the Ocean set the Boundaries to Jekyl Island, 46 miles west of Cumberland Sound. A great Swamp forks from this Stream bearing S. S. E. and

(a) Phennohaloway is a Creek Indian Word, signifies: a Turkey.[35]

(a) in 1771 a Town was laid out on the said Spot and called Brounswig, many are the Petitioners who have applied to the Governors in Council for Properties in this new Town from its Situation extremely promising.[36]

extends on that Course about 20 miles: Some will pretend that this Swamp is part of the famous Oecanphanoko, but the Certainty is yet to be discovered. This Stream is fresh Water and bordered by good plantable Lands, chiefly laid out in Tracts, but as yet not cultivated.

Saint Mary's Stream (thus called by the Spaniards, and by the Indians Thlathlothlaguphka) heads in the renowned and extensive Oekanphanoko Swamp, which is situated with its Southernmost Extent, in Latitude 30°, out of which this Stream takes its first Course N. by E. 35 miles, then with a general Course, N. 73° 45′ E. 29 31/80 miles more, and enters the Atlantic Ocean in Latitude 30°26′49″, and West of Savannah Inlet, 0°41′56″.

In the year 1763 the Governors from Virginia, North and South Carolina, met the Governor of Georgia in a Congress at Augusta upon Savannah Stream with the Deputies sent by the two Indian Nations: the Creeks and Cherokees; in this Congress a temporary Boundary Line was settled between the Settlements and Lands reserved for the Indian hunting Ground, which Line should not be transgressed by cultivating Lands on the west side upon the reserved Lands for the hunting Ground of the Indians, and thereby disturb the Nations in their quiet Possession. This Line was ascertained and concluded upon the 20th day of [*84*] November 1763, and in the year 1766 this Line was regularly laid out and marked by a proper Geometer in the Presence of Georgia Commissaries expert in the Indian Language, and some Indian Deputies. They begun at the Mouth of little River until they came to the Head of one of its Branches, Vulgo called William's Creek; from thence they went South as far as Saint Mary's in the Manner as is laid out in the following Table.

By the above Table [*see p. 151*] appears the general Course; Distance, Difference of Lattitude and Longitude; also the Latitude and Longitude both of the Head of William's Rivulet (vulgo Creek) and of the Pine Stump on Saint Mary's Stream, as also the several Courses and Distances between both.[37]

By the foregoing Account of Streams and Rivers, it fully appears that the Province of Georgia, although only equal with South Carolina as to Planting, yet being watered preferably to South Carolina, [*85*] cannot but have the Preference in the Capacity and Conveniences for Trade and Navigation; first, in respect to the great Number of Streams and Rivers, which are navigable; secondly, that Vessels trading up any of the Streams may unload in fresh Water, or, after they are unloaden, run three or four miles higher up and be in fresh Water, where in 48 hours, the fresh water will dissolve the Sea Salt (the Glue of that Coagulum, consisting in Barnicles, and Sea Weeds) and get the Bottoms clean from all adharent Matters, which will fall off in Scales and kill the Sea Worms, while in other salt Water Ports, 'tis a very expensive Article, for it is to be done there artificially, with great Labour, time and Expence.

GEOMETRICAL TABLE
Containing the Actual Survey of the Indian Boundary

Places set out from	Course	Distance Miles	South Miles	East Miles	West Miles	Places cross'd, or went by	Places arrived at
the head of William's Creek	S.78 45 E.	14	2¾	13½	....	cross'd several Branches of Upton Rivulet	stop'd upon Briar River.
the Place upon Briar River	S.56 15 E.	16¾	9¼	14	....	cross'd Godolphin's Path, by Briar River	Stop'd higher up Briar River.
another Place upon Ditto River	S.45 W.	22½	16	....	16	cross'd head of rocky Comfort Rivulet	stop'd on the S. side of great Ogetchee
a Place S. side of Ogetchee Stream	S.70 09 E.	61.	20¾	57½	....	by the S. side of Ogetchee Stream	came to Apalachicola Path from So. Carolina.
Apalachicola Path from So. Carolina	South	26½	26½	....	....	cross'd the two Ohoopee Paths	To the So. side of Cavanoochee River
Cavanoochee River	South	18½	18½	....	....	cross'd Falls of Weelustee River	to the So. side of Weelustee River
Weelustee River So. Shore	S.19 51 E.	38	35¾	13	....	cross'd five boggy Places	Alatamaha Stream opposite Doctor's Town.
opposite Doctor's Town, upon Alatamaha	East	1¼	....	1¼	....	went down by Water	Landed on So. side of Alatamaha
from So. side of Alatamaha Stream	S.8 36 W.	32 ⎱	43½	....	6½	cross'd River Swamp & Phennehalloway	to So. Shore of great Satilla Stream
So. Shore of great Satilla Stream	S.8 36 W.	12 ⎰	....	....	....	upon Latchokowae Path	made Station in the Pine Land
from Station in the Pine Land	West	8	....	....	8	cross'd part of supposed Oekanphanoko Swamp	made Station in the Pine Land
from Station in the Pine Land	S.19 51 E.	20.	18¾	6¾	....	cross'd a Lake	ended at a Pine Stump, on the west side of S. Mary's Stream.
General Course & Distance	S.21 26 E.	206	191¾	106 / 30½ / 75½	30½		

Difference Latitude ...   2°45'44"   1°20'30". Difference Longitude

Lattd. of the head of William's Creek   33°8'47"   3°8'23" Longitude ⎱ West from Saint Mary's Inlet

Lattd. of the Pine Stump on Saint Mary's   30°23'3"   0°29'19" Longitude ⎰

Chapter 3d

Of the City Savannah, its Latitude, Longitude, Number of Houses in City and Suburbs; its Fortification and Soil of Experiments made in the City; Description of the four principal Salts; of the Savannah Wharfs, of the Sound, its Navigation, Light House, Defence of the Road, the Air of the City of Savannah in particular.

The City of Savannah was settled the first year of General Oglethorp's Arrival in America Anno 1732,[38] in Latitude 32° and Longitude 82°16′: She is laid out 2,115 by 1,425 feet square in her Bounds, this again in 24 Tidings, each of them in 10, in all 240, and 48 Trustee Lots, with six Market Places, each 315 by 270 feet square. Three broad Streets 75 feet wide, runing perpendicular from the Bay, and three other 75 feet wide parallel with the Bay, centrically crossing each other, divides the City in six equal Quarters, each Quarter had four Tidings, each Tiding is run through (parallel to the Bay) by a Line 22 1/2 feet wide, each half Tiding consists in five contiguous Lots, each Tiding as well as Trustee Lot is 60 feet in front, and 90 feet in depth. Trustee Lots are divided from each other as well as from the Tiding Lots by Streets 75 & 37 1/2 feet wide. The City consists of 400 dwelling Houses, a Church, an Independent Meeting-House, a Council-House, a Court-House, and a Filatur.[39] The Plane of the City is at the [86] highest Place, 30 feet above the surface of the Stream, or rather above the Springs under the Quick Sand, and this whole Depth is a meer Sand down to the general Springs in the Quick Sands.

The Author had built in the lowest Part of the City a House in the year 1760,[40] a Season remarkable for extraordinary Drought, he sunk a Well 24 feet deep, wherewith he obtained 18 Inches water, and after 3 hours in vain digging for sinking the Curb deeper in the Quick Sand, he at last had the Well Wall set up, and his Well Water proved, not only of the best kind of this City, but had always Water in Abundance for himself and Neighbours in time of Scarcity: For drawing his Water, he directed an easy Machine of only one Wheel and two Bukets, one going up and the other down, each when drawn up will discharge itself into a Cistern, and run from thence into his Kitchen, under Ground; the Machine is so easy, that his Son in the 7th year of his Age[41] could draw up a Buket and to prevent any Accident proceeding from the Wheels runing by the Weight of the Buket, by which the Person employed in drawing the Water might be hurt, he contrived a double Catch, by which the Wheel, before it could turn an Inch on its Peripherie, it was stopt. Wheels in the City were copied after this Construction as also the Season of sinking them.

The City is since increased by two Suburbs, the one is to the west, called Jamacraw,[42] a name reserved from the Indian Town formerly at this Place of which the famous Thamachaychee was the last King.[43] Another Suburb is to the East called the Trustees Garden, a Place where the Trustees had a famous Garden laid out in order to make Experiments before they were advised to be accounted Objects profitable to be introduced in that Climate; both these Suburbs are increasing since 1760 extreamly fast, so that above 160 Houses are by these Suburbs added to the Number of the Houses in the City.

The prevailing Religion is, what is cultivated by the Church of England, next to this is the Lutheran and the Independent, then Calvinist, the Jews are the least.

Between the City and the Trustees Garden is an artificial Hill upon the Bay, part of which in 1760, was dug through (to open a Communication with this Suburb and the City) whereby a Stratum was opened near the Plane of the City filled with human Bones; this confirmed the History of this Mount, which had traduced it to be an ancient Indian Burying Ground, on which (as Thamachaychee the last Jamacraw King related to General Oglethorp at his Arrival) one of the Jamacraw Kings [87] had entertained a great white Man with a red Beard, who had entered the Port of Savannah Stream with a very large Vessel, and himself came up in his Barge to Jamacraw, and had expressed great Affection to the Indians, from which he hath had the Return of as much. The white Man with his red Beard, intending to present the King with a Piece of Curiosity he had on board his Vessel, for which he signified: some Indians might go down to receive it from his Lieutenant on board, to Whom he wrote a Note, which he desired the Indians would deliver to this Officer, who (pursuant to the Order in the Note) delivered what was demanded, and the Indians brought it up to Jamacraw, at which their King was greatly surprised, but more so, that this white Man could send his Thoughts to so great a Distance upon a white Leaf, which surpassing their Conception, they were ready to believe this white to be more than a Man, as the Indians have no other way to express times passed or to come than by rising and setting of the Sun, by New Moons, by Sprouting of the Trees, and the Number of their Ancestors; the General [*Oglethorpe*] by the nearest Computation and comparing History with Chronology, concluded the Person to have been Admiral Sir Walter Raliegh, who probably entered the Savannah Port in 1584, when on his Navigation upon this Coast.[44]

When the Author in 1757 returned from Fort Loudon to Savannah, it happened that Henry Ellis Esqr., arrived at the same time to take the Reins of Government in his Hands vide, in the Month of February, soon after an Indian War broke out with the Creeks; Governor Ellis assembled the Peoples Representatives to prepare and take such Measures as would most effectually protect a young Province; he also desired the Author's Advice concerning Fortifications, and the necessary Defence of the City, who proposed with a well pallisadoed Intrenchment to envelope the City, so as to make it a Receptacle and Shelter for all the Planters, their Families, Slaves, Etc.[45] The City being open to South Carolina by the Communication which the Navigation of the Stream afforded, so that from that Province Supplies of Ammunition and Victuals might be had in time of Emergency; the Indians would never have it in their Power to do more Mischief than to burn the Houses in the Country, kill some Cattle and steal Horses; but the Colonists are able at any time to go out in Parties to attak and worst the Indians, and thereby would oblige the Remnant to return to their Country without having left them a single Chance of a Scalp by sculking and [88] surprising solitary Plantations, as they use to do, that every Colonist would be more ready to fight the Enemy when he knows that his Family and Property are safe and secured behind good Intrenchment under the Auspice and Protection of the Governor, Council, Representatives, and all the Forces of the Province, surrounded with necessary Stores and Magazines; also be at Liberty to go or Send to Sea, or the Neighbouring Province, from which Benefit they could dread no Probability to be cut off. The Author's Advice met with general Approbation, and he laid two Poligons with three Bastions on the south side, and with two Poligons more (one on the east, and the other on the west side of the City, each ending with a demi Bastion) He joined the Stream. The Soil of Savannah being a meer Sand, to make this keep in a breast work, the Author was obliged to have the outside Talus faced with Pine Saplins set in the Ground, and inclined their Tops in form with the Talus of the Scarp, the Governor improved this Intrenchment with adding wooden Tours Bastioneés (a)—To each Bastion, one of which was placed in the Angle of each Gorge to serve as Cavalierés couvertés, with strong Platforms in their first Stories for Cannons of twelve Pounders to range and command the Country. He altered also the two demi Bastions into small wooden Citadels, each with four Bastions.[46]

Although the Soil of the City Savannah is, as observed before, a single Stratum of Sand from 24 to 30 feet deep down to the general Springs (water Root) in the Quick Sand, on which Dew and Rain strains, as through a wide Sieve, so that without plenteous Rains (which will keep the whole Stratum moist) nothing could grow, was it not for the Mixture of Mould (fine Atoms) in which the Sand accidentally is dissolved on the North side of Edifices or Fances [fences], where the Rays of the Sun never reaches, or by being covered with Boards, Timber, Brigs [bricks], Lime, etc. (Materials for Buildings), they, laying for a considerable time on one Spot, or by mixing Manure, which in itself is replenished with

(a) Copied from these wooden tour's Bastionees executed & erected in the Bastion of Frederica.

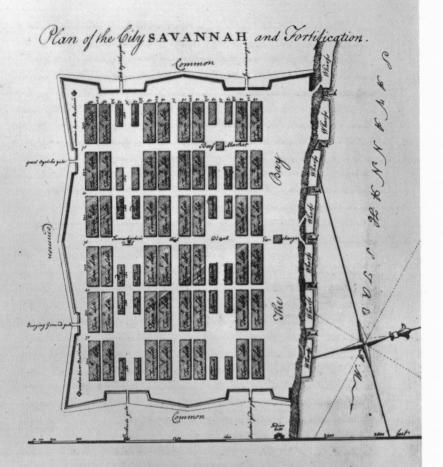

Plan of the City SAVANNAH and Fortification.

Profiles upon a N. 15. E. Line, shewing the Streets, Houses, Bay, Wharfs and Fortification.

the Niter generated in the putrified Animal Excretion, dejected from that most nitrificic Animal Athanor (Matrix specifica for the Generation of the Niter) so as the Ocean is of Table Salt, and as in the Bowels of the Earth is the only matrix of Vitriol, as is displayed below in a short chymical Sciography. By these Means the Gardens in Savannah are productive of all manner of Shrubs, Fruit Trees and Pot Herbs. The many Experiments which are made there, will as inexceptionable Evidences testify the Truth of these Facts. The [89] Author could alledge many which were successfully made before his Arrival in Georgia, by those who had the Care of the famous Trustees Garden: But this usefull Undertaking had been for some years abandoned when the Author came to Savannah, who, however met with two large Olive Trees, some Sevil Orange, Apple, Plumb, Peach, Mulberry, honey Locust, one Apricot and one Amerel Cherry Tree, as Testimonies of the laborious Experiments and good Success. He heard of many other successful Experiments, but not seeing the Vestigia, he will avoid the mentioning of them, and proceed to those made by himself and others during his Stay in this Province; before he enters upon them, [he] will communicate his chymical Sciography on Salts, which he promised above vide;

Nature produces two kinds of Salts,

The one kind consists of three Species, each differing in Gravity, none are fix or permanent in the Fire, and therefore called Acid Spirits vide;

Spirits { the Acid of the Air, next heaviest, but most volatile } not permanent in the Fire, or not able to indure all Degrees of Fire.
also { the Acid of the Sea the lightest, and next volatile
the Acid of the Earth the heaviest, but least volatile }

The other kind consists in two Species, the one is fix and the other volatile; the fix is met with in all Minerals and Vegitables, and the volatile in all Animal Subjects; both are called Alkalins; the fix endures the greatest Degree of Fire, and the volatile flies from the least Degree of Fire; the fix, if cohæres with the Acid Spirits, it makes them all permanent in the greatest Degree of Fire; the volatile, if cohæring with the Acid Spirits, it makes them the more willing to rise in a small degree of Fire.

Although the Acid Spirits differ in their specific Gravity, yet if they have a fix alkalin to the Basis, their Cohæsion to that alkalin is so powerful, that they altogether can endure equally the greatest degree of Fire. The Cohæsion of the different acid Spirits with the alkalin, constitutes the following Products vide, *constitutes on this unsaturated Basis* {

the Acid of the Air, by cohæring with the fix alkalin a Sal Enixum, or Vegitable, called Niter or Salt Petre.

the Acid of the Sea, by cohæring with the fix alkalin a Sal Salsum (or Preservative) called sal comume or Table Salt.

the Acid of the Earth, by cohæring with the fix alkalin a sal medicinale mirabile fixum (or Purgative) called sal Cathartique or bitter Salt.

} *all three fix; or permanent in the fire.*

[90] Any Acid Spirit cohæring with the volatile alkalin, constitutes on this unsaturated Basis a sal mirabile Volatile.

Besides the three first indispensably necessary Salts intended by Nature to support Life and Health (as long as they meet with access, and are admitted to ingress) Nature, by Accident, produces in the Bowels of the Earth, some Salts which are very useful in Oeconomy vide;

Produces as on a saturated basis {

When the Acid of the Earth sufficiently diluted corrodes Copper, by Adhæsion the blue Vitriol

When the Acid of the Earth Ditto . . . . Ditto . . . . corrodes Iron, by Adhæsion the green Vitriol

When the Acid of the Earth Ditto . . . . Ditto . . . . corrodes Lead, or tin by Adhæsion the white Vitriol

But when the Acid of the Earth Ditto . . . . Ditto . . . . corrodes Calx, then on this unsaturated Basis by Cohæsion an Alum, which is not permanent in the Fire.

} *all three volatile, or flying out of the fire*

Although the above are the only Vitriolea made by Nature, yet She has learned the industrious Philosopher, her assiduous Servants, to make what She herself cannot produce, vide, the Vitriols of Gold, Silver and Quick Silver; as also vegitable and animal Vitriols, which are great Rarities and useful Discoveries, and contain the purest Substances of the Animal or Vegitable; as by Vitrification the pure Metals are produced out of the Minera when vitrified. These Animal and Vegitable Vitriols are obtained by Trituration, Evaporation and Crystallisation, agreeable to the new Chymic Hydraulik.

Art may assist Nature also, or rather imitate the production of Salts vide, of

Salt Petre, with phlogiston and Vapour   Putrefaction

Table Salt, with phlogiston and Water   Fermentation

Vitriols, with phlogiston, water & metal   by Maceration   are purified by Crystallisation

Bitter Salt { with fire only . . . . Fusion

Bitter Salt { with water only . . . . Solution

Alkalin, with fire and Water . . . . Deflagration, is purified by Calcination

All Materials inclinable to Putrifaction are fit for the Salt Petre Manufactory; however some are preferable in Capacity.

All Materials disposable to Fermentation in a temperate Place, are fit for the Production of salt Manufactury.

All Materials matalic, animal and vegitable can be triturated in water, and its purest parts obtained in Vitriolic Crystals, or Vitriols can also be obtained by sole Maceration; however this Process requires a very long time.

[91] All Materials disposable to Incineration by an open fire, are fit for the alkalin Manufactury, but the best are, which have the least of Sal commune, or Table Salt adhæring to their outward Texture, which are those that grow near the Seas, but the Alkalin may be delivered from the Table Salt by Crystillisation before it is calcined.

To return again to the Experiments of Vegitable Productions made in the City of Savannah, the Author in the year 1763 planted the tops of several Ananas (v. g. Pine Apple) which took Root and grew whilst he continued in the Province, and so did a Coco-Nut, of which he had the Satisfaction to see it sprouting and growing. The same year [a] few Seeds of the Tartarian Rhubarb were sent to Georgia by John Ellis Esqr., Member of the Royal Society in London,[47] of which the Author had [a] few; these he kept in brown Paper and moistened, whenever it appeared to be dry outside; in this Paper they all sprouted, some the fifth, the rest later, but the last in eight days, as soon as a Seed sprouted, it was planted in a Box filled with 12 Inches of Sand and 3 Inches more of rich Mould. The Box was in February exposed to the Air in day-time, but kept in the House at Night; they all came up exceedingly well, but one Night the Box was neglected to be taken in the House, they died the next day except one, which the Author was very careful of to preserve; when its Leaves became as big as halfpennys, he transplanted it in a small Cask half filled with Loom [loam], and the Remainder with rotten Ground (a). This Cask, in Summer was placed in a shady Spot in the Garden; as long as the Leaves were small the Plant never kept above three Leaves, and when the fourth was sprouting, the Rest decayed and dropt off; but when the Leaves grew to four Inches wide and five Inches long, exclusive of the Stem, the Root was then able to maintain four Leaves, at which time the Plant resembled exactly a young red Beet. The Cask was kept in the same Place through the Summer and next Winter until the Spring the 16 of March 1764, when the Plant dyed, and the Root was not above half an Inch thick. The transplanting of young Trees the Author found practicable at any Month in the year, by only taking up the young Plant with its Soil about it upon a Spade and letting it down in a deeper Hole ready made; then to fill three or

(a) Such is the natural Soil of the Rhubarb about the Chinese Wall in Tartary, which if in shady and moist Places, is esteemed the best for this Culture.

four times a day the same hole with Water, for about one Week, or to slip it into a Calabage (Citrull) whose Bottom is cut out, and it [*92*] is next to the Vine, bored through with a middling Gimblet, and thus set in a hole where no Moisture (as much as can be received by said Calabage) can be lost, except what very gradually (in case of any Superfluity) can through the Gimblet-hole filter into the Sand underneath. This Gimblet hole serves also for the Heart Root of the young Tree to run through, and as the Citrull rots in about 12 months time, its soft Shell will willingly give way to the heart Roots Increase and Extension. The Papaw and plantin Tree has also, as well as the Sugar Cane been experimented in this City, and the Success has proved, that this part of the 5th Climate is not averse to the Culture of Sugar Cane to make Rum, but cannot fill enough and ripen to admit of making Sugar. For which the Canes require twelve Months Growth.

The Lands next to the City are generally the same, as far as it keeps the Level of the City; and is equal to any other Pine Land in this and the Neighbouring Province of South Carolina; and as the natural Products are the same also with those in South Carolina. Reference may be had to the Table of the Pine Land Products in the Description of that Province. Many have pretended a Discovery of Multiplicity of Pine Species; but the Author could never find more than two.[48]

The first is the Pinus, which alters its Bark, Timber and Cones as differently as the Seeds are conveyed by the Wind, Birds, Squirils or Rats indifferent high sandy and dry; high sandy and moist, or high rich and moist Lands; but in all these Soils the Branches of the Pine are bare of Leaves except their Ends, where the Leaves grow out in a Bunch and resemble a Tossel. The Wood or Timber of the first is wide and contregrain'd [*countergrained*] but full of Turpentine.

The Timber of the second is close and smooth grain'd, full of Turpentine (a) fit for all Buildings: and the third is a close and smooth grain'd Timber, but has no Turpentine; it is fit for all inside work in Building, which is not exposed to the Weather. The Turpentine of the four mentioned Pine Trees is yellow, and smells very strong. The second Specie of Pine is the Apies (white Spruce Pine) [*and*] is only met with on the Knowls (small Islands in Swamps), it has not much Turpentine but what it does yield, is of a light Pea green Colour, and of a very sweet Scent. Its Timber is white, therefore it is chosen for flooring-Planks; its Leaves grow all along on its Branches as well as on their Ends.

[*93*] The Savannah Bay is nearly fronted with contiguous Wharfs, the first of a new Construction, was built in 1759 by the Direction of the Author, who advised the Builder (one Thomas Eaton) to drive two Rows of Piles as far assun-

---

(a) This Tree is called yellow Pine, from its inside Colour, when this Pine superannuates, or is cut down and lays on the Ground, it turns to a Pitch Pine.

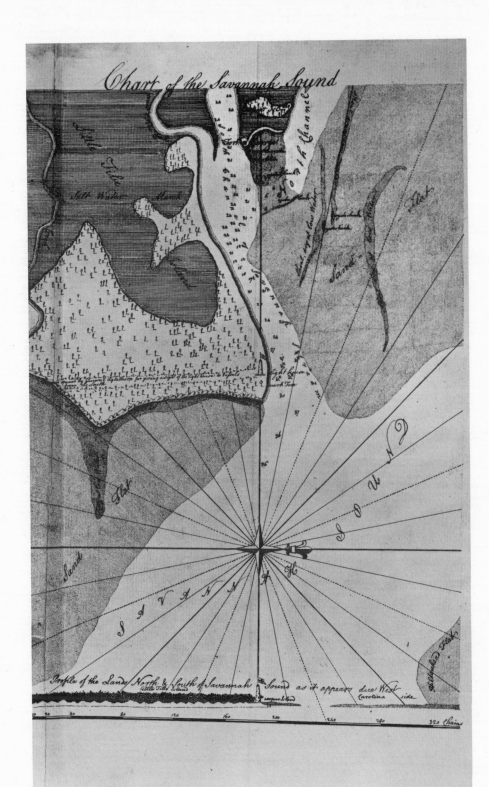

Chart of the Savannah Sound

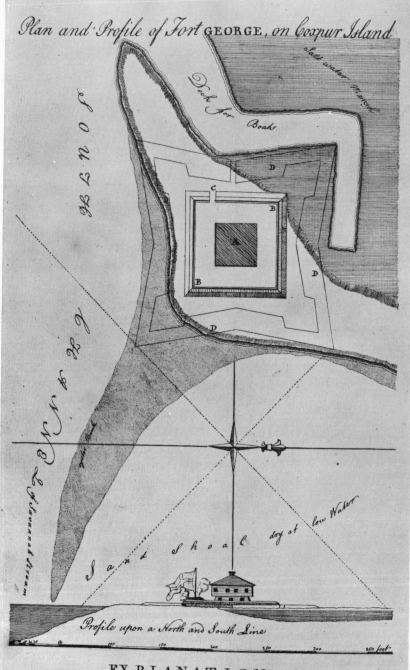

Plan and Profile of Fort GEORGE, on Coxpur Island

Profile upon a North and South Line

EXPLANATION

A. the wooden Tower Bastion, serving for Defence, Barrack and Magazine.
B, Redoubt, built of Earth, and faced with Cabage Tree. C. Gate.
D. Retrenchment not executed.

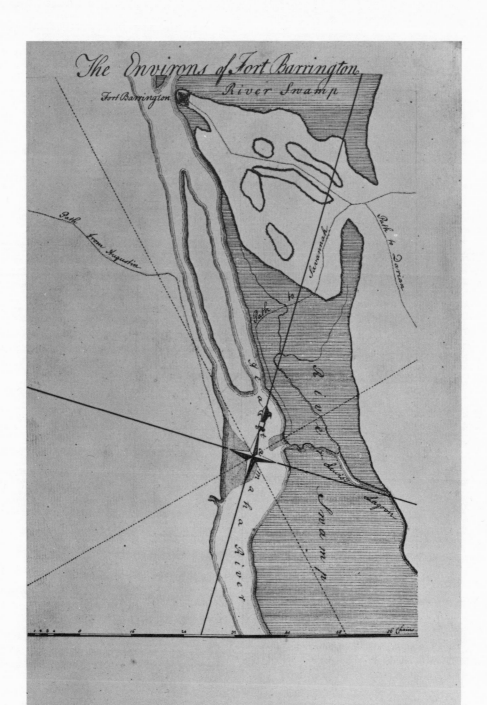

The Environs of Fort Barrington.

Fort Barrington.

River Swamp

View and Plan of Fort Barrington consisting of a wooden Tower Bastionee, and four wooden Caponieres, all built of Renching Timber.

The South View of Fort Barrington

EXPLANATION

The wooden Tower Bastionee is the Center, serves for defence, Officers Lodging, Store and Magazine.
A. the Hall. B. Bed Chamber. C. Store Room. D. Magazine. E. Stair Case.
The wooden Caponieres are in the four Corners, serve for defence and private Men's Lodging.
F. are Beds for 12 Men in each Caponiere. G. Fire Places. The 4 Centry Boxes H. are joined to the Caponieres, with faces and flanks, formed of Pallisadoes. I. the Well. K. Baking Oven.
L. Necessary Houses.

der as he desired his Wharf to be wide, and as far towards the River as low Water Mark; secure their Tops with plates and to trunnel Planks within on the Piles; this done, then to brace the Insides with dry Walls of Stones, intermixed with willow Twigs, and in the same Manner to shut up the Ends of the two Rows with alike Front along the Stream, to build inside what Cellars he had Occasion for, then to fill up the Remainder with the Sand nearest at hand out of the Bluff, or high Shore of the Stream, under the Bay, this Plan has been followed ever since to this day.

The Savannah Stream forms a Sound at its own Outlet into the Ocean, which, altho' it is not barred, yet there are many Banks in the Road between the Sound and City, on a distance of 17 miles, which these 40 years have rather increased in Extent and Shallowness, a Consequence owing to nothing else, but the great Currents yearly wheeling down a distance of 290 miles, especially at the time of great Freshes, by which great Trees with their Roots, and many Shrubs are grubbed up, which, and along with them great Quantity of Ground, Sand and Gravel is hurried down, and before the precipitating Stream breaks into the Sea, the Ocean's Flood checks its Velocity; thus suddenly stopt, the Stream drops its Gravel and Sand on Places where Currents give way to contre-Currents (Eddys). So that a Man-of-War Sloop with Difficulty goes up to the City at this time; when thirty six years ago a forty-gun Ship found no Difficulty to come up and anchor before the Town.

The Sound is formed by a great Sand-flat, which runs from Hilton Head (the north Point of the Sound) three miles to the East, and six miles to the South; and by another Flat, which runs from great Tibe Island (the south Point of the Sound) three miles on a S. E. course. The Breakers of both these Flats have a fine large Entrance into the Sound, which is made, by taking a small Pine Tree (grown on the East of the Light House) a little to the North, so as to bring the Light-house to bear W. 1/2 N., and keep this course until the East Point of Hilton Head bears North, and the west Point bears N. by W. 1/2 W., at which time the North Shoal is cleared, and a Vessel may at Liberty avoid the South Breakers, run up to the Light House, and come a quarter of a mile North of the said Light House to anchor in a very good Ground. The Breakers, from great Tibe and from an Oyster Bank on the North side of the Channel, opposite the Light House, are so visible, that a Vessel needs no written Direction. [94] The least Water from the Light House up to Coxpur Island, which lay East and West a mile from each other, is 12 feet at low, and 19 feet at high Water.

A Light House has been erected by General Oglethorp early in the Beginning of settling this Province, on Little Tibe Island, which is a good Land-Mark for Navigators who touch upon this Coast.[49]

Opposite Coxpur Island is the Mouth of great Tibe Creek on Little Tibe Island, a quarter of a mile off. Between Coxpur and said Tibe Island is the best Channel, of course within Command of Point Blank Shot. The Channel may easily be defended by two Batteries erected, one on Tibe and the other on Coxpur. On the last mentioned Island the Author in 1761 laid out and directed the Construction of Fort George, which is only a small Redoubt, 100 feet square, with a Block House, or wooden Tour Bastionee 40 feet square, in it to serve for a Defence, Magazine, Store House and Barrack; this Redoubt answers more to stop Vessels from going up and down in time of Peace, than Vessels which had a Mind to act in a hostile View; the Reason for so diminutive a Construction was the then prevailing incapacity to raise for this Purpose more than £2,000 Sterling, as many other equally necessary Constructions for the Public Benefit, stood then in Competition before the Eyes of the Legislator.

The City of Savannah continued from its first Settlement, for near 30 years to be accounted a very healthy Place. The South Carolinians used to come there for recruiting their Health, but the Vapours which generally breed in Swamp-Lands and rise by help of its high Trees, as through Chimneys, to gain the free Air, in which by any moving Wind they are carried the Road of the Wind. They had the same Chance in both these Swamps, vide, on Hutchinson's Island, North, opposite the City in the Stream; as also in the low Swamp Land east of Savannah, on which the Trees were higher than the City; so that none of their Vapours could touch the Inhabitants, which were so near to their Rise, but as soon as the Trees on both these Lands were cut down and the cleared Land converted into Rice Fields, the Vapours hanging upon them at present are by a North or East Wind (for want of their living Ladders to ascend by them above the Summit of the City) rolled in it, and all the Streets and Houses filled with them, to the Prejudice of its Inhabitants, whose Diseases are in every respect similar to those in the Neighbouring Province of South Carolina, fully described in the 2d and 3d Chapter of the History of that Province, where Reference being had, the necessary Information both of Pathology, and Materia Medica will fully appear.[50]

[95]

CHAPTER 4th

Of the Inland Communications, Number of Inhabitants, Forces, Negroes, Plan for a Rice Plantation, Export, Riches, and Trading Vessels, of Indians.

This Province is well laid out with Roads, on which, the Laws of the Province obliges all Inhabitants to work twice in the year in order to keep in Repair, what has been made the year before, and add in Breadth in order to widen it gradually; thus they continue until the Roads are all 33 feet wide, after which this Work will cease, except for such times only, when the Roads receive Damage by Rains. These Roads are conducted through the whole Province vide, from the City of Savannah to the Eastward as far as Saint Augustin and Skedoway Creeks; another westwardly as far, as Ebenezer & Augusta; a third southwardly (a), to the Ferry of great Ogetchee Stream below the Mouth of Cowanoochee River, from thence to the Head of South Newport River, where the Road forks, vide, South to Darian and S. W. to Fort Barrington (both Places upon Alatamaha Stream); the many Plantations and Settlements on these Roads make travelling very convenient and easy for Man, Horse and Carriages.

The great Dispatch, Cheapness and Conveniency, which Water Carriage affords from and to all Places in this Province puts Land Carriage almost out of Use, unless it be the Germans at Ebenezer and Bethany for conveying their Cocoons to the Filatur in the City of Savannah, who use Land Carriage in the Season of the year, when the Silk Spinning Manufactury begins, which is generally in the latter end of April and last to the End of May, that is the Carting Business, for the Spinning lasts frequently to the latter end of June or Beginning of July. The Germans used formerly to send their Cocoons down the Stream in Boats, whose Gunwalls were raised and filled with the Cocoons to their very Brim, then covered with Sheets, observing all other necessary Precautions to prevent them from getting wet; this notwithstanding the humid Evaporations from both the Stream & its bordering Swamp and Marsh Lands penetrated them and heated them in a Degree, that (N. B. as they could only be sent at Night, the Heat of the Day being prejudicial) those on the Bottom would be smothered and bruised, and the Worms in the Middle did eat through the Cocoons, [96] whereby a great part of the silk was destroyed before it could be manufactured; which Inconveniences were remedied by a German, who made a long Waggon,

(a) From the Well in the Center of the City, S. 58° W. 12 miles.

filled it with many small Drawers, each in Length equal to the Waggon's Breadth, each Drawer not above six Inches deep, all sides full of Holes, with lathed Bottoms, these Drawers were filled very even, so that one could be placed upon another without bruising the Cocoons within the lower, which was thus carted through the Forrests free from so strong Evaporation, as those of the Stream and its Swamps and Marshes, and delivered to the Filatur without damaging a single Cocoon.

The Inhabitants of Georgia consist in free Men, Women and Children, of 16,000 Persons, of whom are effective and enrolled for bearing Arms in the Militia Regiments 2,500 Men. The first militia Regiment is that of Savannah, the next that of Ogetchee and the third Regiment is that of Augusta; besides these three Regiments is a Squadron of Cavalry, all better trained than formerly a Militia in Europe.

When the Author in 1751 landed in Georgia, he scarce met three dozen of African Servants, and they had not been above ten Months introduced in the Province. Their Sum is since increased to 13,000. Of whom are at least 12,000 employed in the Plantations.

To undertake a Rice Plantation in this Province does by several years Experience prove to attend the following Articles, Expences and Profits.

Supposing the Land to be purchased at 10/ per acre vide, 200 acres	100 -0-0
To build a Barn and Pounding Machine purchased boards & Timber	220 -0-0
To purchase 40 working Hands	1,800 -0-0
To purchase working Oxen and Horses	60 -0-0
To two Carts and Collars	10 -0-0
To Hoes, Axes, Spades, and other Plantation Tools	30 -0-0
To annual Expences for Tax & Quit Rent £5 &	
first year's Provision £50	50 -0-0
To Overseers Wages	50 -0-0
To Negroes Shoes £6-10 Ditto cloath. £20-0 & 13 Blankets	
per annum: £5-6	31-16-0
To a Box of Medicines & Doctor's fees £20-0 for Deaths of	
Negroes per ann. £100	120 -0-0
	£2,476-16-0

The aforementioned Number of Negroes will plant 130 Acres of Rice, making 350 Barrels at 40/ per £700-0-0; also 70 Acres of Provision, will nearly clear £23-5-5 per Cent Interest.

The next year's Provision-Article falling away, the expended Capital will only be £2,426-16-0, and the Interest on it will nearly be £29 per cent. Those who plant Indigo will raise their Interest much higher. N. B. the above Calculation is on Land, which is [97] ready cleared and fenced, for if this is to be done, so full a Crop cannot be expected at the first, and at times not the second year, especially if the Undertaker is not a professed Planter, and has not a very faithfull and industrious well experienced Overseer.

Although Georgia was a Place of Industry ever since its very Beginning, yet its Endeavours consisted only in Experiments, of which it had not for 23 years to load Vessels and to send its Products to any foreign, but only to supply its own Market in the City, which Backwardness seemed only to be owing, first to the Prohibition of introducing African Servants, [and] Jamaica and Barbadoes Distillations; secondly for not being governed in a manner as other Provinces, which have their Governors, Counsellors, Chief Justices and other Officers; as also their Representatives, with the Liberty to make their own Laws; for as soon as this Province became freed from those Prohibitions, and invested with Privileges and Liberties, as other Provinces, which happened in the year 1754, the good Effect proceeding thereof was, that the next years Product proved to consist in 1,899 Tons, value £15,744 Sterling, exported by 9 square rigged Vessels & 43 Sloops and Schooners, which Industry increased during 16 years, in such a Manner, that in 1770 its Products amounted to 10,514 Tons value £99,383 St[erling] exported by 73 square rigged Vessels and 113 Sloops and Schooners. By which it appears that the Products increased in 16 years more than 5 times; their Value more than 6 times, and the Number of Vessels more than 3 1/2 times, the annual Increase is laid down in the following Table—[51]

Producted under the Governors	Year	Tons	Value	square rigged Vessels	Schooners and Sloops	Total	
	1755	1,899	15,744	9	43	52	
John Reynold's Esqr.	1756	1,799	16,776	7	35	42	
	Sum	3,698 —	32,520 —	16 —	78 —	94	Exported out of the Province of Georgia
	1757	1,559	15,649	11	33	44	
	1758	665	8,613	4	17	21	
Henry Ellis Esqr.	1759	1,981	12,694	13	35	48	
	1760	1,457	20,852	7	30	37	
	Sum	5,662 —	57,808 —	35 —	115 —	150	
Total of both Governors......		9,360 —	90,328 —	51 —	193 —	244	

[*98*]

	Year	Tons	Value	square rigged Vessels	Schooners and Sloops	Total	
Producted under the Governor		9,360	90,328	51	193	244	
brought over							
	1761	1,604	15,870	9	36	45	
	1762	2,784	27,021	22	35	57	
	1763	4,761	47,551	34	58	92	
	1764	5,586	55,025	36	79	115	
Governor Wright	1765	7,685	73,426	54	94	148	
	1766	9,947	81,228	68	86	154	
	1767	8,465	67,092	62	92	154	
	1768	10,406	92,284	77	109	186	
	1769	9,276	86,480	87	94	181	
	1770	10,514	99,383	73	113	186	

Sum 71,028 — 645,360 — 522 — 796 — 1,318

Exported out of the Province of Georgia

Total of all the Governors ...... 80,388 — 735,688 — 573 — 989 — 1,562

As the foregoing Table shewed the yearly Increase of the Products in Tonnage, under the three Governors; as also its Value, with the yearly Increase of the Number of trading Vessels; so will the subsequent Table serve to explain in what Articles the above Products and their Exportation consisted; each Article with its total Increase during 16 years in one Sum.

	Barrels		Pounds		Numbers
Rice per		Indigo per		Horses per	
16 years	140,542	16 years	187,082	16 years	1,747
Tar	3,655	Deer Skins	2,167,320	Mules	87
Pitch	2,307	Beaver Ditto	21,997	Cows	452
Turpentine	730	Tann'd Hides ...	411,813	Hogs & Shoats .	7,359
Beef salted	1,945	Raw Silk	8,906	Poultry	9,492
Pork Salted	5,146	Sago Powder ...	34,305	Reeds	54,304
	Bushels				
Rough Rice	27,561	Bees Wax	30,907	Hoops	93,110
Corn	69,104	Tobacco	16,477	Oars	11,014
Peas	4,285	Hemp	1,860	Staves	6,391,362
	Gallons	Tallow	19,184	Shingles	24,334,619
Orange Juice	3,077				Feet
Soy	207			Timber per	
				Board	15,222,088

The whole Amount of Value of the above Articles exported in 16 years is £735,688 Sterling, which divided into 16 equal parts makes the Value of Export one year with another amount to £45,980-10 Sterling. [99] Since the real Increase of the annual Value proves in 16 years to be 6 times multiplied; and in order to make it a 30 years run, which will end in 1785, the Increase will be at the above Rate 11 1/4 times multiplied, and that years Export will be worth £177,120 Sterling.

The Introduction of sawing, Stamp and grinding Mills in Georgia, was almost as early as the settling of the Province; for which Purposes several Streams, Rivers and Rivulets proved very convenient, but some Rivulets have disappeared two or three years after being chosen, and left the Mills dry; for the following Reasons: The Rivulets, as well as all Rivers and Streams are both sides bordered with large Forrests, either low Swamp or high Oak Land, of which the Undertakers of Mills cleared only a small Spot of its Trees for the Mill, above which they carried across the Rivulet a Dam, by which the Rivulet overflowed its Shores, and spread its Water all over the adjacent lowest Land of the Forrest; the Trees of which (being Air Plants) became subject to the Destruction proceeding from stagnant Water, whose Action and Power in a proper Ratiscination is fully advanced in the 4th Paragraph of the second Chapter of the History of South Carolina. In short all the Trees perished, their old Roots shrunk from their Barks, and the young Roots with their Barks shrunk from the Earth, so that either between Bark and Root, or between Bark and Earth Openings appeared, and the Ground thus perforated became like unto a Sieve, through which the Waters of the Rivulets sunk down to the Quick Sand, where they will continue sinking, until these Passages in course of time are stopt up. This Evil might have been prevented, had they laid out the Land intended to reserve the Mill Water into a Field, and planted it for two or three years, and during this time grubed up all Roots, for which Labour the Crops would have richly rewarded, then (when the Field overrun with Grass) had run the Dam across the Rivulet, so they would have kept their Mill Water on their old Fields without Danger of ever losing it.

The Cherokee Indian Towns comprehended in this Province, are Tugelo, Keowee, Kanasetchee, Toxowa, Wawlawsee and Estetowee, all on the west side of Savannah River, they are called the lower Hill Cherokee Towns, Watogo, Johche, Jtaqualejesse, Kiojee, Ajaleste Towns of the middle Settlements, Aiwassee and Natarlee Towns in the Cherokee Vallies.[52]

[100] The Creek Indian Towns included in this Province are Tohowogly and Cawita between eight and ten miles below the Cataract of Chatahutchee River called the Towns of the lower Settlement, or lower Creeks. Little Tallesy and Oweetomkee old Town upon Coosaw River N. W. of Fort Alabamo, Oweetomkee new Town, Mukelossa, Savannow, Coolame, White Ground, Fugoskatchee,

Clually and Ottasee, Towns below the first Cataract of Locushatchee now Tale-pusee River. Nophabee, Tukasatchee and Tallesee are Towns between the first and second Cataract, Hughphala, Lustuhatchee, Oakfusky, Alkehatchee and Suchutopaga Towns above the 2d Cataract of Talepusee. Cojolegee and Oakjoy are Towns upon Cojolegee a Rivulet of Talepusee River, Oktosawsee and Hil-lawbes, Towns on Oktosawsee, another Rivulet of Talepusee River—all upon this River are called the Towns of the upper Settlement, or upper Creeks.[53]

The Number of both lower and upper Creeks consist in 15,000 Men, Women and Children, among whom are above 3,000 Warriors and Gunmen; the Creeks are only in that differing from the Cherokees, that they are esteemed bolder War-riors, greater Politicians, as willing to join the French as the English, and that they exceed the Cherokees in Jealousy: they crop the Ears of an Adulterer; also their Language entirely differs from that of the Cherokees, so that these two Nations cannot converse with each other unless by Interpreters: as to their Manners, Cus-toms, Maxims, and Notions they do in nothing differ from what has been said of the Cherokee Nation in the History of South Carolina.

East Florida

To the Right Honourable the Earl of Dartmouth, His Majesty's principal Secretary of State for the Colonies.[1]

My Lord,

These Sheets, which I have the Honour to deliver into the Hands of your Lordship, comprehend a Full History of Florida, I have traced from the Date, which made this great Continent, (after having remained 5,702 (a) years incognito) known unto its eastern and western Neighbours, with all Actions during a Series of 250 years peculiarizing its Epoches, and therefore worthy of Commemoration from the 20th, of March 1513 to the year 1763; I specifie and distinguish, in particular that part, which, since the last Spanish Epoche in the year 1763 is made known by the Appellation of East Florida, and by the new Settlers, or aboriginal English Inhabitants from the Beginning of a new, vide, its English Epoche in a proper List with their Names, Capacities, and Employs; I have inserted its Climate, Health, Winds, Heat, and Cold, proved by a Continuation of my daily Observations made through 36 months on the Termoscope and herein represented in regular Ephemores, to which I add the Boundaries of the Province with the Capacity of Land in acres by Computation. I prove its Extent of the Coast, all Inlets, and Rivers by the exact Surveys and Mensurations, whose Geometrical Operations I join in careful Copies of the Original Tables; from which the general Map of East Florida is made out, laid down and delivered in June 1772 to the Plantation Office, now part of your Lordship's Department, where I have joined its several Sections in one Sheet of 25 feet long, containing all that part of East Florida which [*102*] contains from the Meridian of Cape Florida a Breadth westwardly of 1°41′41 1/2″; as also in another large Sheet all its Northern Part, situated on the west of the same degree of Longitude,[3] to which I have added two pieces bound in folio, the one containing a History of South Carolina, and the other the same of Georgia, both as an Introduction to this present Work, of which these few Sheets are only the Beginning, and what is mentioned here above; the Continuation will shew the farther Surveys, Soil, Natural Produce, Improvements, Navigation, Botany, Zoology, and several Oeconomical, Chymical and astronomical Observations.

It is a reviving Happiness to me that I have obtained the so much wished for Honour to lay the Product of my unbounded Labors, precious time, and altho'

(a) agreeable to the Dionisian Period[2]

imperfect, yet faithful Endeavours before so impartial, unprejudiced, generous, philosophical, just & consequently competent Judge, who I am sure will not grant his Approbation out of partial Condescension, without a proper Enquiry, nor led by Prejudice, condemn and reject before the Materials are examined; in short I am confident your Lordship will do Justice to my Labors, and grant your Approbation if they really deserve it, and if they are undeserving, justly reject and condemn them; to either of which Events I humbly beg Leave to present them and myself to your Lordship's Justice and Equity. And have the Honour to subscribe myself,

My Lord,

Your Lordship's

Most obedient and

Most humble Servant

William Gerard de Brahm.

East Florida

CHAPTER 1st

From whence the Appellation of Florida, how and when first discovered; when, and what part of it; by whom conquered; when, and how long settled by the Spaniards; when ceded to England, and called East Florida, with a List of its first Inhabitants.

The Derivation of the Name Florida is variously reported; the most ancient and of course most precise and contemporaneous Historian, who wrote upon this Subject is Inka Garcilasso de la Vega born in Perou,[4] his Father was a Spanish Gentleman, who married a Native descending from the ancient Family of the Inkas, this Inka Garcilasso left Perou, and came in 1560 to Old Spain, where he wrote and delivered to the Public the History of the Peruvian Inkas; the Spanish Civil War in that Country, and the General History of Perou; also an Account of the Conquest of Florida, wherein he sets forth, that in the year 1513 (a) the Governor of Porto Rico, Juan Ponce de Leon sailed in quest of the Bimini (one of the Lucayes now) Bahama Islands in two armed Frigates; but after a long unsuccessful Navigation he was in a Gale cast away on Land bearing North from Cuba (the greatest of the Antilles); as this Misfortune happened to him on the 20th of March the day of Pasquas Floridas (Palm Sunday) he in Memory of this day called the Place Florida, supposing it to be one of the Antilles.

Inka Garcilasso does not mention the particular Spot, or from which Point of the Compass that Gale blowed, as whereby one might trace what is so important to render a History precise and exact; however so much can be ascertained for the present, that, if the Wind has been East, the Place is surely to the North of Latitude 25°42' on the western Shore of the Canal (which leads the Waters out of the Gulph of Mexico into the Atlantic Ocean) now called the New Bahama Channel; for had the Governor been cast away to the Southward of Lat. 25°42' he must have wrecked upon the Martyrs long before he could come near any Shore, and even in most places before he could see the Land; in case the Wind has been West, then the Bay formerly called by his Name Ponce, (which the Author of the present History distinguishes by the Appellation of [*104*] Chatham Bay) is the most probable Spot, on which the vast Continent of North America received its original Name, and there remains but little Doubt, that this Bay is possitively the very authentical Spot; for the Spaniards in those days had

(a) The Beginning of the first Spanish Epoche on the Continent of North America

Knowlege of the Eastern Sea Coast of Mexico, but had only a Notion of Lands or Islands being to the Eastward of that Kingdom, therefore not to fall in with it by Night, or by a high Gale in the day-time they stood as far West as possible knowing how to bear away in case they make Soundings or Land to the Westward, and therefore endeavoured to make their Discovery sure by departing from the well known Mixican Shore for Searches to the North and Eastward; this the Author presumes does determine all Probability in favour of Chatham Bay.[5]

When the Spaniards examined the Discovery of the Land made by Sebastian Gabot,[6] who in the year 1496 ⊙ was sent out by King Henry the 7th of England, to find out the west Passage to the East Indies, and was obstructed from proceeding any farther by the Sight of Land in less than sailing the third part of his Longitude from the Meridian of London, he without taking proper Recognizance [*reconnaissance*] of the Land returned to England, which compared with the later Discoveries made before by Ferdinando Soto, the Spaniards not only dropt their Notion, that Florida was an Island, but took it now for granted, that Florida was the Continent, and fixed anno 1544 its septentrional[7] Boundary under the North Pole, but in less than 40 years after Sir Walter Raleigh laying the Foundation of New England distinguished the northern Bounds in 1584 (a) to the Continent (then known to the Spaniards under the Appellation of Florida) by the name of Virginia, the same did the French with their Settlement of Canada, which descending the Mississipi Stream, so as Virginia on the Western Coast of the Atlantic Ocean extinguished the Name of Florida as fast as their Industry obliged them to extend their Cultivation to the Southward, and would at this time have proved the Indolence of Florida by abolishing its Name from the Continent, had not His Majesty, now the sole Lord of that extensive Tract of 66 Degrees in Latitude vouchsafed to let this Name continue on that part of the Continent where it originally took its Rise, and as for the name of Florida was carried by the Tracts of the first Conquerors, in the Reign of Charles the 5th, King of Spain, by whose Order in 1539 Ferdinando Soto[8] (b) the 12th of May set sail from the Havanna on Cuba with an Army of 1,000 Infantry and 250 Cavalrists in all 1,250 Men, whom he landed the 31st of May in the Haven of Tampo or Spiritu Santo, one degree and twenty minutes North from the Middle of [*105*] Chatham (perhaps even at that time called Ponce) Bay; the Haven of Spiritu Santo[9] was then settled by the Hirrigas Indians,[10] of their principal Town Hirrehiguwa six miles up the River (now known by the Name of little Kaloosa) Soto took Pos-

⊙ four years after Christopher Columbus, whom Ferdinand King of Spain sent upon a Discovery of Land to the west of Europe, who sailed from Cadiz in the year 1492.

(a) in the Reign of Queen Elizabeth

(b) one of the twelve Conquerors of Perou, who had share in the taking of the last Inka Intikuti Huallpa.

session, and leaving a Garrison of 120 Men, marched 1,130 to the Northward through the Mukoso Nation (making alliance with some and conquering others) led, with the utmost Difficulty his Army through the famous Oekanphanoko Swamp, at that time bordered on its South by the Urribarakaxes, and on its North by the Akuheras, marched through the Ossachiles, Vitachukos, and Okalehes to Apalache the principal Town of the Apalache Indians on the East side of Apalachicola River; Apalache is situated upon the Gulph of Awute now Apalache Bay or rather Gulph, where Soto rested his Army in Winter Quarters, and were joined by the Garrison, he left at Hirrehiguwa.

The latter end of March 1540 Soto broke up, and moved to the Kofasiki Nation, which was settled on the west side of Apalachicola Stream, discharging itself into the Gulph of Mexico to the East of Cape Escondido at that time bearing the Name of Saint Helene, ever since a Company of seven rich Inhabitants in Saint Domingue fitted out two Vessels, which was about three years after Juan Ponce's Discovery of Florida, in Expectation of finding out gold and silver Mines, and to be the first Adventurers; these two Vessels made this Cape Land on the day of Saint Helene; one Jordon on board of one of the two Vessels was the first, who spyed the Mouth of Apalachicola Stream, for which they stood in, and went up; from this time they called the Stream Jordan in Honour of its Discoverer; the Savages inhabiting that River were the Kofasiki Indians, which admired and treated their Guests very amicably and generously but these Saint Dominguans (after having made an unsuccessful Tryal determined with out Acquisition not to return to their Island, and to have their fellow Insulars laugh in the Bargain) was barbarous enough to allure 130 Indians on board their Vessels with an Intent to carry them as their Slaves to Saint Domingue, took up their Anchors and departed; but the distressed Indians had Resolutions enough to [106] refuse Victuals, and starved themselves rather than to be carried into Slavery, and one of these two Vessels perished in the Passage (a).

Soto after crossing the Apalachicola Stream and the Country of the Kofasiki Indians, arrived with his Army in the Beginning of April 1541 upon Kusaw River, then inhabited by the Chikasaw Nation, attaked and took their Fort called Alibamo, situated in the Fork of Kusaw and Lokushatchee Rivers, built 1,000 feet square, with four Rows of Pallisadoes, three small Gates in each Row, in all twelve Gates in a Line with each other, that is, four in a line in the middle of 500

(a) This particular Narrative is inserted in order to direct those, who are of an uncertainty where to place the Stream Jordan; some will have it in the Gulph of Pensacola, some will that (what is now called Savannah, and divides South Carolina from Georgia) is the Stream formerly by the Spaniards called Jordan; but neither of these places are so near a Cape Land as Apalachicola, nor is there any Cape from this to Cape Romans in South Carolina confining a Stream unless it is Punta Larga, but its River and Entrance is very shallow, and has no water for a Vessel of more than five feet Draught.

feet distance from each Corner, and four Gates answering in a Line each other near both Corners of the Fort; in the middle of which were two lesser Pallisadoes intrenchments, or Retreats. Before Soto arrived upon Kusaw River, and after he left the Kofasikes, he went through the following Towns Guwachule, Ichohi, and Taskalucha, from the Chikasaws he marched his Army into the Chiskaw Nation on the east side of Chukaguha (now Mississipi) Stream 1,500 miles above its Mouth, where he built five Barges, each large enough to hold 150 Infanterist and 30 Cavalrist, in which and some Indian Boats Soto transported his Army diminished to 750 Infanterists and 150 horse in all 800 Men besides Indian Slaves; from thence he proceeded up the Stream to the Kaskins and farther to the Kapahas, where he ended his northerly Course observed since he left the Taskaluchas.

From the Kapahas Soto begun a west Course, with a View to beat his way for Mexico, came to the Colimas, from them he went to the Tulas, and in November he reached the Utiankes, among whom he passed the Winter.

In April 1542 Soto marched to the Natchees, from them to the Guhakanes, where he learned that the western Countries were but barren and inhabited by very few Nations, and they backed with great Deserts without any water or any thing else. Soto conceiving the impracticableness [*107*] of leading farther through barren Lands an Army which had suffered so great a Reduction in plentifull Countries, he shortly deliberated on an Alteration of his Plan of Operation, being sure of the immense Difficulties from so great an inland Distance to hit shortly upon a sure Sea Port, resolved to return, and built upon Mississipi Stream a Town and two Brigantins, with a View of sending them under the Command of his best and most trusty Officers and Men to Mexico, Cuba and all Spanish Ports with Instructions to spread about the favourable account of the Discoveries, thereby to invite and to encourage Spaniards from all Quarters, promising himself, that by their great Concourse all Necessaries would be imported in Abundance. This Plan being resolved upon, he took his Route Southeastwardly towards the Anilkowes, situated on the North side of Anilko, one of the Mississipi Rivers; after passing this River Soto marched with his Army, diminished to 600 Men in the Guhachowiha Nation, which was settled on the west side of the Mississipi, by the Assistance of this Nation and their Boats he intended to set over the Stream, and make himself Master of the principal Quinguwaltankas Town, in order to enjoy their pleasant and fruitful Country, and to receive his Countrymen from the different Quarters in a Country answering his Description, and their Expectation; he no sooner arrived at the Place of Operation, than he immediately made all Preperations for cutting Timber, contriving Cordage &c in order to hurry his Plan in Execution, but was surprised by a violent Fever, being sensible of his Danger appointed the Commander of the Cavalry Louis de Moscoso d'Alvarado to succeed him in Command, called all Officers and ordered

them to take the Oath of Obedience under their new General before him, admonished them and all Soldiers not to give over the Expedition until they have
brought it honourably to its End under the Conduct of so gallant an Officer, as he
has experienced Moscoso to be, and died the third day, on the 23d of June in the
42d year of his Age, generally regretted by both Officers and Men, who provided a Piece of a green Oak Tree seven feet long split, and hollowed them out,
in which they laid in the Night his Corpes, nailed the two Pieces together and
then sunk him in the Middle of Mississipi Stream, for fear if they did bury him in
the Ground the Indians would dig the Corps up and abuse it scandously: After
his Death Moscoso took Council with the Officers to march by Land to Mexico,
especially encouraged by Aniasco, one of the principal Officers (who had been
very successful upon this Expedition in many Discoveries, and was selfsufficient
in [*108*] Geography) yet without knowing the Latitude of Mexico, nor that the
Latitude of their Place of Departure was several degrees to the North of Mexico,
leaded, the 5th of July the Army of 600 Men due west from the Stream in Expectation to hit by this Course upon that Kingdom; this Course Moscoso kept for 300
miles without enquiring or noting the several Nations, through which he
marched; with this Course, and Distance he reached the Ahuchees, and from
them fell in Deserts, which obliged Moscoso to reasume Soto's Plan, and returned
with an E. 3/4 S. course from the Deserts to Mississipi, where he arrived the latter
end of November at two contiguous Towns of the Aminohigas Indians 48 miles
South of the Guhachowihas, from which they had taken their west departure, the
5th of July last; these two Towns were situated upon Mississipi Stream, surrounded with Ditches filled from the Stream, of which they appeared to be
Islands; altho' the Army on a five months frightful Erring [*errand*] in the Wilderness had been reduced to 370 Men, 70 of which were Cavalrists, yet Moscoso
had no other Chance than to take these two Towns from the Indians and keep
his Winter Quarters in them.

The Beginning of February 1543, Moscoso finding his Men recovered from
their Fatigues, set all hands about the Construction of seven Frigates (Carra-
velles), an Employ all Officers and Men seemed to be very fond of, for everyone
was sik of Florida, and wishful to be out of it, so they all joined Hands without
Distinction, and would have been very exact in celebrating the Annals of the 31st
of May by leaving Florida that same day, on which they landed in it four years
passed, had they not been stopped in their Expeditiousness from the 20th of April
to the end of May by the Stream, which according to its (a) custom, overflowed
his Shores for 60 and 70 miles in breadth, so that the Spaniards in their two Towns
did see no ground for 40 days, visited each other in Boats until the first day of

(a) is said to happen once in 14 years.

June, when the Stream had returned to his common Bed and Channel, and all Hands endeavoured to redeem the time lost, which they proved effectually, for in the end of June the whole Army consisting of 350 Spaniards, and 36 Indian Prisoners Men and Women were embarked, from which day the Spaniards were supported by their own Bottom, and no more by that of the Florida Soil, which they had trodden four years, and one Month, and mixed it with the Bodies of 900 Spaniards, with 250 horses, and the Water of Mississipi with the Corps of their General: these seven Frigates fell down the Stream, crossed the Gulph by a Southwestwardly Course, made the Mouth of Pannco, went up that Stream, and landed [*109*] at the Town from which the Stream takes its Name, whence the Troops were marched to Mexico, and discharged; most of them passed the Remainder of their Lives in Poverty or Gloominess.

After this long expensive and unsuccesful Expedition Charles the fifth refused to hear any more, nor to grant Commissions for Governors of Florida, notwithstanding the many Petitions presented to him for that Purpose, until in the year 1549 a Company of Dominican Friars proposed to convert the Florida Indians to Christianism, to which that religious King agreed, and granted his Permission, their Prior Cancel Balbastro landing with his Companions was, besides two more flayed a live by the Indians to revenge themselves for the Injuries they had formerly received from the Spaniards, the rest had the good Luck to escape by reaching their Ship's Decks, and returned to old Spain.[11]

In May anno 1562 one Ribault a Frenchman made the Land and Mouth of Savannah Stream, put in and went up the Creek, which seperates Hilten Head Island from the Main, landed at the Mouth of a River on the West Shore of aforesaid Creek, which Ribaut called May, took Possession for his King, who at that time was Charles the ninth, and built a Fort upon River May in Latd. 32°07' which he called Caroline.[12]

Philip the second being informed of it gave a Commission for the Government of Florida to Pedro Melendez,[13] with order to drive away the French, recognize [*reconnoiter*] and survey the Coast, and remit a Plan of it for the Direction of his Subjects, who should navigate that Coast; in consequence of which Melendez evacuated in 1563 (a) Fort Caroline and Garrisoned it with Spaniards; which (as his principal) Order being executed he now proceeded to the Survey of the Coast, without which he would not have been able to pitch upon the most suitable Place for settling the Seat of his Government, doubtless he did choose it as centrical as possible between the Havanna and Fort Caroline; of course his Surveys would have brought him to Ays (now Hillsborough) Inlet nearest, but the

(a) The Expiration of the first and beginning of the second Spanish Epoche, determining a half Century spent with Effects of avarice, signalized on the Continent of Florida.

Entrance being double-barred, with very little water upon the Bars Channel, nor high Land to settle within; he of course was obliged (no better Inlet being to the Southward of it) to choose the nearest to the North; Muskito Inlet was the first, its bar [*110*] well provided with Water, but no Land to command the Inlet, except what will be overflowed at every Spring Tide: Melendez therefore was obliged to pitch upon the next northern Inlet, which he called Saint Augustin, altho' its bar was not much better stoked [*stocked*] with water than that of the Muskitoes; yet the Land which commanded the Road of the Inlet, and also the open Sea, had to its N. E. the River Talomeko, which seperated it from the Sea Coast forming the north side of the Road; also by Matanze Creek, which cut from the Main Anastasia Island to its S. E. to the West a Rivulet (he called Saint Sebastian) which made the Main to a small Peninsula, of which with little Expence and in a short time by a Fortification Line carried across from Saint Sebastian's Rivulet to Talomeko River,[14] may incompass a Spot of Land to secure and accommodate 1,000 Men if Occasion[*ed*], of course Melendez gave Saint Augustin the Preference, which evidently appears without Conjecture by the Execution of his Plan on that Spot, first as to the Town of Saint Augustin; secondly by the Fortification Line across the Peninsula, and thirdly by the casematted Fort of Saint Marks opposite and commanding the Road of the Inlet.[15]

Melendez was not only the first Spaniard, who made an Establishment in Florida, but also the only who made any Settlement, and it is he with whom the second Spanish Epoche begins on their Continent; his Settlement confines all honour to himself, for little Addition has been made to it after him, altho' his Successors were undisturbed on the Continent of Florida for a Century, yet they shewed no Industry either under Ground moling after what fire will run into Bullion, and exchanges the Goods of the Merchant, nor above Ground plowing after what water and fire will modifie into Bread, feeds the Body and cherishes Life, therefore the Sentence of the unprofitable Servant did justly fall upon them at the end of 100 years vide, in 1663 (a) when Charles the Second King of England drove these Sluggards out of their worm eaten Nest in Carolina, confined them to Melendez's Seat of Government upon Talomeko River and Matenze Creek at Saint Augustin, and teached them by his Example, what good use they might have made both by Industry of the Land, and by Humanity of its aboriginal Inhabitants through a Course of 150 years since Ponce's Discovery, or of 100 years since Melendez's Settlement.

[*111*] At Saint Augustin the Spaniards enjoyed 100 years more Respite to try themselves whether they were the People capable to copy after others, to be as

(a) The Expiration of the second and beginning of the third Spanish Epoche, compleating the first full Century of evidencing the Spanish natural effeminacy and Lasyness.

industrious, to produce the intrinsical Virtue of a Country, as ingenious they had proved themselves of their own accord by inventing a Name for it; but shewing all this while their Effeminacy and Lasyness, [*on*] the Continent of Florida; their Sentence became therefore peremptory with their Crime, and Providence appointed His present Majesty George the third to set, anno 1763 (a) the Period to the Spanish Epoches on a Spot of Land, which they did, or would not know, what to do with, and in lieu of making it flourishing they rather contributed all, they were able, for its fading, at the same time when that part (which had 100 years passed, exchanged both Florida Name and Spanish Masters) has proved itself an industrious Nurse to many thousands in Europe, who would otherwise have shared with the Invalids of Famine; thus the years 1513, 1563, 1663, and 1763 become Objects of Speculation as well as they are special Epochs in the History of America.

The pompous Name Florida, which by extending itself for 250 years on one of the greatest Tracts of the World has contented itself with baffling the Universe is now cancelled from the Lands it hath usurped and is suffered only to continue near its Source, where with a small and perhaps prophetical Adjective of (Orient) it appears afresh under the Name of East Florida under new Masters, in which Reformation it has exerted itself in eight years time preferably to its next Neighbour Georgia, which had not shewen in 22 years what in the least Fraction is equal to East Florida's eight years Industry and Export, altho' East Florida labours under the same Inconvenience, as Georgia did for a course of 22 years for want of a House of Representatives, which want has evidently proved the Cause of Georgia's backwardness from 1732 to 1754; since the first Product and Export of the year 1755 in value consisting of £15,744 Sterling must be allowed to have proceeded from that Liberty, which Georgia enjoyed for the first time under their first General Assembly of Representatives joined to the Authority of a Governor and Council in 1754, and has increased every year after, so that the last of 16 years vide, 1770 the value of its [*112*] Produce and Export amounted to £99,383 Sterling and at this rate in 14 years more vide, anno 1783 the Value of that year's Exportation will be £177,120 Sterling, when Georgia for 22 years vide, from 1732 to 1754, had no General Assembly of Representatives, during which time did not export for the Value of 22 Shillings Sterling; this fully evinces, what East Florida will be in time to come with the Assistance of a General Assembly of Representatives.

East Florida begins its Epoche in Saint Augustin at the Expiration of the third Spanish Epoche, and from the Treaty of Peace made between the two Crowns of England and Spain in 1763, when all the Spanish Claims on the Continent of

(a) The end of the third Spanish Epoche concluding with the second full Century and proving the Spanish Philauty too elated as to copy after any Nation but their own.

North America were given up, and all Spanish Settlements thereon vide, that of Saint Augustin and Pensacola ceded to the Crown of England forever.

The Inhabitants with their Characters from the Beginning of its English Epoche appear in the following alphabetical List.

A LIST
Of the Inhabitants of East Florida, their Employs, Business and Qualifications in Science from 1763 to 1771.

Names	Traders	Innkeepers and Livers in Town	Artificers and Mechanics	Planters, Cowkeepers and Hunters	left the Province	Dead	In the King's Employ and Qualifications as Underneath				
							Draughtsmen	Mathematicians	Navigators	Mariner	In the Surveyor General's Employ
Alexander	Haberdas.										
Albert Frederik				Planter							
Anderson James			Shoemaker								
Bachop Adam							Master of the E. Florida Schooner				
Bagly			Butcher	Planter							
Baker Benjamin				Planter	left Prov.						
Bartram William			Butcher	Planter	left Prov.		Draught.				
Bell		Inn keeper		Planter							
Bernard Charles				Planter							
Bisset Robert Esqr.				Planter				Mathem.			
Blackwell	Store Keeper			Planter		Dead.					
Bollimore			blacksmith	Planter							
Bonsal Roberts				Planter							
Bell			ship corker								
Blathan Nathan											
Box James Esqr.				Planter		Dead.	His Majesty's Attorney General				
Bradshaw Tadeus					left Prov.					Mariner	in Employ
Brandon John				Cow keeper							
Bryan James senior				Planter							
Bryan James junior				Planter							
Bryan Langley				Planter	left Prov.						
Broun			House Carpenter								
Bunckly John											
Burdet Sir Charles							His Majesty's Counsellor				
Burnet John				Cowkeeper	left Prov.						
Burnet John										Mariner	in Employ
Burton Thomas				Planter							
Cadden Richard		Innkeeper									
Cass					left Prov.						
Catherwood Robert Esqr.					left Prov.		His Majesty's Counsellor	Bachelor of Art.			
Caudry Thomas				Planter							
Chapman Arthur					left Prov.					Marriner	in Employ
Chetwood Joseph							Draught.	Mathematician. Messenger of Council.			in Employ
Clark Agnus		Inn keeper		Cow keeper							
Clark Thomas	Store keeper		goldsmith								
Clark William				Planter							
Clements			Ship Carpenter								
Coen	Store keeper				left Prov.						

[113]

Coles				
Colis				
Collins William Esqr.		Attorney at Law		
Comning Walter	Cow keeper		left Prov.	
Cooly Gabriel	Planter			
Cox	Store keeper			
Curvoisieux David	Planter			
Cross John	Planter		left Prov.	
Cunning Witter Esqr.		Navigator		
		His Majesty's Counsellor		
Cunningham Henry Esqr.		Assistant Judge	Dead	
Current Samuel	Planter		left Prov.	
	Planter		left Prov.	

[114]

Dacosta Isaac	Storekeeper		left Prov.	
Davies John	Planter	Draught.	Mathem.	Dead
				in employ
Davies Rober Esqr.	Planter		left Prov.	
Dawson	Planter		left Prov.	
De Brahm William Esqr.		His Majesty's Surveyor General.	not in Prov.	
Delacheroy Nicholas		Draughtsman in the Army.	left Prov.	
Delaire James		Draughtsman. . Mathematician.	left Prov.	in Employ.
Devaux John	Planter		left Prov.	
Dias Casimore Josh.		Marriner.	left Prov.	in Employ.
Dinkinson William	Planter		left Prov.	
Drakis John	Planter		left Prov.	
Drayton William Esqr.		Chief Justice	left Prov.	
Dunlap	Storekeeper			
Dunn John Esqr.		Attorney at Law	not in Prov.	
Dunnet John Esqr.	Planter	His Majesty's Counsellor.	Dead	
Dupont James		Draughtsman. . Mathematician.	left Prov.	in Employ.
Dyason Joseph		In the Army.	left Prov.	
Diamond Thomas		Navigator.	left Prov.	in Employ.

Earl John	Overseer.		left Prov.
Edniston Robert	Planter.	In the Army.	left Prov.
Egleston	Innkeeper.		
Egmont Earl	Planter.		
Elsenor	liver in town.		
English John		Indian Interpreter.	Dead.
Evans Middleton	Ship Carpenter.		Dead.
Evelin John	Mason.	Planter.	

Fairchild Henry		Draughtsman. . Mathematician.	left Prov.	in Employ.
Fairlamb John Esqr.	Planter.			
Fish Jesse	Planter.			
Forbes Jon. Esqr. Reverend		Parson.	Judge. . Admiral. . Counsellor.	
	Store keeper			
Forbes James	Overseer.			
Forbes William	Planter.		left Prov.	
Forne Carlos	overseer			
Frasers N. Reverend		hanged for pirating.		
Fraser William		Parson at the Muskitoes.		
Funck John	Store keeper	Mathematician.		in Employ.

A LIST (Continued)

Names	Traders	Innkeepers and Livers in Town	Artificers and Mechanics	Planters, Cowkeepers and Hunters	left the Province	Dead	Draughtsmen	Mathematicians	Navigators	Marriner	In the Surveyor General's Employ
											[115]
Galahan			house Carpenter		left Prov.						
Gallewin				Overseer	left Prov.					Marriner	in Employ
Gay Benjamin				Planter	left Prov.						
Gilbert Ephraim									Navigator		
Gilbert John			house Carpenter			Dead					
Grahme Thomas Esqr.				Planter	left Prov.		Stamp Master				
Grant James Esqr. Excellency					not in Prov.		Governor in Chief				
Gray Alexander Esqr.				Planter							
Gray Edmond				Planter							
Gray Joseph				Planter	left Prov.		Indian Interpreter				in Employ
Gray William				Planter							
Greening William				Planter		Dead					
Greenwood William				Planter			Naval Officer				
Goodby Joseph				Hunter							
Grondin N.											
Gordon Arthur			Ship Carpenter				Attorney General				
Hainsman Anthony				Planter							
Haly John		liver in town					Deputy Post Master				
Hall N.		liver in town									
Hall N.		Liver in town									
Hamilton Frans.				Planter							
Hancock Anthony				Planter							
Hancock John			Cooper								
Handerson James		Innkeeper									
Hannah George			Mason								
Hannah Thomas			Mason								
Harrahbusky N.	Shopkeeper										
Harvey John				Planter	left Prov.						
Harris Henry			house Carpenter								
Harris Robert				Planter	left Prov.				Navigator		
Hastings Thomas				Planter	left Prov.						
Haughton John			house Carpenter								
Hawksworth Enoch	Haberdasher				left Prov.		Schoolmaster for Augustin.				
Hayman Henry				Planter	left Prov.						
Hazard Richd. senior				Planter							
Hazard Richd. junior				Planter							
Hester William				Planter							
Hewit John	Shopkeeper	Innkeeper	Joiner								
											[116]
Higdon John				Lime burner							

...eson Jeremiah			Planter		
Hog N.					
Holmes John Esqr.			Planter	killed acting as Constable	
Holmes Robert			Planter		His Majesty's Counsellor
Hope		house Carpenter			
Humbert Godfried		house Carpenter		Dead	
Humphrys N.			Overseer	left Prov.	
Hunt Miller Hill Esqr.			Planter	left Prov.	
Jenkin William	Liver in town		Planter	left Prov.	
Johnston John	Innkeeper		Planter	In the Army	
Johnston Joseph			Hunter		
Johnston Timothy	Innkeeper		Planter		
Johnston William		Lime burner			
Johnston William		Shoemaker			
Jollie		Shoemaker			
Jollie George		Turner	Overseer		
Jollie Martin Esqr.			Planter	left Prov.	Assistant Judge
Jones Abraham			Planter		
Jones John			Planter		
Kemp George			Overseer		Surgeon
Kennedy Daniel			Overseer		
Kenward John	liver in town				Store keeper of the Ordnance
Kepp Jacobus			Planter		
Kinlock Frans. Esqr.			Planter	Dead	His Majesty's Counsellor
Laidler Geo. senior	Storekeeper		Planter	left Prov.	
Laidler Geo. junior			Planter	Dead	
Laidler Thomas			Planter	left Prov.	Draughtsman
Laweson John			Planter	left Prov.	
Lee Philip		Cowkeeper			
Letson David		Carpenter			
Letson Robert		Carpenter			
Levett Frans. Esqr.			Planter		Assistant Judge
Lewis Joseph				Mathematician	in Employ
Long N.		house Carpenter	Planter		
Luxenburg N.	Innkeeper	Turner		killed acting as Constable	
Landsford N.			Planter		

[117]

Macdugal William Esqr.			Planter		
Man Spencer Esqr.	Storekeeper		Planter		Notary Public
Manuel George	liver in Town			left Prov.	
Marchal	liver in Town.				
Martin David	Storekeeper				
Mason John		Taylor		Dead	
Mason John	Innkeeper				
McCloud	Storekeeper		Planter	left Prov.	
Magraw			Planter		
McIntosh William	liver in Town.		Planter		
Mckay John	Innkeeper		Planter		

A LIST (Continued)

Names	Traders	Innkeepers and Livers in Town	Artificers and Mechanics	Planters, Cowkeepers and Hunters	left the Province	Dead	Draughtsmen	Mathematicians	Navigators	Mariner	In the Surveyor General's Employ
Mckay William				Planter							
Meech John			Baker		left Prov.						
Mckenzie Collin			Butcher								
Meyer N.		Innkeeper			left Prov.						in Employ
Mills George				Overseer			As Pack horse Man				
Mills Samuel				Planter							
Mills William				Planter							
Mills Thomas				Planter							
Moncrief James				Planter			In the Army				
Mitchell N.			Barber								
Moore John			Butcher								
Morris Thomas				Planter							
Morphay Daniel				Planter	left Prov.						
Moses Meyer	Storekeeper										
Moses Michael	Storekeeper			Planter		Dead.	Chief Justice.				
Moultrie James Esqr.				Planter			Lieut. Governor.				
Moultrie John Esqr.				Planter			In the Army.				
Mulcaster Fr. Geo. Esqr.											
Mulling James				Planter	left Prov.						
Murphy N.					left Prov.						in Employ
Nash N.	Storekeeper			Planter		Dead.					
Noble George				Cowkeeper							
Noland Andrew	Storekeeper					Dead.					
Norelief William					[118]						
Oliver John		Watchman				Dead.					
Oswald Richd. Esqr.				Planter							
Owen William Esqr.							Attorney at Law.				
Parson Thomas			Barber								
Payne Robert	Storekeeper										
Pearson John				Planter							
Pen William				Planter		Dead.	Jack of the Store of Ordnance.				
Penman Hugh								Mathematician.			in Employ
Penman James Esqr.				Planter							
Perry Marmadak				Overseer							
Petit Amos				Planter							
Pig Paul				Planter							
Potton Jeremiah				Planter	left Prov.						
Powell N.							Deputy Provost Marshal.				

Prichard Richd.	Surgeon in the Army
Prusias	hanged for pirating
Purcell James	house Carpenter .. Planter .. Planter
Purcell Joseph	Planter .. left Prov. .. Draughtsman .. Mathematician. Navigator .. in Employ
Rains Cornelius	Planter
Rainsford Andrew	saw miller .. left Prov. .. in the Army
Reddy William	Planter
Richardson John	Storekeeper .. Indian Trader
Ried Thomas	Planter
Robert Benjamin	Storekeeper .. left Prov.
Rodget Barton	Storekeeper .. left Prov.
Rogers Thomas	Storekeeper .. Planter .. Draughtsman .. Mathematician .. in Employ
Rolfes George Esqr.	not in Prov. .. Member of Parliament
Rolle Denys Esqr.	Planter .. left Prov. .. Navigator .. in Employ
Rollin Daniel	Draughtsman .. Mathematician. Navigator .. in Employ
Roman Bernard	house Carpenter . Overseer
Ross N.	Storekeeper .. Planter
Ross Robert	Planter
Ross William	Innkeeper
Rosseter Paul	

[119]

Row John Esqr.	Planter .. Mathematician .. in employ
Row Seton Wedderburne	Mathematician .. in employ
Rupell George Esqr.	left Prov.
Sanders N.	Indian Trader
Sangsten James	Pilot of Saint Augustine .. Marriner .. in Employ
Sax N.	Pilot of Saint Augustine
Senior George	Joiner .. left Prov. .. Navigator .. in Employ
Shneider N.	
Short N.	Storekeeper
Skinner Alexander Esqr.	Naval Officer
Skinner Henry	Planter
Smart Thomas	Planter
Smith James	Pilot of Saint Augustin .. Marriner .. in Employ
Smith Joseph	Planter .. left Prov. .. Marriner .. in Employ
Smith Samuel	Marriner .. in Employ
Smith N.	killed acting as Constable
Spalding James	Planter .. Indian Trader
Spell John	
Steven Richard	Taylor
Stone Thomas	liver in town
Stoneaker N.	Hunter
Storck William Esqr.	Dead .. Oculist, Physician
Stuart John Esqr.	left Prov. .. His Majesty's Counsellor
Stuart Robert	Planter .. left Prov.
Stillwill John	Marriner .. in Employ
Symour William	Planter .. left Prov.
Taylor William Esqr.	Planter .. Colonel in the Army
Turnbull Andrew Esqr.	Planter .. His Majesty's Counsellor.

A LIST (Continued)

Names	Traders	Innkeepers and Livers in Town	Artificers and Mechanics	Planters, Cowkeepers and Hunters	left the Province	Dead	In the King's Employ and Qualifications as Underneath				
							Draughts-men	Mathema-ticians	Naviga-tors	Marriner	In the Surveyor General's Employ
Thomas Joseph		Innkeeper									
Thomas William				Planter							
Thornton Christopher Esqr.		liver in Town			left Prov.						
Tompson N.		liver in Town									
Townsend Thomas Esqr.		liver in Town			left Prov.						
Trout N.			bricklayer		left Prov.						
Terry David				Overseer							
Tweedy Thomas			Taylor								
Vaughan N.			house Carpenter		left Prov.						
[120]											
Ward David										Marriner	in Employ
Warner Josiah							Pilot of Saint Augustin				
Warner N.			blacksmith				Pilot of Saint Augustin				
Way Andrew						killed acting as Constable					
Webly John							Draught.				in Employ
Wells Elton Andrew	Haberdasher							Mathematician			in Employ
Westcot			Butcher								
White Stephen			house Carp.	Overseer							
Wilder Jeremiah				Planter							
Wilkinson George		liver in town, where since he was crippled by the Indians		Planter							
Williams George		Innkeeper								Marriner	in Employ
William Stephen				Planter							
Williams N.				Planter							
Wilson John	Storekeeper					Dead					
Wilson William				Planter							
Wood John			house Carpenter								
Wooldredge Thomas Esqr.				Planter			Provost Marshal				
Woodford Isaac			house Carpenter		left Prov.					Marriner	in Employ
William N.			house Carpenter								
Yeats Davis Esqr.					left Prov.		Deputy Clerk of the Council				
Yeats N.			house Carpenter		left Prov.						
Yonge Charles							Draughtsman	Mathematician	Navigator		in Employ

Number of all Inhabitants and including Women or Children.... 288
Indented Servants from Greece, Minorco imported by Mr. Turnbull.... 1,400
Negroes upwards of 900

[*121*]

CHAPTER 2d

A general Description of East Florida, its Extent, in what Climate, Heat, principal Winds, Health, Pathology, Materia Medica, Regimen and Diet, with Observations on the Termoscope.

EAST FLORIDA, including the Marteers, extends from Lattitude 24°20′ to 30°26′49″, is comprehended in the fourth Climate, which begins in Latitude 23°50′ and ends in 30°20′.

The Beginning of this Climate splits the Entrance of the Gulph of Mexico at 10 minutes north from the Latitude of the Havanna, which lays in 23°40′; the longest day under the Seperation of the third and fourth Climate counts 13 hours and 30 minutes; under its middle (which by Survey falls in 15 1,083/8,000 miles North of Granville's, alias Jupiter Inlet) 13 hours and 45 minutes determine the longest day; and at the Meeting with the fifth (which is 7 5,005/8,000 miles to the North of Nassaw Inlet upon Amilia Island) this Climate allows the longest day to compleat full 14 hours.

By the great Heat which rises in this Climate the Quick Silver on the Termoscope [*climbs*] at times to the height of 121 degrees; this Country would be disinhabitable, were it not for the Trade Winds, which generally begin to blow from the East at nine ante meridiem, when the Earth has passed 45 degrees under the Sun's Inclination, at which time the Sun begins to press powerfully upon the Atmosphere of the Earth, and a Calm ensues, the Winds pressed between the Atmosphere and the Earth (which in its Motion to the East at all times inclines the Winds to assume the same Motion) return in the Night to the East; in the Morning the Earth by her diurnal Rotation opening to the Sun, her Pressure altho' not effectual to repress, yet sufficient to stop the Winds in their course upon the vast Extent of the Atlantic Ocean, where they then lay quiet until the Progression of the Earth's Motion brings them under the Sun's Inclination of 45 degrees, as common, when they laying in an Angle of 135 degrees are, as with a Shove, repressed to the west again. These Winds thus trading to and fro temperate the scorching Heat of the Sun, after She has rarified the Vapours arising from the Marshes, Swamps, Ponds, Lakes, and Rivers; so that the Heat of the Sun in this Climate is not only very agreeably tempered, but also the Air exceedingly serene, of course healthy, even preferably to all more northern Climates, and most on the whole Globe.[16]

[*122*] These Trade Winds do not regularly transgress the northern Limits of

the fourth Climate, therefore they are very seldom and irregularly felt in the next Provinces under the fifth Climate, where the Inhabitants however enjoy regularly the good Effect of its focus from the South, of which mention is made near the end of the 2d Chapter in the History of South Carolina.

A moderate Person willing to observe those Directions for preserving Health mentioned at the Conclusion of the aforesaid Chapter will bring his days to a great Number. Among those 3,000 which evacuated Saint Augustin, the Author is credibly informed, were many Spaniards, upwards of 100 years of Age (observe). This Nation, especially Natives of Saint Augustin, bore the Reputation of great Sobriety; however in case accidental Causes should afflict the new Inhabitants with one or other Disease; the Author has experienced, that early Remedies and such, as he has advanced in the Third Chapter of the History of South Carolina are of quicker Effect, than they prove in any part of the World from the 26th degree East, to the 83d degree west Longitude from London, and from 50° to 24° north Latitude, a Compass of 3,479 square degrees, which he has traversed upon several Rombis, on many of which he has been distressed with sore and herculean Fevers, and has been an Eye Witness of others labouring in similar Cases; He has also, and several of his Ship's Company variously been attaqued with Fevers in East Florida, who with his Prescription of Diet, Regimen, and Medicines, he has experienced them the most flexible, and almost infant Disorders, even after they had been for some time striking Root.

Since all, what has been said in Pathology, Materia Medica, Regimen, and Diet has by Experience proved applicable to this Climate without requiring any Alteration either by adding or subtracting from it, the Author begs leave for refering to the 3d Chapter of South Carolina for Particulars.

In Order to collect, if possible all natural Causes peculiar to the Effect of each Climate in Conjunction with those of the Country under its Dominion, he has with the utmost Care observed and noted the rising and falling of the Quick Silver on the Termoscope, not only in the Shade, but also in the Sun, judging the latter Observation to be the most material, since the Inhabitants and their Cattle cannot always remain in the Shade, and their Nourishment must be produced in the Fields and exposed to the Sun; He has also found the Sky being sometimes clear, then foggy, cloudy or hazy; the Winds in their Changes bringing at times Rain, then Squalls, Thunder or Storms, all [of] which however not always by the same Effect, he therefore has endeavoured to aggregate whatever would present itself opposite to his Attentions, he has continued this Observation near 35 months, vide, from June 1767 to April 1770 as well in [*123*] Saint Augustin as other Places, where his Duty did call and his Surveys would lead him, some of which he had an Opportunity to compare, when he was Possessor of two Termoscopes, and obtained northern & southern Observations of the same date, during which time he never found the Quick Silver to rise above 91 degrees in the shade and 121 degrees in the Sun, and never observed it fell nearer to the Ball than at a distance of 35, which is 20 degrees below tempered. He also observed that different Winds in Combination with the different degrees of heat, altho' they repeated their Power upon the Quick Silver on the Termoscope, yet they had not always the same Effect upon the human Body, nor caused the same Phoenomena, as the following Table of 35 months Observation will shew.

[*124*] [On this folio De Brahm began his "Ephemeris" or daily record of weather conditions during the years 1767, 1768, 1769, and 1770. This record includes temperatures, sky conditions, and wind directions as well as the place and latitude of the observation. It is an interesting and valuable scientific compilation which has been omitted only because of its extended length. Manuscript folios 124 through 152 are entirely devoted to the "Ephemeris" and are omitted here.]

[*153*]

CHAPTER 3d

When and in what manner the Boundaries of East Florida were regulated, what part and by whom surveyed: the Geometrical Operations represented in Tables.

By the Treaty of Peace in 1763 the Crown of Spain has resigned all her Possessions, Rights and Claims of Lands on the Continents of North America, formerly by Her signalized with the Name of Florida, and has the said Continent of Florida, with all her Claims, Rights, and Possessions forever ceded and the Concession solemnly ratified unto the Crown of Great Britain, to hold all Lands on the said Continent of Florida, with all Spanish Claims, Rights, and Possessions forever.[17]

This whole Continent from the North Pole to the Extremity of the Marteers, stretching forth under a Meridian of 66 degrees, or 4,587 English Miles, is now a contiguous lawful Possession and properly annexed to the Realm of Great Britain, which has no small Reason to rejoice in her promising Daughter the Hesperian Albionia, an Acquisition of the two greatest Britons, August Charles the 2d of glorious Memory, who built the Hesporian Albionia, and George the 3d who masted and rigged her, an Honour to the Atlantic Ocean, who glories in his Bed, between a magnificent Europe on its East, and a flourishing ulterior Albion on its West.

By Order of his present Majesty the last Acquisition is divided in two Provinces, the yonder is called West, and the hither East Florida; the Boundaries of the latter are drawn and fixed in the following manner.[18]

[*154*] To the North, beginning at the Fork of the Apalachicola Stream, which branches [*into*] two Rivers, Flint and Chatahutchee (a); from said Fork a Line is drawn (as yet not surveyed) to the Place, where Saint Mary's Stream departs from the famous Ockanphanoko Swamp,[19] in which this Stream takes its Sources, and runs Northeastwardly with the general Course as far as where (this very day) one Sanders keeps an Indian Store for the Conveniency of those Indians,[20] who hunt both sides of said Swamp, which they esteem their best hunting Ground; from Sander's Store the Stream takes a great Sweep with many Meanders, as if determining what general Course to take for its Issue, assumes at last an East Direction, wherewith it discharges its Waters in the Atlantic Ocean in Latitude 30°25'49", and 1°12'22 1/2", West Longitude from Cape Florida.

These aforesaid Traverses set the Boundary between this Province and that of Georgia. The true Distance is 29 31/80 miles from Sander's Store to the Stream's Mouth and was measured by the Author in 1770; the Survey of which appears in his general Map of East Florida, and the Geometrical Operation in the following Tables.

[Folios 155 through 172 consist of a number of mathematical computations and tables titled "Tables Comprehending the General Land Surveys of Part of Saint Mary's River, as the North Boundary and Of the Sea Coast from the Mouth of St. Mary's to Dartmouth Inlet at Cape Florida as the East Boundary of East Florida Adjusted in a General Table by William Gerard de Brahm His Majesty's Surveyor General for the Southern District of North America." They represent the field observations which De Brahm performed in his surveys and are omitted here because of their technical nature and limited interest.]

[*173*] The foregoing General Table comprehends the Survey of the Eastern Boundary of East Florida performed by Land with Chain and Theodolite Geometrically, and the Inlets by taking the unaccessible Angles Trionometrically. By this general Table is proved how difficult it is to avoid in short distances of 30, or 40 miles either to loose or gain upon the Meridian and Parallels, and consequently how necessary it is to adjust a whole Survey of a (3 or 400 miles) Meridian by

(a) seems to have retained the Name from its ancient Inhabitants the Cafasichee, by Corruption of Tradition handed to later Indians and altered into Chatahutchee.

one general distance and Course, in order to obtain the true Length of the Meridian and exact Parallels of the whole Survey.

The Author cannot but observe also, how necessary it is, that the Astronomical Observations on the principal Places are made for two or three days running in Company of three or more Observators especially on the South and North Extremities of the Survey, as otherwise the true Latitudes of the Places and the Magnetical Deviation from the true Meridian of these Places cannot be had exact; the Neglect or want of the Difference, which is between the Magnetical and true Meridian at different Places is of great Consequence, for if the Variation is Easterly, the true Meridians & West Longitudes will decrease in a Survey carried on Southeastwardly, but in a Survey proceeding Northeastwardly the Meridians and West Longitudes will increase, and so vice versa, in case the Surveys are performed Southwest or Northwestward; and all Alterations are reversed, if so that the magnetical Meridian bends to the west of the true Meridian, consequently without the Preciseness of the Magnetical Variation the Differences of Latitudes and Longitudes must be erroneous, and the true shape of the Land cannot be obtained.

Saint Augustin and Cape Florida are the principal Places which the Author has endeavoured to fix in their proper Latitudes by repeated Astronomical Observations, whereby He has made Augustin in Latitude 29°38′59″ and Cape Florida in 25°42′42″, which makes a difference of 3°56′17″. The Survey carried on with the greatest Exactness and the Meridians adjusted at every principal Place, made up no more than a general Meridian of 3°54′48″, which is 0°1′29″ less by Survey than Observation; But when the Author joined all Meridians and Longitudes seperately in one, to adjust the general Distance and Course, after correcting the latter by the Magnetical Variation of the Cape, he found his Meridian to be 3°57′49″ which is 0°3′1″ to the South of the Meridian obtained by the former Operation and 0°1′32″ to the South of the Meridian acquired by Observation, so that there is either a deficiency in the Observation at Augustin or at Cape Florida; if Cape Florida is in its proper Latitude, then it remains in 25°42′42″ and Augustin is in 29°40′31″; but if Cape Florida is not in its Latitude, and Augustin is right, the latter remains in 29°38′59″ and the Cape moves to Lattd. 25°41′10″, as is fixed for the present by the Meridian obtained through the last Operation, which appears in the Conclusion of the General Table.[21]

[174] The Difference existing between the two Operations (vide, the one by adjusting Meridians of 40, 50 or less miles distances, and the other by adjusting a Meridian of 275 3,678/8,000 miles in length) is in the foregoing Survey at a rate of 12 in 1,000 Links, or 10 in 1,000 Seconds; which difference the Author finds no Difficulty to account for and rectify, but the difference of 92 Seconds between

the observed Length of the Meridian and that obtained by an adjusted Survey, the Author (altho' fully convinced of its possibility) does not think accomodable in another and surer Manner, than by the Co-operation of more Mathematicians in one Survey, Observation and the Calculations of both, which especially in surveying flow through several Operations from a quarter of a mile to three and ten; these again to 40 and 50, and so on until They swell in a Sum of 3 and 400 miles, where, if any Error appear the whole Stream of Arithmetical Operations must be traced to its very source which Herculean Labor exceeds all Difficulties in Mathematics, requires therefore a Plurality of Arithmeticians, not only to share the Burden, but to adjust exact Surveys with precise Observations.

The daily Practice and Experience at Sea (where that Exactness is not required, as in Land Surveys) proves a Necessity of several Operators in Observations and Calculations; the more necessary is therefore a Number of Mathematicians to aid each other in Land Surveys, where all the Preciseness in Observations and Calculations is required; the Proof of this Assertion is evident by the great Difficulties in adjusting and comparing the Observations with Surveys and Calculations of the famous Operations performed for discovering the Elipsoide under the Equator in Perou, in which Operations, altho six Mathematicians joined from the year 1736, to 1741, yet they have not flattered themselves with a general Success.[22]

The Instruments in Use both at Sea and Land the Author observes also to want some Reformation, as per instance, the Chart in the Compasses to be made of thin horn rather than Paper; the Reels of the Lock Lines to run in a Frame between two Points in lieu of runing upon a Stick,[23] on which they move with the greatest heavyness. The Minute Glasses not to be cemented of two but blown together of one Glass.

The Observations to be taken with Hadly's Sextants;[24] but as this Instrument requires a North or South Horizon, either of which on all places, as in some Bays upon the Sea Coasts, is not to be had, he advises an Improvement to that Instrument; of a moving triangular Miror, to be bent either to the right side, if the Horizon is West, or on the left side, if the Horizon lays East. The Basis of this Miror is to be equal to the Breadth, and its Perpendicular to the Length of that Miror, which is fixed to the Center of the Sextant; the triangular Miror is joined to the middle of the upper part [175] of the fixed Miror by a small Ball and Socket, so as to humour it to the Angles of Inflection and Reflection, and adapt it to the Horizon's under all Points of the Compass, and the measuring Chain He proposes to be exchanged for a measuring Wheel, expecially upon the Sea Beach and Roads, where nothing obstructs its Procession.[25]

It is said to be an uncommon Instance, that two Observations made by two Persons on one Spot and one day, with equally constructed Instruments, do agree to a Minute, but the Author can assure, that with proper care of those, who observed sometimes with him, he met with such Incident to a Second.

Besides the Geometrical Operations on Shore, the Author has performed also Loxodromical Surveys with two Vessels and Boats upon the Coast, in order to obtain the Soundings, and of the Florida Stream its Settings to the North, as also its distance from the Shore, but as the Loxodromical Tables are very voluminous, and do cover more than twice the Number of Pages (as are filled up by the foregoing Tables) He apprehends the 3d Chapter of the East Floridan History would become tedious.[26] His Reason for inserting the Tables of the Land Survey is to show the Nature of his Method and Practice, by which and with what Preciseness the Meridians and Heighths of Climate, as also the Shape of the Land is obtained, to which a Loxodromical Survey the Author does not think can possibly approach so minutely, notwithstanding of his good Success, between Saint Augustin and Mukoso Inlet, where his Loxodromical difference of Latitude does not differ above a mile from that of his Land Survey. The Author will have an Occasion to join to his future Report a Table of Loxodromical, where He cannot have an Opportunity of a Land Survey, by which a Specimen of his Hydrometrical Method will then appear.

The Southern Boundary of this Province begins at Dartmouth Inlet, and is specified by a Chain of forty eight principal Islands, of which thirty six are laid down in the General Map[27]—these forty eight Islands are made known by the Author with new and old Names vide,

old 1 Biskaino	old 5 Losparadizos	new 9 Pollock
new 2 Oswald	old 6 Soldiers	new 10 Pownall
new 3 Laurens	old 7 Soldiers	new 11 Elliot
old 4 Losparadizos	new 8 Knox	new 12 Jenins

At the End of these twelve Islands, ranks in a Peninsula from the Main, joining the Continent by a very narrow Isthmus, which bears S. S. W. from Dartmouth Inlet, and near West from the S. W. end of Jenin's Island, stretching from said Isthmus upon a S. S. W. Course, a Distance of 33 1/2 miles.[28]

[176] This formerly supposed Island went by the Name of Kayo Larga; but since it is discovered by the Author to be part of the Continent, it is known by the Name of Isthmus Larga ⊙ S. E. of which the two remarkable Islands Fox and Stephen's, alias Rodoriquez and Tabonas seem to have been Capes detached from Larga.

South west of this Peninsula, the rest of the forty eight Islands, partly called by the Author with the following, and partly retaining their former Spanish Names, vide,

⊙ PenInsula Larga

new 15	Bull	27		38	Rice
new 16	Wright	28		39	Jennings
old 17.	Matacombe lamosa	29	These Vacas are a Cluster of	40	Robinson
new 18	Boys	30	Islands appearing as one Island	41	Roberts
old 19.	Matanze (a)	31	towards Hawke Channel.	42	Lyttleton
old 20	Matacombe la Viega old	old { 32 } Vacas	new names	43	Glen
old 21	Vivera	33		44	Oglethorp
old 22	Reynolds	34		45	Edwards
new 23	Ellis	35		46	Fitzherbert
old { 24 25 26 } vacas		36	old	47	Hueso (b)
		37 / Newcastle		48	Tortugas

The whole Chain of the aforesaid Islands and Peninsula, on a general Course from Dartmouth Inlet, runs S. 38° 25′ West, which is S. W. by S. 1/2 W. 163 miles; and from thence across Richmond Bay to Cape Sable which bears from Dartmouth Inlet, S. W. 1/2 W. 74 miles, and from the East End of Matacombe la Viega W. N. W. 32 1/2 miles.

Thus the Southern Boundary of East Florida is fixed by aforesaid natural Marks of forty eight Islands, bordering upon Hawke Channel, which by a Ridge of Rocks and Sand Banks generally called the Martyros, or Marteers, is seperated from the Florida Stream in the Outlet of the Gulph of Mexico.

The general and precise Survey of these Islands has been carried on to the 36th vide, Newcastle Island, and is as far laid down in the general Map: the Survey of which Islands have been executed seperately with Chain and Theodolite, and their Seperations measured trionometrically by obtaining the unaccessible Angle on the opposite Shores of each, by which latter Method are also ascertained the Distances from the east End of Matacombe la Viega, to the Dysom Islands, from them to Cooper's, from Cooper's to Bradshaw's, and from the latter to Cape Sable, by the Spaniards called Punta Yucha, the Meaning of which derives from its Form, being neither round, square, or pointed, that is to say an irregular Figure.

[Folio 176 is the last making up the first bound section of De Brahm's Report, Kings Ms. 210. An error was made in the continuation of the pagination into Kings Ms. 211, the second "Tome." Tome Two begins on folio 173 rather than folio 177. As a result De Brahm's Report contains two folios 173, two folios 175, and two folios 176.]

(a) signifying Massacre, from an unhappy Crew, wrecked on Matacombe, and said to have been massacred thereon by the Caloosa Indians.

(b) signifying Bone, probably thus called from its Figure, resembling a Jaw Bone

TOME 2d,

or the Continuation of the

REPORT

of the GENERAL SURVEYS

In the Southern District of

NORTH AMERICA

By WILLIAM GERARD DE BRAHM *Esqr.*

His MAJESTY's Surveyor General

for the said Department.

To the King's most Excellent Majesty,

Sire,

The 2d of April 1773, I had the distinguished Honour to present to Your Majesty my first report, in which I account for the Provinces of South Carolina and Georgia, with special surveys represented in fourteen draughts, with many observations. To which I joined those I made in East Florida, with a list of the aboriginal English Inhabitants. I have specified the effects of climate in this province on ephemerical tables of one thousand four hundred and twenty days observations, and added the General Survey of the north and east boundaries of said Province in thirteen tables with my remarks thereon.

I have now the honour to present to Your Majesty the second tome or continuation of said report, containing in two sections of accurate maps, the north and southern boundaries, with the general inland surveys, of East Florida, which I express in twenty six tables, specifying all courses and distances of the whole mensuration, from which is laid down that part of the inland, which shall be represented in the northernmost section of the four general maps; also the actual surveys of all practicable inlets from the Atlantic Ocean in the different streams of East Florida, with all Islands, in nine draughts, to each Inlet I join the necessary directions for navigators, as also the direction of the whole sea coast, and from America across the Atlantic Ocean to the English Channel, all from my own careful surveys and observations, to which I add one loxodromical table promised in my first report, and a chart of the Atlantic Ocean of my Hydrometrical performance, and conclude with the object of beacons, to render thereby the navigation on the bars of the inlets upon the Atlantic Ocean practicable in time of bad weather, when Pilots are prevented from venturing out the harbours to bring in vessels, which are either in distress without, or are bound in, which object has carried my attention to a place more anxious for immediate remedy to guide, and aid those, who navigate the gulf of Mexico thro' that dangerous & inevitable passage between the island of Cuba and the promontory of East Florida, where I think it of the utmost necessity, that two Pharusses should be erected, one on the east, and the other on the west extremity of the promontory.

[*176*] These Pharuses signalized with the excellent appellations of George and Charlotte,[29] would eternalize the glory of those Royal Authors, who have streatched out parental hands to facilitate the hitherto dangerous, and inevitable

navigation of that dreadful promontory and terminate Your Majesty's conquest of that great Country, which sets the western bounds of the Atlantic Ocean.

I annex a plan of a Pharus, partly in profile, and partly in its outside view, with a table of measurement, materials & expences.

This performance I most humbly submit as a proof of my unwearied applications, diligence and carefulness to answer the purport of Your Majesty's trust reposed and precise commands layed upon me, who, prostrate at Your Majesty's Throne, am, with the most profound humility,

Your Majesty's

Most dutiful Subject

And Servant

William Gerard de Brahm.

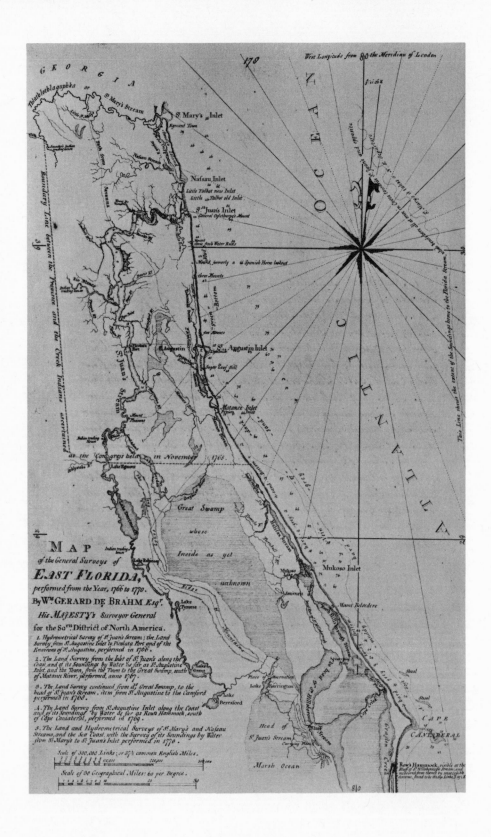

MAP
of the General Surveys of
EAST FLORIDA,
performed from the Year, 1766 to 1770.
By Wm. GERARD DE BRAHM Esqr.
His MAJESTY's Surveyor General
for the South District of North America.

CHAPTER 4th

Of the north and east Boundaries, all Inlets upon the Atlantic Ocean. The Land Survey to three principal Places upon Saint Juan's River from Saint Augustin, viz. to the West, North and South in twenty six Tables. Directions for every Inlet. N. B. all miles mentioned hereafter are geographical, except when positively mentioned common Miles.

1. The North Boundary which separates Georgia from East Florida is (as appears in the foregoing Chapter by the first five Tables of Land Surveys) the part of the Stream Saint Mary's from the Indian Boundary crossing this Stream in Latitude 30°22′03″ and west Longitude from Cape Florida 1°47′46 1/2″ to its outlet into the Atlantic Ocean in Latitude 30°26′49″ and west Longitude from Cape Florida 1°18′50 1/2″, that is a Distance from West to East of 234,159 Links or 0°28′53″ difference of Longitude, which distance on the south side of the River is entirely laid out in Tracts of Land unto private Persons, among which is a Reserve of 10,000 Acres for a Town and Township, 13 miles, according to the Turnings of the River, distant from the Bar of the Inlet. This Town was intended for a Number of Emigrants from the Island Bermudas, who after sailing from said Island was obliged to put in Midway River in Georgia, where they by powerfull Dissuasions were deterred from settling in East Florida, but they all found their Graves in that Province in a short time.[30] Saint Mary's Stream heads in the great and famous Oekanphanoko Swamp, situated by Computation between the Latitudes 28° and 29° and between Saint Augustin and Apalachee Bay. Particulars of this Swamp are mentioned in the Beginning of the first Chapter of Georgia. This Swamp and its contiguous Lands are said to form a Country of exceeding rich Soil. The Jealousy of the Indians has not as yet permitted me to make a Survey of it, for this whole Swamp and its contiguous Country is contained within the Hunting Ground reserved by the Indians at the Congress held at Picolata in November 1765 between James Grant and John Stuart Esqrs., the former for that time being Governor of East Florida, and the latter Superintendant of Indian Affairs with the head Men of the Indians, at which time the latter fixed the above described Line between the Land ceded to His Majesty, and the hunting Ground reserved for themselves. This Line was to begin at the Pine Stump upon Saint Mary's Stream where the Georgia Boundary Line stops, and to continue as far as Okleywahaw River.[31]

[*180*] 2d. The Inlet of Saint Mary's is the best on the Atlantic Ocean in this Province, on the Bar of this Inlet are 9 1/2 feet at low water mark, neep Tide, and 15 feet at high Water full and change. This Bar is formed by a Sand Bank,

which resembles a Lobster's Claw, and is made by taking the South Point of the Inlet (which is the north Point of Amalia Island) in a W. 1°39′ South Direction: (This Point lays 2 1/6 miles of the Bar) or in a clear day by bringing the North Point of the Inlet (which is the south Point of Cumberland Island), in a W. 6 3/4 Nr. Direction. The Distance from the Bar to said Point is 1 1/9 of a League, the same depth of Water (which is on the Bar) can be carried up to the Indian Line. Concerning the Soil I will not be particular here, as I intend to give a general Account of it throughout the whole Province in the next Chapter. (a)

3d. From the Mouth of Saint Mary's to Dartmouth Inlet on Cape Florida,[32] the Atlantic Ocean sets Bounds to that part of the Province which fronts the East, on which, viz. East Boundary of this Province are sixteen Inlets, of which Saint Mary's Inlet is the first; but having advanced all that is remarkable of it in the foregoing Paragraph, I shall proceed to the next, viz.

[185] 4th. Nassau Inlet is situated in Latitude 30°13′24″ and 0°5′33 1/2″ East of Saint Mary's Inlet, its Bar lays E. S. E. 1/6 E. from the North Point of Little Talbot Island, 5/6 of a mile, and is made by taking said Point (being the south Point of the Inlet) in a W. 15 3/4 N. Direction.[33] The Bar has 9 feet at low Water

(a) The only sure Method to lay down Surveys of large Territories in Draughts is from the magnetical Meridians, which are discovered by Observations on principal Places differing from each other ten or more Miles in Longitude and Latitude; between these Places is formed a regular Trapezium by continuing their Meridians as far to the North and South until they be both of an equal Length, and can be joined by Parallels; these Parallels are divided in as many equal parts as they contain Geographical Miles of Longitude in their respective Latitudes; through every of these miles from one to the other Parallel are drawn as many Meridians, as the Parallels contain Miles, from each of these Meridians is laid down the Survey of that part of the Territory, which was made next to it, each of these Lines is the magnetical Meridian of such Place, to which it is nearest, thus it will not be attended with any Difficulty to note the Variation of the Compass to such Place or Places, which are to be specified in the Map or Chart, on which the solar Meridians are drawn through Places of Observation laying under one Meridian on a distance of one or more degrees from each other. The Angles of Intersections made by this solar or its neighbouring Meridians with those of the Magnetical are particularized by splitting the Cardinal North Point of the Star and Flower de Luce, and laying one half of it on the Radius, which notes the magnetical Meridian (Variation of Compass) and the other half on the Line which is drawn [185] through the whole Map or Chart in order to direct by the two cardinal Points to the true North and South Poles of the Globe, from which Line viz. the solar Meridians, which are next to each Inlet, are drawn the several Directions for navigating through the respective Channels of Bars, as they were washed up at such Places, where the opposite Forces of both Ocean and Streams Waters contested last, before I performed the Surveys of them; a Navigator therefore will allow for every course of my Direction such Variation of the Compass, as is (if any) specified to every North Point of the Stars and Flowers de luce laid down on every solar Meridian next to the respective Inlets, as per instance at the forementioned Saint Mary's Inlet the Variation of the Compass being 1°39′ East, a Navigator will direct his Course by the Compass due West, in case he takes the south point of the Inlet for his Object, or a W. 1/2 N. 1°8′ N. in case he pilots by the N. Point of the Inlet. The distance from the N. to S. Point is full 20 seconds or 1/3 of a mile difference of Latitude.

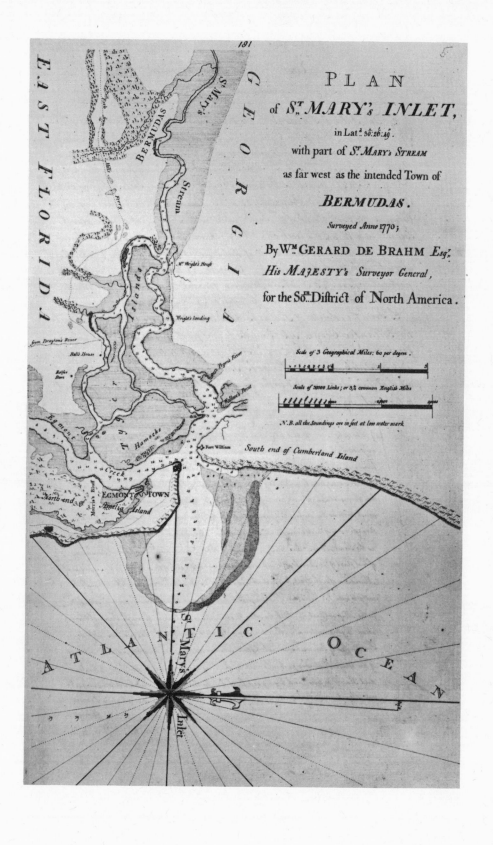

PLAN
of S.ͭ MARY's INLET,

in Lat.ᵗ 30:26:49.

with part of S.ͭ MARY's STREAM

as far west as the intended Town of

BERMUDAS.

Surveyed Anno 1770;

By W.ᵐ GERARD DE BRAHM Esq.ʳ

His MAJESTY's Surveyor General,

for the So.ͭʰ District of North America.

Scale of 3 Geographical Miles; 60 per degree.

Scale of 50000 Links; or 5½ common English Miles.

N.B. all the Soundings are in feet at low water mark.

EAST FLORIDA

GEORGIA

BERMUDAS

S.ͭ MARY's

Stream

Islands

Mr Wright's House

Wright's landing

from Drayton's River

Bell's House

Refuse Store

Egmont

Bay

Hamocks

Creek

Pigeon River

Mallow's Point

Fort William

South end of Cumberland Island

North end of Morris's Bluff

EGMONT TOWN

Amelia Island

ATLANTIC   OCEAN

S.ͭ MARY's Inlet

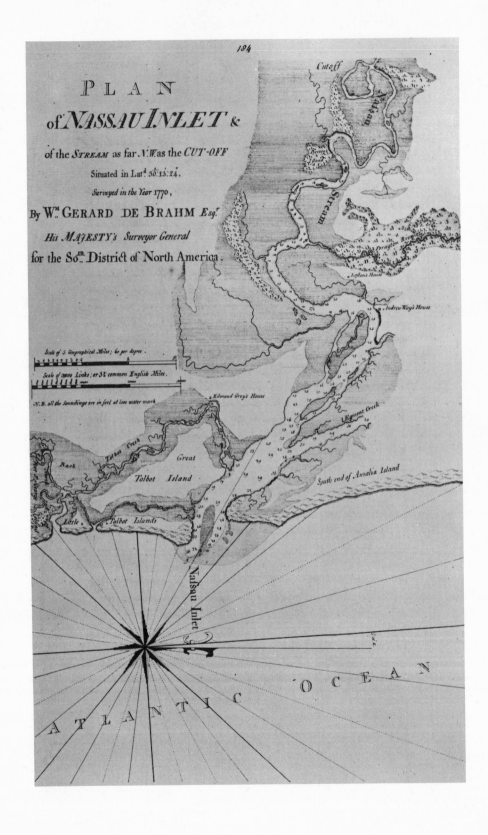

PLAN of NASSAU INLET &

of the STREAM as far N.W. as the CUT-OFF

Situated in Lat.ᵈ 30:13:24.

Surveyed in the Year 1770,

By Wᵐ. GERARD DE BRAHM Esqʳ.

His MAJESTY's Surveyor General

for the Soᵗ. District of North America.

Scale of 3 Geographical Miles; 60 per degree.

Scale of 2000 Links; or 3¼ common English Miles.

N.B. all the Soundings are in feet at low water mark.

Mark, and rises 5 feet at high Water full and change. Nassau Stream is by its Meanders for a distance of 18 miles navigable for Vessels which can sail over the Bar. They will find rather better water in the Stream than upon the Bar. The Land on both sides of this Stream, up to the very head inclusive, is laid out for private Persons. This Stream runs from its Bar West, a distance of two hundred thousand Links, or twenty five common English Miles. Near half of its Borders from the Inlet is Marsh, the other half up to the Stream's Head is Swamp Land; the same Nature of Soil extends North and South from the Stream on a Meridian of ninety thousand Links, or eleven and a half common English Miles, and covers a Country of one hundred seventy nine thousand, eight hundred and forty Acres of plantable or otherwise profitable Land, all contiguous to the Stream's Navigation, either by being bordered upon it with high Land, or calculated to admit artificial Access by Wharfs. This although short Stream, renders its Environs, altho' in a small Compass, one of the most advantageous Countries in this Province for Trade and Navigation.

[*186*] 5th. Between this and Saint Mary's Inlet is situated Amalia, now Egmont Island, containing between 8 and 9,000 Acres of Land; the northern part of which affords the greatest Quantity of plantable Land. A Town is laid out anno 1770, by the late Earl of Egmont, which is situated on the first Bluff from the north Point of Egmont Island, on Egmont Creek. This Island is encompassed by the Ocean, Egmont Creek, and the two Inlets Saint Mary's and Nassau, is the greatest and best of the nine Islands in this Province, which are situated upon the Ocean and its Salt Water.[34]

> The Names of the nine Islands are
> Amalia
> the three Tygers
> great
> little { old / new } Talbot
> Fort Saint George
> Anastasia

The three Tyger Islands are situated within and surrounded by Egmont Creek, Saint Mary's Stream, and three of its Creeks, as laid down in the Plan of Saint Mary's Inlet.

Great and the two little Talbot Islands are cut off from the Continent by great and little Talbot (Creeks of the Ocean) and by part of Fort Saint George Creek. They appear in the Plan of Nassau Inlet.

Fort George Island is made by Saint Juan's Stream, the Ocean and its Creek called Fort Saint George. This Island is distinguished in the Plan of Saint Juan's Inlet.

Anastasia Island is separated from the Main by the Ocean and its Creek called Matance, and the two Inlets, Saint Augustin and Matance; the northern Part of this Island is laid down on the Plan of Saint Augustin Inlet.[35]

6th. The third and fourth called New and Old Talbot Inlets are barred up with the Sand Banks in a manner that they are unserviceable for any Vessel greater than a Boat.

[*191*] 7th. The fifth is Saint Juan's Inlet in Latitude 30°6′49″ and 0°6′30 1/2″ East of Saint Mary's Inlet. The General's Mount, a high Sand Hill, makes the South Point of the Inlet.[36] To the West of this Mount appears a Sand Bluff, its Northern Extremity is a good Land Mark; two Miles from this Bluff E. 4°15′ N. lays the South Bar, and is made by keeping said Bluff in a W. 4°15′ S. Direction, and ranging it in that Direction a half Sails Breadth to the South of the South Point of the Woods on Fort Saint George Island. Both Bars have only 4 feet at low-water Mark, on which the Sea rises 5 feet at full and change; the same, yea much better Water can be carried up to Lake Dartmouth. The Land on the North and West of the Stream is all laid out in private Properties as far as Okleywahaw River; but on the South and East Side as far South as to the Head of Saint Juan's Stream, to the Carrying Place out of this into South Hillsborough Stream, which is due West 21 common miles from Cape Caniaberal [*Canaveral*]. Saint Juan's is more a Lake than a Stream, widens itself in many Places into large Lakes, and contracts again in narrow Channels between said Lakes. This Stream is famous for Mollets[37] which come down from spawning every year in such a Quantity that they take in one tenth of the Stream, they being met at Flood time by the Bass and Porpoises jumping by thousands on the dry Banks of the Stream perish rather than become a Prey to their Enemies. The Bar of this Stream is so very shallow, and the Stream all at once seven times deeper obliges the Sea Water at Flood Tides to precipitate itself over the Bar into the Stream, and runs on the Bottom of it, so that the Stream gradually swelling continues its Ebb as long until the Sea Water underneath is almost half Flood when, and not sooner, the Stream reverses its natural Course to run Flood with the Sea, which on account of the little Pressure or Fall of Water in the Stream, will run Flood as long until the Sea Water underneath has run near half Ebb. When great Freshes happen after a long Spell of Drought and Easterly Winds, the Stream will be divided in Spots, some of salt water and others of fresh water, and each Spot of several miles in Length, because the several fresh-water-Runs and Rivulets pour into the Stream so much fresh-water that their moving Weight forces the standing salt-water swelled up the Stream by Easterly Winds to contract in separate

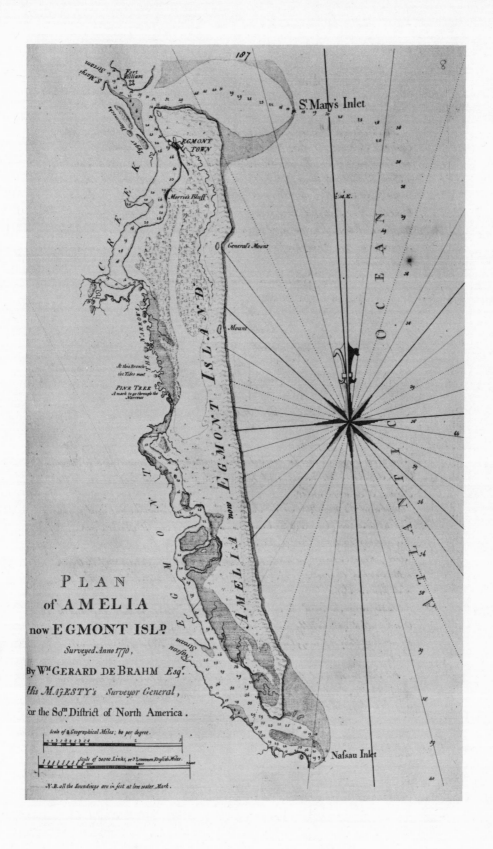

PLAN
of AMELIA
now EGMONT ISLⁿ

Surveyed Anno 1770,

By Wᵐ GERARD DE BRAHM Esqᵗ.

His MAJESTY's Surveyor General,

for the Soⁿ District of North America.

Scale of ¼ Geographical Miles; 60 per degree.

Scale of 5000 Links, or 3½ common English Miles.

N.B. all the Soundings are in feet at low water, Mark.

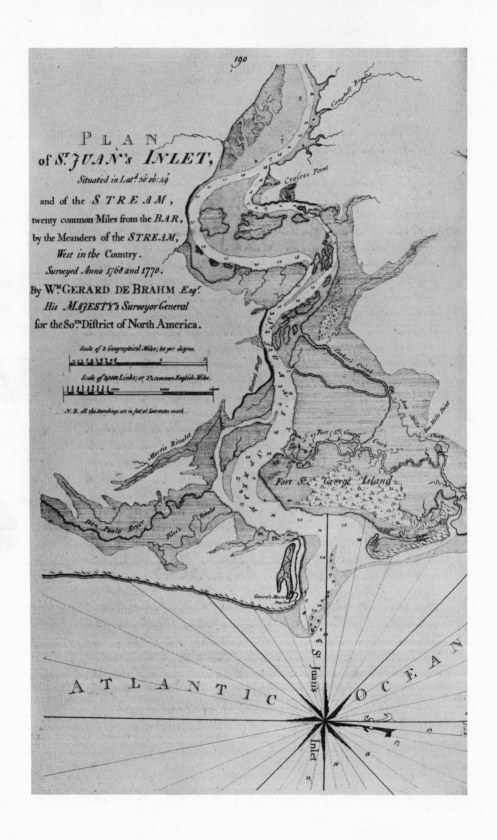

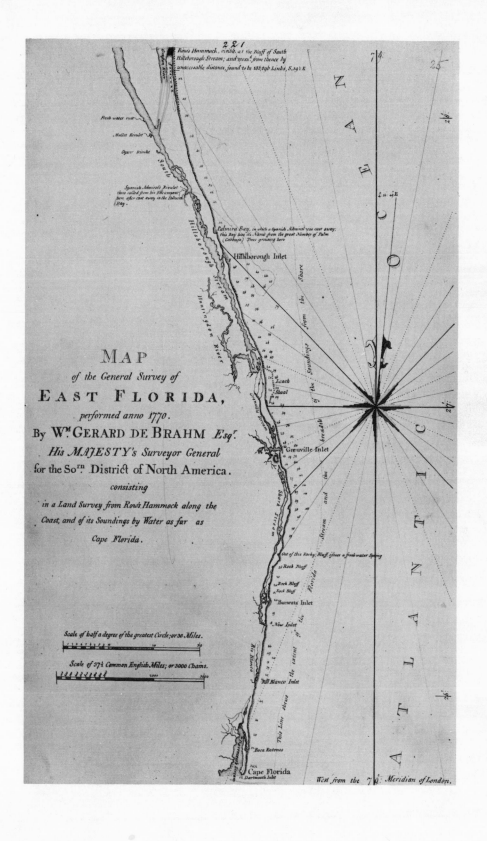

Row's Hammock, visible at the Bluff of South
Hillsborough Stream; and meas.d from thence by
unaccessable distance, found to be 18h,99h Links, S.39½ E.

Fresh water rivlt

Mullet Rivulet

Oyster Rivulet

Spanish Admiral's Rivulet
there called from his Encampment
here after cast away in the Palmira
Bay.

Palmira Bay, in which a Spanish Admiral was cast away;
this Bay has its Name from the great Number of Palm
(Cabbage) Trees growing here

Hillsborough Inlet

Leach
Shoal

Grenville Inlet

MAP
of the General Survey of
EAST FLORIDA,
performed anno 1770.
By Wm. GERARD DE BRAHM Esqr.
His MAJESTY's Surveyor General
for the Sorn District of North America.
consisting
in a Land Survey from Row's Hammock along the
Coast, and of its Soundings by Water as far as
Cape Florida.

Out of this Rocky Bluff issues a fresh water Spring
Rock Bluff
Rock Bluff
Rock Bluff
Barseota Inlet
New Inlet
Rio Blanco
Rio Blanco Inlet

Scale of half a degree of the greatest Circle; or 30 Miles.

Scale of 37½ Common English Miles; or 3000 Chains.

Boca Ratones

Cape Florida
Dartmouth Inlet

West from the 70. Meridian of London.

Places (a) which uncommon Phænomenon with that of the Tides, [*192*] seems
to many Navigators on this Stream to be Wonders of Nature. I have surveyed
Saint Juan's Stream anno 1766 by Water, from the Inlet up to the South End of
Barrington Jervis Lake,[38] which distance anno 1767 I also surveyed by Land from
the Inlet of Saint Juan's along the Sea Coast, across the Inlet of Saint Augustin;
the Survey of which has appeared in the 5th Table of my General Surveys from
the North Point of Amalia Island in the foregoing Chapter: Also anno 1766 from
the Inlet of Saint Augustin to the Barrier Gate of the Town of Saint Augustin,
and to Governor Grant's Farm Lot N. W. corner, and thence a due west Line to
Saint Juan's Stream, 9,266 Links North of Fort Picolata.[39] Item anno 1768 from
said Barrier Gate to the Cow ford upon Saint Juan's Stream.[40] Lastly anno 1768
from the said Barrier to Barrington Jervis Lake, and farther to the Head of Saint
Juan's Stream. These three general Land Surveys appear in the following twenty
six Tables. I have designedly omitted my Loxodromical Tables of the Coast
Survey which I performed by Sea anno 1765 from the Inlet of Saint Augustin
to Cape Florida; but as this Survey cannot be accounted equal to the Mensuration
with a Chain on Shore, I esteem it only a good Investigation of a Country heretofore superficially known; I have therefore thought it sufficient to give a Specimen
of my Operation at Sea, by joining to the Atlantic Pilot in the 7th Chapter
hereafter, my Loxodromy and Observations in a Table and Map of the Atlantic
Ocean, performed in July, August and September 1771: Nor have I thought it
necessary to increase the Pages of this Report with the Tables of the General
Surveys performed of different Situations and inland Streams, Rivers, Rivulets
and the Road from Saint Augustin to Smyrnea [*New Smyrna*].[41]

[Folios 193 through 219 consist of De Brahm's "Twenty six Tables Of Land
Surveys and Observations I Made from the Meridian of the South Point of Saint
Augustine Inlet to Saint Juan's Stream near Picolata. II from the Meridian of the
South Point of Saint Augustin Inlet to the Cow-Ford of Cape Saint Nicola on
Saint Juan's Stream. III from the Meridian of the City of Saint Augustin to the
Head of Saint Juan's Stream. By William Gerard de Brahm Esqr.; His Majesty's
Surveyor General for the Southern District of North America." Like his other
tables of surveys they are omitted here because of their technical nature and
limited interest.]

[*223*] 8th. The Sea on the Bars, mentioned before the Tables, and in short on
all Bars fronting the East are ruled by its own natural Respiration or Zimosis, and
by the different Effects of Winds. The Description which I have advanced, is of
the Effect of West, and Westwardly, South and Southwardly Winds; but the

(a) the same Circumstances and Effects I have met with in Halifax Stream anno 1765.

North, East, and Eastwardly Winds bring more Water on all Bars upon the Atlantic Coast. Of these Effects more shall be said in the seventh Chapter.

9th. The sixth Inlet is Saint Augustin, in Latitude 29°38′59″ and 00°04′03 1/2″ East of Saint Juan's, or 00°11′03 1/2″ East from Saint Mary's. The North Point of Anastasia Island, makes the south Point of this Inlet. From this Point runs a Sand Flat 1 1/6 mile from the Shore of Anastasia Island. From the North Point of the Inlet runs a Bank Southeastward 2 1/5 mile long to meet the Sand Flat at the Bars Channels; the Marshes on the Main bear from the Bar's South Channel N. 38°52′ W. 3 1/6 m[*iles*] & The Light-House on Anastasia Island N. 68° W. 1 6/7 mile from the Bars South Channel. This Light-House has been constructed and built of Mason-Work by the Spaniards; and in 1769 it was by Order of the Brigadier General Frederick Haldimand Esqr.[42] raised 60 feet higher in Carpenter's Work; had a Cannon planted on the Top, which is fired the very Moment the Flag is hoisted for a Signal to the Town and Pilots, that a Vessel is off. The Light-House has two Flag Staffs one to the South and the other to the North on either of which the Flag is hoisted, viz. to the South, if the Vessel comes from thence, and to the North if the Vessel sails that way. This Light House is now observed at a greater Distance to the Northward, viz. where formerly a Point of Land obstructed the Sight of it to Coasting Vessels. The Bar of the Inlet has two Channels separated by a small middle Ground in the Bar. The North Channel is made by ranging a black Bush on a white Bluff with the said Light-House on a N. 79°16′ West Course. The South Channel is made by ranging a white Spit, runing Northwardly from Anastasia Island about the Length of a Sail's Breadth to the North of the Indian Church, situated North near a quarter of a Mile from the [224] Town of Saint Augustin in a N. 67°30′ W. Direction. The best Entries are made with Easterly Winds, at which time the Sea stands 8 feet deep at low Water in the Channels of the Bar. The Tide rises five feet at full and change. It must be observed however, that the above Directions were suitable only for that Bar in 1765, when I made the Survey of it. The Channels have since frequently shifted and will in all Probability not settle itself for some time to come, if ever. The Situation of the Town of Saint Augustin is mentioned in the first Chapter, and eleventh Paragraph of East Florida. I have only to add, that the town is situated in a healthy Zone, viz. in the fifth degree and forty ninth Minute of the fourth Climate; is surrounded with salt water Marshes not at all prejudicial to Health; their Evaporations are swept away in the day time by the Easterly Winds trading to the West, and in the Night Season by the Westerly Winds trading back to the Eastward. At the time, when the Spaniards left the Town, all Gardens were well stocked with Fruit Trees, viz. Figs, Guava, Plantin, Pomgranates, Lemons, Limes, Citrons, Shaddock Pergamot,[43] China and Seville

PLAN
of St. AUGUSTIN INLET
and TOWN,
with its ENVIRONES.
Surveyed in the Years 1765 & 1766,
By Wm. GERARD DE BRAHM, Esqr.
His MAJESTY's Surveyor General, for the
Sorn. District of North America.

Scale of 5 Geographical Miles; 80 per degree.

Scale of 50000 Links; or 3¾ common English Miles.

N.B. all the Soundings are in feet at low water mark.

Path from Mount Pleasant

Villa Rubera

Rivolata

R. Mills

Fountainball River

St. Sebastian's River

Mukoso and Smyrnea

Fountainball

Wilson Rivulet

Path

St. AUGUSTIN

Gui. Gramin Farm

Tolomato Stream

Mon plaisir

bella vista

Matanca Creek

Black Point

Five Mounts

Lighthouse

ANASTATIA ISLAND

Clam Pond

hard - grey - Sand

-Vein

Auguating Mount

Soft green

muddy

- Bottom

- sandy -

St. Augustin

White

St. Augustin Inlet

ATLANTIC OCEAN

Oranges; the latter full of Fruit throughout the whole Winter Season; and the Pot-herbs, though suspended in their Vegitation were seldom destroyed by Cold. The town is three quarters of a Mile in Length, but not quite a quarter wide; had four Churches, ornamentally built with Stone in the Spanish taste, of which one within, and one without the Town still exist. One is pulled down, viz. the German Church, but the Steeple is preserved as an Ornament to the Town; and the other, viz. the Convent Church, and Convent in Town is taken in the Body of the Barracks. All Houses are built of Masonry; their Entrances are shaded by Piazzas, supported by Tuskan [*Tuscan*] Pillars or Pillasters against the South Sun. The Houses have to the East, Windows projecting 16 or 18 Inches into the Street, very wide, and proportionably high. On the west side their Windows are commonly very small, and no Opening of any kind to the North, on which side they have double Walls 6 or 8 feet assunder, forming a kind of Gallery, which answers for Cellars, and Pantries. Before most of the Entrances were Arbours of Vines producing plenty of very good Grapes. No House had any Chimney.

[227] The Spaniards made Use of stone Urns, filled them with Coals left their Kitchens in the Afternoon, and set them at Sun-set in their Bed-Rooms to defend themselves against those Winter Seasons, which required such Care. The Governor's Residence has both sides Piazzas, viz. a double One to the South and a single One to the North; also a Belvidere and a grand Portico, decorated with dorick Pillars and Entablature.[44] On the North End of the Town is a casamatted [*casemated*] Fort, with four Bastions, a Ravelin, Conterscarp and Glacis, built with quarried Shell Stones (a) and constructed according to the Rudiments of Marchal de Vauban. This Fort commands the Road of the Bay, the Town, its Environs, and both Talomeko Stream and Matance Creek. The Soil in the Gardens and Environs of the Town is chiefly sandy and marshy. The Spaniards seem to have had a Notion of manuring their Land with Shells, for the rich Soil is near one ninth part Shells, one foot deep. The Inhabitants (Garrison

(a) is the only stone met with in the northern part of this Province, and consists of Shells congeled together with Sea-Salt, which by repeated Solution and Coagulation has lost its Acid and become silenitic. Some are of course Shells, & others not bigger than a sand grain. This latter will bear to be cut in all Shapes, & even in small ornaments. The former are adapted for [228] Grotto Work in European Gardens: also in such Vaults of Fortifications where Strength and Lightness are required, both which Qualities are combined in these Stones, however they must be well cemented over with Paris Plaister and coated with a thin Brick wall in form of a Roof before it is covered with Ground, or according to more skillful Invention; or else the Rain and other Moisture is very apt to find its Passage through them, for which reason they will fully answer for vaulting Cisterns both in Fortifications and on-board of Men of War to filter Rain and Salt water provided they have their proper Strata of Pebbles and a Variety of Sand.

accepted [*sic*]) consisted, anno 1770 of 124 Persons, of whom 50 were married and 74 unmarried. N. B. Women and Children are not comprehended in this Number.[45]

10th. The seventh and eighth Inlets, are Matance and Penion, as they are chiefly barred by the Effect of continuing easterly Gales, of course without a Channel, they consequently serve for nothing but Boats.[46]

11th. The ninth Inlet is Mukoso, alias Muskitoe,[47] situated in Latitude 28°54'00", and 00°27'24" East of Saint Augustin and 00°38'24 1/2" East of Saint Mary's. The Channel of this Bar has near the same Water as that of Saint Augustin, when I surveyed it in 1765 I made my Land Marks the northernmost Bluff on the South Point of the Inlet. This Bluff I took in a S. 1/2 W. Direction, by which I made the Channel, but since that time the Channel has shifted several times, the same as that of Saint Augustin. The Bar is not much above 60 feet over, the Channel was then about 300 feet wide; I had 9 feet Water in the Bars Channel at 3/4 Flood, at that time neep-tide, and the Wind at N. N. E., which is one of the Winds that rises the Sea upon the Bars, and tho' the Winds blew but moderate, the Tide run up 6 feet (b) so that that day the Bars Channel had 10 1/2 feet at high water mark, which I doubt not may at other times be more when the easterly Wind blows fresh. [*228*] This Inlet has high Sand hills on both North and South sides, whose Distance I measured 2,900 Links from North to South. The Soundings increase gradually from 10 1/2 feet on the Bars Channel to 36 feet within the Harbour. Ten feet Water may be carried for 11 miles from the bar up Halifax,[48] which is the North Stream; and the same Water for 5 miles up North Hillsborough,[49] which is the South Stream; both which Streams form the Mukoso Harbour, in the Mouth of either of these Streams a Vessel at Anchor is Land-locked against all Winds. All the Lands upon Halifax and North Hillsborough Streams are granted to private Persons, and many of them improved. The Town of New Smyrnea, has been settled upon North Hillsborough Stream, in 1768, by Doctor Andrew Turnbull, with 1,400 Minorcans, among whom were some French, and 75 Greeks. The Town has two Churches, one for English Protestants, and the other for Roman Catholicks.[50]

[*233*] 12th. The tenth Inlet is to the Southward of Cape Canaveral, called Hillsborough, alias Indian, alias Ays Inlet,[51] situated in Latitude 27°30'53" and 1°1'18 1/2" East of Saint Augustin or 1°12'22" East of Saint Mary's, has two Bars; the first had anno 1765 (when I recognized [*reconnoitered*] it) five Channels, the second from the North had 18, and the second from the South had 12 feet; the second Bar had 2 Channels to the South and 2 Swashes to the North.

(b) the common Rise and Fall of Flood and Ebb is 4 1/2 feet.

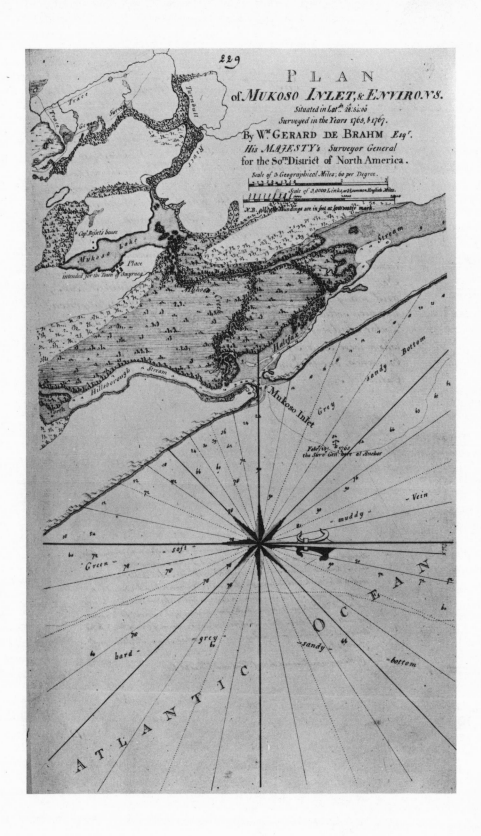

PLAN
of MUKOSO INLET, & ENVIRONS.
Situated in Lat. 28:54:00
Surveyed in the Years 1765, & 1767.
By W. GERARD DE BRAHM Esq.
His MAJESTY's Surveyor General
for the So. District of North America.
Scale of 3 Geographical Miles; 60 per Degree.
Scale of 3,0000 Links, or 84 common English Miles.
N.B. all the Soundings are in feet at low water mark

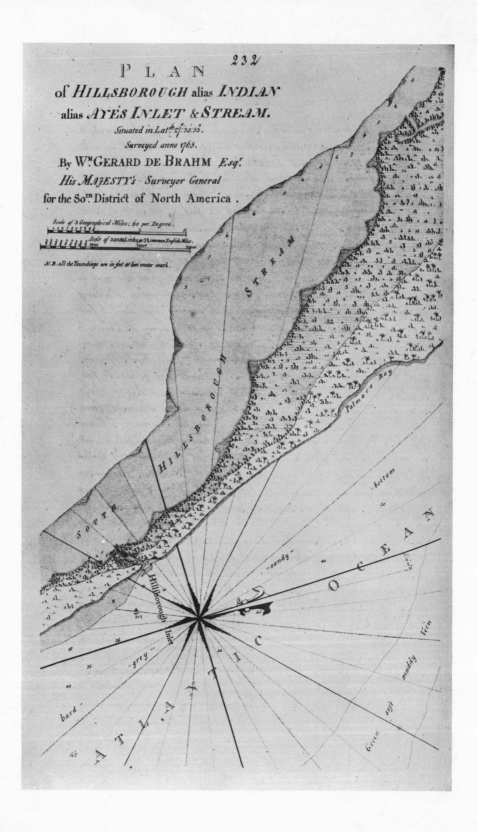

PLAN
of *HILLSBOROUGH* alias *INDIAN*
alias *AYES INLET & STREAM.*
Situated in Lat. 27:30:55.
Surveyed anno 1765.
By W.ᵐ GERARD DE BRAHM Esq.ʳ
His *MAJESTY's* Surveyor General
for the So.ᵗ District of North America.

Scale of 3 Geographical Miles; 60 per Degree.

Scale of 30000 Links, or 3½ common English Miles.

N.B. all the Soundings are in feet at low water mark.

STREAM

HILLSBOROUGH

SOUTH

Hillsborough Inlet

Palmara Bay

bottom

sandy

grey

bard

muddy

Green soft

Veia

ATLANTIC   OCEAN

The Tide rose 4 feet the 12th of March, which was two days before Neep Tide. I entered the Harbour in my Boat, had 12 feet, near high Water in the second Channel, from the South on the first Bar, and in the South Channel of the second Bar I had 5 feet, when another of my Boats entering the North Channel of the second Bar had 6 feet Water (a). This Inlet is 1,500 Links wide from its North to its South Point; is to this day frequented by Spanish-fishing Schooners from Cuba, the South Hillsborough, alias Ays Stream, and Huntingdon, alias Santa Luz,[52] River are famous for Mullets and Bass. Upon which Stream and River they send their Boats, and leave their Schooner in the Harbour, from whence they do not return to Cuba before the Schooner is laden with Fish; these Schooners have sometimes been obliged to wait several Weeks, the Bars Channel being shut up by Easterly Gales, until they could go out with the first Ebb at full or change soon after these Gales; for although they shut up the Channel, yet they flood constantly the Sea Water in the Harbour, and admit of no Ebb, of course restore in Water the Obstruction, which they cause unto Navigation, by filling the Bars Channels.

13th. The Eleventh Inlet called Grenville alias Jupiter,[53] is situated in Latitude 26°20'34" and 1°15'17"—East from Saint Augustin, or 1°26'20 1/2" East of Saint Mary's; it was the 30th of November 1770, four days after Neep-tide, when I examined this Bar, and surveyed the Harbour. The Bar [234] runs from the North Point of the Inlet due South, and joins some Rocks, which range from the South Point along the Coast for three hundred yards Distance; to the North of said Range of Rocks is the Channel through the Bar, which was made by ranging the second Sand Point, and a Palmetoe Tree on the South Side of the Inlet in a West Direction, until near the Bar, then standing in W. by N. over the Bar I had that day 7 feet at high Water Mark; the Wind then at N. W. which is one of the Winds, that bends the Sea from the Coast and makes lower Tides, than common Neep-tides in a Calm. My Tender in the foregoing Night, over shutting [shooting?] this Inlet sailed in the Morning from the Southward to join me at Anchor to the North of the Bar. She endeavouring to beat up against the Wind by making too much Sail carried her Main Mast overboard, so that I was obliged to send her in the Inlet, where She refitted herself; the 6th of December she sailed out with 8 feet water in the Bars Channel at the Beginning of Ebb, four days after full Moon and the Wind at N. by W. a little inclining to bend the Sea of the Coast; by this it is plain, that this Channel with Easterly Winds will not be

(a) by entering with a W. Course I followed by Eye between the first & second So. Breakers until I ranged the North Breakers N. N. W. & W., then run up N. W. 1/2 N. to the So. Channel of the 2d Bar. In this Harbor Inlet with [was?] a Papaw full of young Sprouts. The Criterion of a Climate fit for Sugar.

inferior to Mukoso Inlet, and much preferable to that of Hillsborough. In the year 1765, when recognizing [*reconnoitering*] this Western Atlantic Coast, I found this Inlet intirely shut up, but in the year 1768, Surveys being made to the North of this Inlet by my Deputies, they found it open. This Harbour is formed by Grenville Stream, issuing out of South Hillsborough Stream, and spreading four Branches westwardly of the Harbour. The same Water, which is upon the Bar can be carried up three Miles upon the Main Stream. The Channel lays on the West Side near the Hammok Land. N. B. a fine and large Body of Rice Land lays between, and at the Heads of said 4 Branches.

14th. The twelfth, thirteenth, fourteenth and fifteenth Inlets, called Barracuta, alias Dry Inlet, Rio Nuovo, (a) Rio Blanco, and Boca Ratones are only fit for Boats.

[*239*] 15th. The sixteenth is Dartmouth Inlet, in Latitude 25°44'11", and 1°7'49 1/2" East of Saint Augustin, and 1°18'53 1/2" East of Saint Mary's. Cape Florida is the North Point of this Inlet, and the north Point of Biskaino Island is the south Point of this Inlet; 12 feet water may be carried to the southernmost Point of the Cape, where a Vessel may lay Land-locked against all Gales, except from the S. E.; for this Wind comes right up the Channel of the Inlet; this Inlet leads into the Northern part of Sandwich Gulf.[55] N. B. The Regularity of Ebb and Flood begins at this Inlet and runs 6 hours Flood and 6 hours Ebb all the way to the Northward upon the western Coast of the Atlantic Ocean. Sandwich Gulf has more Inlets to the Southward, the greatest of which is Dartmouth Sound; this Sound lays between the south Point of Biskaino and Oswald Islands, is 3 1/2 miles wide from North to South, and the Gulf is here 8 miles over from East to West. In this Sound one Tide floods 5 and ebbs 5 hours, and the next Tide floods 7 and ebbs 7 hours, but the farther southward, the less Regularity is kept by the Tides, viz. from the North End of Hawke Channel to Hueso Island, where in the adjacent Egmont Channel it floods 5 and ebbs 7 hours, and next it floods 7 and ebbs 5 hours. Thus far I have minutely laid down, first my Actual Surveys of the most principal Parts of East Florida in thirty nine Tables, besides the Table of my Hydrometrical Survey across the Atlantic Ocean, by which thirty nine Tables (should some or all my Draughts be lost) the principal Situations and the General Map of my Surveys may be restored many Ages hereafter. Secondly, I have accounted for the different degrees of Climate and the Effect of solar heat (agreeable to common Notion) (a) in Ephemerical Tables of one thousand four

---

(a) The great Rains in May 1765 filled this River & its Marshes with so much water that its weight within & the Sea without by Force of the N. E. gales demolished the Bank & made this Inlet between 25th & 30th May 1765.[54] 17 common miles to the No. of this Inlet is a fine fresh water Spring, issuing out of a Rock upon the Beach.

(a) the Body of the Sun is neither hot or cold.

PLAN

of *GRENVILLE INLET* Situated in Lat.d 26:20:34 ;

with it's *STREAM,* and *FOUR BRANCHES.*

Surveyed anno 1770

By WILLIAM GERARD DE BRAHM Esq.r

His MAJESTY's Surveyor General

for the So.rn District of North America.

Scale of 50,000 Links for 3½ common English Miles.

Scale of 3 Geographical Miles; 60 per Degree.

all the Soundings are 16 feet at low water mark.

South end of the Leech Shoal Rocks.

Grenville North-west Great Branch

Grenville

Grenville South-west Branch

Grenville Little South-west Branch

Grenville Rocks

Grenville South Branch

Grenville Inlet

Bottom

Sandy

Grey

hard

ATLANTIC OCEAN

Florida Stream no soundings

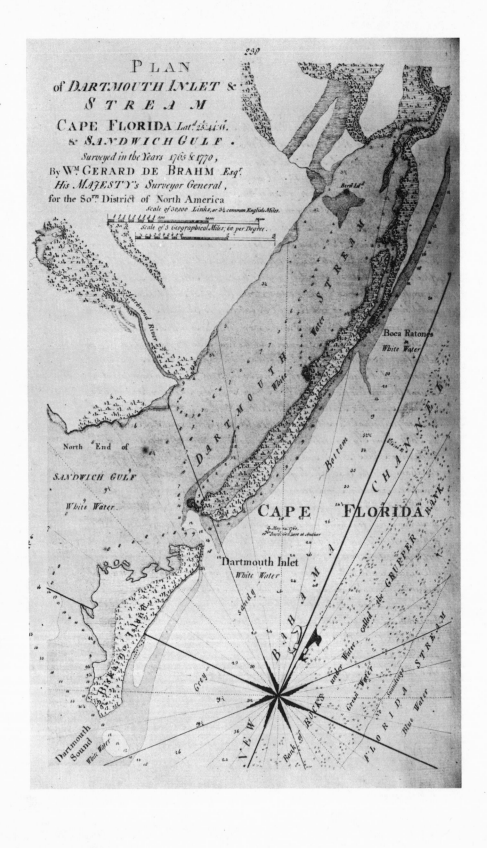

hundred and twenty Observations, which will be a Guide forever. Thirdly, my List of the Aboriginal English Inhabitants will be a Record for the Generations hereafter. Fourthly, the Variation of the Compass at the principal Places, as also the Directions for navigating the several Inlets, being both subject to Vicissitudes of Time, Weather and Winds Effects, will serve to compare the future changes. In Obedience to the Instructions received from the Right Honorable Lords of Trade and Plantations I will now proceed to the different Soils, their natural Productions, to Manufacturies, to Oeconomical, Pathological, and Architectonical; as also to Directions for navigating the Florida Stream near the Martyrs, Cape Florida and the Western Atlantic Shore.

[240]

CHAPTER 5th

Of the Soil, natural Productions, what Experiments made with foreign Plants and Seeds; necessary Advices for New Settlers, how to transport from Europe, and what Plants and Seeds; how to improve the Soil; in what manner to build houses, how to preserve Health by Diet and Regimen.

1st. In the second Chapter of East Florida, and by the general Table inserted in the third Chapter I have shewn, that this Province in its Extent to the South, occupies six degrees of the fourth Climate; and of the fifth Climate it takes off from its Beginning two Miles and three Seconds. From which Proximity to the Æquator one should be apt to judge, that the Heat must be intollerable; This would be really the Case, were not the easterly Breezes (which trade from nine in the forenoon to three in the Afternoon from East to West, and returns from West to East again in the Night) such a Remedy, by which in this Province, especially near and at Cape Florida the Heat is made as tollerable in Summer, and Winter, as the Spring Heat is in England; Altho' it is situated between the eighth and ninth Climates, from thence it proceeds; that in East Florida is a very short, but at Cape Florida no general Cessation of Vegitation in the Winter.

2d. From the Mouth of Saint Mary's up as far as Sander's Store, or the Indian Boundary Line in Latitude 30°22'03" and 29'19" west Longitude from the Mouth; the Soil consists of much fine low Land for the Culture of Rice; of few high Oak Land for Indigo, and the rest is all Pine Land, well stocked with fine Trees fit to be manufactured into Timber; those not fit for Manufactury may be tapped for drawing the Turpentine, and they laying on the Ground (generally called Hurricane Trees) with the Limbs broken down by high Winds, together with the Remainder of those Manufactured may be burnt in Kilns to extract the Tar, which to convey with little Expense to Markets, Saint Mary's River affords good Communication, it being navigable above Sanders Store, and probably would be so to its very Source in Oekanphanoko Swamp, were the River not impracticable on account of [*241*] Cypress and other Trees, which, ten miles above Sander's, begin to lay across and barricade the River, torn out of their rich and loose Ground by high Winds, that happen in March, and September. These Pine Lands afford fine Pasturage for Cattle and Horses.

3d. The Soil upon the Atlantic Coast, from the Mouth of Saint Mary's River to Cape Florida and Dartmouth Inlet, a distance of 339 miles, is all Sand, and in most Places barren; but the South Coast detached in a Number of Islands, is chiefly a rich Marl of a bluish-Cast, and continues even to mix with the Sand, or cover the Rocks under Water of its Sea as far as I could take Soundings; wherever I was obliged to come to an Anchor, I brought up the Flooks [*flukes*] covered with this Marl, which the Salt water blanches white as Chalk. This Sea in a Calm is so clear that the Fish, Corals, Rocks, Spunges, Sea Feathers, and Tortoise Grass alga, or Algue (a) can be clearly discerned in four fathom Water, and the Sea Water as far as it covers these Soundings assumes in a Calm the Colour of a Beryl, and a stormy Sea bringing up this fine Soil resembles unto Milk; so that a Meridian Observation can only be taken by good Connoisures, who are able to distinguish the Horizon from the Sky. The Rocks, which are under Water or on the Shore are either Coral Rocks, or Flints, some grey, some white, some dark blue. These Rocks are the Foundation of all the Islands, and covered with Marl; the Parts overflowed with the high Tides of the Sea produce only Mangrove (an ever green Tree) whose Leaves resemble nearly those of the Bay, has three Barks, the Outside grey, the next green, and the third crimson (b). Its Wood is very close, and fine grained, after cut and dried grows as hard and near the Colour of Lignum sanctum, takes a very fine Polish. The Coals of this Wood burn clear, and leave little or no Ashes (a Sign of its prevailing sulphureous Principle). Its Seed is a Pod which divides this Genus in two Species, the first is a tall straight Tree, and grows in all from the first to the middle of the fourth

(a) a Salt called Cali is made of it in Spain and Portugal.
(b) it is said the Spaniards dye Morocco Leather with the red Bark of Mangrove.

Climates. The second is a short and crooked Tree, met with in the Northern Part of the fourth Climate, and not farther; its Pods (which are not plucked off by the Winds) continue growing, until they reach the Ground, then strike Root, and give Nourishment to the Tree, to which they serve [242] as Shrouds to the Masts of Vessels, or the Lines to a Tent; and as the Mangroves grow very near one to another, their Shrouds interfearing with each other, form such a Texture, that it is impossible, without cutting a Road to make a Way of ten yards through them in an hour (c). The Pods of the first Species drop, when about six Inches long, and from the Moisture of the Ground swell, and strike Root out of the one End, and issue Branches from the other, thus grow up to a Tree. The Soil, which produces the Mangrove is, as said above, a Marl, but of a very dark blue Colour. The richest of the kind is full of salt Particles, therefore unfit for Cultivation, unless dammed in, and sweetened with Rain Water for one or two years, then cleared of its Trees. The high Lands, which are not overflowed, are covered in Places with Sand, on which little or nothing grows; in other parts they have a Stratum of bluish Marl, on which flourish the following Species.

Aloe Plant	Madeira Tree, specie of mahagony
Cinnamon wild	Mamhenilla Tree
Cotton Tree	Mangrove Tree
Elemigum Tree	Opuntia, prickly Pear, Indian Fig
Grape Wine Tree	Papaw
Grape Vine	Papajos
Hicocoplum Tree	Pine
Iron Wood Tree	Sapadilla Tree
Lignum Vitæ Tree	Spice Tree
(Lignum sanctum)	Squilla Plant
	Torch Tree

On some of these Islands are Ponds and Wells in Rocks of exceeding good fresh Water; of which Notice is taken in the general Map, which makes it probable that the same can be met with by the Laborious on all Islands.

4th. As far as my Land Surveys have been carried upon the Streams, Rivers and Rivulets mentioned in the adjoining List, I have observed that the Inlands afford as good, but not in the same Proportion, that Quantity of plantable Land from the Hand of Nature, as is met with in the more northern Provinces of Georgia & South Carolina. [243]

(c) is fit to be planted in Fortification Ditches, from the Scarp to the contrascarp in order to fill up the whole Ditch.

East Florida is watered by the following

Streams	Rivers	Rivulets
Saint Mary's	Saint Mary's	Purcell, alias Pigeon
Nassau	Don Paulo	Joseph, alias jumping
Saint Juan	Trout	Drydon's, alias Cowpen
Talomeko	Sebastian	Hazzard
Matance	Tonyn, alias Rio blanco	Laidler
Halifax	alias blake	Maxon
No. Hillsborough	Fountain Hall	Davies
alias Mukoso	alias woodcutter	Popo
So. Hillsborough	Matance	Picolata
alias Ays	Oklywaha	Rainsford
Grenville	Greyhurst	Jenkin
Shark	Tomuko	Lower Observation
Rio Blanco	Turnbull	Upper Observation
Rio Ratones		
Dartmouth		

I distinguish the running Waters in Streams, Rivers and Rivulets; the last as not navigable Branches of Rivers or Streams. The Rivers as navigable Waters emptying into Streams, and the Streams as navigable Waters disemboguing into the Ocean.

5th. The Variety of Soil is distinguished by the following Lands, viz. Pine Land if low is of a black Soil, if midling high it is of a white Sand, and if very high its Soil is of a Sand as yellow as Oker [*ocher*]. The black Soil produces a shrubby Pine, only fit for the Benefit of drawing from them Turpentine and Tar; is chiefly covered with wire Grass, not fit for Pasturage, and mixed with Cabbage Trees (a). The white Sand produces a tall Pine Tree, but not of the best kind for Manufactury, and has on its higher Ridges the white Spruce Pine. Its Grass is of the wire kind, [*244*] but mixed with Bunch Grass. Near the Head of Saint Juan's River I have met this kind of Pine Land all covered with young Canes (the sweetest Pasture of any); but the yellow Sand produced yellow Pine very tall and straight, without Limbs for upwards of 30 feet, the finest Tree

(a) is a Species of Palma, they bear about a bushel of small Cacao Nuts, all in one heap, shaped as a Piramid upon the top of the Trunk between the Leaves covered and interwoven with a rough brown Net. Each Nut receives its Nourishment thro' a fine string from the Tree, whose Heart near the Top is upwards of 30 inches long and 4 in diameter, consisting of young tender Leaves; this Heart is taken out of the Tree when cut down and is eatable boiled or raw, has much the Taste of young Wallnuts. I have met with cabbage Trees near 100 feet in heighth, and 12 Inches in Diameter.

for Timber. The Pasturage on this Soil is bunch Grass, next to Cane Grass the best Food for Cattle and Horses. It is very remarkable that in all my Surveys I have not met with a Pine Tree above 14 inches in Diameter, and they were all young Trees.

6th. The next Species of high Land differs very little in Soil from the midling Pine Land, and produces live and red Oak Hickery Nut, and wild Mulberry Trees; but this kind of Land is only met with in Groves (by the Americans called Hammoks[56]) not exceeding one hundred Acres of Land. There are also on the same Soil very small Groves consisting of nothing else than sour and bitter sweet Orange Trees. These latter Groves have been planted by the Spanish horse Party, scouting from Saint Augustin, which always carried a Provision of those Oranges with them, and planted the Seeds wherever they halted to refresh or incamped. These Orange Seeds sprouted, grew to Trees, bore Fruit in three or four years time, and increased themselves from the dropping Oranges which rotted on the Ground, became Dung to the Seeds, and were covered by the Winds with Earth.

7th. The third Species is divided in five different low Lands, viz. Mangrove Swamp, which is only met with near the Sea Coast, and upon the Islands on the south side of this Province; this kind of Swamp is already described in the 3d Paragraph. The next kind of low Land is called Maple Swamp, its Soil is rich, appears black, mixed with white Sand, on which the Rain-Waters remain a long time before they sink through this Soil or is dryed up by the Sun; this Swamp is generally overrun with Canes; its highest and thickest, tho' all young Trees and Canes stand in the Middle of these Lands, and are surrounded with a Nursery of younger Trees and Canes from all Ages down to one year. The third kind is called Cypress Swamp; its Soil is richer and blacker than that of the Maple, has also a Mixture of some white Sand, but is not overgrown with Canes. Its Center Trees are also young, but not above 15 Inches in Diameter, equally surrounded with a Nursery of younger cypress Trees, gradually down to one year's Age. The young Trees as far as to those of 15 feet high are rather in a very sandy Soil; but from thence to the Center the Soil increases in Richness; the Rain Waters are so well [245] sheltered by the Trees that they hardly dry up in these Swamps, unless in the hottest Seasons. The fourth kind is also of a black Soil, but mixed with a great deal of white Sand, and goes by the Name of Loblolly Bay Swamp, bordered on both sides with high Pine Land, therefore has not that Nursery; for this kind of Tree require an ever moist Ground; this Land is always overflowed by running Water, and Freshes caused by Rains. In this Swamp the Trees are also young, but seem older, than any of the foregoing Trees both on high or low Pine Land. The Loblolly Bay Trees (as they are called in America) may justly be ranged among the Magnolias, bearing Resemblance both to their

Flower and Cone. Its Leaves are small, and spear shaped, dark green on the upper and light blue on the lower side. The Tree rises in Height near one hundred feet, has two Barks, the outside grey, very coarse and thick, and the inside a fine crimson Colour. The Wood is very white and spungy. This Tree is an evergreen. The fifth are the great and open Savannahs (Meadows), some twelve miles across, on which grow bunch Grass, Cotton Snake Root and the blessed Thistle. They are covered for the greatest part of the year with Rain Water on account of their rich Soil having scarce any Mixture of Sand, of course no Passage for the Water to sink through, and their Beds are so level that hardly any Water can drain off, but intirely depends from the Sun's Exhalation. Although I have passed over them in a dry Season, when they had no Water, yet the Soil was so loose and moist that my Horse only with a slow and easy Gate could traverse them, and yet every Step made three or four Inches deep Impression. These Savannahs are spattered over as it were with little Groves of twelve or twenty Trees, some Pine, of the worst kind, some Cabbage and Maple Trees, and are chiefly surrounded by Maple or Cypress Swamps, which seem to extend themselves upon said Meadows; from which and the Youth of the Trees (which I observed all over the Country) convinced I have drawn the Conclusion that East Florida, especially its southern Extent, is the last in making of the whole North American Continent in His Majesty's Possession; wherefore no doubt that (as it will go on increasing its Forrests) the Land which is now covered with a sandy Soil will in time to come receive a Stratum of yearly dropping Leaves and Limbs, be shaded and consequently preserved against the Sun's Exhalation; whence a Putrefaction will ensue, an acid generated and the Sand corroded into a fine Marl; this will make its Impression yearly deeper by degrees, as the Stratum will increase to thicken itself with the deciduous Leaves &c: this is perhaps the [246] Reason, that Providence has wisely prevented its Population to this day, in order to give the necessary time to this part, for making its Soil plantable.

8th. The Experiments in the Culture and Manufacturies, chiefly by Europeans, unacquainted with the planting Business, yet willing and endeavouring to do their Best, were made with Vines, Coffee, Cotton, Sugar Canes, Ananas, and Indigo; in all these Experiments with their scant Knowledge, they however have had some tollerable Success; but the Indigo has really been brought to Perfection, equal to that made at Quatamala [*Guatemala*] in New Spain, which is estimated the best manufactured in the World, they have in 1771, among a few Planters made upwards of 1,200 Weight equal to the Quatalama Indigo (a). The Ex-

(a) Two Inconveniences attend the Indigo Plant, viz. Drought and Caterpillars; the first is without Remedy, but the last has been conquered by making a Trench 3 feet wide round the infected part of the Field, then by cutting down the Indigo within, the latter deprived them of the necessary shade against the scorching Sun, and the former prevented them

periments which succeeded in this as well as in the Provinces of Georgia and South Carolina were made by a few Europeans partly, but chiefly by Native Americans and Emigrants from Northern Colonies, and consisted in Rice, Rye, Indian Corn, Potatoes, Pease, Lantils, Lucern, Turpentine, Tar and Pitch, in all manner of European Garden plants, and Pot herbs, in Cypress, Cedar and Pine Boards, as well as Timber, in burning of Lime and in quarrying of Stones.

9th. That all Europeans (which incline to cultivate this Province) may proceed like unto the Americans with Boldness and reasonably account before hand for their Success, not meeting with those Disappointments obvious hitherto for want of Experience or Information: The most ingenious of them are advised to enquire into the Nature of their own Climate, in which they are born and educated; the Power of the Sun by Inflection and Reflection; their Nourishment and Medicines accustomed to; they are to accquire Information of the Climate, Power of the Sun, Mode of Living and Culture of the Climate they intend to move to; they are to collect such Plants and Seeds as they are sure will be worth transplanting, either for Refreshment of Life, Preservation or Recovery of Health, or for Market and Profit; they are [247] (if able) to lay in a good Stock of Furnitures, Garments, Provisions and Medicines, such as they have been used to, and which they have no Probability to meet with in a New Province; thereby to do Justice to their Constitution, private Interest, and to the general Good of Society.

10th. As America is the general Object of those who out of Necessity, or Inclination of making Experiments, become Emigrants or Adventurers; and East Florida in a special manner is here the Object treated upon, in which Province I have resided and surveyed from 1765 to 1771, to its southernmost Extent, both by Land and Sea; after endeavouring to collect all possible Experience from Culture, Surveys and Travels, in Georgia and South Carolina, from 1751 to 1765, I think it therefore my Duty to pour out for His Majesty's Interest, and the Good of the Public, all my Experience gathered by Observations & Experiments during twenty years time. I will endeavour, in the most concise Style and Sense, to deliver up my Observations, which in a general View will be serviceable for all parts of America, but in a more particular One are meant for East Florida.

11th. The general Opinion prevailing is, that Emigrations of Man and Trans-

---

from taking Refuge in the sound part of the Field; thus the Caterpillars perished. I advised to gather these Vermin, squeeze their substance thro' a hair sieve, mix it with lime water and elixivate it, or to come off with less Trouble, drown the Caterpillers in lime water, then dry them in the shade and put them up for use, convinced from Experience that all Plants breed their special Caterpillar, Bug or Worm, which contain the Quintessence of the plant ready manufactured for use, of course the best Indigo must be in the Caterpiller of its Plant.

plantations of Vegitable Plants best succeed in the same Climate. This Opinion is so plausibly well grounded, that it cannot miss to receive a favourable Reception in Theory: But by Experience I know, that the Winds and Effluvies of Earth and Water cause such Alterations, that the Effects almost differ in every degree of Longitude in the same Climate, and the bad Effects of these Differences are generally without Remedy; to illustrate this with Examples as the surest Teachers, I observe that the Spaniards have taken from the best Grape Vine at Madeira, situated in the v Climate, and transplanted them near in the same Climate upon the Coast of California about six thousand miles to the West of their Original and Native Place; but the Wine produced from the California Cultivation is much inferior to the best Wine exported from Madeira. The Query is now, if the same Climate does not prove successful for transplanting its own Native, carried a Distance of several thousand miles; which Climate is to be preferably chosen, that more northwardly, or another more southwardly; If it were unexceptionable to draw Arguments de minori ad majus, we might be contented to enter European Gardens, where the Sowing is performed in common Soil, and the [248] Transplantation in a better Soil, viz. in such which by Manure is made susceptible of more Warmth; this will decide at once that a Plant used to a certain degree of Heat, caused by the Inflection of the solar Rays, or any other artificial Warmth, would not prosper in a lesser degree, but require a Climate or Construction which affords more Heat, as per instance, a Climate nearer the Æquator where the Plant receives more Warmth; this can be affirmed from another Experiment made by the Hollanders, who took from the best Vines in Burgundy, situated in the viii Climate on the North side of the Æquator, and transplanted them at Cape good Hope, which lies in the v Climate on the south side of the Æquator. The Wine obtained from the good Hope Production is highly delicious, and much superior to the Wines made in Burgundy. This Experiment, in Company with the first of California, sufficiently proves the Error of the above Opinion. I would however give this Caution, not to exceed the viii Climate northwardly in the Choice of Plants and Seeds to be transplanted in the iv Climate, viz. East Florida, because the Proportion between the Climates may perhaps be as well too great as too little; and those Plants which are used to Rays of very oblique Inflection, not so much multiplied by reflecting Rays of the Sun, may not all at once be able to bear the Rays generated by near perpendicular Inflection, and multiplied by Reflections in infinitum. For East Florida (as I have abovementioned) lays under the iv Climate, where in Summer the Inflection of the Sun's Rays, especially at Cape Florida, are near perpendicular; and this Province is one Climate nearer the Æquator than Good Hope; altho' I make no doubt that Rhenish and Mosel Vines, laying under the ix Climate would succeed at Cape Florida; yet I would advise a small Trial of them first;

so much is certain, that the Wine Grapes seem to accommodate themselves to each Climate by assuming in cold Climates a thick, and in warm Climates a thin skin to cover and digest the Juice in the Berries, in which latter, viz. thin skins, the best Digestions is performed, and the best Musts are prepared; as from the natural Inclination (which spontaneously produces the Grape Vine and Grape Tree (a) as observed above). I am convinced that the Culture of Grape Vines will answer in East Florida preferably to any more Northern Province.

[249] 12th. To know what Plants, besides Vines, principally are to be chosen in Europe, it will be necessary, first to enquire, what Plants are not as yet introduced in America; next what Plants are both in America and Europe. Thirdly what Plants, from Experience, cannot be transplanted from Europe to the southern Climates of America. Fourthly, what Grains transplanted from Europe have proved equally as well or better in southern Climates of America. Fifthly, what Plants from strong Supposition of those happily cultivated in the same Climate (but on the south side of the Æquator) may be worth trying on the north side. I will subjoin the different Lists of them.

A List
Of European Fruits, as yet not introduced in America

Almonds	Pinioli
Currans	Pistacho
Olives	

Of these are neither Genus or Species to be met with. Olive Trees I have seen both in South Carolina and Georgia, transplanted from Europe, but never saw any Fruit, or did I hear they ever bore any.

Fruits common to Europe, and also to America

China Oranges	Lemons, or Limons
Citrons	Seville Oranges

Of these East Florida produces a greater Perfection of its Fertility than Europe, or even any other American Province or Island. And they have many Species in this Province which are scarce known in Europe, viz. the Orange has three Species, as the bittersweet, the Pergamot and the Shaddock. The Species of Lemon is a small Fruit called Lime, its Acid is stronger than that of the Lemon.

(a) is a natural Plant of East Florida, and one of the Tropic Products. The Stem and Branches resemble a Fig Tree: its Leaves are circular round, and about six Inches in Diameter. One Tree makes a fine Arbour, takes in a Circumference of near thirty feet in diameter.

This Tree does not grow higher than 14 or 15 feet. Its Leaves are not above an Inch and half long, and an Inch broad, are oval-spear-shaped, and indented all round. The Lemon Tree grows something taller; but all Orange Trees grow near 30 feet high, and their stem one foot in Diameter. [*250*]

Fruits, which by Experience degenerate when they are transplanted nearer the Æquator than the VI Climate.

Apples	Pears
Cherries	Prunes
Peaches	

Grains, which by my own Knowlege and Experience, joined to those of others, have proved equal, or rather better in Quality, being transplanted in the V and IV Climates, to what they are in more northern Climates.

has been planted in Carolina and Georgia...........Barley		Oats......in So. Carolina & Georgia	
in Georgia.................Flax		Pease.....in So. Carolina, Georgia & E. Florida	
in Carolina & Georgia.......Hemp		Rye......In So. Carolina, Georgia & E. Florida	
in East Florida............Lentils		Wheat....in So. Carolina and Georgia	

N. B. The above Grains are not propagated by the Inhabitants of the Sea Coast, as they have more profitable Objects to take in hand, therefore rather purchase what they want of the above Articles; but the back Settlers rather plant than purchase them.

Plants, which are cultivated in the four viz. I, II, III and IV Climates on the south of the Æquator; also in the three, viz. I, II, and III Climates north of the Æquator & prosper equally alike are,

Ananas	Indigo
Bananas	Plantin
Cacao	Rum
Cashew Nut	Sugar } from the Canes
Cochonille plant opuntia	Tobacco
Cotton	

East Florida, as far North as Hillsborough alias Ays Inlet, in Latitude 27°24′45″ by Observation, may, from the Nature of its Climate be judged equal to that of

Paraguay, where the Zona terminates, which produces the Tropic Plants, commonly called West Indian Products; for in the southernmost Extent of Paraguay the Sugar Cane is still cultivated viz. in the IV Climate, on the south side of the Æquator, and the Sugar which is [251] manufactured in that Country is conveyed, and sold at Santa Fe in the Province of Buenos Ayres, consequently the same may be expected from the Nature of the East Florida Climate, as far North as Lattitude 27°24′46″ the more so, as Canes have been planted with success farther northwardly unto Lattitude 29°00′00″.

13th. The Manner how to preserve European Plants and Seeds, in order to bring them from any part of Europe, Asia or Africa to America without Prejudice, without much Expence, and with the least Trouble, and greatest Advantage. I would propose to pack up immediately all Roots, Suckers, Vines, &c (after collected in any of aforementioned parts of the World) in tight, strong Iron-bound Oak Casks, of different Sizes, then headed, and through the Bungs to fill the Casks with Oil, and closely bung'd; the Seeds to be put in Bottles, filled after with Oil and well corked; out of which Oil the aforesaid Articles hereafter are not to be taken until the Ground is determined on, and prepared, then and not before the Oil is drawn into empty Vessels, the Plants and Seeds, after being well wiped, are to be rubbed with dry Ashes so long, until the Ashes come off dry; after these small Pains have been carefully taken, they may be regularly planted or sowed. The Oil which is not diminished in Virtue and Taste can be disposed of for oeconomical Use in the Family and in Markets; and the Casks, some sawed thro' the Middle in two will serve in new Plantations, viz. the bigger for Tubs, and the lesser for Pails and Buckets; some left whole for the Use of sending in them the Oil to the Markets; this Method will require no Attendance at Sea or on Shore, consequently give no Trouble more than packing, boarding, and Landing; other Methods, as for instance, to pack them in Earth cannot keep out, but must admit the Air, which will enter the Pores of the Plants, and with Assistance of its Warmth, swelling the closed Germs, disposes to sprout; this happening, whilst packed up in Ground and Casks, the young Sprouts of the Plants cannot obtain sufficient and free Air; Putrefaction of course ensues, and the Plants or Seeds are destroyed: but in case they can obtain the necessary free Air, they require to be frequently watered; but the Expence of laying in a sufficient Provision of Water at Sea, beside the Labour connected therewith is too extravagant, as also at the time of unruly Seas, and when they are to be landed from the Vessel on Shore, the hurry is so great that most of the Plants are bruised, and destroyed before they can reach their destined Ground, which perhaps for some Weeks, with any Propriety, cannot even be [252] pointed out, much less prepared; during which time the Labour, which should be bestowed on other Necessaries, must be divided in order to attend the Plants, which if not done they chance to be neglected and perish, and if done, other pressing Business, numerous in setting out a new Place must be retarded probably to great Prejudice; therefore to keep the Air from the Plants and Seeds is the only Remedy, and cannot be more effectually executed, than to surround them with Wax or Tallow, which is attended with many Inconveniences and Niceties, or preserved in Honey; which on a long Voyage, in great Warmth with the Moisture in the Plants and Seeds, is apt to ferment, therefore best in Oil, else all the Premisses stop effectually the Pores of the Plants and keep out the Air. This stopping of the Pores may seem pernicious and apt to prevent the Seeds and Plants from sprouting in the Ground, when sowed or planted; but if they are all carefully wiped, some if not all Pores disposed by the subterraneous warm Moisture will swell and open to give Passage to the Air under Ground, and require perhaps one or two days more time than ordinary to open them all, which the Fatness of the Oil was able to close up, but becomes insufficient to hinder the Air from penetrating, where the Fat has separated from the Lips of the Pores; beside the Warmth of the Ground (if dry) will by Rarification and Evaporation consume, but if moist by Coagulation and Contraction dislodge it from the Texture of the Seed's Husk, or of the Plant's Bark.

14th. I venture to recommend this Method for preserving the Silk-worm seed (Eggs) from hatching or giving vent to the inclosed worm sooner than the Mulberry Trees or Shrubs are sufficiently sprouted and afford the necessary Quantity of Leaves to feed them; which unhappy Incidents have proved frequently great Backwardness in the Georgia Silk Culture, altho' the Industrious endeavoured for want of Mulberry Leaves to feed them with young black Berry or Sallad Leaves, but the Worms became sick and died, or weak and made very imperfect Cocoons; wherefore many would not take any Trouble, but let the young Worms perish at once for want of food. The way of wiping these Seeds or Eggs, when taken out of the Oil, is by mixing them with fine and dry Ashes, and by moving them mixed with the Ashes on blotting Paper so long and so often repeated with fresh Ashes and Paper, until no mark of Oil remains in the Ashes or on the Paper.

[253] 15th. I have made above the most precise and faithful Report of the Soil and natural Products of East Florida, but am afraid the Description of the Coast, being the most preferable Place for Health, and Conveniency, will for the Sake of its sandy Disposition, bring Reflection on the whole Continent, and discourage those from settling who would prefer that Situation before any inland, and whose Eyes are used to Marl and other rich Soil; This Imperfection however need not discourage European Emigrants from making Choice of such Land, provided the Situation has otherwise most desirable Advantages both of free Air and easy Access; for the quick Sand, which contains the subterraneous Universal Water Source lays in this Province under a Stratum (in case it is Sand) generally not above six feet thick; but where it is Marl (which generally is supported by a coral

Rock) there the quick Sand lays about four feet under the Surface, and is met with after piercing through the coral Rock. The sandy Stratum I have experienced in the dryest Seasons never to be above two feet under the Surface exhausted of Moisture, so that Vegitable Plants which strike the Fibers of their Roots more than two feet deep, received always Nourishment from below, and the Night-dews refreshed the Plants as far as they had been over Ground withered in the day time; the infallible Truth of this is obtained by the daily Experience since 1765 in this very Province, both in regard to cultivated and such natural Products which are peculiar to the different degrees of Climate in this Country.

16th. However as I cannot expect my eight years Experience on sandy Soil should be sufficient to out-do the through many thousand years entertained Notion, from a want of fair Trials and Experiments in different Climates, and on different as well a shallow as deep laying quick Sand, and dispose European Emigrants to trust to a Fertility in a thin Sand stratum, but must expect they will rather desire a Marl or otherwise manured Soil, for which I do not mean to reproach Man's good Care of making sure and depending best of his own Experience. They need not however to exchange or refuse occupying a well situated, and for many Advantages well calculated Place on account of being sandy, and elect another inconveniently situated because its Soil is manured or a Marl. They may in rainy Seasons cover any part they please, and intend for Gardens or Fields, with a Stratum of Stones or Shells about six [254] Inches thick, in case Leaves, Grass, Straw, or Rushes &c are handyer than a foot thick; this Stratum will absorbe the fiery Particles (Phlogiston) conveyed by the inflecting Rays of the Sun, and hinder the reflecting Rays from exhausting the subterraneous Moisture reaching the Earth's Surface.[57] Whoever will bestow his leisure hours upon such useful and profitable Undertaking, he will, in about twelve Months time be convinced of its good Effect, when he in another rainy Season removes said Stones, Shells &c by forming Passages and Rows, each six feet wide, clears all Materials out of the Passages, and lays them upon those remaining in the Rows, will find in the Passages than an Acid has been generated under the stratum, that this Acid has corroded (alkuholized) the upper part of the sandy Soil into a fine Marl, which after it is hoed or plowed about six Inches in Depth with and under the Sand, in order to stop the wide Interstices between the sandy Grains, and hinder the quick Passage of the Rain through them to the Refreshment of what is sowed or planted there, that consequently this Method will richly reward him with a fine Crop in the Passages, and there remains no room for Doubt, when the necessary Pains are taken a little before the next ensuing planting Season to move the Stratum of Stones &c out of the Rows into the Passages last planted, so as to make them Rows, and the Rows to Passages, it will be discovered that a two years stratum has made a much deeper Impression of corroded Sand into Marl, and will consequently pay that Trouble with a second and richer Crop. It must be observed, that the Seeds or Plants are to be sowed or placed on both sides of the Passages, next to the Stratum of the Rows, so as to give them the Benefit of the Moisture constantly retained under the Stratum. Thus annually or once in two years removing the Stratum from the Rows into the Passages will afford a perpetual Renewal and enriching of the Ground. Secondly, be a Destruction to all wild and pernicious Seeds and Roots of Grass as well as of Weeds, a Method preferably answering to that of the northern and cold Countries, where the Farmer by plowing up the Roots of the Grass and Weeds and by exposing them to severe Frosts, endeavours to extirpate them, however no Frost can destroy the Seeds which are dropped from the ripe Grass and Weeds in the Ground, which the artificial Stratum will smother & perfectly destroy, and save laborious hewing [hoeing] and plowing in the Summer Season to exterminate the Grass and Weeds out of the planted Fields, so that this Method is saving of much Labour and procuring a richer Crop than common Methods. Thirdly, [255] this Mode of making such Stratums, will, though with little Industry, acquire the same Benefit in these parts, what Ice and Snow occasions to the Soil in those Countries which are favoured by Nature with Ice or Snow Stratums not depending from any Industry. Thus I have given a Remedy to those who will or cannot trust a Crop on a shallow sandy Soil. I am sure it will prove in future time when this Method is once introduced and becomes common, that by these means the best Manure is procured in all, especially hot Climates, where Dung increases rather the Heat more, than is necessary, besides infecting the Ground with Worms and New Seeds, and where the hewing [hoeing] and plowing to loosen and mellow the Ground for the easier absorbing the airy Night-dews, or even Winds, are so much required, and will in a Soil free of Grass and Weeds become an easy Labour. Observe that the Fields in East Florida are never to be hewed [hoed] or plowed in the hot hours of the Day, whereby much of the Moisture is exposed to the Sun's Exhalation, which Moisture is to be increased, at least preserved. The only times for hewing [hoeing] or plowing are before Sun-rise; but better at the hours of the trading Sea Breezes, and best at sun-set, but in a rainy Season all hours of the day are proper, unless at such, when the Clouds grow thin, and more so if they begin to move from before the Sun.

17th. I have above advised, with good Reasons, drawn from Experience, that the Vines should not be taken from Countries situated to the North of Burgundy, I would now recommend Lucca,[58] situated upon the Mediterranean in the VII Climate, for gathering the Olive Plants, as that Country is renowned for the Production of the best Olives, viz. the great Ones, which when ripe yield the best Oil; and the lesser kind commonly called Picholini are the best for pickling, when green, as the pickling of the Olives is performed with Sea-salt water, it being the principal Ingredience: this Province, especially Cape Florida, which is bordered by a Sea much richer of Salt than that of Lucca, the Preference will be given to the Olives pickled in this Province.

18th. Although I have advanced several necessary Observations, which I think worthy of Attention, and which chiefly fall within the Bounds of the European's Recognizance; whilst on their side of the Atlantic Ocean, I shall however have much more to say hereafter, relative to Occurrences strictly concerning East Florida, when they land these Shores.

19th. Since all good Success in such great Undertakings of cultivating and improving Deserts chiefly depends from the Vigour and Health of the Body [256] and Constitution, I think it highly necessary to shew from my twenty years Experience in the v and iv Climate, by what Diet and Regimen new Colonists may preserve their Vigour and Health from the time of changing the European, and for the time of continuing in a new and warm Climate, and to make every Man a Judge and Guardian of, and over himself, my Advices are, First, to abstain in hot Seasons from boiled Meat and Fish, from all manner of warm Broth or Liquids, and to eat no warm Victuals but such as are roasted, and drink none but moderately cold Draughts in common Diet, although in cold Weather both boiled Victuals or warm Liquids may be used; and when a Regimen of Perspiration requires them to be warm, of which I shall be more particular hereafter. No Draught should be pure Water, but mixed with a little good Rum (bad Rum is by all means to be avoided for the Reasons given in the 2d Chapter of South Carolina); if good Rum is not at hand, the Water must be corrected by calibiating it with quenching in it a red hot Iron. At no time Freedom is to be taken with immoderate Draughts of strong Liquors, nor overcharging the Stomach with Victuals; neither is it safe to sleep in a Room between two Openings (Doors or Windows) where the Wind has a free, be it ever so small a Draught. Secondly, New Settlers must by all means avoid wetting their Bodies, or even only their Feet in Rain, and more so in Dew; but if by Chance or Necessity it will so happen, they who thus become Sufferers are to increase their Motion, until they reach their Habitation, then take a good and repeated Draught of warm Tea, warm but weak Coffee; warm Water, and Rum or Wine; warm Water mixed with sweetened Juice of Limes, Lemons or Oranges; but in case none of these Premisses are to be had conveniently, then warm calibiated Water, uncloath themselves, enter their Beds, and promote, under sufficient Coverts a moderate Perspiration for the Space of thirty minutes, then dress themselves dry, and take a gentle Exercise. Should any hereafter find himself feverishly disposed he must repeat the aforesaid Regimen of Perspiration as often until that Disposition is expelled; for more Advice in the medicinal Way, Reference may be had to the third Chapter of South Carolina. Thirdly, New Comers are to avoid hard work in the hot (calm) hours, as thereby they will exhaust too much of their necessary Humours by Perspiration; but Necessity will make it some times an obligation to work hard at these hours; such therefore as expose themselves at those hours are to quit their Work, when [257] finding the Perspiration to be violent, and put on a Blanket or other warm Coat, therein retire to a shady, but not windy Place, and take very moderate often repeated but moderately cold Draughts of calibiated Water, or cold Water mixed with a little good Rum, Wine or sweetened Juice of Limes, Lemons or Oranges. Fourthly, In case a sudden cold Wind or Rain should surprise them, whilst in a (altho' small) Perspiration, before they are well covered with Cloaths, they are to take Recourse to the sweating Regimen above directed. Fifthly, They are not to go out in the Sun with an uncovered Head, their best head Cover in Summer is a Straw Hat with a broad Rim, to be light and give Shade to their Faces and Shoulders; these Hats are to be white or whitish, in order to absorbe none but reflect all Sun's Rays inflecting on them; as also those reflecting from the Ground. Sixthly, Their Dress in general is to be light coloured, wide and light as far as to their Knees; but farther down to their Soles they are to be (Summer and Winter) warmly dressed in Cloth, Flannel or Shrouds, and good Shoes. In order to make this Dress convenient, they have two square Pieces of Flannel or Shrouds, in them they wrap up their Legs, and confine them with Garters below their Knees; the rest loosely covers their Feet and Heels home to the Ground, which will prevent (altho' wet) to get any Cold in their Feet; and the Rattle Snakes, which commonly bite about the Heels, (if they do bite at all) they will think themselves sufficiently revenged on the Cloth for having been disturbed by them, and the Person will not be offended or hurt from such Bite. Seventhly, The American Woods and Forrests, especially near the Sea Coast, shelter an infinite Number of Gnats (Muskitoes) during the time that Plantations are only small, of course the Forrests near; when the Winds have no great Power to dissipate them; these Insects are very troublesome after Sun Set, and throughout the whole Night, by which the weary Man is deprived of that Rest he needs, to recover and recruit new Strength; in order that they may make themselves private and keep off such troublesome Company, they are to have over each Bed a Pavillion made of thread or silk-net (Gauze) in a Form of a Bell-tent, twenty four feet wide, running up seven feet to a Point fixed on a Ring, to be hanged thereby over the Bed, and to spread over it at Night, so as to touch the Ground about the Bed. The Remedy for driving these Insects from the Tents or Houses in the Evening before Bedtime is by making several Smoak-Fires round the same; this Method will force the nearest to leave the Tents or Houses, and hinder those which are at a [258] Distance to draw near them; the Inflamation which the Muskitoes cause with their Stings, and form little Tumours in the Skin of New Comers, is best and soonest cured, by rubbing the diseased Places with Spirit of Camphire [*camphor*]. None must set upon a rotten Tree or Stump, as they are full of a small Bug, not bigger than the Point of a dull Needle, and only visible in the light of the Sun, by seeing a scarce visible red speck in motion, they bury themselves in the Pores of the Skin and cause itching Tumors, which by much scratching sometimes mortify; Spirit of Camphire [*camphor*] is the best Remedy to ease the Itching; the Bug in a short time will perish, and the Tumor dissipate. The Ticks are another Plague, especially the Seed, or young Ticks not bigger than a Sand-grain, and brown; their Plague has thrown delicate Persons into a Fever; they may be soon destroyed by rubbing those parts of the Body (where they are) with sweet Oil, which closes their Orifices & chokes them instantaneously.

20th. The Dwelling Houses are to be built lofty, so that the Rooms may be at least nine but not above eleven feet high; the Windows are to reach the Floor, the same as the Doors, on all four sides of the Houses; though I have observed that all American Spaniards make neither Door or Window on the North Side of their Houses; they build on that side a double Wall of eight feet or more, distant from each other, forming a Gallery, as I have mentioned in the 9th Paragraph of the 4th Chapter. These double Walls of the Gallery excluded the Rawness of the North Air, which perhaps they judged pernicious to their Health. This Judgment I doubt not was entertained by a Notion from a pretended Experience, of which they could have had in 200 years a greater Share than I pretended to, yet I have not followed their Practice, but built Doors and Windows on the North side of my House in Saint Augustin, and fixed on that side a Landry [*laundry*] and Pantry with good Success in keeping Victuals and Liquors of all kinds, without prejudicing the Health of any of my Family. My Reason for not following the Spanish Rules of Architecture was, from Experience, that an inclosed could not be so wholesome as a free circulating Air; however the Spanish Method may be tryed first, and mine afterwards, as the former will save time and Expence, and the latter may be applied after the first Experiment does not give Satisfaction. As I suppose the Want of Boards will prevent new Settlers from making their Ground Floor three feet high from the Surface of the Earth, as is necessary to prevent Jiggers [*chiggers*] and other Vermin from nesting in their Floors; by frequent cleaning, washing and airing the House; by [*259*] throwing the Doors and Windows open, from nine in the forenoon to three in the Afternoon. I advise to burn Shells into Lime and to mix it with twice the Quantity of unburnt pounded Shells; these Materials together, to be made up into a Mortar; this Mortar must not be mixed with fresh, but salt-water taken from the Sea (this salt-water in all Buildings will prove to make a better Mortar, soon petrifying, than fresh-water, whose Mortar soon putrifies. (This I have from my own Experience in both cases, on my Buildings in Saint Augustin.) After the Ground-Floor of the House is well rammed with heavy Pestles; the above Mortar is to be laid on four or six Inches thick, and beat by three or more Persons with light Pestles all over, gently and quickly until nothing of the Mortar will stick to the Pestles, then a brush of Linseed Oil must be given all over and continue beating until the oil disappears. This brushing with Oil and beating is to be repeated until the Floor is hard, smooth and shiny; such a Floor will prove near equal to Marble, very lasting, cold, easy to be cleaned with a wet Mop, and aired to keep out Jiggers [*chiggers*], beside all manner of Bugs and Vermin.[59] In East Florida the Expence of Glass Windows may be saved, as they are of little Service, unless it is in stormy and rainy Weather, which the Doors and Shutters on the Weather side will shut out much better than Glass Windows; in lieu of which I advise to make Use of Gauze Blinds (the same Stuff the Pavillions are made of) both in the Door and Window Openings, and to keep them shut all day long, or at least to have them shut before Sun-set, thereby not only to enjoy the free Air, but also to keep out of the Houses both sand-Flies and Muskitoes during the Evening Conversation before Bed-time, at which the Blinds are to be opened and the Shutters and Doors to be shut. Least this Advice should alarm any Person and give cause to suspect as if the Night Airs were unwholesome as it is in the I, II and III Climates both North and South of the Æquator, to the contrary I must observe and can from my own Experience warrant the Night's Airs in the IIII [*IV*] Climate, viz. in East Florida, as far South as Cape Florida, to be the most inoffensive, least dangerous and most healthy in the Universe, as far as I have been, from the 26th degree of East Longitude to the 83d degree West Longitude from the Meridian of London, and from the 55th to the 25th North Latitude, a difference of eight Climates on the North side of the Æquator. I can assure that myself and People with me have slept many Nights in the Woods and on the Sea Coast (when on my General Surveys) [*and*] never any of Us felt the least Inconvenience, so that I can advise the Inhabitants to choose the outside of their Houses for their Night's Rest, in order to [*260*] enjoy the Benefit of the Air, provided tempestuous Weather will not prevent them, and provided also they hang their Pavillions on a Branch of a Tree and spread it over their Beds for keeping of the Muskitoes and Sand-Flies. Altho' they lay now in the free Air, yet this Air has not as in Houses a Draught over but surrounds them; a Draught of Air and its Effect can be compared to a Brasier's blowing through a soldering Pipe, which little Draught incensed by the Flame of the Lamp will smelt a Piece of Metal in a few seconds, which the quiet Flame will not effect even in many years. This Paragraph should have been the nineteenth in lieu of the twentieth, but as in New Plantations the clearing of Land and planting what is necessary for Provision are the first Things to be undertaken, the Planters build Tents of Bushes and cover them with Earth or live in Canvas Tents until they have secured their Crop and make the Construction of their Barns the next, and their Houses the latter Object.

21st. Beside the above Advices and Instructions it will not be superfluous in hinting to new Settlers, that probably they will meet at their Arrival with Persons in the southern (the only vacant) Part of East Florida; or in other more northern Parts, if they should touch any, who will endeavour to prepossess their Minds with many Prejudices in regard to Climate, Soil, Insects, Wild Beasts, Tempests, Indian, French and Spanish Wars: To this I can with Truth observe that no Person beside those in my Service in any part of America ever has been on the southern Main, or if he has, he never took proper pains, or inclined to enquire minutely, so as to form a fair Judgment of the southern Part of East Florida; and the Persons, as may be met with especially at, or near Cape Florida, they have interesting Reasons which induce them to look with a jealous Eye upon New Settlers, who they are sure will become Sharers in their Advantages immediately, nay will cut them off from many Profits, as for instance, from Wrack's [*wrecks*], Fishery and Mahagony Timber, notwithstanding the Benefit they themselves will enjoy from new Settlements, which to foresee, their Avarice stands in their own Light. I have therefore given a full Account of the Climate, and communicated proper Means against the worst; I have given it in the Power of New Settlers to turn the Soil (be what it will) to their Views; I have shewn how to fix Barrier between themselves and the Insects, and to make the nestling impracticable to Bugs, as to wild Beasts and Vermin; as Bears, Panters [*panthers*], Basilisks (rattle Snakes) and Crocodiles (Alligators) which are the only offensive Ones, yet they have never been known to hurt a Person, unless when they being attacked were obliged [*261*] to defend themselves; they all will fly at the Sight of a human Specie, except Basilisks, they cannot fly, but when a Person comes near them they will give warning with rattling their Tail, which is equal to the Noise of mounting a Watch, at which one may stand off. Crocodiles indeed will attack a grown Person, but not otherwise than in the Water a-swimming; I have heard of Instances that they have attacked Children without the House, and carried them off from the Land into the Water, but cannot vouch for its Truth. Tempests will be seen more in that than any other part of the Globe, especially at Cape Florida, as the Main is there situated open to the Gulf of Sandwich within and the Florida Stream without the Sound of Dartmouth, in which Stream the Winds between North and East have great Power, and cause Turbulations of disagreeable Effects, but only to those on the Stream in Vessels, and not to them on shore in their Houses, the first Sight will no doubt affect their Mind, until repeated Sights will render them familiar to it when their Apprehensions will be much less to what they can be in Hurricanes in any part of the Main in Europe. As to the Indians they will prove themselves to new Settlers rather friendly, useful and necessary; if any in their way of hunting (being unlimitted) should come near them, as they came to my House in 1763, which I erected in the Wilderness of Georgia, when they endeavoured to gain my Acquaintance and Friendship by supplying Me with Venison, of which they did make a Practice, as I always presented them with a little Corn, Rice or Salt, but never let them know I had stronger Liquor in my House than Water; they would never come in the House when I was absent, altho' my Wife desired it; they readily will trafic with new Settlers, and exchange Skins, Furs, Bears Oil, Wax and Honey for such Articles as are mentioned in the Sixth Chapter of South Carolina; however new Settlers are not justly entitled to this Trade, unless they have sollicited the Governor for a Licence, without which they are by no means to make a Practice of it. The Indians will not break out into War, nor be jealous about new Settlements, or even complain of it out of a political Pretence, provided the Governor is requested to send Invitations to the Head Men of the Seminolskees (Indians which have separated themselves from the Creek Nation, living by small Tribes in Towns lately built to the West and South of Saint Augustin, are thus called by the Nation Seminolskees, signifying a wild Indian).[60] Their head Men may easily be satisfied by an Information that His Majesty thought it necessary Settlements should be made along the Atlantic Coast in East Florida by His Subjects, in order to give Assistance and Relief to so many distressed who yearly suffer Shipwrack on that Coast; a few Presents of Coats, Waistcoats, Shirts, Blankets, Bracelets, Guns, [262] Powder and Balls, to the Value of £50 Sterling, distributed among the head-Men (which are in all about six or seven) will make the Settlements upon the Sea Coast as far as Cape Florida, an Object if not agreeable at least a matter of Indifference to these Barbarians.[61]

22d. As to French and Spanish Wars, I must observe in general, that such a Plantation, Farm, Country Seat, Village, Town, City or Fortification has, as yet not existed, which could claim a Right or boast of Assurance not to be attacked or molested in time of War, for even the best fortified Places (which if any might have expected that Prerogative) have been worse treated, than open Places, when the latter met frequently with good Treatment. In the year 1762 I then had done fortifying Savannah in Georgia for some time, but for want of Subsidies it could only be made to defend against Indians on the Land side, the River side was quite open; French and Spanish Privateers frequently entered the Mouth of Savannah River, one of which came to an Anchor and allured a Party from Savannah frolicking in the River on board his Vessel, and took them Prisoners; the Captain sent his Barge well manned in the Night up to Savannah, when they might have burnt us all in our Beds, for nothing hindered them from landing and taking a View of the Town; however they meeting with no Resistance were satisfied with the Token they could give to their Prisoners before they were set at Liberty that they positively had been in the Town of Savannah. Settlers especially at Cape Florida will be much better off than all others on any Place I know upon the Eastern Coast of America; for the new Bahama Channel is the principal Outlet of the Gulf of Mexico for all Vessels bound for the Northern Provinces, or Europe; consequently in time of War King's Ships and English Privateers will be constantly cruising at and about Cape Florida, and serve to its Inhabitants as Guards, on whose account Enemies will not venture to stop and molest the Inhabitants, but endeavour to crowd all Sails for running by these Quarters as fast as possible. I must also observe, that all the East India Treasures collected at the Manillas, all the Riches of Mexico, New Spain, Peru and Cili [*Chile*] are hived in the Havannah on Cuba Island; and from thence under the Auspice of a Spanish Admiral escorted to Old Spain, by the Way of the New Bahama Channel.

[*263*]

CHAPTER 6th

Of Pearls, their Climate and Generation; Manufactury of Table Salt; of Baril Ash (Pot-ash, salalkali), item of salt Petre and Asphaldus [*asphalt*]; what profitable Vegitables and Animals are in East Florida.[62]

1. The natural Products of East Florida which invite new Comers to collect them for Manufacturies suitable to European Markets, as well as for Oeconomical and Medicinal Uses appear in the following List.

Subject	Class	Subject	Class	Subject	Class
Alkekenge	Plant	Hare	Beast	Salt Petre	Manufactury
Aloes	Ditto	Hog red	Fish	Salt common	Ditto
Ash-Baril	Manufactury	Honey wild	Electrum	Sheepshead	Fish
Asphaldus	Electrum	Jew	Fish	Snipe	Bird
Albicores	Fish	King	Ditto	Snapper	Fish
Angel	Ditto	Lumber	Manufactury	Spice Tree	Plant
Bear	Beast	Mackarel	Fish	Squile Sea Onion	Ditto
Baracuta	Fish	Mollet	Ditto	Tar	Manufactury
Bass	Ditto	Oyster	Ditto	Tortoise	Amphibious
Bone	Ditto	Papaw	Plant	Turpentine	Manufactury
Bonita	Ditto	Papaja	Ditto	Turkey	Bird
Cinamon wild	Plant	Plum wild	Ditto	Trout	Fish

Subject	Class	Subject	Class	Subject	Class
Cochoneal	Worm	Pearl	Fish	Turbot	Ditto
Cavallo	Fish	Pitch	Manufactury	Wax {Bees	Electrum
Deer	Beast	Partridge	Bird	Wax {Myrtle	Plant
Duck	Bird	Pigeon	Ditto	Wine Grape	Ditto
Gum Elemi	Plant	Possum	Beast	Wood-cock	Bird
Groan	Fish	Porgus	Fish		
Grupper	Ditto	Porpoise	Ditto		
		Prawn	Amphibious		
		Raccoon	Beast		

[*264*] 2d. Inka Garcilassa de la Vega observes in his History of the Florida Conquest, that the Spaniards, (who under the Command of Muscoso returned from the Florida Expedition to Panuco, in the Kingdom of Mexico) reported that the Indians of Florida understood the Pearl Fishery, and wore them about their Necks and Arms. The Gulf of Mexico was in them days settled all round by several Indian Nations. This Gulf lays with the Persian Gulf in the same climatic Zona, viz. in the IV Climate on the North side of the Æquator. It is well known that the Pearl Fishery is one of the great Treasures of Persia, as besides the climate these two Gulfs resemble each other also in the Situation viz. a Sea to the East and South, and Land to the North and West. I cannot help concluding that they must equal each other in the Production of Pearls, and easily give Credit to Garcilasso's Account that the Florida Indians wore and possessed great Treasures of Pearls, although the Modern Indians living only upon fresh Rivers, and far off from the Sea, grind the purple or blue Spot out of the Oysters in round Shapes and wear them; such Beads they esteem of the greatest Value and call them Wampum. These Indians have after so many Generations entirely lost the Knowlege of Pearls. I should not be so apt to draw with so much Assurance a Reference from the Gulf of Persia had I not another plausible Instance before me, viz. the Island of Ceylon in the East Indies, and the King's or Galeres Islands in the Bay of Panama have one Zona (viz. the second Climate on the North Side of the Æquator), common, as also a rich Pearl Fishery; the Pearls of Ceylon are reckoned the best, because those from Panama are never exported, except a few indifferent Ones, for the good Pearls fished at Panama find near and good Markets at Quito, Lima, Cusco, and La Plata in Peru and Saint Jago [*Santiago*] and La Conception in Cili [*Chile*], where they are sold at a higher Rate than the Price they would be valued in Europe: for the Ladies in those parts prefer Pearls before Diamonds, and other precious Stones. The finest Pearls are found in Places where no River or Rivers (be they fresh or salt) are near; for they wash at times of Freshes the Mud from the Main into the Sea in great Clouds, and force a Passage to the very Bottom of

the Sea, where the River Mud mixes with that fine Mud on which the Pearl Oysters and Muscles feed; although they use to grow fat, feeding upon that Mixture, yet their Slime becomes unclean, which they perspire; and with which they incrus-[265]tate by degrees both the inside of the Pearl Mother and the Pearl Itself, which originally was a small Grain of Sand accidentally shut in the Oyster or Muscle; in consequence of this unclean Slime, the Incrustation will be of an unclean Water (Lustre), such Pearls are thrown and sold among the River Pearls for Medicinal Use in which case they sell for more Money than the finest Pearls; but the Effect does not exceed that of Medicinal Preparation made of common Oyster and Egg Shells. Where no River or Rivers are near, this Mixture of the River and Sea Mud cannot happen; for altho' the Winds will stain sometimes with this Mud the Soundings on a Distance of several Miles, yet for want of Gravity it cannot sink and is thereby kept floating on the Surface of the Sea, gathering into a Scum and thrown by the Flood on Shore. In these Places the Oysters feed on the pure fine vitresible Earth, which the saline Acid in its Saturation precipitates as superfluous for its Basis in the Generation of Salt. I have (when refining Salts by Crystallisation) often received such an Earth much resembling the Flores Benzoe. Successful Enquiries and Searches after fine Pearls are to be made First, in the four first Climates both North and South of the Æquator. Second, on Places where no River fresh or salt is near. Third, where they are covered by the Land against the East and North Winds, on the North side of the Æquator, and against East and South Winds on the south side of the Æquator. Fourth, where they may be freely and long irradiated by the western Sun generating the Dews. First, because in the four first Climates, the Sun impregnates the Sea by its perpendicular Inflection with more Salt or Acid than with its oblique inflection in the more southern and northern Climates, therefore secondly the Interstices of the Waters in the south Ocean are so filled with Salts that the foreign Earth Particles from the Main carried by the Winds only (unless they be Sand) cannot get a Passage to the Bottom of the Sea to adulterate the pure vitresible Earth (Mud) on which the Oysters feed. Thirdly, the East Winds are hot and dry and the North Winds are cold and dry on the north side of the Æquator, and on the south side the south Winds are the same, which two opposite Effects of hot and cold are so powerfully penetrant that neither Glass or Stone can bear their Vicissitudes without being split and calcined in time, much more will it effect the tender Pearl in its Crustation although several Fathoms under Water. Fourthly, the Rays of the Sun are the Conveyors of the Universal Sperma through the Air and Water and sow it all over the Face of the Earth and Bottom of the Sea, where it has no more [266] than the time of the Night to form itself into crystallin Bodies, which being very volatile acquire the Protection of a cold Shade, or else the Rising-Sun being hot and dry is very apt to absorbe them.

3d. From the Premises I have fully evinced, that the IIII [*IV*] Climate governing this Province calculated for the manufacturing of common (Table) Salt, which may be perfectioned with little Labour, viz. the Manufacturer fixes upon a small Lake near the Sea Coast, which has no Communication with any Run or Rivulet, and runs dry at low Water; across the Mouth of this Lake he carries a Dam about eight Inches lower than high water Mark Spring Tide; at the Bottom of the Dam he lays two or three or more Troughs, made of four Planks 12 Inches wide, provides them with Flood-doors in and outside the Dam; the Bottom of this Lake must be made very even. The highest Spring Tides are let in by the Trough, and over the Dam, in order to fill the Lake which when filled the Flood-doors are shut in order that the salt water in the Lake can have no Supply before the next Spring Tide, the Sun mean while will exhale great part of the Water, so that the Salt can form itself in cubical Crystals, one or two days before the next Spring Tide the Doors in the Troughs are opened at low Water and Bags applied on the outside in order to receive the Salt which the draining Water carries along, when the Lake is dry or before the Flood comes up to the Dam then the Doors must be shut again that the Salt may be raked up, washed in Sieves with clean salt water, and spread on a clean Floor under the Shade to dry gradually. This washing of the Salt may be done near the Lake, so that the Water being very salt may run into the Lake; this method produces Salt as hard as a Rock, and succeeds best in dry hot Seasons; cold, moist and rainy Weather retards it in some degrees, however, there are long Spells of suitable Seasons, that the Manufacturer will have sufficient Reward for his Labour.

4th. As the Coast produces the Barilla in great Plenty besides other Weeds equally rich of a vitresible Earth, the Manufactury of Pot-ash, (Baril ash or alcali) is the next salin Object in this Province to be undertaken with Profit, viz. the Weeds are gathered by two or three Persons, and carried to the Spot, where a fourth Person digs a hole about three feet deep and four feet in Diameter at the Top, fixes a large Iron Pot or Iron Copper in the Bottom, and plaisters the sides above the Copper with Clay up to the Top, the Weeds are laid round the Hole and dryed as Hay [*267*] with the dryest a Fire is made in the Copper, which when blazes is smothered with green Weeds, they again are covered with dry Weeds, this Process is continued until Night when the Fire in quenched with fresh Water; next Morning before the above Process is reassumed the loose Ashes which are uppermost are taken out with a Hoe (a) and the Fire is continued until Night as the day before and quenched with fresh Water. This Process is repeated every day until the Copper is full of hard matter, then the Copper or Pot is taken out of the Holes if the Matter appears white with green and blue Spots or Veins;

(a) made into a thin Pap, therewith besmear the fresh Weeds N. B. With this Pap made out of the Ashes before these Weeds are laid on so as to burn all Ashes over again.

the Pot Ash is finished and requires no more than to be dug out with a Chisel and Mallet; if the Matter is brown and unclean (commonly called a Magma), it must after it is dug out be dissolved in fresh Water, which Solution, after the Dregs are settled to the Bottom (b) is boiled up in the Copper with a middling Fire, so as not to make the Matter boil over the Copper, when the Matter begins to thicken the Fire is increased all about the Copper so as to bury it in the Fire as long until the Copper is red, then the Fire is taken off and the Pot Ash taken out with Spades and Trowels whilst hot, which makes an End of this Process.

5th. The third salin Object to be taken in hand is the Salt Petre. I have observed that the cold Winds in December and January surprise the Fish which with the Flood approach the Shore in great Sholes, benums [benumbs] them with cold in a degree that they loose the Faculty of Swimming, fall on their Backs and are left after high Water on shore, where part may be salted and dryed for Provision; the rest are junk'd and mixed with unslacked Lime, buried under a long Shade in a Ditch, and covered with Lime and Swamp Mud or Dung of Animals, especially of Sheep; in six Months time one end of this Ditch is laid open with a Spade; if the Fish are quite rotten this Earth is well mixed by digging and moulded in the Form of small Bricks, which when dry are elixivated with hot water in large Tubs; the clear Extraction is boiled in a Copper and so long supplied with fresh Extraction until a Crust of Ice appears all round on the Copper, or until a few drops crystalize on a cooled Iron; at this Appearance the Fire is taken off and a large Broom is let down, so that the Ends of it spread on the Bottom of the Copper, which after some hours (when all is quite cold) is taken out and the Crystals of Salt Petre are broke off the Broom on a Shed spread in a Shade [268] to dry; the Copper is heated afresh and the boiling or rather evaporating Lixivia is supplied with fresh Extraction until the above sign appears again, and so the Process is continued as long as there is Earth to be elixivated; the elixivated Earth is laid up under the Shade until the next Supply of the benummed [benumbed] Fish which are to be covered after the Lime with the above Earth; it must be observed that all manner of animal Bodies, even Vegitables thus putrified are Original Materials to manufacture in the above Way this necessary Article of Salt Petre.

6th. The Manufactury of Turpentine, Pitch, Tar and Lumber is so common that I need not to engross these Leaves with those Articles and their Processes.

7th. I therefore proceed to describe the Benefit that accrues from the Collection of the Asphaldus [asphalt], which I have gathered in Pieces from one ounce to one hundred Pounds Weight on the Coast in my general Surveys on Shore: The Indian Women in Mexico chew it to clean their Teeth; I have melted it with a

(b) when the Dregs are settled, the clear Solution must be decanted before it is boiled a second time.

little Addition of oil or Animal Fat, the Savings on board, and painted my Vessels and Boats Bottoms with it, which in appearance and Goodness was equal to Japan, and held out longer without taking Grass and Barnacles, than common Bottoms from which it may easily be judged that its Usefulness will extend to many purposes in Oeconomy, besides that it is well calculated for giving the Body in all black Balsams and Emplastres, and is no doubt when dissolved with Alcohol vini sharpened with spirits Urinæ, then distilled with several Cohobitions to obtain its Tincture, or if pounded mixed with Sand, is distilled out of a Retorde [retort] to receive its Oil that both Products will not be inferior to those extracted from Amber Grease.

8th. Cochoneal is a Bug not above the tenth part of an Inch big, the Description of which and its Commodity are mentioned in the first Chapter of South Carolina.

9th. The Process of extracting the Myrtle-Wax appears also in the same Chapter after the Cochoneal, Opuntia and Barilla.

10th. Bees-Wax and Honey may be gathered out of the hollow Trees in the Swamps and Pine Lands, of which I have met many in my general Surveys and have had frequent Supplies of Honey for myself and People but was always obliged to have the Tree cut down, which never could be done without great Destruction of the industrious Bees, and is the [269] Method used both by the Europeans and Indians, this notwithstanding these indefatigable and very thriving Inhabitants of the wild American Forrests, doth not seem to diminish, but increase from their own Stock and those young Swarms, which by Neglect of their European Keepers escape from the Hive and cultivate the Wilderness.

11th. The wild Cinnamon Tree grows very plenty upon the Martyr Keys (Islands), its inner Bark is of a light straw Colour, rather sharper than the East Indian Cinnamon, with which (when mixed equal parts) soaked in Madeira Wine fourteen Nights and distilled, yields as fine a Cinnamon Spirit as any made of the East Indian only.

12th. The Gum Elemi Tree is also very common upon all the Islands of the Martyr's; it's Gum is of a very agreeable Scent, and will approve itself as a Balsamicum in Pills alterants and digesting Emplasters, which require such Ingrediences.

13th. Of the Virtue, and Use of the Aloes as one of the Martyr Plants, I need not mention more than that the Concretum of its Juice is a Mixture of a Gum and a Resina, the former a gentle Catharthicum and the latter a principal Vulnerarium, after the Juice is coagulated into a dry Massa, then pounded, out of which the Gum is separated from the Resina by Elixivation with Rain Water, and this evaporated again in Balneo Vaporis.

14th. The Plums commonly called Hiccoca (which means a Fig Plum) are met with all along the Sea Coast of this Province, especially to the southward of Cape Canaveral; these Plums are one of the Articles preserved and exported among the West Indian Sweet-Meats.

15th. The Alkekenge is a Plant which over runs all shady Places of old Fields and Gardens in this Province, its Fruit is yellow, resembling a Cherry covered with a thin Bag or Bladder; the Root of this Plant is exceeding bitter, one dram of it (after it is reduced into a Powder) soaked in four or five Ounces of cold Water, and after twelve hours steeping is taken on an empty Stomach before Bed time, and the Patient does not go abroad but confine himself in a temperate Room during the Operation of this Remedy, which lasts four or five days, or as long until the Evil is removed; this Remedy disposes itself to the Circumstances of the Patient, is an Emetic when Nature requires an Evacuation upwards or a Chezanane when downwards, it removes all Obstructions, Disorders and Pains of [270] the Stomach, Histeric, Nephritic, Collic, Sciatic, and accelerates the Birth; in short it is a paliative against all Pains, and so safe a Remedy that it may be given to Children one year old. A Wine made of Alkekenge is very diuretic and a Specificum AntiNephriticum when a Wine Glass full is drunk in the Morning.

16th. The Papaw is a Plant which produces a Fruit like a Melon, about three Inches in Diameter; this Fruit and the young Sprouts of the Plant are among the Articles comprehended in the West Indian Sweet Meats, where this tender Plant stands the Winter Season without receiving any hurt; it is an infallible Criterion of the Climate in that Country, being favourable to the Cultivation of the Sugar Cane.

17th. The Papajos is a small Tree resembling a Fig Tree as to its Trunk and Limbs; but its Leaves are four Inches in Diameter, round and smooth, with a deep green on their upper side, and wooly with a light brown on their underside, at a distance in a sun shiny-day they appear as green enameled Gold; its Blossum is the same as that of the China Oranges, rather of a more agreeable Scent; its Fruit is shaped as a Lemon, yellow as an Orange, full of small Seeds, which are coloured shaped and as big as Lentils; this Fruit is only eatable, when brown and rotten, and relishes much like Cheese-Cakes; this Tree is an evergreen; bearing all the year round Blossum, green, yellow and rotten Fruit.

18th. The Wine Grape Tree is very large, resembles with its Trunk and Limbs the Fig Tree and Papajos, I have seen some whose Trunk was near a foot in Diameter; its Leaves resemble those of the Papajos, but much larger, and appear with the same Lustre as those of the Papajos in a sun shiny day; its Limbs spread horizontal twelve or more feet from the Trunk, so as to form an agreeable Arbour and Shade of 24 feet in Diameter, 75 in Circumference and 452 square feet Area Room sufficient to shade 50 Persons sitting under it. The Grapes are in large

Clusters, their Berries red, of an agreeable Taste, but on account of their large Seeds they contain but little Juice. This Tree does not appear in the End of the IIII [IV] Climate, (at least the northernmost I met with) grew in Latitude 29°. The Wine Grape Tree is a deciduous, which as well as the Papaw when sprouting indicates the Season to commence planting; although this Climate protects the Wine Grape Tree, it nevertheless favours also the Grape Vines; but they are only met with in Swamps, and proves that East Flori- [271] da is peculiarly calculated for the Culture and Product of Wine. It seems Nature directs that the Wine Grape Tree should be cultivated in Groves, and the Grape Vine planted near its Root, to run up this Tree spread upon its Limbs, and enjoy the Benefit of its Shade, both to keep off the cold Spring Winds, sometimes prejudicial to the Blossum, and prevent the Sun from exhaling the Moisture, and Dew from the Soil, which covers its Roots. In this and the foregoing Chapter I have in two Lists enumerated vegitable Objects, those in the first are Productions of the Martyr Islands, and the southern part of the IV Climate only; the next List comprehends Objects which did strike my Attention in regard to immediate and beneficial Use; that it may not appear as if this Province presented no other vegitable Product to the Eyes of Inhabitants and Visitors. I have thought proper to annex a List of such vegitable Objects, which are common to the whole, but chiefly to the Northern part of the IV Climate.

List of Plants, as yet not mentioned

Ash .... Tree
Asp .... Ditto
Barilla .... Herb
Bay { flowring, laurus, swamp, sweet } .... Tree
Beach .... Ditto
Birch .... Ditto
Botton snake root .... Herb
Cabbage species..... Tree
Cane .... Weed
Cedar .... Tree
China root...Convolvulus
Cherry .... Tree
Chincopin .... Ditto
Citron .... Ditto
Cyprus .... Ditto

Grass { Bunch, Cane, Cattail, Crab, Marsh, Salt, Fresh, Oats, wild, Sword, Wire }
Guava .... Tree
Gum .... Ditto
Hickery .... Ditto
Holy .... Ditto
Iuka...alias silk grass
Indian Pride Tree...Tree
Indigo Wild......Weed
Lemon & Lime......Tree
Magnolia Species...Ditto

Orange { Bittersweet, China, Pergamot, Seville, Shadoc, Sour-sweet } .. Tree
Palmetoes ....Shrub
Palmetoe royal......Tree
Passion Flower......
Convolvulus
Peach .... Tree
Persimon .... Ditto
Pine { yellow, spruce, swamp } .. Ditto
Plantin .... Ditto
Pomgranate .... Ditto
Poplar .... Ditto
Quinoh .... Ditto

Chicasaw Plum.....Ditto	Maple ....Ditto	Santonicum ....Herb
Cujan Pepper.......Ditto	Mulberry ....Ditto	alias Jerusalem Oak
Dogberry ....Tree	Myrtle ....Ditto	Sassafras ....Tree
Dogwood ....Ditto		Sea Potatoe..Convolvulus
Elm ....Ditto	Oak { Live / Red / Water / White } .....Tree	Sloe ....Shrub
Fern ....Ditto		Tallow ....Tree
Fig ....Ditto		Thistle Blessed .....Herb
Fringe ....Ditto		Tupelo ....Tree
		Wallnut ....Ditto

[272] 19th. I come now to the useful Animal, among which the Bear deserves the Preference, for its Meat is by many relished above Pork, his Fat is rather an Oil, and sweet as that of Almonds, and his Skin makes the best under Bed in Summer both in Houses, and in the Woods, for it is cold and gives no Passage to the Moisture of the Earth to prejudice those Travellers, who are obliged to camp in the Forrests; makes also a good Cover over the Pack-Horses to keep the Baggage dry in rainy Seasons, and in a Temperature against the Heat of the Sun.

20th. The Deers are from three to four feet high, their Skins are a good Commodity to exchange for European Goods, and their Meat is wholesome, and relished by every One. The Hunter walks up to them, when they are feeding, but he must stop without the least Motion, as soon as the Deer shakes its Tail, for then the Deer intends to raise its Head in order to look about, as soon as it inclines its Head down again to the Pasture, the Hunter walks up nearer until nigh enough for his Gun or Rifle.

21st. Raccoons are a kind of Foxes with Monkies Feet and Toes, they live upon Fish, Oysters and Birds; their Fur is much the same as those of Badgers; some of the Inhabitants think their Meat very delicious, especially their Hams when smoaked.

22d. The Possum is in Shape and Figure like a large Rat, as big as a midling Fox, they are grey when young, and white when old. Their Fur is not regarded, and their Meat by very few admired. I mention this Genus as having no Species, and being extreamly curious in part of their Structure. Nature has not provided them with a Matrix, but only six or eight Dugs out of and on which their young Ones grow, as a Fruit on a Tree; they can shut up their Belly with two Valves of Skin, as close as two Lappels of a Coat will cover the Breast, so that their young Ones do not appear, and when they are ripe, their Mouths will dissolve from the Dug on which they are grown in a manner (as I have tryed to pull them off) that the places of Separation will bleed as a Wound, and the young Ones had no Power any more to hold fast to the Dug, as long as the young Possums are not above the Bigness of a common Rat, they will creep into that Belly or Bag to take Suck, or when any Danger is nigh, that the Mother is obliged to escape, She takes in her young Ones, shuts her Valves and flies; they climb up the highest Trees, and let themselves down from one Limb to another by slinging their Tail round a limb (as a Monkey) & hold fast until they can reach with their Fore-feet any of the lower Limbs.

[273] 23d. The Hares are not bigger than the grey Rabbits sold in the Streets of London, they do not burrow and breed under Ground as Rabbits, but as Hares in Thickets under Bushes; their Meat is as white as that of Rabbits, and very palatable; they will increase themselves in Plantations without the Planter's Trouble, provided they are protected against Dogs, Foxes, Cats, Eagles and Turkey Bussarts, and are not hunted too much.

24th. Turkies are in great Abundance, their Weight exceeds sometimes twenty four Pounds; they are bigger than any tame Turkey I ever saw in Europe; their Feathers are brown, tipp'd with black; their Meat is exceedingly delicious; they feed upon Acorns, Palm and Palmetoe Nuts, Grasshoppers and any Worm or Snail they meet with in the Forrests and Savannahs, they hatch twenty or thirty young Ones at a time; Hunters catch them by walking first gently after them and increasing the Motion in Conformity with those of the Turkey, which at last by a long Walk and Trot are so fatigued, that they cannot fly, but must sur-render to the running Hunter; or the Hunter makes several Traps with Poles four and five Inches in Diameter, and nine or twelve feet long, which he piles up in a Square as four Walls of a House, of seven or eight Poles about four feet high, over a hole two feet deep and seven or ten feet square, in which leads, by a Slope, a Communication from the outside of the Poles; on this Communication as well, as in the hole they scatter a few Pease or Beans, as the Turkey picks going along without raising its head he will gradually be led into the Hole under the Trap, which is covered at the Top with Poles also, when after consuming the Bait, willing to leave the Place the Turkey in its Fright, seeing himself sur-rounded and covered with Poles, lifts up his Head to search for a Passage, misses the Communication, through which he was introduced, and thus is caught. The Method of hunting them is with a small Dog; which by their barking will oblige them (when on the Ground) to take the Tree, where he will keep his Eyes fixed on the Dog; the Hunter mean while approaches from another side and shoots him down; dexterous Hunters will bring them down with a Ball fired out of a Gun or Rifle from the highest Tree, without the Help of a Dog.

25th. Woodcocks are not in great Number, therefore seldom met with, they reside in low swampy Places well shaded with Trees and Bushes.

[274] 26th. The Snipe is a Bird scarce more frequent than a Woodcock, they stay in open Places where stagnant Waters are bordered with Marshes.

27th. The Ducks are in an incredible Quantity, especially in the Winter

Months, when they leave the cold Northern Provinces to enjoy the agreeable Climate on the open Ponds, Lakes and Rivers of East Florida.

28th. All the wild Pigeons on the Continent of North America seem to make Georgia and East Florida their Home during the Winter Season, when their Game affords Diversion, and supplies the Table in lieu of Poultry. Their Meat is equal to Pigeons in general.

29th. The Partridges will [in]habit and hatch about the Planters Gardens and Fields, if not shy'd will become so tame as to feed with the Poultry in the Planter's Yard; I had frequently that Diversion to see them feeding in my Plantations in Georgia with my Fowls. They are not bigger than the Quails in England. Their Meat is white, tender and relishing.

30th. East Florida produces three kinds of Tortoise in very great Numbers, viz. the Loggerhead, Hawk bill and green Tortoise, from ten to one hundred Pounds in Weight, of which the green Tortoise is only admired and relished at Tables. Vessels are loaded with them and brought to the Georgia and South Carolina Markets where they sell for nine pence per Pound weighed with the Shell. The Loggerheads are caught for the Sake of their Shells only on which the Scales are very large and thick, and sold under the Title of Tortoise Shells. All Tortoise lay their Eggs on the Sea Shores in the Sand, in which they make with a sharp square Nail about three Inches long loosely fixed in a Stick an Inch and a quarter thick and six feet long; the Nail is tied in its Middle on the end of a strong fishing Line latched from one to the other end of the said Stick, the Remainder of the Line which contains from 60 to 100 fathom lays on the Bottom of the Boat; as soon as the Fishermen has struck a Tortoise the Nail will fix itself in the Shell and part with the Stick; the Fisherman then humours the Tortoise by giving him as much Scope to swim away as the Length of the Line will admit of, then pulls it back again as long as his Force is superior to the Tortoise, but when it grows superior to him he gives it a fresh [275] Liberty to take its own way; by these Spells the Fisherman rests himself, but the Tortoise is constantly fatiguing, so that at last over fatigued by these repeated Changes will suffer itself to be pulled near the Boat, taken in and laid on its Back. The Tortoise lay their Eggs on the Sea Shores in the Sand, in which they make big Holes and arch it over with a Vault of Sand cemented together with their Slime, leave a small hole of an Inch and a half in Diameter, through which they drop their Eggs in the holes in a manner as the Shell Snails; their Eggs are near an Inch and a half in Diameter, covered with a hard Skin in lieu of a Shell. Each Tortoise lays between two and three hundred Eggs; at these times the Fishermen surprise them upon their Nest, or if they fly, run after and turn them upon their Backs before they can reach the Water; thus a Fisherman may in a few Minutes catch a Dozen; for it is impossible for a Tortoise laying on its Back upon dry Land to turn itself upon its Fins. The Hawk-Bill is by the Fishermen and Sailors eaten, and by them much praised, but their Approbation is not received by Epicures, they therefore never make their Appearance upon the public Markets.

31st. Oysters are not only very plenty, but whole Rocks of one hundred or more Fathoms in Length met with which are nothing but oysters cemented together. The Oysters are generally three times as long as they are broad, when in Season they are very fat and of so agreeable a Saltness, that they who have been long in America, cannot relish English Oysters on account of their strong copperish Taste; Mukoso Creek which issues out of Mukoso Lake and runs into Mukoso Harbour, has its Bed between two almost continuing Banks of Oyster Rocks. All Oysters are open when the Water runs from them, and they lay dry. Raccoons which prey at Ebb Tide after them (if not carefull) are sometimes caught by the Oysters, which at the least Touch shut themselves, and thus confine the Paws of the Raccoons until high Water, who are then drowned.

32d. Prawns grow to the Weight of five Pounds, and upwards each; amazing Numbers of them live and spawn in the holes of the coral Rocks (generally the fundamental Stratum of the Mangrove Islands) on the north side of Hawke Channel. These Prawns are by the West Indians improperly called Lobsters, although they have not the two Claws as Lobsters; they are beautifully spotted with red, yellow, blue, green and some black; all which Colours change into one red Colour by boiling. [276] My People brought some on board which they catched at the Matance Island, of which several were so large that their Bodies only (beside the Tail) was too great a Meal for Me, although my Appetite was very good.

33d. Of the Fish I shall only mention that they all are very plenty, as I have mentioned in the 5th Paragraph, where I give Directions for the Salt Petre Manufactury. A Family will never want Provision, if they do but chuse to take the Pains of catching them on the Shores of the Sea, Streams, Rivers and Rivulets; some of them are very delicious. The Jew Fish is reckoned the best, next to him is the Sheepshead and Mullet; the middle sort is the Trout, Angel Fish, Porgus, Bass and the Turbot; the rest are of an inferior kind. The Baracuta is a Sea Pike seldom eaten unless on board of vessels. In the West Indies many have been poisoned and lost their Lives by eating of them; for this Fish preys upon those small Fishes, which feed upon the West Indian Copper Banks, on which the small Fish, on account of their Nourishment, and seldom being caught, live without Disturbance; it will happen sometimes that Negroes out of Ignorance go there a-Fishing, and as many as eat of those Fish, prove by their Death the fatal Certainty of their poisonous Quality, the Information of which had such an Effect on my Apprehensions, that I never could relish Baracutas, although they were

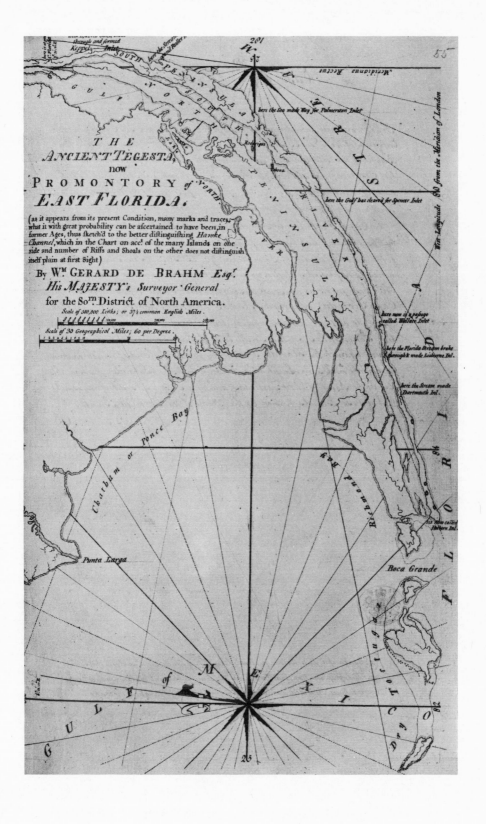

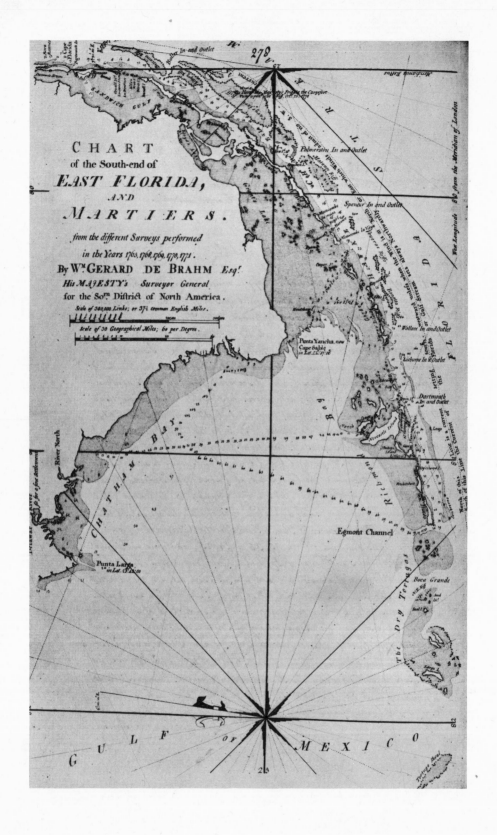

CHART
of the South-end of
EAST FLORIDA,
AND
MARTIERS.

from the different Surveys performed
in the Years 1765, 1768, 1769, 1770, 1771.
By Wᵐ GERARD DE BRAHM Esqʳ
His MAJESTY's Surveyor General
for the Soᵗʰ District of North America.

Scale of 300,000 Links; or 37¼ common English Miles.

Scale of 50 Geographical Miles; 60 per Degree.

Punta Yancha, now
Cape Sable
in Lat 25. 25. 00

Punta Larga
in Lat 25.21.00

River North

CHATHAM BAY

Egmont Channel

Boca Grande

The Dry Tortugas

GULF OF MEXICO

G

F L O R I D A

glutted by my People on board my Vessels; I did however taste of them not catched in the West Indies, but on the Atlantic Coast, where they are not pernicious. I found them to be of that dryness in their Meat which the fresh water Pikes used to be.

[279]

CHAPTER 7th

Necessary Directions for Navigation in the Florida Stream, from the Gulf of Mexico, upon the Eastern Coast of East Florida, Georgia and South Carolina, &c, or the

Atlantic Pilot.[63]

1st. Cape Florida has not in Appearance to transient Navigators the Characteristic of one of the Southern Capes of the Promontory of East Florida (in former times scarcely known to the World, save by its bare Name and Existence, unless in parts by those who in their Navigation near it became unfortunate by suffering Shipwrack). I should not contend with such as refuse or hesitate to admit it among the Number of Capes, because it almost joins (when discovered from the Southward) a Ridge of Islands on its South, with scarce less visible Distinction, than it joins the Continent to its North, and in deed it has in all Probability, in former Ages been part of the Main. This by the Plan I have Sketched of its probable ancient Figure, drawn from Judgments obtained by concluding from its present Shape and Condition, I endeavour to shew more fully, however because of the last Bend, or Course of the Florida Stream at this Place, where it enters, (after several Changes in its Course) the New Bahama Channel with a N. by E. Direction, because of the Inlet being here made by Force of the said Stream into Hawke Channel (which Channel runs from Latitude 25°35′ to 24°25′, contains one Degree and ten Minutes difference of Latitude, and one degree forty three Minutes difference of Longitude; and has its Bed between the Martyr Reefs and Shoals on its South and the Martyr Islands on its North. Also because of this Place being at present the south End of the Western Atlantic Coast, and the Beginning of the Southern Main, forming that part of the Gulf of Mexico, which lays between Cuba, and East Florida; they both meet here in an Angle of 150°; and likewise as all Vessels departing from the Havannah on Cuba or Panna Matance if properly laid up, discover generally this Place first and is their criterion of having passed the Martyr Reefs, and they may hence with [280] Safety continue standing Northward; here they are sure to be in the Entrance of the New Bahama Channel, and take from thence the Benefit of the Florida Stream through the said Channel into the Atlantic Ocean; for all which Reasons I think myself justified for having ranked this Place among the Capes and particularized it as such in my General Hydrogeographical Map.

2d. Cape Florida is situated in North Latitude 25°42'42" N. B. by Observation; but by Survey in 25°44'11" and in West Longitude from the Meridian of London (a) 79°25'56". The Suns and magnetical Amplitudes differ here with 6° East Variation of the Compass. All these parts at present distinguished by the Appellations of Cape Florida, Martyr Islands, Martyr Shoals, and Martyr Reefs do appear to have been in times past contiguous, forming two Peninsulas on the South End of that Promontory fortified as it were, against the Florida Stream by broken Islands, which contain near forty miles in Longitude and twelve miles in Latitude, known this day by the Name of Dry Tortugas, and by a Reef (out sight of any Land) West of these Islands, known by the Name of the Tortuga Bank.

[*284*] This folio is entirely devoted to De Brahm's "Table of the Hydrometrie from Charles Town in So. Carolina to London Performed in 1771 by Wm. Gerard de Brahm Esqr. His Majesty's Surv. Genl. for the Southern District of North America." It, like the tables of his land surveys, is of limited interest and is omitted here.

Most of the material contained in the manuscript version of the "Table" is included in the "Table of Loxodromy and Observation, from which the Map of the Atlantic Ocean is laid down, by William Gerard De Brahm, Esq.," found in *The Atlantic Pilot* (London, 1772).] [*287*]

Of the southernmost Peninsula, whose Isthmus now constitutes Cape Florida, there remains only the Trace among the Shoals, and Reefs of the Northern Peninsula, whose Isthmus lays west of Sandwich Gulf, there are extant many valuable Islands, beside the Tract of its whole Shape. Between these two Peninsulas, and the Main are to this day parts of one River, now called Grant's Lake, and the whole Channel of another, now called Hawke Channel; both issuing, viz. the former from the Northward of the (formerly called Island, now) Peninsula Larga, and the other out of the Gulf, now known by the Name of Sandwich, and both with a parallel Course, viz. Grant's Lake, after sweeping the North Beach of the Northern Peninsula and South Shore of the Main, and Hawke Channel, after watering the South of the Northern, and the North Shore

(a) By a careful Hydrometric performed in 1771 of which the Loxodromical Table and Hydrographical Map, laid down from the same Table and containing the Atlantic Ocean between America and Europe are adjoin'd after the Draught of the Cape.

of the southern Peninsula both emptying themselves to the North, and South of Dry Tortugas into the Gulf of Mexico, and its Stream. The Islands still in being, as Remnants of the Northern Peninsula, are many, and go by the general Name of Martyr Islands, or commonly the Keys, whose Original Spanish Names are not at all known, or which never have been named, of such the remarkable and nameless are distinguished, and mentioned with their proper Names, as they are recorded in the latter End of the 3d Chapter of East Florida of which Hueso Island is the south Point of the former Northern Peninsula, as the Shoal of Sombreros, with its barren Sand Hills is the south Point of the Southern Peninsula. Between Hueso, and the Tortugas continues the former Creek in very good Condition, situated in Latitude 24°25', and in 81°10'33" west Longitude from the Meridian of London, where the magnetical differs 6°25' East, from the solar Amplitude, which I have made known by the Name of Egmont Channel, and affords a very good Passage to and from Pensacola and Places contiguous. An E. N. E. Moon makes there high Water; the Rise and Fall of Flood, and Ebb is 3 1/2 feet at neep Tide, and 6 1/2 feet at full and change. The best Water lays on the East side of the Channel, which is five Miles in Length, bears S. S. E. and N. N. W. and (where narrowest) is a quarter of a mile wide; it floods in this Channel at times from South to North five hours and ebbs seven; at other times it floods seven hours moderately, so that a Vessel with a leading Wind may easily stem its Current: but it ebbs five hours [288] from North to South with Precipitation across the Hueso Banks, and sets over upon the Tortuga Shoals, so that a Vessel cannot with a leading Wind stand against it without Danger of being set on Shore on the Tortuga Bank. The Soundings in this Channel run between 36 3/10 and 16 1/2 feet high Water, neep Tide, and from 39 3/10 to 91 1/2 high Water Spring Tide upon white Sand on the South End, which lasts for about two Miles, then upon Rocks, and Sand for near two miles more, and end upon white Marl, from which they fall upon quick Sand to the North of the said Channel, and increase in Richmond Bay on a sandy Bottom.

3d. The great Weight of the Sea inclosed within the vast Extent of the Mexican Gulf is set in Agitation by the Trade Winds, as is generally agreed, whereby the famous Florida Stream is supposed to be effected, and thence called Gulf Stream, by which Nature conduces both to the Health, and Conveniency of that Region. But this Stream is in Reality carried into the Gulf of Mexico by these Trade Winds, and therein circulates at large; but at the Place of its Issue anxiously compressed by the Islands Cuba, and Bahamas on one side, and the Promontory of East Florida on the other is constrained to curb its Current suddenly and often, in order to take its Vent on the East Side of the said Promontory at Cape Florida through the new Bahama Channel into the Atlantic Ocean, with a N. by E. Direction; which Direction at Cape Canaveral, in Latitude 28°20'50", by Observation; but by Survey in 28°22′09″; it exchanges with a N. N. E. Course, in which it continues as far, as Charles Town in South Carolina, from whence it runs with a N. E. turn to Latitude 42°, and 68° west Longitude from London; then E. by N. to the Banks of Newfoundland, and unites about 40° west Longitude from London, with the Currents issuing out of Saint Laurence's Gulf, Baffin's Bay, and Hudson's Straits, with which it takes a S. E. Departure towards the Western Islands; probably joins the Current setting out of the Strait of Gibralter (a) and proceeds, as far, as the Coast of Africa, [*289*] until it falls in with the Trade Winds again, and returns, after its Rotation into the Ocean to the Gulf of Mexico; North and N. E., as also East Gales press the Florida Stream home to the Atlantic Coast, and confines it in a very narrow Channel, at which times the Florida Stream runs as a Torrent. S. E. and South Gales have not that Effect upon the Stream, because it then runs in its natural Channel, which is wider, than the Channel, it occupies between the Pressure of the Gales from North to East, and the Shore, on which the Stream with southwardly Gales leaves a great Space, in which a part of the Stream returns by an Eddy southwardly. S. W. and N. W. Gales extend the Stream still further to make its Channel in the Ocean; consequently beyond its natural Eastern Boundary; by which its Current is but moderate, because first being so much extended, and spread upon the Atlantic Ocean; Secondly its Motion being also diminished for want of that Pressure, it receives in its Confinement between the Islands Cuba, and Bahama, and the Promontory of East Florida from all other Gales. For Particulars, Reference may be had to the Hydrographical Map of the Atlantic Ocean between the English Channel, and North America, terminating with the Martyrs; where the Stream according to the Interceptions of Gales contrary to its assumed regular Course, and by reason of its sudden Change in its Procession on the Promontory from S. to S. E. to E. to N. E. and at Cape Florida to N. N. E. forced in the New Bahama Channel to N. by E., strikes more or less Force on the narrow Head of the said Promontory in such manner, that the Continent has been, and is to this day subject to yield its Limits foot by foot to the Stream. Myself, and People employed by Me in this Service have during three years observed many Places, where fresh Encroachments appear to this Effect; even the vast Quantity of scattered large old Trees washed out with their Roots on all Shores of the Islands, and out in the shallow Sea, now called Grant's Lake between the Islands and Main testify, that they lay on the Spot of the former Continent, and Peninsulas, where their Genus and Species formerly flourished; but none of us on the many Places, we frequented, have met with a Spot, where the Continent has taken Possession of Limits de-

(a) That is to say the Florida Stream sets in the Straits with the upper Waters and runs out again with the ground Waters in the same manner, as I have observed at Saint Juan's Inlet, and mentioned in the 7th Paragraph of the 4th Chapter.

serted by the Stream; these are Testimonies, if not evident Proofs, that [290] the Stream not satisfied with its confined sudden turns endeavours to extend; but does not give up any of its Acquisitions, or exchange old Possessions in lieu, as Seas, and Rivers are well known to do in all Parts of the known World.

4th. This Encroachment of the Stream has torn these naturally low Peninsulas, and the Continent, where lowest, at times of Inundations, (caused by the great Gales, and Hurricanes, aggravated by the Accompanyment of Moons full and change) into so many Subdivisions, as are in being under the different Names and Appellations mentioned above. In the Month of September 1769 happened such an Inundation, which then covered the very Tops of the highest Trees on the Peninsula Larga, and the Islands Fox, Stephens, Jenyns, and Elliot with three feet Water, if the Report can be credited, which was spread by John Lorain, Master of the Litbury Snow, who with the N. W. Current of the Stream by a N. E. Gale, was forced over the Cary's Fort and Litbury Reefs on the Rocks, of which he started his Rudder, came to Anchor in Hawke Channel over the south end of Elliot, where he found his Vessel next day high and dry, passed all Remedy to get her off, disposed of his Cargo, and burnt the Vessel to save the Iron, which Action has brought upon him the Reproach of Imprudence; perhaps his Report of the Inundation may have no other Merit, than that of Necessity. The Land on the Island is at least 6 feet higher, than the Sea; the highest Trees on the Island are about sixty feet high, the Inundation by his Report being three feet higher than the Trees, is together 69 feet. The highest Rocks on the Reefs scarce project three feet above the Surface of the Sea, of course Captain Lorain had 66 feet Water under his Vessel when he run over the Reefs; how he could start his Rudder in eleven fathom Water is inconceivable to Me; but if he has struck in eleven feet Water the Trees must have been 52 feet above Water, of course the Mistake must be in the Inundation, for that he started his Rudder is certain.

5th. None of the Martyr Islands are inhabited by human Species, but constantly visited by the English from New Providence, and Spaniards from Cuba, for the Sake of Wracks [wrecks], Madeira Wood, Tortoises, Prawns, Fish and Birds.

[291] 6th. The Shoals, especially Sombreros, south of Fitzherbert, and the Shoal Loup (a) south of Roberts, both border upon the Florida Stream, distinguishing themselves by shewing their Sand Hills above Water visible at four and five Miles Distance, evidently appear to be the Remnant of the Southern Peninsula, torn first into Islands, which deprived of their natural Products, and rich Soil retain only at this time their barren Sand cover over their rocky Foundation; from which I am induced to conclude, that the rocky Reefs are the Number of those Islands formed by Force of the Stream out of the southern Peninsula

(a) has its Name from the Loup-Man-of-War being lost on it.

above mentioned, but washed clean of all, that the Violence of the Stream could move thereon, and remain awfull and dangerous Wharfs in that Sea, to the great Prejudice of the many Vessels wracked [*wrecked*] thereon in times past, and almost weekly to this day; these Rocks in some Places project, in others level the Surface of the Sea; nevertheless they fathom in their Intervals from eighteen to forty eight feet water, so that Vessels have crossed these Reefs on those Intervals without touching. I have observed in my Surveys of the Martyrs, that the Florida Stream at its regular Seasons and uninterrupted Course in fair Weather forms a remarkably visible glazed Line of Division; but in many Places out sight of Land from the Deck; outside of which Line the Stream appears in some Places as blue boiling Water; in others bursting and fermenting like Cataracts, even at times of the greatest Calms, beside being fathomless in these very Spots, and within the aforesaid Line is an Eddy quite smooth, changing gradually as it approaches Hawke Channel & the Islands from the Stream's deep blue, to a beautiful Sea-green, and at last into a milk white. The Soundings under the blue coloured Water are on fine white Marl, under the Sea-green on the said Marl, with Spunge, white Coral, Sea Feathers, Tortoise Grass, and sometimes Banks of Rocks, and under the white-coloured Water the Soundings are on white Marl, with Banks of Rocks, or white Sand; this Eddy takes its Current in an opposite Direction from that of the contiguous Stream, viz. Southwestwardly.

[*292*] 7th. The Soundings in the Eddy (that is to say in case no Reef is in the way) between the Stream and Hawke Channel fathom from two hundred and eighty to sixteen feet, and where Reefs, and Shoals divide the Stream and Hawke Channel, the Soundings in some Places run from bottomless at once to sixty eight feet.

8th. After these Discoveries, Vessels may with Safety proceed and avoid hereafter the Eddy, or make Allowance for it in their daily Calculations, that is, if they cannot help falling into the Eddy (after they have taken all Precautions by sounding early in blue Water, and when they had Bottom endeavoured to stand off in the Stream) they will naturally subtract, what Longitudes they make in the Eddy from what they had made in the Stream, and begin a new Departure; be precise in their Morning and Meridian Observations, and when they find themselves with 6°25' East Variation in Latitude 24° which is nearest Hueso Island, the Sombreros, Loup Shoal, Holborn and Dartmouth Inlets, they are to make an East Offing of a hundred and forty miles, if with 7°30' East Variation in Lattd. 24°40' which is nearest Matance Island, and Spencer Inlet; to gain an East Offing of sixty miles when with 7°32' East Variation in Lattd. 25° which is nearest Tabona, now Stephen Island and Palmerston Inlet, then to try for an East Offing of thirty miles, before they stand North for the New Bahama Channel. But in case they are with 6° East Variation in Latitude 25°40' which is nearest Cape Florida, and to the North of all Reefs, they need no Offing provided they see no land to their West.

9th. Many Vessels bound through the New Bahama Channel were lost in fair Weather; unacquainted with the Stream's Eddy and of Soundings being under blue Water, they were swept insensibly by the Eddy to the westward, and when they found by their Calculations, that they had a good Offing East of Cape Florida, they stood North, in lieu of entering the New Bahama Channel, run straight upon a Reef.

10th. As the Meridian Observations south of Lattitude 25°40′ are no Directions, and the Morning and Evening Observations useless as long as the Variations of the Compass on the different places of the Promontory have not been heretofore known; I have [293] therefore with the greatest Care taken the Variations on Cape Florida, the Matance and Hueso by Morning Amplitudes, which on this Promontory are the surest, for the Evening Observations (as I have experienced on Places, where I could have both in one day, and on one Spot) do not so nearly agree with a Meridional Operation (I make Use of at times) which though very tedious, is however infallible.

11th. I mentioned before, what Effect the different Gales have upon the Florida Stream. I think it necessary to observe now, that this Stream is also subject to an Alteration from another Cause, by which as well, as by the Gales it is either pressed on or off the Coast, viz. by the full and change of the Moon, which according to its Position have all the different Effects upon the Stream, however not in equal Power with those of the Gales; and the Disposition of the Stream is encreased to its superlative, if the Effects both of the Gales and Moon are combined; for at this time the natural Zimosis of the Ocean rises highest; this Zimosis regulates the Flood and Ebb, and divides them in proportioned times, and consequently directs and increases them with the Assistance of easterly Moons, and Gales to the West, and of westerly Moons and Gales to the East, so that the West and East Shores are at times deprived of, and at other times overflowed by Tides occasioned by these Vicissitudes.

12th. The boisterous East N. E. and North Gales begin generally in September, and are frequent during the Season, when the Sun is in the southern Latitudes, viz. until March, at which time their Period is mostly expired, and in general ceases, for the Atmosphere of the Sun at that time balances, and divides the Atmosphere of the Earth, and forces the prevailing Pressure from the North Pole to its Station by giving Room to that from the South Pole, by which encroaching, and recoiling of both Pressures generally a Gale or Hurricane ensues, in case the Pressure of the Moon in its full or change should join in Alliance; if then Vessels happen to be in the Mouth of the Gulf of Mexico, that is between the Island of Cuba, and the Promontory of East Florida, they best endeavour to make the Bahama Islands, or at least the Soundings of them, and proceed under their lee side; but when they are to [294] the North of these Bahama Islands, then to keep in the Eastern Extent of the Florida Stream; or else they will not be able to clear their Way through the New Bahama Channel, nor along the Coast of East Florida, Georgia or South Carolina, either go on Shore of the Martyr Reefs, Cape Florida, or Cape Canaveral, if not, upon the Beach either between the Capes, or to the Northward of them, which is the least Evil of the two; for thus the Crew and Cargo may be saved; and some Vessels may also be brought off provided the Storm slakes before the Vessel is made a Wrack [wreck] of; but if at this or any other time westwardly Gales should happen, then the Atlantic Coast affords the most eligible Lee for Navigators, who do not chuse to take the Stream.

13th. Two Instances of the same Nature I experienced, one in February the other in December 1770: viz. December 25th. Then Moon's change being in the Gulf Stream, in the Morning I made Fox, alias Roderigos Island, stood in for Cary's Fort Reef, fell in very soon (after I had Sight of said Island) with the Stream's Eddy, and it was then by the Land very visible how much I was swept to the Southwestward by the Eddy: At Noon I was opposite the Matance Island; in the Evening almost lost Sight of it: All this time I was becalmed till 5 o'Clock in the Evening; when the Wind came from the Northeastward I stood E. S. E. with which course I took my Departure from the Matance (still a little visible, and bearing Northeastwardly) out of the Eddy into the Stream, run all Night at the Rate of five Knots until four o'Clock in the Morning, of the 26th when the Wind shifted to the East and blew very high; sure of being twelve Miles East of Cape Florida, without allowing for Current then in my Favour, I suffered my Master to lay the Vessel N. N. E. for the Mouth of the New Bahama Channel; about eleven discovered Land to the Northwestward, which by the Meridian Observation as well, as by approaching it nearer to Sight, proved to be Cape Florida, which with a southwardly Wind would have been an agreeable Aspect; before the Observation the Wind had already blown a high Gale, so that I was obliged to unship my fore-top Mast, and take in my flying Jeeb Boom, as by every Slide the Vessel made from a Wave She run her Head into the Sea, so that the Sailor, which took in the Jeeb and unshipped the Boom was three times under the [295] Sea, and myself in the greatest Apprehension of his Danger, finding the Florida Stream setting Northwestwardly: viz. on Shore of the Promontory and on the Vessel's Weather Side, I attempted to tack to the S. S. E., but soon discovered, that both Wind, and Current hurried the Vessel towards the North End of Biskaina Reef; I stood N. N. E. again, but having upon both Tacks Gale and Current joining on one side, the Vessel was swept so near the Land that no more than a fifteen Minute's Run would have set a Period to my Navigation. My

HYDROGRAPHICAL MAP
of the
ATLANTIC OCEAN,
Extending from the Southernmost part of
NORTH AMERICA to EUROPE.

Shewing the different Variations of the Compass, the settings and changes of the Currents in the Ocean, as well caused by the FLORIDA commonly called GULF STREAM, than those coming from Baffin's Bay, and Hudson's Straights; especially the true distance from EUROPE to AMERICA, as ascertained by a late Hydrometrical Operation, the Table of which is joind and the Operation laid down in the Tract on the Map.

performed in 1771,
By Wm. GERARD DE BRAHM Esqr.
His MAJESTY's Surveyor General,
for the Som. District of North America.

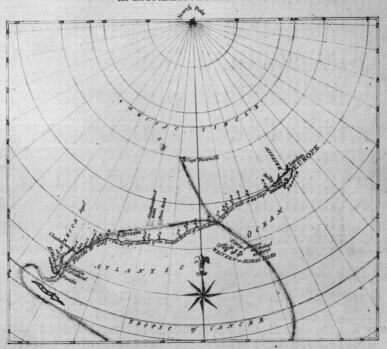

Master ran to the Helm, sat the Vessel about to the S. S. E. a second time, which however would only have determined our Catastrophe upon the Reef; whereas on the other Hand the N. N. E. Tack would have brought the Vessel to the Beach of the Cape, for the Main and Reef bore N. N. E. and S. S. W. the Vessel lay with its Larboard Tack parallel with the Main; the Current from the S. E. bearing upon the Weather Quarter afforded no Room for lee Way between the Vessel, and the Main; and the Vessel with her starboard Tack, although She made four Points with the Reef, because the Current was setting upon the Weather-Bow would fetch the Reef within the End of her lee Way; but that very instant the Wind shifted to the E. N. E., which brought the Stream in a narrower Channel home to the Main, and changed the N. W. into a N. N. W. Current, of course under the lee Bow of the Vessel besides laying then six Points from the Reef, was now able to obtain a sufficient Offing, and gained the lee of the Bahamas. All that Night and after until December 29th the Wind waved between North and East, during which time I had much a do by frequent Southeastwardly Tacks to regain the Eastern Extent of the Stream, through which every Northeastwardly Tack had swept the Vessel even within Sight of Land, and it was only owing to Recourse taken to the Southeastwardly Tacks, that I bewared of Cape Canaveral Shoal, and the Coast of East Florida, Georgia and South Carolina.

14th. I should not have enlarged these Discoveries with the preceeding particular Narrative of my Adventure, had I not thought it a Circumstance important, and giving Weight to my Observations, and Discoveries premised. Besides as I am [296] determined at any time (if it should by my Lot to fall in with the above Seasons in that Sea) to make my Offing good in the Soundings of the Bahamas; this obliges me to communicate my Reasons and Judgment in these critical Cases to the World for the Benefit of those, who are bound from the Havanna on Cuba to the Atlantic Ocean.

15th. After this necessary Digression, I return to the ancient State of the Promontory and the Effect of the Stream, by which the abovementioned River, now Grant's, terminating in Lloyd's Lake is entirely filled up with the Soil torn from both the Main, and Northern Peninsula; so that a Passage Northeastward of the Matacombes has not as yet been met with, for even a Vessel of three feet Draught to communicate between the Martyr Islands, the Main and Peninsula Larga. I was obliged to employ a Battoe, and Yawl of not above nine Inches draught to perform the Survey thereof. The River between the two Peninsulas, now Hawke Channel affords a very safe Communication between the Martyr Reefs, Shoals, and Islands; as also a safe Reception for Vessels in Distress finding their Way through the Inlets, which I will specify hereafter. This Channel has upwards of forty five feet water in deep places, and not less, than 14 1/2 feet in the shallowest Places, of which the first is opposite Elliot's south and Jenyns North Points in

Latitude 25°18′30″, and the second opposite the North Point of Larga in Latitude 25°18′00″.

16th. Hawke Channel has eight Out- and Inlets, safe Communications from the Florida Stream through the Reefs, and Shoals of no less, than eighteen feet Water; the first in Latitude 25°35′16″ N. W. from the South Point of Biskaino Island called Keppel Inlet, the second called Buller opposite Elliot, bears due East and West between Biskaino and Litbury Reefs in Latitude 25°28′31″; the third called Palmerston, between Hays and Matance Reefs bears due East, and West from and to Tabona (now Stephen Island) in Latitude 24°56′35″ (N. B. fourteen miles North of this Inlet His Majesty's Ship the Cary's Fort was run by the Pilot upon the Reef, now known by the Name of Cary's Fort the 23d of October [*297*] 1770) and was brought off by the Master, Mister Hunter's Skill and Diligence, and is the first Vessel to my Knowlege which got clear. The fourth Inlet called Spencer, is about eight miles wide, between Matance and the last of the Viveres Reefs, in Latitude 24°42′30″ opposite the Island Matance. The fifth called Wallace, south of the southernmost of the Vacas Islands, and the south End of Bonetta Reef, in Latitude 24°32′30″. The sixth called Lisburne, S. E. of Edward's Islands, in Latitude 24°27′30″. The seventh called Dartmouth, six Miles and a half to the Eastward of the Loup S. by E. of Robinson's Islands and E. by S. of Huntingdon Harbour in Latitude 24°27′16″. The eighth and last called Holborn Inlet, is west of the Sombreros, and South of Egmont Channel in Latitude 24°20′. Besides these Out or Inlets, are three Passages through the Martyr Islands into Richmond Bay for Vessels of little Draught to shorten their Voyage to and from Pensacola; the Northernmost called Onslow, has its Inlet on the South of Matacombe la Viega in Latitude 24°45′, opposite Spencer Inlet, runs on the South of the Islands Jenkinson, Dyson, Townshend, Cooper and Bradshaw (alias sandy Key) and under the North of Vivera has six feet Water in the shallowest Places; the next is Gordon, in Latitude 24°35′ enters through the Vacas; viz. by the east End of the last westernmost but one, N. by E. of Wallace Inlet, runs North of Ellis, and its shallowest Water is 8 1/2 feet. The third Passage called North in Latitude 24°33′ Inlets East of Jennings Island N. by E. of Dartmouth Inlet, and W. by N. of Lisburne Inlet, and runs on no less than six feet Soundings under the N. E. side of New Castle Island, but Vessels of twelve feet Draught, taking Hawke Channel bound to and from Pensacola or its contiguous Places, must cross the Martyr Islands through the more Southern Passage called Egmont Channel, of which I have advanced fully what was necessary; I will therefore conclude with the Direction through Egmont Channel. The southernmost Point of Hueso Island is remarkable by the Rocks thereon mostly above Water. Vessels from the Southward in the Stream stand in through Holborn Inlet; as also Vessels coming down Hawke [*298*] Channel, after clearing the said rocky Point in Hueso stand in due North half a mile to the West of Hueso, and run up until they bring the said rocky Point to bear S. S. E. astern, then lay N. N. W. and pursue that course until the Shoals both of Hueso and Tortugas are cleared; from which time they will soon increase their Water as they advance in Richmond Bay. Vessels again coming from the Northward of the Gulf of Mexico see the said rocky Point when within 16 1/2 feet Soundings before the Tortuga and Hueso Banks draw up both sides of the Channel, whence they bring the rocky Point in a S. S. E. Direction ahead and follow that Course (consulting Eye and Lead) until they shut up the two Points of the first small Bay on the North Side of Hueso, then come to a safe Anchor, or stand due South out through Holborn Outlet into the Stream, with which they will meet after four Knots run, provided they chuse the Outside of the Shoals and Reefs of the Martyrs, but in case they chuse the Inside of the Shoals and Reefs thro' Hawke Channel, then clear the rocky Point with a south Course of a full half-mile's Run, and draw up E. by S. along the south Shores of the Islands Hueso, Fitzherbert etc. further keeping an Offing from the Islands in general of a League parallel to the Range of them all (consulting Eye and Lead), will meet with the best Water to anchor every Evening and to proceed as far as Biskaino Island, where without Difficulty (if the Wind is westward or southward) they may run into the Florida Stream which is there in Sight.

17th. Before I conclude I think it necessary to observe that Flood and Ebb keep equal Tides upon the Atlantic Coast, as far South as Oswald, Laurence, Soldiers, Knox and Pollock Islands, where it floods seven hours and ebbs seven hours, after which it floods five hours and five hours it ebbs, but from hence along the Martyr Islands it never keeps any Regularity as far as Hueso where it observes a Regularity again, as mentioned in the 2d Paragraph of this Chapter, as also the end of fourth Chapter.[64] And that the Tides upon the Atlantic Coast in this Province regulate their Currents by the different Bearings of the Coast on which they run and parallel with them they set to and from the Bays and Inlets from North to South with a South and S. E. Winds, but with East North and N. E. Winds they set from the South to the North; an E. S. E. Moon nearest [299] makes high Water at full and change on all the Inlets upon this Coast. The best Entries are made with East and Eastwardly Winds, at which time the Sea rises highest in the Channels; South and S. E. Winds make the smoothest Bars. North and N. E. Winds cover the Bar with a raging Sea; West and N. W. Winds bend the Sea from the Coast, and leave the Bars at times near dry. The Inlets upon this Coast are all Subject to the Inconveniency of having their Bars shifted by East, North and N. E. Gales, by which they loose their old and obtain new, sometimes better Channels; viz. when great Freshes happen at that time which fill the Rivers and Streams to their very Sources, and besides being increased with Sea Water rolled in by the Gales, they then force themselves through the new Bar with great

Power at the End of the Gale, either deepen the old Channel through the Bar, or break through on another Place and make a new Channel deeper than the former has been: But when these Gales happen at a time of a Drought, the Waters within the Inlets, altho' swelled with the Sea for a Distance of several miles from their Outlets have not sufficient Weight, nor are able to hold out long enough in order to wash a new Channel through the Bar as deep as the former Channel has been, or to restore the latter, this shifting of the Bars requires always new Land Marks; to establish them effectually [*it*] would be best to fix a Beacon on a Place within the Harbour centrical to the Bar from Point to Point of the Inlet, and have at high Water Mark a Flag-Staff erected in a manner that it can be moved and ranged (when necessary) between the Bar's Channel and the fixed Beacon; on this Staff is occasionally hoisted a Flag of two Colours red and white; either of which Colours are visible in any Weather. Proposals have been once made at Saint Augustin to lay Buoys without the Bar, and move them with the Changes of the Channels, which although a good Invention I objected against them, because they could be of no lasting Service in these Sands which are quick and floating, as also Barnicles, which grow in four weeks time, would give Occasion for Worms to eat through and sink them, which besides the Loss of many Anchors, proves too expensive.

18. Since I have entered upon the Conclusion of the seventh Chapter with the Object of Beacons to render thereby the Navigation on the Bars [*300*] of the Inlets upon the Atlantic Ocean, practicable in time of bad Weather, when Pilots are prevented from venturing out the Harbours to bring in Vessels which are either in Distress without, or are bound in; I think it necessary not to give up this Object with so short an Observation, but to expatiate upon it for the good of those who navigate out of the Gulf of Mexico through that dangerous and inevitable Passage between the Island of Cuba, and the Promontory of East Florida, as from which Navigation depends the good Success of the Spanish Flota, which conveys from Cuba all the Riches collected there from the Manilles, Mexico, Perou and Cili [*Chile*]; altho' this Flota consists but of few Vessels, yet their Cargoes are precious; this Passage is navigated by a great Number of English Vessels, which trade in the Gulf of Mexico, the number of those who unhappily end their Navigation in this Passage are English Sailors; with the Causes and Remedies of their Disasters I have enlarged this whole Chapter as far, as it was in my Power, and as far as it depends from astronomical Observations and Navigation, but since good Observations too often fail for want of Opportunity, many unhappy Navigators will end their Periods upon the low Promontory of East Florida, which shews no land-mark in the highest Places at a greater Offing, than four Leagues, at which distance Vessels in Danger are generally passed all Remedies. My Duty of Office, Humanity, fellow feeling and public Interest call upon me to shew: by what

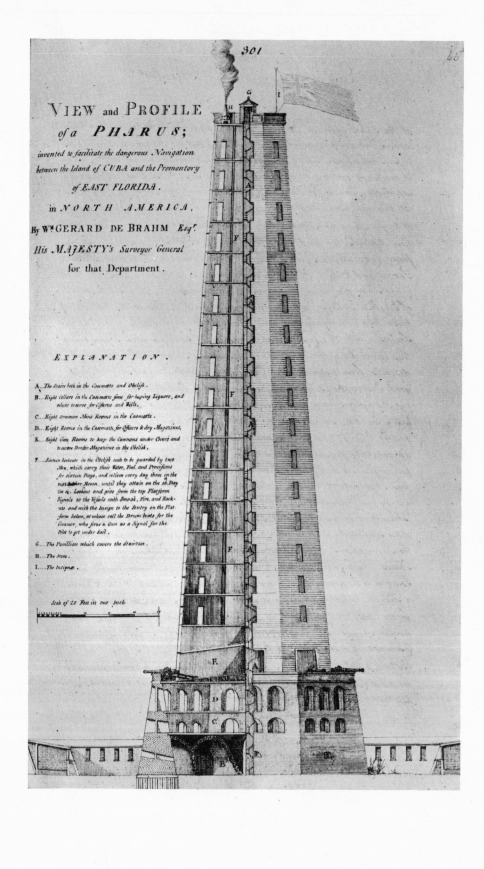

means this Navigation may be made safe, and those be relieved, as are Sufferers by the Violence of irresistable North, and East Winds; the west and east Extremities of the dreadfull Promontory of East Florida (whose Banks altho' scattered with numerous Rocks, yet they all could be covered with the Inscriptions of the many, who ended their Navigations on it) are the Places which solicit for two Pharus's, to be constructed upon them, each Pharus to be provided with a Sloop and Barge; on each of these Pharus's a Fire be entertained day and night, so that its Smoak may be an Object for the Day, and its Light, with a Sky Rocket lighted every half hour, for the Night; the Construction of these Pharus's should be an octagonal Case-matte of two Stories, 74 feet diameter, its Walls to be 10 feet at the Bottom, 4 feet thick at the Top, and 36 feet high with Rooms suitable for a hot Climate to accommodate for its Defence 100, and upon Occasion 450 Men, 24 pieces of Cannon, Provision and Amunition in proportion [303] with great Convenience; on and in this Casematte is raised an Obelisk of Carpenter's Work 214 feet high, its Center contains the Stairs of 500 Steps which leads to the Top on which is to be railed in a platform with a large Iron or Brick Stove, contrived in a manner so as to conceal Fuel against Wind and Weather, send up its Smoak and Flame without Obstruction and Danger to the Obelisk to give Signals for Navigators. Constructions of such kind would not only procure infalliable Means for judging of Currents, for accounting of Longitude, keeping a proper Offing and getting proper Pilots through this Passage, but would also be an effectual Assistance and Relief from the Sloops and Barges of either or both Pharuses, besides saving half the Insurance now paid for Trading Vessels bound through this Passage.

CHAPTER 8th

Of the Indian Boundaries.[65]

1st. Great Britain has preferably to all Kingdoms in the Universe always cultivated that Reverence which is due to the Right of Possession, as sacred to the Possessor whoever, even to the very American Savages, who unto this day possess more Land, than they know, what Use to convert it to else, but to hunt upon it.

2. The Method used, from the time of Queen Elizabeth's Reign unto His pres-

ent Majesty's was to obtain from those Indians who accepted the King's Peace, by regular Requests on the one [*304*] Hand, and Voluntary Cession on the other Hand such Lands which are now held under English Titles. For which Purposes the respective Governors of the different Provinces invited the Head-Men of those Nations (who were then the Possessors of the Lands in View) to a Congress at an appointed place; to which the Governors repaired with such Persons as was acquainted with the Lands in the Country, which they intended to treat for with the Indians; the Head Men of the latter appeared in Company of such of their own Nation who had a full Knowlege of their Country, which was to be ceded. The Indians received from the Governors in Presents such Goods as suited their Purposes, and the Governors insinuated to the Indians the Necessity of having a certain Country by them ceded for the Use of His Majesty and his Subjects, to which or part thereof the Indians consented; artificial and natural Boundaries were then agreed on, and the principal Men of the Indians in the Presence of their Company and those with the Governors confirmed their voluntary Cession of the Lands requested by subjoining their Marks in lieu of their Names on the Bottom of the Instrument, which contain'd the Cession of the Land.

3. This Method has been observed even with American Provinces, altho' they were by Conquest obtained from the last Possessor, either the Crown of Spain or France; thereby to prevent the Indians from claiming their Original Right under Pretence, as if France or Spain had violently dispossessed them.

4. Anno 1765 in the Month of November I had then actually finished a Plan of East Florida as far, as I had at that time investigated by repeated recognizing [*reconnoitering*] in two Expeditions, and possessed a general Idea of the Province; at this time Lands could not with Safety be granted by the Governor as the Limits were not known, to which the Indians were willing to agree; therefore His Excellency the then Governor James Grant Esqr., invited the Head Men of the Creek Nation to meet him at Fort Picolata (a) on a Congress [*305*] in the month and year as above.[66]

5. As I had not been invited to the congress nor previously consulted to its purposes; convinced also that His Excellency studied the greatest frugality in order not to cause unto Government more than the most necessary expences besides that Fort Picolata afforded either conveniencies nor entertainment for Volunteers, I judged it improper to intrude myself.

6. At this Congress the limits between East Florida and the Creek Indians were drawn from a pine tree upon Saint Mary's Stream. This tree is laid down in my General Map, and expressed in the first table of my land surveys from Sander's Indian store, and comprehended in the third chapter of East Florida. This

(a) a Casematte built by the Spaniards on the east Side of Saint Juan's Stream; in 15 common English miles, west from Saint Augustin.

pine tree determines the Georgia Boundary, between the Settlements and Indians. The survey of this boundary appears at the end of the second chapter of Georgia. The line agreed upon from said pine tree was not to exceed the south side of Oklywahaw River, but turn with the said river home to its mouth, and from thence another line was to be drawn towards sun rise (due east) to the Atlantic Ocean.

7. Of the transactions or limits agreed upon at the Congress, I never received a copy to guide myself, as well in my surveys, which I was to perform as Surveyor General of Lands in the Southern district; as also to avoid transgressing the Indian limits by laying out private tracts of land for Grantees, it being the function of my office as Provincial Surveyor.

8. What is peculiarly admirable in the capacity of the Indians is their natural knowlege in Geometry. For in my future surveys, their first line, which they joined to that of Georgia, viz. from the pine tree, to the River Oklywaha, proved to be a parallel with the Atlantic Coast. This line contains 610,000 links in length, and the due east line measures 345,000 links, which two lines, Saint Mary's stream and the Atlantic Coast inclose a tract of 1,899,975 acres of land, too much for a County, and too insignificant for a Province, which by the Indian Boundaries extends from latitude 30°22′03″ no farther south than lattitude 29°16′50″ which is 1°05′13″ in lattitude, and 0°50′47″ in longitude; all lands to the south from [306] Lake Gordon, the great Swamp, and the head of Halifax Stream, comprehending the following tracts of lands laid out by the deputy Surveyors on His Majesty's Warrants and the Governors private orders are within the Indian Reserve.

List of the Proprietors, whose lands, and what
quantities lay within the Indian Reserve.

1.	Barrington Samuel Esqr. .... Captain	20,000
2.	Beresford John and William	40,000
3.	Besborough Earl of	20,000
4.	Bisset Robert Esqr. .... Captain	5,000
5.	Bradshaw Thomas Esqr.	10,000
6.	Bret Richard Esqr.	10,000
7.	Cassilis Earl of	20,000
8.	Cooper Grey Esqr.	20,000
9.	Crowl William Esqr.	10,000
10.	Dartmouth Earl of	40,000
11.	Duncan Sir William	20,000
12.	Faucitt William Esqr. .... Col.	20,000

13.	Fitzherbert William Esqr.		20,000
14.	Fortrey James Esqr.		10,000
15.	Garbrant Caleb Esqr.		5,000
16.	Gordon Lord Adam—out of 20,000		6,000
17.	Grant Alexander Bart.		20,000
18.	Grant Archibald Bart.		20,000
19.	Grant Duncan Esqr.		10,000
20.	Greyhurst John Esqr.		20,000
21.	Jerveys John Esqr.	Captain	20,000
22.	Jones Arthur Esqr.		5,000
23.	Lillingston Luke Esqr.		10,000
24.	Mason Kenter Esqr.		5,000
25.	Moira Earl of		10,000
26.	Morray John Esqr.	Captain	10,000
27.	Morrison James Esqr.		5,000

[307]

28.	Oswald Richard Esqr.		20,000
29.	Penman James Esqr.		10,000
30.	Rickets William Esqr.		20,000
31.	Robertson James Esqr.	Coll.	15,000
32.	Southwell Edward Esqr.		20,000
33.	Taylor Peter Esqr.		10,000
34.	Taylor James Esqr.		10,000
35.	Temple Lord		20,000
36.	Townsend Thomas		10,000
37.	Townshend Charles Esqr.		20,000
38.	Turnbull Andrew Esqr.		33,000
39.	Tutchet Samuel Esqr.		20,000
40.	Tyrone Earl of		20,000
41.	Upton Cothworthy Esqr.		20,000

679,000

Besides those tracts which are laid out
unknown to me when in the Province and
since my absence from America, which
increase the above sum to more than a
million of acres.[67]

9. I must observe, that from November 1765 to October 1773 I was kept unacquainted, that a due east line had been agreed upon to be drawn from the mouth

of Oklywahaw, to the Atlantic Ocean, to be a boundary, but am informed since that the Indian Invasion intended against the Muskitoe (alias Mukoso) Settlements (which happened anno 1770, when I was out on my general Surveys) had been intended to resent the Injury done to the Indians by trespassing that very boundary, and taking violent possession of their reserved lands.

10. The Town of Smyrnea [*New Smyrna*] was the point in view of the Indians; there they appeared all in arms and painted with black (their token of war). Doctor Turnbull by distributing among the Indians, what he had in his Magazine, which they would have taken violently, had he not prevented it by making all over to them in presents, atoned so far to the Indians, for the Injuries, that they, for that time in expectation of being called to a congress by the Governor, was prevailed on to withdraw; but no invitation to a congress has as yet been issued.

[*308*] 11. The Indians will probably renew their claim as often, as they can agree among themselves for that purpose, in order to have such presents repeated, and will, if not prevented by an early Congress, perhaps refuse to appear at any hereafter, finding the demand of the not binding presents from individuals, for which they may ask as often as they please to be more advantageous to them than the binding presents given at the Congresses, and in course of time form a claim of right to a tribute to be payed to them by the Inhabitants, to which they may easily be led by the instinct of their own politic discretion, seconded by the inspiration of those vagabond Europeans, who live among them, and heightened by their boldness, which is become unbounded ever since the cruel murders by them committed anno 1767 upon the Saint Mary's settlers, at which, to this very day has been winked with too much condescension and resignation into the Indians discretion.

12. It happened soon after the commission of these murders, that I performed the two Land Surveys, viz. one from Saint Augustin to the Mukoso Settlements, and the other from Saint Augustin, intended across the Promontory to the Gulf of Mexico; but a stop was put to that expedition, when at the head of Saint Juan's Stream; for my Indian guide refused to proceed any farther because he had observed some Indian parties scouting on the east side of Saint Juan's Stream; thus a mensuration, so highly necessary to obtain the longitude of the promontory by a land survey, preferable to any, even the best astronomical observation was suspended.

[Folios 309, 310, and 311, headed "Table of measurement, materials and expences attending the building of the Pharuses upon the extremities of the Promontory of East Florida," end De Brahm's manuscript Report. They are omitted here.]

Notes on the Introduction

1. Emanuel Bowen, "An Accurate Map of North America Describing and Distinguishing the British, Spanish, and French Dominions on This Great Continent According to the Definitive Treaty Concluded at Paris 10th February 1763." This map accompanied a report from the Board of Trade to King George III, summarizing the board's opinions concerning the disposition and administration of the newly acquired territories. Both the map and the report are now retained in the Public Record Office, London. The report is filed under Colonial Office Records, America and West Indies (original correspondence, etc.), Vol. 65, p. 67; the map is separately filed as MR–26. The Colonial Office Records, America and West Indies includes such valuable materials as the original correspondence and entry books of the Board of Trade and the secretary of state. Acts, sessional papers, and miscellanea are arranged under the following subdivisions: Carolina (Proprietary), North Carolina, South Carolina, Connecticut, East Florida, West Florida, Georgia, Maryland, Massachusetts, New England, New Hampshire, New Jersey, New York, Pennsylvania, Rhode Island, Vermont, Virginia, Proprietaries. In all 1,450 volumes and bundles dating from ca. 1606 to 1807 are included in this artificial class of documents. For brevity, footnote citations to these materials will appear as follows: C. O. 5–65, p. 67. For a somewhat dated but still valuable guide to the Public Record Office, see Charles M. Andrews, *Guide to the Materials for American History to 1783, in the Public Record Office of Great Britain*, 2 vols. (Washington, D. C., 1912, 1914).

2. Colonies General, Original Correspondence, Vol. 15, p. 105. Many of the original source materials used in the preparation of this book are found in the Public Record Office, London. The class of papers known as Colonies General, Original Correspondence (short form C. O. 323), is made up of documents which usually concern more than one colony or no one colony in particular. The whole class is comprised of 1,868 volumes dated from 1689 to 1943. The earlier volumes of C. O. 323 include the valuable series of Board of Trade papers called Plantations General, which were of particular value in this study. Hereafter the short form of footnote citation to these materials will be employed, i.e., C. O. 323–15, p. 105.

3. C. O. 323–16, p. 189ff. This document was titled, "Hints relative to the Division and Government of the conquered and newly acquired Countries in America." In his article bearing this title in *The Mississippi Valley Historical Review*, VIII (Mar. 6, 1922), 367–73, Verner W. Crane stated that "Hints" was the key document in the series which culminated in the proclamation of Oct. 7, 1763.

For a fuller discussion of the British land policy in America, see Louis De Vorsey, Jr., *The Indian Boundary in the Southern Colonies, 1763–1775* (Chapel Hill, N. C., 1966).

4. C. O. 5–65, p. 63.

5. Extracted from an anonymous tract of 1730 entitled, "Some considerations relating to the present Condition of the Plantations With Proposals for a Better Regulation of them," C. O. 5–5, p. 313.

6. Exchequer and Audit Department Records, Accounts, Various, Vol. 140, n. p. These papers consist primarily of the particulars of accounts, vouchers, and other documents associated with them. In all, 1,430 rolls and bundles dating from 1539 to 1886 make up this class of documents in the Public Record Office, London. For brevity, footnote citations to these materials will appear as follows hereafter: A. O. 3–140, n. p.

7. Ibid.

8. Ibid. For a discussion of Holland's life and work see Willis Chipman, "The Life and Times of Major Samuel Holland, Surveyor General, 1764–1801," *Ontario Historical Society Papers and Records*, XXI (1924), 11–90.

9. C. O. 323–17, p. 123ff.

10. Ibid.

11. Holland suggested that the general survey be mapped at a general scale of one inch to the mile with particular "places of note such as channels and harbours, by a scale of four inches to a mile." Depth soundings of all harbors and channels were to be included. Astronomical observations were to be used in fixing "the latitudes and longitudes of all Capes, head lands, etc." In addition to maps and charts, "a natural and historical description of the countries, the rivers, and lakes, and whatever other remarks shall be thought necessary" was to be recorded by the surveyors general and their deputies.

To assist in the conduct of these important and comprehensive geographic surveys Holland recommended that an armed cutter or some other small, armed vessel with two whale boats and a large longboat be assigned to the surveyor general. In his Northern Department such craft would, he felt, be useful in the actual survey and also in preventing smuggling on the St. Lawrence River by French agents. In his estimates of the costs of the survey, Holland made provisions for the several assistants necessary in conducting it. A paid deputy was to be provided to act in Holland's place as Quebec's provincial surveyor of lands so that he could continue to hold that office and enjoy its emoluments while on the business of the general survey. Two assistant surveyors and one draftsman would be engaged with him on the general survey, supported by a military contingent made up of a sergeant, a corporal, and twelve men. The latter would be employed as "camp colour and chain men and to make signals along shore and on the tops of mountains." An amount was also to be provided for horses and guides as needed.

12. A. O. 3–140, n. p.

13. C. O. 323–17, p. 281.

14. For a discussion of the administrative procedure followed in De Brahm's appointment, see Andrews, *Guide to Materials in the Public Record Office*, I, pp. 233–34. The warrants appointing De Brahm to his East Florida post and the sur-

veyor generalship of the Southern Department are found in Colonies General, Entry Books, Series I, Vol. 52, pp. 37, 39 (1662–1872, 175 vols.). Hereafter cited as C. O. 324-52, pp. 37, 39.

15. For biographical sketches on De Brahm, see Allen Johnson and Dumas Malone (eds.), *Dictionary of American Biography* (New York, 1930), V, pp. 182–83; Wilbur H. Seibert, *Loyalists in East Florida, 1774 to 1785* (De Land, Fla., 1929), II, pp. 337–38; Whitfield J. Bell, *Early American Science: Needs and Opportunities for Study* (Williamsburg, Va., 1955), p. 53; Thomas D. Clark (ed.), *Travels in the Old South: A Bibliography* (Norman, Okla., 1956), I, pp. 188–90; D. E. Huger Smith, "An Account of the Tattnall and Fenwick Families in South Carolina," *The South Carolina Historical and Genealogical Magazine*, XIV, No. 1 (Jan. 1913), 3–19; *Who Was Who in America Historical Volume 1607–1896* (Chicago, 1963), p. 141.

16. Johnson and Malone (eds.), *Dictionary of American Biography*, V, p. 182. Unfortunately this early and most available biographical sketch of De Brahm includes several factual errors which have been repeated frequently by later authors. For example, both Carita Doggett Corse and Charles L. Mowat, in their articles which appear in the *Florida Historical Quarterly*, identify De Brahm as a Dutchman. See "De Brahm's Report on East Florida, 1773" and "That 'Odd Being', De Brahm" in Vols. XVII and XX of that journal.

17. In a memorandum to Lord Dartmouth dated Jan. 10, 1774, De Brahm wrote that he was no longer going to encourage German artisans to emigrate to America. He referred to Germany as "my native country" in this document, while in another place in the Dartmouth correspondence he wrote of "my German family." See Dartmouth Manuscripts D1778 II 788, and D1778 II 748, Staffordshire County Record Office, Stafford, England. Hereafter citations to material in this valuable collection will use the abbreviated form Dartmouth Ms. D1778 II 788. Writing to the Commissioners of Fortifications for South Carolina on Mar. 10, 1756, De Brahm indicated that he had been born in Germany. This letter is included in the entry for Mar. 15, 1756, in the manuscript "Journal of the Commissioners of Fortifications," examined in microfilm at the South Carolina Archives Department in Columbia. (Hereafter cited as S. C. Arch.) Gov. Reynolds of Georgia, in a letter addressed to the Board of Trade, dated Jan. 5, 1756, referred to "Mr. William De Brahm who is a German Gentleman of Great Honour and Ingenuity." This letter is found in the unpublished typescript "Colonial Records of Georgia," XXVII, p. 238, located in the Georgia Department of Archives and History, Atlanta. (Hereafter cited as Col. Recs. of Ga.) Finally, in the obituary notice of De Brahm's deceased widow, Mary De Brahm, née Drayton, Germany was specified as the place of his birth. For this obituary, see the *Savannah Republican*, Mar. 22, 1806. In her will, Mary De Brahm provided that a portion of her estate would go to assist her late husband's relatives then in Germany. They were four nieces: Marie Walburgha de Brahm, Francisca de Brahm, Baroness de Wenz, and Ann Louisa de Brahm. For a copy of this will, see the typescript volume "Wills–Charleston County Will Book D 1800–1807," XXX, Book C, p. 952, S. C. Arch.

18. Dartmouth Ms. D1778 II 617.

19. Ibid.

20. *Documents Connected with the History of South Carolina* (London, Printed for Private Distribution, 1856), p. 157.

21. "That 'Odd Being', De Brahm," *The Florida Historical Quarterly*, XX (Apr. 1942), p. 323.

22. "A Map of Savannah River beginning at Stone Bluff or Nexttobehell, which continueth to the Sea; also the Four Sounds Savannah, Hossabaw and St. Katherines with their Sounds Likewise Newport or Serpent River from its mouth to Benjehova bluff." This colored, manuscript map is filed in "Faden Collection" of the Library of Congress, Geography and Map Division as Faden map number 45.

23. *Savannah Republican*, Mar. 22, 1806.

24. Dartmouth Ms. D1778 II 980.

25. Dartmouth Ms. D1778 II 617.

26. Ibid.

27. Dartmouth Ms. D1778 II 980.

28. C. O. 5–71, p. 7.

29. Exchequer and Audit Department Records, Claims, American Loyalists, Series II. These records include 141 bundles of claims by American Loyalists during the period 1780 to 1835. Hereafter footnote citations to these materials will appear as follows: A. O. 13–137, p. 126.

30. Ibid.

31. C. O. 5–372, p. 280. The other foreign member was Christian de Munch (Chretien von Munch), a prominent Augsburg banker.

32. C. O. 5–372, p. 281.

33. C. O. 5–374, p. 63.

34. Col. Recs. of Ga., XXXI, p. 512.

35. Allen D. Candler (ed.), *The Colonial Records of the State of Georgia* (Atlanta, 1904–11), XXVI, p. 311.

36. Ibid., p. 319.

37. William P. Cumming called De Brahm "the most prolific map maker in the Carolinas during the third quarter of the eighteenth century." See *The Southeast in Early Maps* (Chapel Hill, N. C., 1958), p. 54.

38. Candler, *Colonial Records of Georgia*, XXVI, pp. 347–48. From De Brahm's description plus what is known of his surveying efforts during the months following his arrival in Georgia, it might be suggested that this map was similar or identical to the map described in note 22 above.

39. Ibid., II, p. 518.

40. Ibid., XXVI, pp. 347–48.

41. De Brahm was apparently acting as an agent for Christian de Munch and his three sons, each of whom was to receive a grant of 500 acres near Ebenezer. For details of this arrangement see Col. Recs. of Ga., XXXI, p. 508.

42. Glen was something of a geographer and military engineer in his own right. For evidence of his geographical talents, see Chapman J. Milling, *Colonial South Carolina: Two Contemporary Descriptions* (Columbia, S. C., 1951). In a letter written to the Board of Trade in 1750, Glen boasted of his knowledge of fortification engineering. He mentioned having been instructed "by Mr. Mullar and some of the ablest masters in Europe" in this science. This letter is found in the "Letter

Book of James Glen, 1745–52," on Reel 1 GD45/2/1, Dalhousie Muniments microfilm, S. C. Arch.

43. For a review of Glen's often stormy relationship with the South Carolina provincial assembly, consult M. Eugene Sirmans, *Colonial South Carolina: A Political History, 1663–1763* (Chapel Hill, N. C., 1966), especially Chapter XI, "Tinkering with the Constitution."

44. Ibid., p. 293.

45. "Journal of the South Carolina Commons House of Assembly," XXVII, pt. 2, p. 440, S. C. Arch. Glen had expressed his concern regarding the erosion of the royal prerogative in South Carolina shortly after his arrival in the province. In the letter he drafted to report the conditions which he found as he began to function as the colony's governor he stated, "I found the whole frame of government unhinged and the governor divested of that power which His Majesty's instructions and the Constitution place in him, and his power parcell'd out to many hands under different denominations, but chiefly under that of Commissionares." Quoted from Public Record Office Photostats, XXI (1743–44), p. 235, S. C. Arch.

46. Ibid., p. 438.

47. Ibid., p. 437. See also C. O. 5–734, p. 62.

48. Ibid., p. 440.

49. Ibid., p. 548. The attitude of the assembly toward "foreigners" might explain De Brahm's change of prefix in his surname from "von" to "De" at about this time.

50. "Council Journal," no. 20, pt. 1, p. 321, S. C. Arch.

51. Ibid., p. 325.

52. Ibid., p. 384.

53. Quoted from a letter written by Henry Laurens, dated Oct. 12, 1755. See Philip M. Hamer (ed.), *The Papers of Henry Laurens* (Columbia, S. C., 1968), I, p. 358.

54. From "A Short Description of the Province of South Carolina . . . Written In The Year 1763" by George Milligen Johnston, reprinted in Milling, *Colonial South Carolina*, pp. 128–30.

55. "Journal of the South Carolina Commons House of Assembly," XXVII, pt. 2, p. 581, S. C. Arch.

56. Ibid., p. 612.

57. Both the report and the plan are located in the Public Record Office, London. The plan is filed as C. O. 700, Carolina/14. It is incorrectly dated as 1742 in the Public Record Office records and as ca. 1755 by William P. Cumming in his *Southeast in Early Maps*, p. 223. The report is filed separately from the plan as C. O. 5–374, pp. 66–67, in the same archive.

Of major value in the preparation of this book were the maps of early America found in the Public Record Office. These were acquired from a variety of sources over a very long period, the most important single source being the Colonial Office Records. In all, there are about 1,600 maps cataloged under the classification "Maps and Plans" (C. O. 700). In recent years the Public Record Office map collection has been undergoing a re-indexing, and a new system of map referencing has been introduced. Such designations as M. R. and M. P. G. for maps in the Public Record Office are the products of this new system. As such they may be unfamiliar to readers who are familiar only with the older scheme of referencing. While working on this book in the Public Records Office during 1968, the author was allowed to consult the typescript pages of the guide to the maps of North America which was being prepared for publication by Her Majesty's Stationery Office. When this volume appears it will be a most valuable addition to the carto-bibliographic literature concerning this continent.

58. C. O. 5–374, p. 66.

59. "Journal of the South Carolina Commons House of Assembly," XXVIII, pt. 1, pp. 85–88, S. C. Arch.

60. Candler, *Colonial Records of Georgia*, VI, p. 384.

61. Reprinted in Alfred Coxe Prime, *The Arts and Crafts in Philadelphia, Maryland, and South Carolina, 1721–1785, Gleanings from Newspapers* (Topsfield, Mass., 1929), p. 35. De Brahm had given notice of his intentions to produce such a map in the *South-Carolina Gazette* of Oct. 23, 1752. These efforts finally culminated in the publication of "A Map of South Carolina And A Part of Georgia . . . ," by Thomas Jefferys on Oct. 20, 1757. For a description see Cumming, *Southeast in Early Maps*, pp. 227–28.

62. Candler, *Colonial Records of Georgia*, XXVI, p. 461.

63. Ibid., VII, p. 128.

64. Ibid. A second memorial on this topic was sent on Nov. 7, 1755. On this occasion Noble Jones, Georgia's original surveyor, was also ordered to surrender his many maps and plots of surveys to Yonge and De Brahm.

65. Ibid. p. 131. This site is shown on Harry A. Chandler's "Map of a Portion of Historical Savannah" (Savannah, Ga., 1917).

66. For a review of Reynold's tenure as governor of Georgia, consult W. W. Abbot, *The Royal Governors of Georgia, 1754–1775* (Chapel Hill, N. C., 1959), pp. 34–56.

67. Col. Recs. of Ga., XXVII, pp. 244–52. Abbot, cited in note 66 above, was apparently unaware of this representation which Reynolds forwarded to his superiors in the winter of 1755. As a result, his treatment of the governor is more harsh than might otherwise have been the case.

68. The map which accompanied Reynolds's representation is now filed as C. O. 700, Georgia/12, in the Public Record Office, London. The sheet of fortification plans is located in the same archive as C. O. 700, Georgia/11. It has been reproduced in *Collections of the Georgia Historical Society* (Savannah, Ga., 1913), VII, pt. III, p. 11.

69. Candler, *Colonial Records of Georgia*, VII, p. 163. See also the original Grant Book A, 1756–1758, Surveyor General Department, Atlanta.

70. Candler, *Colonial Records of Georgia*, XVIII, pp. 202–11.

71. For references to De Brahm's official positions and services to the colony of Georgia, see ibid., VIII, pp. 63, 426, 499, 541, 701; XIV, pp. 40, 54, 78, 102; XVIII, pp. 205, 343, 413; IX, pp. 179.

72. For description of De Brahm's land acquisitions in Georgia see ibid., VII, pp. 344, 588, 839; VIII, pp. 93, 46, 502.

73. "Council Journal," no. 6, pt. 1, p. 210, Public Record Office Photostats, S. C. Arch.

74. Ibid., p. 239.
75. For an example, see two letters written by Henry Laurens during July 1755, in Hamer, *Papers of Laurens*, pp. 300, 305.
76. This appointment and commission is recorded in the miscellaneous records of the secretary of the province, Book KK, 1754–58, p. 203, S. C. Arch.
77. *South-Carolina Gazette*, weeks of Aug. 21–28, 1755, and Aug. 28–Sept. 4, 1755.
78. See the "Miscellaneous Record Book," KK, 1754–58, p. 219, S. C. Arch., and "Council Journal," no. 6, pt. 2, p. 379, Public Record Office Photostats, S. C. Arch.
79. "Miscellaneous Record Book," LL, pt. 2, 1758–63," pp. 592–93, S. C. Arch.
80. Henry A. M. Smith, "Beaufort—The Original Plan and the Earliest Settlers," *South Carolina Historical and Genealogical Magazine*, IX (July 1908), p. 155.
81. For both background and detailed information concerning Glen's policies and activities during the crisis-ridden early 1750s, see John R. Alden, *John Stuart and the Southern Colonial Frontier* (Ann Arbor, Mich., 1944), pp. 38–56.
82. William L. McDowell (ed.), *Documents Relating to Indian Affairs, 1754–1765* (Columbia, S. C., 1970), p. 99.
83. Alden, *John Stuart*, pp. 49–50.
84. Quoted in John P. Brown's *Old Frontiers* (Kingsport, Tenn., 1938), p. 61.
85. McDowell, *Documents Relating to Indian Affairs, 1754–1765*, p. 115.
86. "Council Journal," no. 25, p. 325, British Public Record Office Photostats, S. C. Arch.
87. Ibid.
88. "Register Kept by the Rev. Wm. Hutson, of Stoney Creek Independent Congregational Church and (Circular) Congregational Church in Charles Town, S. C., 1743–1760," *South Carolina Historical and Genealogical Magazine*, XXXVIII (Jan. 1937), p. 33.
89. McDowell, *Documents Relating to Indian Affairs, 1754–1765*, pp. 169–70.
90. Brown, *Old Frontiers*, p. 63.
91. McDowell, *Documents Relating to Indian Affairs, 1754–1765*, pp. 214–20.
92. The reader should, at this point, consult pp. 100–102 of De Brahm's Report.
93. Demere complained of this as early as Oct. 26, 1756. See McDowell, *Documents Relating to Indian Affairs, 1754–1765*, p. 232.
94. Ibid., p. 224.
95. Ibid., pp. 232–34.
96. Ibid., p. 241.
97. Ibid., p. 250.
98. Ibid., p. 274.
99. Ibid., pp. 271–74.
100. Ibid., p. 287.
101. *South-Carolina Gazette, Supplement*, Feb. 3, 1757.
102. *Old Frontiers*, pp. 62–71.
103. *John Stuart*, note, p. 36.
104. McDowell, *Documents Relating to Indian Affairs, 1754–1765*, p. 224.
105. The Mar. 12, 1795, edition of the *Georgia Gazette* contained a long letter which De Brahm addressed "To the President of the United States." In this rambling letter the aged De Brahm expressed his great concern for the Cherokee Indians who were, in his opinion, being threatened by land speculators in the vicinity

of Muscle Shoals, along the Tennessee River. Apparently, the Indian claim to the territory was being challenged on the ground that it had been ceded to the British earlier. De Brahm refuted this by stating that only the 700 acres which surrounded Fort Loudoun had been legally surrendered by the Cherokees. He concluded his letter with the following paragraph: "To be thus precise, I (presuming [*to be*] the only one who remains of those that officially know of this matter) feel myself in duty bound to give in evidence the matter of fact concerning the surrender which the Cherokees made to the Crown of England in 1756, to wit 700 acres only, and no more, for a fort and garrison to defend this nation against the Janees [*Shawnees*], but not to take and hold possession of the Jasoo [*Yazoo*] country."

106. See "Report of the Journey of the Brethren Abraham Steiner and Frederick C. De Schweinitz to the Cherokees and the Cumberland Settlement (1799)," in Samuel C. Williams, *Early Travels in the Tennessee Country, 1540–1800* (Johnson City, Tenn., 1928), pp. 443–525.

107. Ibid. It is difficult to conclude which of De Brahm's several published works on religio-chronologic themes this "small printed work" might have been. An educated guess might select *Time An Apparition of Eternity*, printed in Philadelphia by Zacharaiah Poulson in 1791. Williams astutely observed that "there was much of the mystical in De Brahm's mental structure, . . . this appealed to many of the Cherokees who remembered him with esteem for a generation or more." *Early Travels in the Tennessee Country*, p. 187.

108. Col. Recs. of Ga., XXVII, p. 237.

109. Ibid., p. 238.

110. *The History of Georgia* (Boston, 1883), I, p. 510.

111. Col. Recs. of Ga., p. 11.

112. Ibid., p. 10.

113. Ibid., p. 11.

114. See pp. 153–54, below.

115. In his letter to the Board of Trade, dated Aug. 25, 1760, Governor Ellis described Savannah's improved fortifications as follows:

> . . . and at the North East Angle of this town one (a log fort) is built at the Public Charge, of two hundred feet square, regularly laid out with four Bastions; in each of which is a Tower mounting four Cannons; the whole work is as defencible and substantial as our Materials of Wood and Earth can make it. At the North East Angle, I have at my own expense (the Colony being unable to do it) built another Fort, which has cost me upwards of four hundred pounds Sterling. This is 120 feet square, flanked with four Bastions also, and a tower is raised in the center, mounted with four Cannons: Upon the two other angles of the Town, we have Erected Block Houses, each capable of bearing three cannons, picquitted round; which are likewise very tenable.

Quoted from Col. Recs. of Ga., XXVIII, pt. 1, pp. 458–59.

116. One such study was included by Howard J. Nelson in his article "Walled Cities of the United States," which appears in *Annals of the Association of American Geographers*, Vol. LI (Mar. 1961), pp. 1–22. It should also be noted that Nelson, in his study of Charleston, completely overlooked De Brahm's considerable contribution to the fortifying of that "walled city."

117. Col. Recs. of Ga., XXVIII, pt. 1, p. 459.

118. Candler, *Colonial Records of Georgia*, XIV, p. 40.

119. Ibid., p. 54.

120. Ibid.

121. Ibid., p. 78. This map has never been identified and must be presumed lost.

122. Ibid., p. 102.

123. "South Carolina And A Part of Georgia . . . Composed From Surveys taken by the Hon. William Bull Esq. Lieutenant Governor, Captain Gascoign, Hugh Bryan, Esq: And the Author William De Brahm . . . Engrav'd by Thomas Jefferys . . ." (London, Oct. 20, 1757).

124. "Original Conveyance Book C–1," pp. 181–83, Ga. Arch.

125. Ibid., pp. 261–63.

126. Candler, *Colonial Records of Georgia*, VII, p. 588.

127. Ibid., p. 700.

128. Ibid.

129. Ibid., p. 839.

130. Ibid., VIII, p. 93.

131. "Register of Grants Book B," Ga. Arch.

132. Candler, *Colonial Records of Georgia*, VIII, p. 464.

133. Ibid., p. 502.

134. Ibid., XVIII, p. 343.

135. Ibid., VIII, p. 63.

136. Ibid., XVIII, p. 413.

137. Marked "Mr. De Brahm's order for Tea Sepr. 3rd 1759" in Duke University Library Manuscript Collection.

138. Abbot, *Royal Governors of Georgia*, pp. 84–183.

139. Candler, *Colonial Records of Georgia*, VIII, p. 541.

140. Ibid.

141. C. O. 5–648, p. 144.

142. Ibid.

143. See De Vorsey, *Indian Boundary in the Southern Colonies*.

144. *Journal of the Congress of the Four Southern Governors and The Superintendent of That District, With The Five Nations of Indians, At Augusta 1763* (Charles Town, S. C., 1764).

145. These maps are described by William P. Cumming in his *Southeast in Early Maps*, p. 232. After a study of both maps and a comparison with others known to have been drawn by Yonge and De Brahm it was concluded that Yonge drew the British Museum copy while De Brahm drew the Clements Library copy. Christian Brun apparently misread De Brahm's map when he prepared a description of it which appears in his *Guide to the Manuscript Maps in the William L. Clements Library* (Ann Arbor, Mich., 1959), p. 152. In this description, the date of Oglethorpe's cession from the Creeks is given as "1759." This is incorrect and should read "1739."

146. It is probable that this map has become separated from the original letter and is in fact the copy done by Yonge which is now located in the British Museum. See *Catalogue of the Manuscript Maps, Charts, and Plans, And of the Topographical Drawings In The British Museum* (London, 1861), III, p. 513. Wright's letter can be found in Col. Recs. of Ga., XXVIII, p. 813.

147. Ibid.
148. Candler, *Colonial Records of Georgia,* XIV, p. 102.
149. For an excellent description and discussion of this valuable map, see Cumming, *Southeast in Early Maps,* pp. 227–28.
150. Quoted by Cumming in ibid., p. 228.
151. Ibid., p. 54.
152. Reprinted in Prime, *Arts and Crafts in Philadelphia, Maryland, and South Carolina,* p. 35.
153. On Apr. 12, 1764, De Brahm published the following in the *Georgia Gazette:*

> William De Brahm esquire, has finished for publication four maps containing the provinces of North Carolina, South Carolina, and Georgia; also, the Cherokee and Creek nations; with all the boundaries, rivers, creeks, towns, forts, roads, isles, inlets, the soundings in particular, as well as the soundings in general, of the whole sea coast, from latitude 31 to 36.
>
> For the satisfaction of the gentlemen connoisseurs and curious, this performance may be seen at the author's house in Savannah. For 100 copies only subscriptions will be taken in, at One Guinea per set, for which receipts will be given, and a list of their names, and the number of the receipt given will be published as often as the same list increases six in number. Mr. Thomas Jefferys, a skillful geographer in London will be the engraver of these maps, which will be executed within less than 12 months time, and delivered in Savannah by the author, or his attornies, and in Charlestown by John Gordon, esq.

> There is no record of this ambitious cartographic scheme ever being completed. It might be that the desired subscriptions failed to materialize. Perhaps it is even more likely that De Brahm's departure from Savannah to take up the duties of surveyor general in East Florida caused him to abandon this project. It is also possible that Thomas Jefferys's financial difficulties and bankruptcy in 1766 killed the project at his end. For details on Jefferys see J. B. Harley, "The Bankruptcy of Thomas Jefferys: An Episode in the Economic History of Eighteenth Century Map-Making," *Imago Mundi,* XX (1966), pp. 27–48.

154. Col. Recs. of Ga., XXVIII, pt. IIB, p. 66.
155. C. O. 324–52, pp. 37, 39.
156. C. O. 324–17, dated Aug. 15, 1764.
157. Ibid.
158. Most of this material is found in the British Public Record Office, London. One extremely valuable set of maps and descriptions which De Brahm forwarded to the Board of Trade in July 1765 was turned over to the Admiralty. This action is mentioned in the published *Journal of the Commissioners for Trade and Plantations, January 1776–May 1782* (London, 1938), pp. 212–13. A search of the Naval Library, Ministry of Defense, and the Hydrographic Department of the British government failed to uncover these charts. Surprisingly they were located in the collection of the Library of Congress, Geography and Map Division. These and other De Brahm maps now held by the Geography and Map Division are described by P. L. Phillips in *The Lowery Collection* (Washington, 1912), pp. 340–41. Mr. Richard W. Stephenson, of the Geography and Map Division, sug-

gests that these De Brahm maps of the Florida coast were acquired by the library in 1867 with the Peter Force collection of Americana which was purchased in that year by the Congress of the United States. (Personal communication, Nov. 15, 1968.)

159. C. O. 324–17, n. p.

160. C. O. 323–18, pp. 114–16.

161. Ibid. De Brahm appears to have determined his latitudes by observing the sun on the meridian and consulting solar tables. These tables usually included the sun's declination for each day of the year. This sort of observation was best made on shore away from the heaving deck of the ship. De Brahm frequently mentions going ashore to perform this demanding task with greater accuracy.

162. C. O. 323–18, p. 163. The *Times Atlas* places St. Augustine at latitude 29°54′ North. On Aug. 20, 1766 (C. O. 323–24, p. 77) De Brahm reported a corrected latitude for St. Augustine. He shifted its position 50′ farther north to 29°38′15″. He ascribed this change to "the difference in the quadrants I used; for last year I observed with a mahogany quadrant graduated by 3,600 seconds per inch and this year with a brass quadrant by ten degrees per inch." The Feb. 21, 1765, edition of Savannah's *Georgia Gazette* carried the following report on De Brahm's arrival in and impressions of his new home, St. Augustine:

> Mr. Printer,   St. Augustine, Feb. 2, 1765
> I have the pleasure to acquaint you of my arrival in St. Augustine the 25th of January. The bar, with a southerly or easterly wind, is as safe as any in America. Great injustice is done to this place on this head, and as much to the soil of this town and its environs, which I find much superior to that in and about Savannah. I have taken the latitude of this town, which is in 29 deg. 37 min. and 25 sec. The number of petitioners for land is greater than I could have imagined which has detained me longer than I intended, but shall proceed on my survey, if nothing obstructs me, on the 5th inst. The high winds would not admit to take the latitude of Tybee Light-house. I am, Sir, your humble servant,
>   William De Brahm
>   Surveyor-General for the Southern
>   District of North America.

163. De Brahm was probably referring to the instrument usually known as Hadley's quadrant, equipped with a vernier scale. Hadley's quadrant was the immediate forerunner of the nautical sextant. For a description see Charles H. Cotter, *A History of Nautical Astronomy* (London, 1968), pp. 77–83. Finding longitude by observing Jupiter's satellites was considerably simplified in 1765, when the first *British Nautical Almanac* appeared containing "tables of eclipses of Jupiter's Satellites."

164. See Ralph H. Brown, "The De Brahm Charts of the Atlantic Ocean, 1772–1776," *The Geographical Review*, XXVIII (Jan. 1938), pp. 124–32; and Lloyd A. Brown, "The River in the Ocean," *Essays Honoring Lawrence C. Wroth* (Portland, Me., 1951), pp. 69–84.

165. The De Brahm–Goffe charter, dated Dec. 17, 1764, is found in the British Public Record Office as C. O. 323–18, p. 239.

166. C. O. 323–18, pp. 168–78.

167. Ibid.

168. Ibid., pp. 164–66.

169. In an essay titled "The Bibliographical Way," which appears in *The Colophon*, n. s., III (spring 1938), Lawrence C. Wroth wrote about his own doubts concerning the credibility of De Brahm's scientific writing. Wroth first knew of De Brahm as the eccentric author of a "mathematico-mystical treatise" entitled *The Apocalyptic Gnomon*. . . . After a considerable amount of research Wroth discerned De Brahm's true stature as a scientific surveyor. Concerning De Brahm's map of the Gulf Stream which appeared in *The Atlantic Pilot*, Wroth wrote the following:

> I found that the Gulf Stream map was not a point in space unrelated to anything else but an integral part of a book on the navigation of the North Atlantic; that it was indeed, the graphic representation of a long and arduous experiment, the result in graphic projection of innumerable observations of position, courses, drift, and other nautical factors entering into the comprehension of that great ocean current.

170. In a letter to Lord Dartmouth dated May 3, 1777 (Dartmouth Ms. D1778 II 364), J. Wooldridge, an East Florida resident and agent for Dartmouth stated, "Mr. Grant may be an excellent officer but he is a most Tyrranical Governor." Cf. Charles Loch Mowat, *East Florida as a British Province, 1763–1784* (Gainesville, Fla., 1964), p. 45.

171. C. O. 5–570, p. 26. The grant with the attached plat of "William Gerrard De Brahm Town Lot No. 1 Governor's Quarter" is found in Treasury Papers Expired Commission Etc., East Florida Claims Commission, Bundle 4, n. p. Public Records Office, London. Hereafter cited as T. 77–4, n. p.

172. T. 77–4. De Brahm's two St. Augustine town lots were listed in the manuscript "Book on Register of City Lots (Bdl. 409)" found in the library of the St. Augustine Historical Society. He was also shown as a property owner on James Moncrief's "Plan of The Town of St. Augustine," dated Mar. 1, 1765. A full-scale photostatic copy of this map is in the collection of the St. Augustine Historical Society.

173. *Georgia Gazette* (Savannah), Oct. 3, 1765, p. 3.

174. C. O. 5–540, p. 178.

175. "Abridgement of Governor Grant's Deportment against the Surveyor General William Gerard De Brahm," Dartmouth Ms. D1778 II 497.

176. C. O. 5–540, pp. 181–82.

177. On this score, Governor Grant observed: "Mr. De Brahm's commissions as Surveyor of the District and as Land Surveyor of the Province are worded nearly in the same way and he makes no distinction in the nature of the offices, as the business of both is carried on in the same manner: for he remains in his office in Town and Trusts the General Survey to the Provincial Deputies, who are very unequal to such a task, tho they may be fit enough to measure and locate particular tracts of Land in the Province." Quoted from C. O. 5–551, p. 25.

178. Ibid.

179. From "Abridgement of Governor Grant's Deportment against the Surveyor

General William Gerard De Brahm," Dartmouth Ms. D1778 II 497. The following notice which appeared in the Nov. 3, 1766, edition of the *South-Carolina Gazette* indicates that De Brahm undertook the construction of a vessel for use on the survey:

> William Gerard De Brahm, His Majesty's Surveyor-General for the Southern District of North America Gives this Public Notice. That he is building a schooner rigged galley of 60 tons burthen on St. John's River in East Florida, for the service of the general survey, to be continued to the southernmost promontory within his district, upon which he proposes to set out in May next (1767): And that he shall have occasion to employ in the said service a Master equally qualified in the Theoretic and practical parts of Navigation, and acquainted with the Keys on the South shore of East Florida particularly with Cayo Largo and the Martiers on the East, and the Dry Tortugas on the West of the said shore: also a well qualified geometrician, who is well versed in Navigation. Such as may be inclined and can be well recommended for sobriety and capacity, to engage in this service, may expect all reasonable encouragement by applying to said De Brahm in St. Augustine. And any gentlemen who are inclined either for their own improvement or curiosity, to make a *Parti voluntaire*, on said survey shall be welcome to a passage, by applying as above.

In an official letter to the Board of Trade dated Oct. 1, 1766, De Brahm explained the vessel he was building in the following terms: "[*I*] am actually building on St. Johns River in this province a schooner rigged galley with conveniencys not common in other vessels, have master, mate and sailors in monthly pay (and) hope by this method to have it in my power to proceed when I think proper, leave off surveying . . . and return to it again without consulting agreements, charter partys, master, mate, etc." He went on to estimate that the ship would cost £500 to construct. Quoted from C. O. 323–24, p. 211.

180. Ibid.
181. C. O. 5–551, p. 27.
182. Ibid.
183. Ibid.
184. Ibid., p. 28.
185. C. O. 5–551, p. 31.
186. Dartmouth Ms. D1778 II 497, p. 6.
187. C. O. 5–551, pp. 25–36. By far the best published account of the De Brahm–Grant controversy is found in Mowat, "That 'Odd Being', De Brahm."
188. The notice of Mulcaster's marriage to "Miss De Brahm, daughter of William Gerard De Brahm Esq; Surveyor-General of the Southern District of North America," appeared in the July 10, 1769, edition of the *South Carolina and American Gazette*. Governor Grant commented on De Brahm's annoyance with his son-in-law in a letter to Hillsborough dated Oct. 2, 1770. He wrote, "I mentioned . . . that Mr. Mulcaster was married to Mr. De Brahm's daughter, an only child, but is at variance with his son in law, as he is with all mankind." Quoted from C. O. 5–545, p. 23.
189. C. O. 5–551, p. 89.

190. C. O. 5–72, p. 245.

191. The Apr. 4, 1771, edition of the *South-Carolina Gazette* carried the following advertisement announcing De Brahm's "over hurryed" sale of his possessions:

> To be sold by public Vendue at the House possessed by Mr. De Brahm, in Johnston Street Charles Town where William Cattell Esq. lately lived, on Monday the 15th day of April, 1771, at Ten o'clock in the Forenoon: Eleven Valuable Negroes amoung which are, Cooks and Washer Women, also five Boat negroes, Household-Furniture new and fashionable Plate, a schooner as she lies on the Rappoo Marshes and a sloop with all the appurtinances mentioned in the inventory, Also an elegant new house built of stone, in St. Augustine; a Tract of 1,000 acres 25 miles from said Town, and another of 150 acres 5 miles from Said Town, both convenient for Water and Land carriage. All the premises lately the Property of William De Brahm Esq. by Andrew Hiblen.

192. C. O. 5–154, p. 28.

193. Dartmouth Ms. D1778 II 497.

194. Treasury Papers, Minute Books, Vol. 43, pp. 52–442, Public Record Office, London. Hereafter cited as T. 29–43. Dartmouth Ms. D1778 II 677.

195. T. 29–44, p. 23.

196. Dartmouth Ms. D1778 II 310.

197. De Brahm expended a great deal of time and energy toward encouraging a group of Swiss and other Protestants to emigrate as a colony and occupy a portion of Dartmouth's huge landholding in southern Florida, in the vicinity of present-day Miami. See for example his detailed description of the area with recommendations for successful settlement entitled "To the Cape Florida Society," Dartmouth Ms. D1778 II 607. B. F. Stevens, in his Introduction to *The Manuscripts of the Earl of Dartmouth, American Papers* (London 1895), II, p. x., attributed the failure of the Cape Florida Society to De Brahm. While De Brahm may have contributed to the scheme's failure it seems manifestly unfair to lay the whole blame on him as Stevens has.

198. An eloquent insight into the relationship existing between Dartmouth and De Brahm is provided in the following paragraph written by De Brahm in a letter to Dartmouth on Aug. 24, 1774: "The 28th of July I was ordered to answer before a full Board of His Majesty's Treasury upon the Several Complaints of Governor Grant, which I did in the simplest manner offering to produce my two personal Evidences, office books and other original papers, which however was not desired, but Lord North was pleased to declare myself reinstated into provincial office of East Florida; the whole transaction lasted but 15 minutes, an event for which I am indebted to your Lordship patronage which will continue for ever in gratefull remembrance before me."

199. C. O. 5–70, p. 333.

200. C. O. 5–72, pp. 43–44.

201. C. O. 5–72, p. 308. The present location of the map described here has not been determined.

202. Dartmouth Ms. D1778 II 380.

203. Dartmouth Ms. D1778 II 496. There are two manuscript maps in the Public Record Office, drawn by the same hand, which may have formed De Brahm's 25-

foot-long General Map. They are: C. O. 700, Florida/53, "A Survey of the Part of the Eastern Coast of East Florida from St. Mary's Inlet to Mouth Halifax. Showing the ascertained boundary between East Florida and the Creek Indians," and one which adjoins it to the south, C. O. 700, Florida/3, "East Florida East of the 82nd degree of Longitude from the Meridian of London . . . Surveyed by William Gerard de Brahm. . . ." C. O. 700, Florida/3 is now mounted on a roller in two sheets, each about 10' long by about 5' wide. C. O. 700, Florida/53 measures about 4'4" by about 6'.

204. Dartmouth Ms. D1778 II 578. Unfortunately this map is not found with the letter which served as the source of this quotation and is presumed lost. Dartmouth's interest in the development of his East Florida landholdings was great during this period. Dartmouth Ms. D1778 II 495 b is a folio-sized notebook containing another copy of De Brahm's history and description of East Florida. In essence, it is another copy of the British Museum's Kings Ms. 210 "East Florida Chapt. 1st." with the dedication to Dartmouth. There are some minor differences: for example, the Dartmouth Ms. lacks one week of the "Ephemoris" and includes 291 names in the table of East Florida residents, which is 3 more than in the British Museum Ms.

205. Dartmouth Ms. D1778 II 579.

206. Report, pp. 61–194.

207. Dartmouth Ms. D1778 II 696.

208. C. O. 5–551, p. 25.

209. Dartmouth Ms. D1778 II 709.

210. The Houghton Library, Harvard University, provided a photocopy of the manuscript, "History of the Three Provinces, South Carolina, Georgia, and East Florida," by William Gerard De Brahm Esq., which has been compared with the British Museum's Kings Mss. 210 and 211 in the preparation of this book. In a prefatory letter bound in the Harvard manuscript addressed to the High Commissioners of the Treasury, written and signed by De Brahm, it is stated that the Harvard manuscript along with additional materials was delivered to "Phineas Bond, consel [sic] General of Great Britain for the United States of America" on Nov. 2, 1798. In the words of Charles M. Andrews and Frances G. Davenport, "The History of these volumes cannot be traced, but eventually two of them fell into the hands of Henry Stevens of London, who sold them in 1848 for £ 12-10s, to the Library of Harvard University, where they now are. The two Ms. present a number of points of difference. The Harvard College Library is bound in one volume and covers many more pages than the British Museum copy. The address to the king in Harvard College Library has two additional paragraphs, also an address to the Treasury, and an appendix in Latin, of a philosopho-mystical nature entitled 'Hercules ex rore sub flora corona', which was written in 1763, but is not found in the British Museum copy. The maps and plans are the same in both copies, with slight differences in the wording of the titles." Quoted from *Guide to the Manuscript Materials for the History of the United States to 1783, in the British Museum, in Minor London Archives, and in the Libraries of Oxford and Cambridge* (Washington, 1908), p. 27. De Brahm forwarded "Hercules ex Rore Rosatus Vet Categorico-Analytica Ecphansis . . . Johannem Wilhelmum Gerhardum S:R:F:E: de Brahm Suas Magnas Britanniae

Majestatis Georgii III archimetreta Geirguas Americanae 1763," to Dartmouth on Nov. 1, 1769. See Dartmouth Ms. D1778 II 311.

211. Dartmouth Ms. D1778 II 730.

212. De Brahm's account of Georgia from the Harvard manuscript was privately printed in a limited edition of 49 copies under the title, *History of the Province of Georgia: With Maps of the Original Surveys*, by George Wymberley-Jones (Wormsloe, Ga., 1849). His account of South Carolina from the Harvard source was also privately printed. This account, lacking the maps and "Compendium" of the Cherokee language, is included in Weston (ed.), *Documents Connected with the History of South Carolina*, pp. 155–227. Only 121 copies of this book were printed for Weston's private distribution. Of De Brahm's description of South Carolina, Weston wrote:

> The original of the following treatise is, I believe, in the Library of Harvard University, accompanied by many maps and plans, which I have not in my copy. More than one transcript is in existence: mine was purchased at a sale in New York, three years back. This portion has never been printed, though that concerning Georgia has been edited by Mr. G. Wymberley Jones, in folio, 1849, with great typographical elegance; the edition being confined to forty-nine copies.
> Beyond the particulars in the author's advertisement I know nothing of De Brahm's life; but [*that*] he lived within the memory of persons now alive, much addicted to alchemy, and wearing a long beard.

A more recent source by Samuel Cole Williams, entitled *Early Travels in the Tennessee Country*, pp. 187–94, includes De Brahm's description of Fort Loudoun with the map "Profile of Fort Loudoun." This material is also from the Harvard manuscript source.

213. H. Roy Merrens recently suggested that the inaccessibility of De Brahm's writings has resulted in his underemployment by present-day scholars. See "The Physical Environment of Early America," *The Geographical Review*, Vol. LIX (1969), pp. 530–56.

214. *The Atlantic Pilot*, London; Printed for the Author, by T. Spilsbury, in Cook's-Court, Carey-Street; And Sold By S. Leacroft, Opposite Spring Gardens, Charing Cross, MDCCLXXII.

215. *The Monthly Review; or Literary Journal*, XLVI (London, 1772), pp. 536–37.

216. Bernard Romans, *A Concise Natural History of East and West Florida* (New York, 1775), pp. 292–300. For details on Romans's relationship with De Brahm see P. L. Phillips, *Notes on the Life and Works of Bernard Romans* (Deland, Fla., 1924). Romans's criticism of *The Atlantic Pilot* is very widely known. It was, however, somewhat offset by other late eighteenth- and early nineteenth-century authors who commented favorably on important aspects of the work. For examples see the following: George Gauld, *Observations on the Florida Keys, Reef and Gulf* . . . (London, 1796), pp. 17–20; Andrew Ellicott, *The Journal of Andrew Ellicott* (Philadelphia, 1803), pp. 257, 270; James Grant Forbes, *Sketches, Historical and Topographical, of the Floridas; More Particularly of East Florida* (New York, 1821), p. 97.

217. *Recherches faites par Ordre de sa majeste Britannique, depuis 1765 jusqu'en 1771,*

*pour rectifier les cartes & perfectionner la navigation du canal de Bahama . . .
Traduite d l'anglois de W. Gerard De Brahm, ecuyer Hydrographe general au
departement due sud de l'Amerique Septentrionale* (Paris, 1788).

218. R. A. Skelton, "Cartography," Chapter 20 of Charles Singer et al. (eds.), *A History of Technology* (Oxford, 1965), IV, p. 605.

219. Both papers appear in the Royal Society's *Philosophical Transactions*, LXIV (London, 1774). See pp. 158–70 for "M. De Luc's Rule for Measuring Heights by the Barometer, reduced to the English Measure of Length, and adapted to Fahrenheit's Thermometer, and other Scales of Heat, and reduced to a more convenient Expression" by the Astronomer Royal, and "M. De Luc's Rules for the measurement of Heights by the Barometer, compared with Theory, and reduced to English measures of Length, and adapted to Fahrenheit's Scale of the Thermometer; with Tables and Precepts for expediting the Practical Application of them" by Samuel Horsley, LL.D., p. 214.

220. Dartmouth Ms. D1778 II 895.

221. Dartmouth Ms. D1778 II 942.

222. *The Levelling Balance and Counter-Balance; Or, The Method of Observing by the Weight and Height of Mercury, On any Place of Terra-Firma on the Terrestrial Globe, the Exact Weight and Altitude of the Atmosphere Below and above the Place of Observation; Thereby to ascertain how much the Horizon of the Sea is lower than the Place whereon the Observation is made* (London, 1774).

223. See Ms. "Journal Book of the Royal Society," Vol. XXVIII from Feb. 17, 1774 to Feb. 13, 1777 (the President's Copy), f. 118, 10 Nov. 1774.

224. Dartmouth Ms. D1778 II 443.

225. Ibid., D1778 II 576.

226. Board of Trade Minutes, Vol. 81, p. 21, Public Record Office, London. Hereafter cited as C. O. 391–81.

227. Dartmouth Ms. D1778 II 846. It is interesting to note that the *Cherokee*, the ship eventually assigned for De Brahm's use, does not appear in the list of ships included with this letter.

228. C. O. 324–18, p. 480.

229. Dartmouth Ms. D1778 II 1004.

230. Ibid., 1026. The need for "general maps" to comprehend the whole of the vast southern region was deeply felt during this period. See Louis De Vorsey, Jr., "The Southeast on an Accurate General Map," *The Southeastern Geographer*, VI (1966), 20–32. Such a map by De Brahm has not been identified.

231. Admiralty Papers, Master's log 1639, Public Record Office, London. Hereafter cited as Adm. 52–1639.

232. Dartmouth Ms. D1778 II 1519. In his article, "Charles Town Loyalism in 1775: The Secret Reports of Alexander Innes," *The South Carolina Historical Magazine*, LXIII (Jan. 1962), 134, B. D. Bargar incorrectly suggested that De Brahm was in Charleston during the month of June 1775.

233. Houghton Library, Harvard University. See Ralph H. Brown, "The De Brahm Charts of the Atlantic Ocean, 1772–1776," *The Geographical Review*, XXVIII (Jan. 1938), 129.

234. Dartmouth Ms. D1778 II 1519. See also De Brahm's letter to Gen. James Ogle-

thorpe dated Oct. 17, 1775, reprinted in R. A. Roberts, *Calender of Home Office Papers of the Reign of George III, 1760–1765* (London, 1878), p. 448.

235. Adm. 52–1662, p. 143.

236. Mabel L. Webber (comp.), "Death Notices from the *South Carolina and American General Gazette*, and its continuation *The Royal Gazette*, May 1766–June 1782," *South Carolina Historical and Genealogical Magazine*, XVII (Apr. 1916), 93. His son-in-law, Mulcaster, claimed that De Brahm's second marriage was not altogether a happy one. See his letter to Grant dated Oct. 3, 1775, reprinted in Peter Force's *American Archives* (Washington, D. C., 1843), IV, p. 331.

237. Dartmouth Ms. D1778 II 1519. In a letter to Governor Patrick Tonyn of East Florida, dated Oct. 15, 1775, Alexander Innes mentioned that "the Cherokee is a great acquisition to us. . . ." He went on to note that "De Brahm . . . has been plaguing us with his being impeded in carrying on the service he was order'd but the Governor (who has moved from the *Tamer* to this ship) has cut him very short. A fine time to talk of his surveys of a country that we are in a doubt to who it may belong. . . ." This letter is included in "Papers of the First Council of Safety of the Revolutionary Party in South Carolina, June–November 1775," *The South Carolina Historical and Genealogical Magazine*, III (Apr. 1902), pp. 75–76.

238. C. O. 5–77, p. 16. This major manuscript is now found in the Houghton Library, Harvard University. It is titled "Continuation of the Atlantic Pilot. Chap. 9." De Brahm clearly intended that it should represent a continuation of his Report. It was, like his personal copy of the Report, turned over to Phineas Bond, the British consul, in 1798 (see note 210, above). It is hoped that this manuscript, which represents a milestone in systematic oceanographic research, can soon be edited and published to join De Brahm's Report herein presented.

239. C. O. 5–77, p. 115.

240. C. O. 5–78, p. 164. His latitude agrees with that given in most reference atlases today. In terms of longitude, De Brahm's determination is within a few minutes of that usually recorded for Charleston in present-day reference volumes.

241. Ibid.

242. C. O. 323–29, p. 241.

243. Edward McCrady, *The History of South Carolina in the Revolution, 1775–1780* (New York, 1901), p. 145.

244. Williams, *Early Travels in the Tennessee Country*, p. 187.

245. C. O. 323–29, p. 241.

246. Ibid., p. 243.

247. Lord William Campbell, the royal governor, had fled Charleston in 1775 and served as a volunteer with the British force during the 1776 attack.

248. Brun, *Guide to the Manuscript Maps in the William L. Clements Library*, p. 92. For a brief note on Ferdinand De Brahm see Peter J. Guthorn, *American Maps and Map Makers of the Revolution* (Monmouth Beach, N. J., 1966), p. 9.

249. F. B. Heitman, *Historical Register of Officers of the Continental Army During the War of the Revolution, April 1775, to December 1783* (Washington, D. C., 1893), p. 97.

250. Julian P. Boyd (ed.), *The Papers of Thomas Jefferson* (Princeton, 1955), II, p. iii.

251. Ibid., XIV, p. 627.

252. The editor is indebted to William L. McDowell, Jr., Deputy Director of the South Carolina Department of Archives and History, for valuable information concerning disbursements made in connection with the fortification of Charleston and to Ferdinand De Brahm for his many services to the Provincial Congress of South Carolina.

253. C. O. 5–78, p. 103. The anonymous author of the tract entitled *A Letter to the English Nation, On the Present War With America* ... (London, 1777) included a bitter complaint regarding the unavailability of good maps and charts of America. He further observed, "The surveys of De Brahm, which might have been useful, have been made a present to the Congress by that Gentlemen, who had very ingeniously contrived a scheme to present them with the *Cherokee* armed schooner, which was alloted him for the duty he was employed on, but which miscarried by an accidental discovery of his intentions" (p. 57). Who the author of this accusation was is unknown, as is the source of his information concerning De Brahm's alleged plot. For some unexplained reason, Lloyd A. Brown attributed the authorship of *A Letter to the English Nation* ... to De Brahm. See Brown's "The River in the Ocean," *Essays Honoring Lawrence C. Wroth*, p. 80.

254. A. S. Salley, *Marriage Notices in the South Carolina and American Gazette from May 30, 1766 to February 28, 1781* ... (Columbia, S. C., 1914), p. 24.

255. Smith, "An Account of the Tattnall and Fenwick Families in South Carolina," 6–8.

256. *Georgia Republican*, Mar. 28, 1806, p. 3.

257. T. 29–49, p. 104.

258. British Museum, Additional Ms. 24322, p. 46.

259. C. O. 324–18, p. 516. There is an inconsistency on this point in the documents. Another "Estimate" for 1778 shows no allowance at all for De Brahm. This is C. O. 5–79, p. 62. On Mar. 3, 1778, De Brahm requested that the Board of Trade continue his allowance for the survey. According to the *Journal of the Commissioners for Trade and Plantations*, p. 171, De Brahm was told that the allowance he had received for 1777 was made "as a support during his confinement" only. The Board of Trade went on to observe that "he being now liberated from that confinement, the reason for making any extraordinary provision in their opinion now ceased." In a memorial addressed to the Board of Commissioners for the American Loyalists ten years later, De Brahm stated, "In 1778 I received ½ years Salary as Surveyor General." A. O. 13–137, p. 126.

260. A. O. 13–137, p. 126.

261. C. O. 5–81, p. 4.

262. Dartmouth Ms. D1778 II 1919.

263. Ibid.

264. T. 77–4, n. p. In addition to the two town lots described on page 40, De Brahm owned a thousand acres of land on the east side of St. Johns River a few miles south of present-day Jacksonville. The manuscript plat of this property is found in T. 77–4, n. p. It was strategically situated between the river on the west and the "path from the Cowford to St. Augustine" on the east.

265. A. O. 13–137, p. 128.

266. De Brahm had mentioned the death of his daughter in St. Augustine in Nov. 1773, leaving two motherless grandchildren. Dartmouth Ms. D1778 II 748. De Brahm's Florida-born grandson was to become Sir Frederick William Mulcaster (1772–

1846), lieutenant-general, colonel-commandant royal engineers, and inspector-general of fortifications. *The Dictionary of National Biography* (Oxford, 1937–38), XIII, p. 1171.

267. "Journal of the Senate of South Carolina, Jan. 6–Mar. 26, 1784," p. 114, S. C. Arch. This petition was referred to the General Committee on Confiscations, which later removed De Brahm's name from the Confiscation List.

268. See for example, "Petition to the Court of Chancery of the State of South Carolina . . . ," reprinted in *The South Carolina Historical and Genealogical Magazine*, VIII (Oct. 1907), 222.

269. A. O. 13–137, p. 128.

270. This material is quoted from a letter in the Royal Archives through the gracious permission of Her Majesty Queen Elizabeth II.

271. T. 77–4, n. p.

272. For examples, see A. O. 13–137, pp. 126–28, and Chatham Papers, bundle 116, Pt. I, pp. 18–19, Public Record Office, London. Hereafter cited as P. R. O.

273. P. R. O. 30–8–116. It is interesting to note that De Brahm, unlike most others, ascribed the king's indisposition to physical rather than mental causes. Until very recently it had generally been assumed that George III was insane. Recent research by two physicians has shown, however, that the king was in fact suffering from a very rare and exceedingly painful metabolic disease. See Ida Macalpine and Richard Hunter, "Porphyria and King George III," *Scientific American*, CCXXI (July 1969), 38–46.

274. A. O. 13–10, folder marked, "Various Papers C–E" (Nos. 47–74).

275. A. O. 13–137, pp. 126–28.

276. P. R. O. 30–8–116, p. 19.

277. Information provided by Mr. T. Roth of the Reading Room, The Historical Society of Pennsylvania, Philadelphia.

278. "An Account of the Tattnall and Fenwick Families," 9.

279. Quotation from a manuscript note found in a copy of *Apocalyptic Gnomon . . .* described in Catalog No. 47 of Ludwig Rosenthal's *Antiquariaat*; see P. L. Phillips, *Lowery Collection*, p. 340. Other mystical books published by De Brahm are: 1) *Voice of the Everlasting Gospel* (Philadelphia, 1792); 2) *Zeite Rechenschaft* (Ephrata, Pa., 1794); 3) *Sum of Testimonies of Truth* (Philadelphia, 1795?). These materials have not been thoroughly analyzed in preparing the present study since they were written long after the Report. At least one author who has turned his attention to De Brahm's mystical writings found his philosophy, as disclosed in the *Apocalyptic Gnomon . . .* , "unquestionably a modern philosophy." See A. J. Morrison, "John G. De Brahm," *South Atlantic Quarterly*, XXI (July 1922), p. 258. The biographer who attempts to construct an accurate and comprehensive profile of this fascinating figure of colonial American and early United States history could ill afford to neglect his voluminous mystical writings.

280. Harry M. and Margaret B. Tinkcom, *Historic Germantown from the Founding to the Early Part of the Nineteenth Century* (Philadelphia, 1955), p. 59. In his book, *Ancient and Modern Germantown, Mt. Airy and Chestnut Hill* (Philadelphia, 1889), p. 76, S. F. Hotchkin stated that "William Gerhard de Brahm, Surveyor General of His Majesty dwelt here. He wrote the 'American Military Pocket Atlas' and the 'Atlantic Pilot'." On page 250 Hotchkin noted, "Thomas

Jefferson once occupied the house in which Watson dwelt. John De Braines a French-German astronomer, had lived there still earlier."

281. De Brahm's Will, from a ms. copy in the collection of The Historical Society of Pennsylvania, Philadelphia.

282. Anne D. Mears, *The Old York Road* (Philadelphia, 1890), p. 25.

283. Ibid.

284. See note 280 above.

285. S. F. Hotchkin, *York Road, Old and New* (Philadelphia, 1892), p. 49.

286. In the typescript volume "Wills—Charleston County Will Book D 1800–1807," Vol. 30, Book C, p. 952, S. C. Arch.

287. *Savannah Republican*, Mar. 28, 1806.

288. Charles R. Barker's manuscript volume, "A Register of the Burying-Ground of Philadelphia," I, p. 130. This is located in The Historical Society of Pennsylvania, Philadelphia.

289. Personal communication from Louis and Madeline De Vorsey to the author, Sept. 5, 1968.

Notes on South Carolina

1. De Brahm used the term "Climatic" to describe a band of the earth's surface bounded by two designated parallels of latitude. In this scheme the longest day along the parallel nearest the pole was one half hour longer than the longest day along the parallel nearest the equator. His climates began at the equator with number one and progressed poleward. "Climate 5," which embraced South Carolina, was thus a band, six degrees and sixteen minutes in width, which began at latitude thirty degrees and thirteen minutes north and ended at thirty-six degrees and twenty-nine minutes north. Modern atlases usually record Charleston's latitude as thirty-two degrees and forty-seven minutes north. For a fuller explanation of this system, see *De Brahm's Zonical Tables For the Twenty-five Northern and Southern Climates* ... (London, 1774).

2. De Brahm erred in using 1663, the year in which Charles II granted the Carolina charter, as the beginning date for South Carolina's settlement. It was not, however, until 1670 that the first permanent British settlers established themselves at Albemarle Point on the Ashley River, across from the present site of Charleston.

3. South Carolina's boundaries were the cause of frequent disputes during the colonial period. Marvin L. Skaggs, *North Carolina Boundary Disputes Involving Her Southern Line* (Chapel Hill, N. C., 1941); A. S. Salley, *The Boundary Line Between North Carolina and South Carolina*, Bulletin of the Historical Commission of South Carolina, No. 10 (Charleston, S. C., 1929); and Louis De Vorsey, Jr., *The Indian Boundary in the Southern Colonies, 1763–1775* (Chapel Hill, N. C., 1966), should be consulted for detailed discussions of the early boundaries of South Carolina.

4. Lewis Gervais earned a reputation for his success with vineyards in the area of New Bourdeaux. James Cook's "A Map of the Province of South Carolina . . . ," (London, 1773), shows "New Bourdeaux" on the Little River in present McCormick County. This map also shows the name "jervais" near two houses in the immediate vicinity. See also, Arthur H. Hirsch, *The Huguenots of Colonial South Carolina* (Durham, N. C., 1928), pp. 205–7.

5. "Opuntia" is the name given to a large genus of cactaceous plants. De Brahm has used the term here to describe what is commonly known as prickly pear. Cochineal was a dye stuff which was made from the dried bodies of the insect *Coccus cacti*, found on several species of cactus in various parts of the world.

6. Barilla is a maritime plant long employed in southern Europe to produce an impure alkali for use in soda, soap, and glass production.

7. This was doubtless the Yaupon (*Ilex vomitoria*), which belongs to the holly family and grows along the southeastern coast of North America. It has long been used by Indians and Europeans.

8. That is, sealed with pitch or wax to make them airtight.

9. Probably the cabbage palmetto (*Sabal palmetto*).

10. For the location of the many settlements, rivers, and other features mentioned by De Brahm, the reader should consult "A Map of South Carolina and A Part Of Georgia. . . ," engraved and published by Thomas Jefferys in 1757, and "A Map of South Carolina And A Part of Georgia . . . , Republished with considerable additions, from the Surveys made and collected by John Stuart Esqr. . . . , By William Faden, 1780." For details concerning these important maps, see William P. Cumming, *The Southeast in Early Maps* (Chapel Hill, N. C., 1962), pp. 54–55, 227–28.

11. Although De Brahm's ideas concerning the causes and spread of disease seem bizarre and fanciful, it should be remembered that they were typical of his period and persisted well into the nineteenth century. Indeed, many of these ideas persist among older rural dwellers to the present day. For a concise review of early medicine in America, consult Richard H. Shyrock, *Medicine and Society in America, 1660–1860* (New York, 1960).

12. De Brahm has provided an excellent discussion of the controlled use of fire as a tool in land management. This is a topic which has been gaining in interest among a wide range of researchers in recent years. Much of this research is summarized and reported in the annual *Proceedings* of the Tall Timbers Fire Ecology Conference, published by Tall Timbers Research Station, Tallahassee, Florida.

13. The experiment from which these data were derived was conducted by Dr. John Lining (1708–60), a well-known Charleston physician. See George Milligen Johnston, *A Short Description of the Province of South Carolina . . .* (London, 1770), p. 46.

14. Valerius Cordus (1515–44) is usually credited with the authorship of the first pharmacopoeia (1535) used in Germany and the discovery of sulphuric ether.

15. Frederic Hoffmann (1660–1742), a German physician and experimenter who espoused the use of chemistry in medicine.

16. Sir Nathaniel Johnson, colonial governor of Carolina from 1702 to 1708. Johnson was very active in building the defenses of the colony during the period of Queen Anne's War. De Brahm was not alone in misspelling the name of the fort and governor. For details concerning the building of Fort Johnson see Harry S. Mustard, "On the Building of Fort Johnson," *The South Carolina Historical Magazine*, LXIV (1963), 129–35.

17. Plate 2 illustrates De Brahm's proposed new fortification to occupy the site of Fort Johnson. Like many of his schemes it was too costly and never constructed.

18. Plate 3, with its "Explanation," illustrates De Brahm's ambitious scheme to make Charleston into an island. Needless to say, it was not executed.

19. For details on "cowpens," see Gary S. Dunbar, "Colonial Carolina Cowpens," *Agricultural History*, XXXV (July 1961), pp. 125–31.

20. James Glen served as royal governor of South Carolina from 1743 until 1756. He is remembered for his great energy and activity in improving the colony's de-

fenses during this critical period. Glen was one of De Brahm's most important supporters in South Carolina.

21. De Brahm's involvement with the fortifications of Charleston began even before 1755. On Nov. 24, 1752, he presented Glen with his elaborate "Plan of a Project to Fortifie Charles Town Done by Desire of His Excellency the Governour in Council by William De Brahm Captain Ingeneer in the Service of his late Imp: Maj: Charles VII." The "Plan" or map is now separated from De Brahm's written report explaining its details. The map is filed under Colonial Office Records, "Maps and Plans," Carolina 14 (hereafter cited as C. O. 700, Carolina/14) in the Public Record Office, London, while the written text of the "Plan" is filed under Colonial Office Records, America and West Indies, Vol. 374, pp. 66–67 (hereafter cited as C. O. 5-374), in the same repository. The "Plan" has been erroneously dated 1742 in the Public Record Office. Although it is based on an excellent map which De Brahm drew after "recognizing and Sourvaying the Terrene of Charles-town," it should not be considered as a map of Charleston as it appeared in 1752. It incorporates many features which were De Brahm's proposals only and which were never to become a part of the Charleston scene.

22. Colonel Othniel, or Othneal, Beale, was a member and president of the South Carolina council. In 1742 he was employed to draw up plans for the fortification of the southern and eastern portions of Charleston. Roy W. Smith, *South Carolina as a Royal Province, 1719–1776* (New York, 1903), p. 199.

23. Probably "grillage," meaning a framework made of wood used to sustain foundations and prevent the irregular settling in soils of unequal compressibility.

24. "Fascine" was the name given to bundles of faggots extensively employed in eighteenth-century fortifications. They were used to raise batteries, fill ditches, strengthen ramparts, and for many other purposes.

25. The fortifications which De Brahm is describing were not begun until 1755. The South Carolina assembly had blocked Gov. Glen's earlier efforts to have him undertake the project in 1752. Their refusal to consent to De Brahm's employment was made on grounds of security. The South Carolinians strongly objected to allowing the German engineer to sound the channel and design the fortifications for their metropolis. Glen, however, maintained that only a competent military engineer should be commissioned to devise the plans. After three years of bickering and piecemeal repairs to the dilapidated and hurricane-damaged defenses, the city in 1755 was in a perilously exposed state. The distrust and dislike of the "foreigner" De Brahm was finally overcome and he was invited to begin work in the spring of that year. After making a careful survey of the town and harbor, De Brahm presented an elaborate plan for defending Charleston from any conceivable attack. Apparently, it was deemed too costly and not entirely necessary and De Brahm was forced to undertake a much more modest scheme.

For details on De Brahm's role in the design and construction of Charleston's fortifications see the ms. "Journal of the Commissioners of Fortifications 1755," South Carolina Historical Society (microfilm copy at South Carolina Archives, Columbia, S. C.). There are also many extended discussions of his employment in both the ms. South Carolina "Council Journal," and "Journal of the Commons House of Assembly," in the same archives. These manuscript accounts should be read in the light of De Brahm's "Plan for fortifying Charles Town, South Carolina, as now doing, with additions and Improvements July 1757." For a description of this map, consult Cumming, *Southeast in Early Maps*, p. 227. A favorable contemporary account of the works was provided by the editor of the *South-Carolina Gazette* in the edition of May 6, 1756.

26. Fort Loudoun on the Little Tennessee River. See the map *Vonore*, 139 SW–2 Tennessee 3¾ Minute Quadrangle, U. S. Tennessee Valley Authority, Chattanooga, or Knoxville, Tennessee. This map is printed at a scale of 1:12,000 and shows the area surveyed and mapped by De Brahm in great detail. For a review of the intended function of South Carolina's fort amidst the Overhill Cherokee towns on the Little Tennessee River, see Glen's message to the Cherokee chief Little Carpenter, in William L. McDowell (ed.), *Documents Relating to Indian Affairs, 1754–1765* (Columbia, S. C., 1970), pp. 99–100. The present editor read it in page proof, July 1969.

27. See "Plan of the Environs in the Neck of Tanassee and Talequo Rivers about Fort Loudoun and Little Tamothly, the westernmost of the Upper Cherokee Towns," Plate 5. De Brahm shows "Taskigee Old Town this place the Indians proposed for a Fort," just one quarter mile upstream from Fort Loudoun, facing Thirty Acre Island. This site was certainly far more exposed and vulnerable than the nearby ridge where De Brahm laid out Fort Loudoun. Opinion as to the correctness of De Brahm's choice of the site for the fort has varied widely both among his contemporaries and among historians of the present era. For a strident criticism by the fort's commander, Raymond Demere, see his many letters addressed to Gov. Henry Lyttelton, reprinted in McDowell (ed.), *Documents Relating to Indian Affairs, 1754–1765*. Robert L. Meriwether, on the other hand, discusses De Brahm's contribution in the siting and construction of Fort Loudoun in very favorable terms in *The Expansion of South Carolina, 1729–1765* (Kingsport, Tenn., 1940), pp. 213–14. The present editor is of the belief that De Brahm's scheme for a fort amidst the Overhill Cherokee towns was far more grandiose than the needs of the time demanded. In Demere's words, De Brahm conceived of his fortification "as if the River was navigable for Men of War," rather than for Indian dugout canoes and other small craft of the day.

28. De Brahm was correct in stressing the Cherokees' longstanding request for a fort to be built and garrisoned amidst their western towns. John Richard Alden, *John Stuart and the Southern Colonial Frontier* (Ann Arbor, Mich., 1944), p. 32.

29. Tellico River.

30. Spelled "Tamothly" on "Plan . . . Fort Loudoun and little Tamothly, the westernmost of the Upper Cherokee Towns," Plate 5.

31. For a highly readable and well-illustrated account of Fort Loudoun's construction and historic role based on extensive archival and field investigation, see Paul Kelley, *Historic Fort Loudoun* (Vonore, Tenn., 1961).

32. As he indicated (p. 101), De Brahm's relations with the officers of the Fort Loudoun contingent were strained from the outset of the project. They did not improve as work on the fort progressed. In his account of the affair, De Brahm naturally tended to cast himself in a most favorable role. The military commander, Capt. Raymond Demere, was, as mentioned in note 27 above, exceedingly critical of De Brahm's performance. De Brahm did not remain to see Fort Loudoun completed, returning to Charleston after a bitter row with Demere a few days be-

fore Christmas in 1756. Demere abandoned De Brahm's design for the fort and pressed his men to erect a wooden pallisade on the German engineer's elaborate earthworks.

On Jan. 4, 1757, Gov. Lyttelton presented "The Plan and Profile of Fort Loudoun Lattitude 36°7ᵐ Projected by William De Brahm his Majesty's Surveyor Genll in Georgia," for consideration by his council. This "Plan" shows several differences from the one which is included here as Plate 6. The "Plan" which Lyttelton presented in 1757 is now found in the collection of the Henry E. Huntington Library and Art Gallery, San Marino, California. For a reproduction see Paul Kelley, "Fort Loudoun: The After Years, 1760–1960," reprinted from *Tennessee Historical Quarterly*, XX (Dec. 1961), 9.

33. There is a rust-encrusted cannon on display at the Fort Loudoun Visitor Center Museum which is believed to be one of those carried over the mountains by Indian trader John Elliot.

34. Lending a note of authenticity to the present-day reconstruction of Fort Loudoun are a number of young locust trees planted in the ditch before the ramparts.

35. There has been a good deal of misunderstanding concerning the role which William Byrd III and his force of Virginians played in the attempted relief of Fort Loudoun. For a concise discussion of the matter listing most of the available sources, see Stanley J. Folmsbee's annotations to the reprint of J. G. M. Ramsey, *The Annals of Tennessee to the Eighteenth Century* . . . (Kingsport, Tenn., 1967), pp. 750–52.

36. Probably Holston River.

37. For an account of Montgomery's abortive attempt to deliver Fort Loudoun, see John P. Brown, *Old Frontiers* (Kingsport, Tenn., 1938), pp. 96–100.

38. Capt. John Stuart, who later became His Majesty's Superintendent for Indian Affairs in the Southern Department. See Alden, *John Stuart*.

39. In his "Compendium of the Cherokee Indian Tongue in English," De Brahm gives "Skaigunsta" as the word meaning "warrior." This is similar to "aya-sti-gi" which Brown lists as meaning "warrior" or "fighting man," in his Cherokee vocabulary. See Appendix A of Brown's *Old Frontiers*, p. 547. "Dutchee" probably represents "Deutch" or "German" rather than "Dutch" in the sense of one from the Netherlands. De Brahm was thus "the German Warrior" to his Cherokee acquaintances.

40. De Brahm's identification of the northern Indians with the lost tribes of Israel is in keeping with the prevailing opinion of the day. His use of the idea of continental separation or, as it is now phrased, continental drift, to account for their location in the New World is, on the other hand, quite novel and interesting.

41. The thesis that the southern Indians are descendants of the ancient Carthaginians is an intriguing one which is being actively investigated at the present time. It is to be regretted that De Brahm did not leave sketches of the "Hieroglyphics" which he mentions, as did Bernard Romans in *A Concise Natural History of East and West Florida* (New York, 1775), p. 103.

42. This "Compendium," like De Brahm's maps and sketches, was not included with the transcript which Plowden C. J. Weston acquired and published in 1856. See Plowden C. J. Weston (ed.), *Documents Connected With the History of South Carolina* (London, Printed for Private Distribution, 1856), pp. 155–227. De Brahm gives no clue as to whether the "Compendium" is the result of his or someone

else's efforts. An earlier German resident among the Overhill Cherokee, Christian Priber, was also credited with having compiled a "Cherokee dictionary." Priber's manuscripts were reported to have accompanied him to Fort Frederica where he was imprisoned and died sometime after 1744. Samuel Cole Williams, *Adair's History of the American Indians* (Johnson City, Tenn., 1930), p. 257.

1. Pierre Francois Xavier de Charlevoix (1682–1761) was a well-known French Jesuit priest, explorer, and historian. He recorded his accurate observations of interior America in his *Histoire de la Nouvelle France*, first published in 1744.
2. Don George Juan, unidentified.
3. Antonio De Ulloa (1716–95) was a Spanish naval officer and colonial administrator. His several reports on conditions in Spanish America were translated and widely circulated in the mid-eighteenth century.
4. Louis Antoine de Bougainville (1729–1811) was a French navigator and aide-de-camp to Montcalm in Canada in 1756. His *Voyage autour du monde*, a description of his circumnavigation of the world, was published in 1771.
5. The Georgia charter was granted to "The Trustees for establishing the Colony of Georgia in America," on June 9, 1732. The original charter describes the area from the Savannah River south to the Altamaha River and west from the heads of these two streams to the "South Seas," as the Pacific Ocean was then called. The trustees formally surrendered their charter to the Crown twenty years later on June 23, 1752, when Georgia became a royal colony.
6. For an excellent account of these three colonial governors and conditions in Georgia during the period of their tenure, see W. W. Abbot, *The Royal Governors of Georgia, 1754–1775* (Chapel Hill, N. C., 1959).
7. De Brahm was in error on this point. "An Act for constituting and dividing the several Districts and Divisions of this Province into Parishes . . ." was passed by the Georgia general assembly in Feb. 1758. See *Acts Passed By The General Assembly of the Colony of Georgia, 1755 to 1774* (Wormsloe, Ga., 1886), p. 190. Gov. James Wright did not assume his office until the autumn of 1760. For a map of the parishes, see Thomas Wright, "A Map of Georgia and Florida." Reproduced as Plate 60 in William P. Cumming, *The Southeast in Early Maps* (Chapel Hill, N. C., 1962).
8. The territory between the Altamaha River and Spanish East Florida was claimed by South Carolina by virtue of original charter rights. A royal proclamation in 1763 awarded the disputed area to Georgia and designated the St. Mary's River as the boundary between Georgia and the newly created British colony of East Florida. Edward M. Douglas, *Boundaries, Areas, Geographic Centers and Altitudes of the United States and the Several States*, U. S. Dept. of the Interior, Geological Survey Bulletin 817 (Washington, D. C., 1932), pp. 152–54.
9. John H. Goff suggested that this tongue twisting name be pronounced as "Hla-

hlo-hla-kuff-ka." See his "Short Studies of Georgia Place Names," *Georgia Mineral Newsletter*, XII (spring 1960), 39.

10. Okefenokee Swamp. De Brahm would appear to be in error regarding the meaning of this Indian word. Most authorities agree that "Okefenokee" originally meant either "Trembling Water" or "Trembling Earth."

11. Chattahoochee River.

12. Fort Prince George was a South Carolina post near the Cherokee town of Keowee. It was built by Gov. James Glen during 1753. For a contemporary description of it see Wilbur R. Jacobs (ed.), *The Appalachian Indian Frontier: The Edmond Atkin Report and Plan of 1755* (Lincoln, Neb., 1967), p. 54. The site is now inundated by the waters of Lake Keowee of the Keowee-Toxaway Project of the Duke Power Corporation.

13. De Brahm would seem to have described Big Junction peak in this colorful footnote. Big Junction has an elevation of 5,472 feet and would have provided him with an excellent vantage point from which to look northwest to the valleys of the Little Tennessee and Tellico Rivers. See *Chattanooga* and *Knoxville* sheets (NI 16-3 and NI 17-1), Army Map Service, Series V501P, scale 1:250,000. "Hughnaky" indicates the mountain range now identified as "Unicoi" on the maps mentioned above. James Mooney suggests that "Unicoi" and "Unaka" are corruptions of the Cherokee word "unega," meaning "white." See *Myths of the Cherokee* (Washington, 1900), p. 542.

14. "Tehotee" and "Tehutaco" represent De Brahm's spellings of the important Overhill Cherokee towns of Chota (Chote) and Citico (Settico).

15. The Tellico River, which flowed through the Cherokee towns known collectively as the Valley Settlements. "Talequo" and "Tehahekee" represent De Brahm's spellings of the Cherokee Valley towns of Great Tellico and Charique (Chatuga) which were located in the vicinity of the present-day town of Tellico Plains in Monroe County, Tennessee. The best eighteenth-century map to consult for the locations and names of southeastern Indian towns is the large manuscript map drawn by Joseph Purcell in 1775. For a reproduction of this map see Louis De Vorsey, Jr., "The Colonial Southeast on an Accurate General Map," *The Southeastern Geographer*, VI (1966), 20-32.

16. For information and notes concerning Fort Loudoun, see the preceding chapter.

17. In this paragraph De Brahm indicates his awareness of the topographic variety of the coastal plain which formed such an important part of South Carolina, Georgia, and East Florida. The belt of "Hills" which he described at about 37 miles from the coast are recognized today as the severely eroded remnants of the older series of Georgia coastal plain terraces. William Bartram also described these coastal plain terraces as he passed from Savannah to Augusta in 1773. Francis Harper, *The Travels of William Bartram: Naturalist's Edition* (New Haven, Conn., 1958), pp. 19-21. De Brahm is original, however, in utilizing distribution of the epiphyte commonly known as Spanish moss to mark the extent of his "Salt Air Zone" or coastal plain. Recent research has shown that the distribution of Spanish moss in the southeastern United States is limited to the area between the fall zone and the sea coast. See R. E. Garth, "The Ecology of Spanish Moss (Tillandsia Usneoides): Its Growth and Distribution," *Ecology*, VL (summer 1964), 470-81.

18. Bishop Samuel Urlsperger of Augsburg in Germany was one of two non-British members on the Board of Trustees for Establishing the Colony of Georgia in America. He actively promoted the colony's growth by encouraging and assisting displaced German Protestants to settle there. As indicated in the Introduction to this volume, Urlsperger financed De Brahm's migration to Georgia in 1751.

19. Christian de Munch (Chretien von Munch) was an Augsburg banker and the only other foreign member on the Board of Trustees for Establishing the Colony of Georgia.

20. De Brahm was certainly not suffering from any sense of modesty when he wrote these paragraphs regarding the state in which he found Georgia upon his arrival in 1751. It should be noted, however, that the colony was at a very low ebb during this period, so his description is not to be entirely discounted. For a review of the trying years immediately prior to Georgia's becoming a royal colony, see Chapter VII, "The Utopia Fails," in E. Merton Coulter's *Georgia: A Short History* (Chapel Hill, N. C., 1960), pp. 64–80. The map to which he alluded was presented to the government of Georgia by De Brahm on Mar. 24, 1752. See Allen D. Candler (ed.), *The Colonial Records of the State of Georgia* (Atlanta, Ga., 1904–11), XXVI, pp. 347–48. It is possible that this map may have been similar or identical to "A Map of Savannah River beginning at Stone Bluff or Nexttobethel, which continueth to the Sea; also, the Four Sounds Savannah, Hossabaw and St. Katharines with their Islands Likewise Newport or Serpent River from its mouth to Benjehova bluff. Surveyed by William Noble of Brahm Late Captain Ingenier under his Imperial Majesty Charles the VII." The ms. original of this map is now found in the Faden Collection of the Library of Congress, Geography and Map Division.

21. For a documented account of this first significant immigration of propertied planters into Georgia, see Abbot, *Royal Governors of Georgia*, pp. 21–22.

22. Slavery had been prohibited through most of the period of the trustees' control of Georgia. It was allowed, in a limited way, by a system of rules which the trustees instituted in 1749. By 1750, these regulations, like most others peculiar to Georgia under the trustees, were removed and slave labor was becoming commonplace in the colony.

23. There is a large and growing body of literature concerning Georgia's early German settlers, the Salzburgers. An interesting and informative general review is provided in R. L. Brantley, "The Salzburgers in Georgia," *Georgia Historical Quarterly*, XIV (Sept. 1930), 214–24.

24. For a review of the rise and decline of silk production in Georgia see Mary Thomas McKinstry, "Silk Culture in the Colony of Georgia," *Georgia Historical Quarterly*, XIV (Sept. 1930), 225–35. On the topic of Salzburger agriculture in general, consult Hester Walton Newton, "The Agricultural Activities of the Salzburgers in Colonial Georgia," *Georgia Historical Quarterly*, XVIII (Sept. 1934), 248–63.

25. For an account of schooling, divine services, and the use of the English language by the Salzburgers, see Hester Walton Newton, "The Industrial and Social Influences of the Salzburgers in Colonial Georgia," *Georgia Historical Quarterly*, XVIII (Dec. 1934), 344–48.

26. De Brahm's classification of colonial Georgia's towns and settlements was reproduced by Charles C. Jones in *The Dead Towns of Georgia* (Savannah, Ga., 1878), p. 245. This source should be consulted for further information regarding these settlements, many of which long ago disappeared from the Georgia scene.

27. See Marguerite Bartlett Hamer, "Edmund Gray and His Settlement at New Hanover," *Georgia Historical Quarterly*, XIII (Mar. 1929), 1–12; and Alex M. Hitz, "The Wrightsborough Quaker Town and Township in Georgia." *The Bulletin of Friends Historical Association*, XLVI (spring 1957), 10–22.

28. See E. R. R. Green, "Queensborough Township: Scotch-Irish Emigration and the Expansion of Georgia, 1763–1776," *William and Mary Quarterly*, 3d ser., XVII (Apr. 1960), 183–99.

29. De Brahm has confused the position of Tugaloo River. His "Toogelo" is the Tugaloo which enters the Savannah about eighty-five miles upstream from Augusta.

30. De Brahm shows this property clearly on "A Map of South Carolina And A Part Of Georgia . . . ," drawn in 1757. This Little Ogeechee (Ogetchee) River should not be confused with the better-known stream of the same name found in present-day Washington and Hancock counties.

31. De Brahm's description of these extensive ruins on Demetrius Island has been the cause of a good deal of speculation as to their origin. J. Randolph Anderson was probably correct in taking De Brahm to task for not suggesting that the ruins might have been the vestiges of a Spanish mission. "The Spanish Era in Georgia, and the English Settlement in 1733," *Georgia Historical Quarterly*, XVII (June 1933), 91–110. It may be that De Brahm's Demetrius Island corresponds with the area known as Harris Neck, shown on the Sapelo River, Ga. Quadrangle, scale 1:62,500. John Tate Lanning shows the mission and Indian village Tupique in this general area of his map, "The Spanish Missions of Georgia." John Tate Lanning, *The Spanish Missions of Georgia* (Chapel Hill, N. C., 1935), p. 53.

32. Located on Seneca Creek near Walhalla, in Oconee County, S. C. Mooney, *Myths of the Cherokee*, p. 541. De Brahm may have confused this Cherokee town with an abandoned Creek town located near present-day Milledgeville, Ga. It was this Creek town which lent its name to the river which unites with the Ocmulgee to form the stream known as the Altamaha River.

33. Towaliga River.

34. Tobesofkee River.

35. Penholoway Creek. Goff, "Short Studies of Georgia Place Names," VIII (spring 1955), 22–23.

36. Present-day Brunswick, Georgia. George McIntosh was assigned to lay out the town of Brunswick in 1770. See "The Case of George McIntosh," *Georgia Historical Quarterly*, III (Sept. 1919), 132.

37. For a discussion of the evolution of this and other Georgia Indian boundary lines during the colonial period see Louis De Vorsey, Jr., "Indian Boundaries in Colonial Georgia," *Georgia Historical Quarterly*, LIV (spring 1970), 63–78.

38. De Brahm has confused the year of Oglethorpe's arrival. He arrived to begin the colony on Feb. 12, 1733. The charter to the trustees, as mentioned in note 5, was issued during the preceding year.

39. For a description of Savannah during this period, see John P. Correy, "The Houses of Colonial Georgia," *Georgia Historical Quarterly*, XIV (Sept. 1930), 181–201.

40. The site of De Brahm's house is shown on Harry A. Chandler's "Map of a Portion of Historical Savannah." This useful map is available from the Georgia Historical Society, Savannah, for $1.00.

41. This was doubtlessly De Brahm's son George Charles. See Introduction, p. 20.

42. Yamacraw, the Indian town site, is located immediately to the east of the southern approach to the present-day Eugene Talmadge Memorial Bridge.

43. Tomochichi, the famous chief of the Yamacraw Indians.

44. For a discussion of this local legend, see Dolores Boisfeuillet, "The Legend of Sir Walter Raleigh at Savannah," *Georgia Historical Quarterly*, XXIII (June 1939), 103–21.

45. De Brahm had produced a comprehensive survey of Georgia's defense requirements for Ellis's predecessor Gov. John Reynolds the year before. See "A Representation of the Forts, and Garrison's that are necessary for the Defense of Georgia, and an Estimate of the Expense," with its enclosed sketches of proposed fortifications and a map of Georgia showing the places to be fortified. A typescript of the "Representation" is found in the unpublished "Colonial Records of Georgia," XXVII, pp. 244–52, Georgia Department of Archives and History, Atlanta. The sketches have been reproduced at a reduced scale in *Collections of the Georgia Historical Society*, VII, pt. III (Savannah, Ga., 1913), p. 11. A copy of the map is on file at the Office of the Surveyor General of Georgia, Archives Building, Atlanta. On July 19, 1757, De Brahm was named as one of the commissioners designated to execute the provisions of a Georgia legislative "Act for the Security and Defense of the Province . . . by Erecting Forts. . . ." Candler (ed.), *Colonial Records of Georgia*, XVIII, p. 205.

46. For detailed drawings of several of De Brahm's Georgia fortification plans see the reproduction of "The Profile of the Whole Citadelle of Frederica . . . Profile to the Projects for Savannah and Harwick . . .," in *Collections of the Georgia Historical Society*, VII, pt. III (Savannah, Ga., 1913), facing p. 11.

47. John Ellis (1710–76), highly regarded London naturalist, was appointed agent for West Florida in 1764. Bernard Romans, one of De Brahm's better-known deputies, dedicated his book on the Floridas to Ellis in 1775. Bernard Romans, *A Concise Natural History of East and West Florida* (New York, 1775). This book has been republished as a facsimile reproduction by the University of Florida Press (Gainesville, Fla., 1962).

48. For a discussion and description of the various southern pines consult the appropriate sections of U. S. Department of Agriculture Forest Service, *Sylvics of Forest Trees of the United States*, Agricultural Handbook No. 271 (Washington, D. C., 1965).

49. See "A view of Tiby Light House, at the entrance of Savanna River, Georgia, Dec. 1764," King George III Topographic Collection, p. cxxii. 77. C., British Museum, London.

50. Ideas similar to De Brahm's concerning the influence of trees on human health were to persist well into the nineteenth century in Savannah. In 1806, Dr. J. E. White was vigorous in urging his fellow Savannahians to plant promenades of

trees because they presented a "barrier to the progress of impure exhalations." Dr. J. E. White, "Topography of Savannah and its Vicinity: A Report to the Georgia Medical Society, May 3, 1806," *Georgia Historical Quarterly*, I (Sept. 1917), 240–41. Significantly, the following year the city council appointed a superintendent of trees and appropriated $500 for his use. Thomas Gamble, Jr., *A History of the City Government of Savannah, from 1790 to 1901* (Savannah, Ga., 1900), pp. 83–84. The deleterious effects of flooded rice fields, too, became widely appreciated. In 1817, the Savannah city council passed an ordinance prohibiting rice cultivation. Nearly $9,000 was provided from city funds to assist local planters in draining their lands and shifting to dry-culture farming. Ibid., p. 142. It is interesting to note that maps of the Savannah area following this date frequently indicate "dry culture" in the fields surrounding the city.

51. Bernard Romans (*Natural History of Florida*, p. 104) used data similar to these, "An Aggregate and Valuation of Exports of Produce from the Province of Georgia . . . from the year 1754 to 1773. Compiled by William Brown, Comptroller and Searcher of his Majesty's Customs in the Port of Savannah."

52. For the locations and preferred spellings of these Cherokee towns, consult James Mooney, *Myths of the Cherokee*.

53. For the locations and preferred spellings of these Creek towns consult John R. Swanton, *Early History of the Creek Indians and their Neighbors*, Bureau of American Ethnology, Bulletin 73 (Washington, D. C., 1922).

1. The earl of Dartmouth, to whom De Brahm addressed this dedicatory letter, was William Legge, second earl of Dartmouth (1731–1801). In Aug. 1772, he succeeded Lord Hillsborough as Secretary of State for the Colonies and President of the Board of Trade and Foreign Plantations. He retained these positions until Nov. 1775, when he became Lord Privy Seal. Dartmouth, who has been described as an "amiable pious man . . . entirely without any administrative capacity," enjoyed a very close association with George III. De Brahm came to look upon Dartmouth as his patron and enjoyed his confidence. There are a large number of manuscript letters, reports, and other communications from De Brahm to Lord Dartmouth preserved in the Dartmouth Papers now housed in the Staffordshire County Record Office, Stafford, England. For a description, see Historical Manuscripts Commission, *The Manuscripts of the Earl of Dartmouth* (London, 1895), II, pp. x and passim. This section of the Report, including De Brahm's first three chapters devoted to East Florida and the dedication letter, was first prepared for Lord Dartmouth. The Dartmouth Papers include this material in the form of a large notebook cataloged as D1778 II 495 b, Staffordshire County Record Office, Stafford, England. There are differences between the Report here presented and the Dartmouth notebook, however. For example, the Dartmouth copy has a few more persons named in the list of East Florida inhabitants. Also, the "Ephemeris" in the Dartmouth version lacks one week in length as compared to the Report.

2. Dionysian Period, a period of 532 Julian years, after which the changes of the moon recur on the same days of the year; introduced for calculating the date of Easter.

3. The large maps which De Brahm describes are still extant. The northern part is filed under Colonial Office Records, "Maps and Plans," Florida/53 (hereafter cited as C. O. 700, Florida/53) in the collection of the Public Record Office, London. This meticulously drawn manuscript map is inscribed, "A Survey of the Part of the Eastern Coast of East Florida from St. Mary's Inlet to Mount Halifax. Showing the ascertained boundary between East Florida and the Creek Indians." It is approximately 4′4″ by 6′ in size. The remainder of the Florida east coast, south to the Keys, is shown on the map now cataloged as C. O. 700, Florida/3, in the same collection. This manuscript map was drawn by the same accomplished cartographer and adjoins Florida/53. It is inscribed, "East Florida East of the

82nd degree of Longitude from the meridian of London Pursuant to the Directions from the Right Honorable The Lords of Trade and Plantations Surveyed by William Gerard de Brahm Surveyor General For the Southern District of North America." Because of its large size this map is now stored as two 10′ by 5′ sheets on a large roller. To gain an idea of the area covered by these large-scale depictions of pre-Revolutionary Florida, visualize the three regional maps reproduced here as Plates 15, 20, and 26 mosaicked to form one large map.

4. Inca Garcilasso de la Vega (1539?–1616), the son of a Spanish cavalier of noble lineage and an Inca princess, was born in Cuzco, Peru. Following the death of his father, Garcilasso went to Spain and saw service with the army campaigning against the Moors. He is best remembered as the author of *La Florida del Inca: Historia del Adelantado Hernando De Soto* (1605). For an edited translation, see John Grier Varner and Jeanette Johnson Varner (eds.), *The Florida of the Inca* (Austin, Tex., 1951).

5. De Brahm is not alone in placing Ponce's landfall in southwestern Florida. Many early maps show a bay named Juan Ponce in the area which De Brahm designated as Chatham Bay on his map, Plate 26. Modern scholarship has indicated, however, that Juan Ponce de León made his first continental landfall somewhere in northeastern Florida, probably a beach located between present-day St. Augustine and the mouth of the St. Johns River. See T. Frederick Davis, "Juan Ponce De Leon's Voyages to Florida," *The Florida Historical Society Quarterly*, XIV (July 1935), the whole issue. Davis's map of Ponce's track in 1513 was reprinted in Rembert W. Patrick, *Florida under Five Flags* (Gainesville, Fla., 1945), p. 3.

6. Sebastian Cabot.

7. Northern.

8. Hernando De Soto. For an excellent review of the De Soto expedition, see *Final Report of the United States De Soto Expedition Commission* (Washington, D. C., 1939).

9. Tampa Bay, probably at Terra Ceia Island. Ibid., pp. 137–38.

10. Spelled "Hirrihigua" in the translation of Garcilasso's *Florida of the Inca* (see note 4 above). These were the Ocita Indians, who probably spoke a language related to the Timucua group. They appear to have occupied the towns of Ocita and Orriygua located on the southeast side of Tampa Bay, *Final Report of the De Soto Commission*, p. 53. This excellent source should be consulted for the identity of the other Indian tribes, villages, and natural features which De Brahm mentions in this extended recapitulation of Garcilasso's narrative.

11. This is an account of the tragic episode experienced by the Dominican monk known as Fray Luis Cancer de Barbastro. See Woodbury Lowery, *The Spanish Settlements within the Present Limits of the United States, 1513–1561* (New York, 1911), pp. 411–27.

12. Jean Ribault, the French Huguenot leader, built Fort Caroline on the south bank of the St. John's River in 1564. See Jacques le Moyne's contemporary drawings of the fort in Charles E. Bennett, *Settlement of Florida* (Gainesville, Fla., 1968), pp. 21–23. Le Moyne was the official cartographer attached to Ribault's expedition. His excellent depictions of Fort Caroline were invaluable aids during the recent construction of the replica which is now open to visitors.

13. Pedro Menéndez de Avilés, founder of St. Augustine.

14. Tolomato River.

15. For a colored portrait of Menendez and annotated translations of his letters, see Bennett's *Settlement of Florida*, frontispiece and pp. 147–76.

16. De Brahm uses the phrase "Trade Winds" in an interesting manner to describe the onshore-offshore diurnal alteration of local winds. His "Trade Winds" shift or "trade" back and forth in direction. Present-day usage usually reserves the term to describe the relatively steadily flowing winds which move from the earth's subtropical high-pressure belts toward the equatorial low-pressure belt. When discussing his theories concerning the Gulf Stream and oceanic patterns of circulation (pp. 243–44), De Brahm utilizes the term "trade wind" in the more generally accepted manner. The pioneering treatise describing the pattern of world wind systems, *Concerning The Cause Of The General Trade Winds*, by John Hadley, had been published in London in 1735, and so was widely known by navigators in De Brahm's period.

    Modern visitors to Florida's beaches, like De Brahm, are frequently relieved by the brisk sea breeze which blows onshore during the heat of the day. Conversely, evening promenades along the same beaches are made more bracing by the shore breeze which blows toward the sea as the land cools in the dusk. It should be added that the lack of elevation which characterizes so much of the Florida peninsula serves to accentuate the effect of these breezes.

17. It should be recalled that Spain had belatedly allied with France in the war against the British and so was a signatory to the Peace of Paris in 1763. Spanish Florida, as well as the French ports and settlements along the Gulf of Mexico, was included in the immense territory which the victorious British acquired on the North American continent in that eventful year.

18. An emphasis on the "original thirteen" American colonies which evolved into the United States has often resulted in a lack of appreciation of the significance of the two Floridas in the imperial schemes of eighteenth-century Britain in America. Two excellent monographs, however, are available and go far in offsetting this lack. They are: Charles L. Mowat, *East Florida as a British Province, 1763–1784* (Gainesville, Fla., 1964); and Cecil B. Johnson, *British West Florida, 1763–1783* (New Haven, Conn., 1943).

19. This boundary between Georgia and Florida has been the occasion for an inordinate amount of tension and debate through the more than two centuries which have elapsed since it was first proclaimed. See Edward M. Douglas, *Boundaries, Areas, Geographic Centers and Altitudes of the United States and the Several States*, U. S. Dept. of the Interior Geological Survey Bulletin 817 (Washington, D. C., 1932), pp. 157–59. De Brahm's Chatahutchee and Ockanphanoko are, of course, the Chattahoochee River and Okefenokee Swamp.

20. "Sanders Indian Trading Store" is clearly shown on Plate 15.

21. The location of St. Augustine is given as 29°53′ N. 81°21′ W., in *Goode's World Atlas*, 12th ed. (Chicago, 1966). A sundial mounted on the front of the present-day Cathedral of St. Augustine indicates that its position marks latitude 29°53′19″ N. and longitude 81°18′26″ W.

22. De Brahm is alluding to the French expeditions which measured arcs of the meridian in high and low latitudes (in Lapland and Peru) between 1736 and 1745.

The findings of these ambitious projects established the earth's shape as being that of an oblate spheroid.

23. The log line was a line or cord fastened to a small weighted board or "log" and wound on a reel. The unreeling of this line or cord, as the log was allowed to float behind a moving ship, was indicated by knots or marks. The length the cord unwound in a given time indicated the rate of the ship's sailing. The time interval was determined with a sandglass, called, by De Brahm, a "minute glass." In general practice, the number of knots and parts of a knot unwound from the reel in half a minute was the number of miles and parts of a mile which the ship ran in one hour.

24. John Hadley (1682–1744) invented Hadley's quadrant in 1731. In about 1757, Captain (later Admiral) John Campbell increased the instrument's arc to 60° in order to facilitate the measurement of angles up to 120°. The quadrant then gave place to the sextant. An American optician, Thomas Godfrey (1704–49), is also credited with the invention of a reflecting instrument for measuring altitudes and lunar distances at the same time as Hadley. E. G. R. Taylor, *The Mathematical Practitioners of Hanoverian England, 1714–1840* (Cambridge, Eng., 1966), pp. 123–24.

25. De Brahm's "measuring wheel" is better known as an odometer. During the eighteenth century the term "perambulator" was also used.

26. De Brahm utilizes the word "loxodromic" to identify his surveys made from shipboard as opposed to those made on land. In navigational parlance, the term pertains to oblique sailing by rhumb line.

27. See Plate 26.

28. The small scale of Plate 26 makes it difficult to follow De Brahm's detailed description of the geography of the Florida Keys. The interested reader is advised to consult his printed "Chart of the South End of East Florida and Martiers," included with *The Atlantic Pilot* (London, 1772).

29. De Brahm proposed naming his two Pharuses or lighthouses after Britain's Hanoverian monarch George III and his queen, Charlotte.

30. See Mowat, *East Florida as a British Province*, pp. 63–64. For De Brahm's plat of this proposed town, see his "New Bermuda in East Florida," a manuscript sketch bound as p. 118 in Colonial Office Records, America and West Indies (original correspondence, etc.), Vol. 548 (hereafter cited as C. O. 5-548), Public Record Office, London.

31. On the matter of Indian boundaries, De Brahm is not always to be relied upon for accuracy. His relationship with John Stuart, the Superintendent for Indian Affairs, was not an easy one. Stuart had served with Raymond Demere at Fort Loudoun and shared Demere's exceedingly low opinion of De Brahm which had developed there. As a result, De Brahm was not privy to the developments taking place under Stuart's guidance. For details concerning and maps of the Indian boundaries of South Carolina, Georgia, and East Florida, see the relevant chapters on each colony included in Louis De Vorsey, Jr., *The Indian Boundary in the Southern Colonies, 1763–1775* (Chapel Hill, N. C., 1966). The Okleywaha River is now identified as the Oklawaha River. For suggested meanings of this name, see William A. Read, *Florida Place-Names of Indian Origin and Seminole Personal Names* (Baton Rouge, La., 1934), p. 25.

32. "Dartmouth Inlet" was De Brahm's name for the passage into what is present-day Miami Harbor. See Plate 25.

33. Nassau Inlet is currently known as Nassau Sound. Nassau River today serves as the boundary between the Florida counties of Nassau and Duval.

34. The name "Egmont" did not adhere and this large island along Florida's north-eastern littoral is known today as Amelia Island. The site of Egmont Town is now occupied by the town of Fernandina Beach.

35. See Plate 21. The inlet called "Matance" by De Brahm is properly named the Matanzas.

36. Shown on Plate 19.

37. The fish, mullet, still highly regarded by Florida's countless fishermen.

38. De Brahm's "Barrington Jervis" lake as written here probably represents the "Lake Barrington" shown on his map, Plate 20. If this is correct it seems probable that his Lake Barrington is identified on present-day maps as Lake Haney in Volusia and Seminole counties, Florida.

39. The royal governor of East Florida, James Grant (1720–1806), was a veteran military commander who had served with distinction in the war between the South Carolinians and Cherokees a few years earlier. Fort Picolata was an old Spanish strongpoint on the east bank of the St. Johns River west of St. Augustine. It was the scene of East Florida's first formal Indian congress in 1765. Today the area is known as Picolata, St. Johns County.

40. The "cow ford" or crossing of the lower St. Johns River has been incorporated into the growing metropolis of Jacksonville, Florida. See T. Frederick Davis, *History of Jacksonville, Florida and Vicinity, 1513 to 1924* (St. Augustine, Fla., 1925), pp. 25–27.

41. Correctly spelled "Smyrna," this was the settlement of 1,400 people of Mediterranean origin established by Dr. Andrew Turnbull sixty miles south of St. Augustine in 1767. Carita C. Doggett, *Dr. Andrew Turnbull and the New Smyrna Colony of Florida* (Jacksonville, Fla., 1919); E. P. Panagopoulos, *New Smyrna: An Eighteenth Century Greek Odyssey* (Gainesville, Fla., 1966); Bruno Roselli, *The Italians in Colonial Florida* (Jacksonville, Fla., 1940).

42. Frederick Haldimand (1718–91) was a Swiss-born officer who rose to the rank of lieutenant general in the British army. He was the military commander in Florida from 1767 through 1773.

43. Shaddock is the name applied to a species of large oranges (*citrus decumana*) with white pulp, named after a Captain Shaddock, the man who introduced it to the West Indies from the East Indies.

44. In recent decades the citizens of St. Augustine have done much to make their historic city one of the chief tourist attractions of northern Florida. Thanks to their efforts, some of the colonial atmosphere of the old town dominated by its fort can still be appreciated by the present-day visitor.

45. An accurate estimate of St. Augustine's population for this period is not available. For information on population, see Mowat, *East Florida as a British Province*, especially Chapter 4, "Peopling the Sandy Desert."

46. Present-day Matanzas Inlet.

47. Present-day Ponce de Leon Inlet.

48. Halifax River, now a part of the Intracoastal Waterway.

49. De Brahm's North Hillsborough is now called Indian River.

50. For references to New Smyrna see note 41 above. The name persists in the area today, being applied to the town of New Smyrna Beach in Volusia County.

51. De Brahm shows Hillsborough Inlet clearly on both Plates 20 and 29. This inlet to the Indian River no longer exists and so is not shown on present-day maps of the area. It was probably located just to the south of Melbourne Beach.

52. The Santa Luz or Huntington River is the present-day St. Lucie River.

53. Jupiter Inlet. For an account of the survey of Grenville Inlet by two of De Brahm's deputies in 1769, see James Grant Forbes, *Sketches Historical and Topographical of the Floridas; More Particularly of East Florida* (New York, 1821), pp. 97–99.

54. Carita Doggett Corse wrote that this note by De Brahm cleared up speculation on the origin of the New River Inlet at Fort Lauderdale. See her article, "De Brahm's Report on East Florida, 1773," *The Florida Historical Quarterly*, XVII (Jan. 1939), 225.

55. De Brahm's Dartmouth Inlet is the passage between present-day Key Biscayne and the southern tip of Miami Beach. His Sandwich Gulf is present-day Biscayne Bay. He is inconsistent in his placement of Cape Florida. On his "Chart of Cape Florida according to the Surveys made May 13 and 29, 1765 by W. G. De Brahm," Library of Congress, Geography and Map Division, he correctly identifies the southern extremities of Key Biscayne as Cape Florida.

56. Usually spelled "hammock," designating "in general . . . a comparatively dense forest composed mostly of trees other than pines, not subject to innundation . . . in a region where open pine forests or prairies predominate." Quoted from Roland M. Harper in Francis Harper, *The Travels of William Bartram: Naturalist's Edition* (New Haven, Conn., 1958), pp. 523–24.

57. In her article cited in note 54 above, Carita D. Corse stated that "many fields so treated are still to be found in northeastern Florida." "De Brahm's Report on East Florida, 1773," 225.

58. Lucca, a town in northwestern Italy near Pisa.

59. Carita D. Corse reported that floors of this construction were still to be found in certain houses in the old part of St. Augustine. "De Brahm's Report on East Florida, 1773," 225.

60. Seminoles. The Seminoles were an offshoot from the Lower Creek Indians who were actively populating the peninsula of Florida during the last half of the eighteenth century. The word "Seminole" comes from the Creek *siminole*, which meant "separatist." Thus the Seminoles were looked upon as a breakaway group from the Creek Confederation during De Brahm's period. Read, *Florida Place-Names and Seminole Personal Names*, p. 31.

61. A condition which has drastically changed in recent years. The Seminoles have won a suit lodged against the government of the United States for lands unjustly taken from them in Florida. The Oklahoma and Florida bands of the Seminole Nation will be compensated for some forty to fifty million acres of Florida real estate. For background, see *Before the Indian Claims Commission. Docket No. 73, The Seminole Indians of the State of Florida, Petitioner; Docket No. 151,*

The Seminole Nation of Oklahoma, Petitioner, Versus United States of America, Defendant. Defendants Requested Findings of Fact, Objections to Petitioner's Proposed Findings and Brief (Washington, D. C., 1963).

62. A thorough annotation of this chapter of De Brahm's manuscript description of East Florida would run to an extended length and is not possible within the present edition. The reader is, however, advised to consult Francis Harper's authoritatively edited and annotated *Travels of William Bartram.* Bartram traveled over much of the same terrain as De Brahm and skillfully described its flora and fauna in detail. It is possible that the two were associated for a period during De Brahm's conduct of the Florida surveys. In any event much of what Bartram saw and described is also discussed by De Brahm in this chapter. Although De Brahm was not a professional botanist his work in this field did attract Thomas Pownall's attention and praise. In his book, Pownall noted, "The Botanists & particularly the ingenious Mr. William Gerard de Brahm give long lists of trees & shrubs which form the natural vegetation of these [*Coastal*] parts. . . ." See Thomas Pownall, *A Topographical Description of the Dominions of the United States of America . . .*, ed. Lois Mulkearn (Pittsburgh, Pa., 1949), p. 92.

63. Much of this chapter, including engraved versions of Plates 26 and 28, was published by De Brahm as *The Atlantic Pilot.* This is a rare book, but copies are held by several research libraries in the United States and the United Kingdom. Although Bernard Romans, in *A Concise Natural History of East and West Florida* (New York, 1775), referred to De Brahm as a "Bedlamite" and stated that *The Atlantic Pilot* bore marks of insanity, other contemporaries hailed it as a useful and valuable work. The reviewer of the London magazine, *The Monthly Review; or Literary Journal,* was most favorable in his report, which appeared on pp. 536–37 of Vol. XLVI during 1772. He stated, "The author (Mr. Gerard De Brahm his Majesty's Surveyor-general of the Southern district of North America) received orders, in 1764, for making discoveries with regard to those seas, and for carrying on a regular survey of the countries to which they set bounds; and he seems to have executed his commission with great fidelity, accuracy, and diligence." In the *Critical Review,* XXXIV (1772), *The Atlantic Pilot* was recommended by the reviewer as a "small but elegant performance," which testified to the author's ability both as surveyor and navigator. George Wood, the Charleston bookseller, was quick to import a supply of *The Atlantic Pilot* for his clientele. He advertised the arrival of a consignment of copies on Aug. 6, 1772. See Hennig Cohen, *The South Carolina Gazette, 1732–1775* (Columbia, S. C., 1953), p. 154.

At a slightly later date even more highly qualified critics—George Gauld and Andrew Ellicott—were moved to praise and employ De Brahm's work in their own publications. Gauld made extensive use of De Brahm's description of the southern Florida coast and Keys in his book, *Observations on the Florida Keys, Reef and Gulf,* which was published by William Faden in London in 1796. See especially p. 19, subheading, "Description of the East Shore of Florida by M. Gerard de Brahm." Andrew Ellicott, the well-known boundary commissioner and mathematician, in writing of his experiences with the Gulf Stream, mentioned that they were similar to those reported by De Brahm earlier. Ellicott clearly felt that De Brahm's ideas concerning the Gulf Stream were in many respects more accurate than those of the more widely known Benjamin Franklin.

See *The Journal of Andrew Ellicott* (Philadelphia, 1803), pp. 257–67. *The Atlantic Pilot* was translated into French and published in Paris in 1788 with the title, *Recherches faites par ordre de sa Majeste Britannique, depuis 1765 jusqu'en 1771, pour rectifier les cartes & perfectionner la navigation du canal de Bahama . . . Traduite de l'anglois de W. Gerard de Brahm, ecuyer Hydrographe general au departement due sud de l'Amerique Septentrionale*. This work went into at least two editions in 1788. For recent evaluations of *The Atlantic Pilot*, see Ralph H. Brown, "The De Brahm Charts of the Atlantic Ocean, 1772–1776," *The Geographical Review*, XXVIII (Jan. 1938), 124–32; and Lloyd A. Brown, "The River in the Ocean," *Essays Honoring Lawrence C. Wroth* (Portland, Me., 1951), pp. 69–84.

64. From this point onward, the manuscript contains material which was not published in *The Atlantic Pilot*.

65. This chapter apparently was not originally a part of De Brahm's outline for this "Tome" of his Report. In a letter to Lord Dartmouth dated Oct. 23, 1773, he wrote:

> The Report is finishing under my hand with all speed agreable to the received directions, and as soon as it is accomplished, will beg leave to deliver it into your Lordships hands.
>
> Few days ago arrived a Gentleman from St. Augustine from whom I had such information, which made it necessary to increase my present Report with the Eight Chapter relating all what concerns the Indian Boundary, which otherwise should have been in my future report.
>
> I humbly beg leave to inclose a copy of the Eight Chapter, which is so very material, and I will insert it in the Book, if Your Lordship will be pleased to indulge me with the return of it for a few days.

Quoted from D1778 II 730. As pointed out in the Introduction, De Brahm's strained relationship with both John Stuart, the Indian superintendent, and James Grant, East Florida's governor, excluded him from most of the important Indian negotiations which took place in the province.

66. For a review of the congress at Fort Picolata, see De Vorsey, *Indian Boundary in the Southern Colonies*, pp. 190–95.

67. During De Brahm's absence, his son-in-law Frederick Mulcaster functioned as East Florida's surveyor general and continued to record grants of land. For an example, see the plat for 20,000 acres surveyed for Samuel Fouchett by Bernard Romans, which is in the collection of Yale University. William P. Cumming, *The Southeast in Early Maps* (Chapel Hill, N. C., 1962), Supplement, p. 218.

Selected Bibliography

DE BRAHM'S PUBLISHED WORKS

Apocalyptic Gnomon Points Out Eternity's Divisibility Rated With Time Pointed At by Gnomon Siderealis. Philadelphia: Francis & Robert Bailey, 1795.

De Brahm's Zonical Tables For the Twenty-five Northern and Southern Climates.... London: T. Spilsbury, 1774.

History of the Province of Georgia, With Maps of Original Surveys. Wormsloe, Ga.: Privately printed, 1849. (Limited to 49 copies.)

Recherches faites par ordre de sa majesté britannique, depuis 1765 jusqu'en 1771, pour rectifier les cartes & perfectionner la navigation du canal de Bahama ... Traduite de l'anglois de W. Gerard De Brahm, ecuyer, hydrographe général au départment du sud de l'Amerique Septentrionale. [Paris, 1788]

Sum of Testimonies of Truth. [Philadelphia? 1795?]

The Atlantic Pilot. London: T. Spilsbury, 1772.

The Levelling Balance and Counter-Balance; Or, the Method of Observing by the Weight and Height of Mercury, On any Place of Terra-Firma on the Terrestrial Globe, the Exact Weight and Altitude of the Atmosphere Below and Above the Place of Observation; Thereby to Ascertain How Much the Horizon of the Sea Is Lower Than the Place Whereon the Observation Is Made. London: T. Spilsbury, 1774.

Time an Apparition of Eternity. Philadelphia: Zachariah Poulson, Jr., 1791.

Voice of the Everlasting Gospel. Philadelphia: Zachariah Poulson, Jr., 1792.

Zeite Rechenschaft. Ephrata, Pa.: Salomon Mayer, 1794.

BOOKS

A Letter To The English Nation, On The Present War With America ... By An Officer Returned From That Service. London, 1777.

A State of the Province of Georgia Attested Upon Oath In the Court of Savannah, November 18, 1740. Collections of the Georgia Historical Society, Vol. II. Savannah, Ga.: For the Society, 1842.

Abbot, W. W. *The Royal Governors of Georgia, 1754–1775.* Chapel Hill, N. C.: University of North Carolina Press, 1959.

Acts Passed by the General Assembly of the Colony of Georgia, 1755 to 1774. Wormsloe, Ga.: Privately printed, 1886.

Adams, George. *Geometrical and Graphical Essays.* London, 1791.

Alden, John Richard. *John Stuart and the Southern Colonial Frontier.* Ann Arbor, Mich.: University of Michigan Press, 1944.

American Husbandry: Containing an Account of the Soil, Climate, Production and General Agriculture of the British Colonies in North America and the West Indies. 2 vols. London, 1775.

Bartram, William. *Travels Through North and South Carolina, Georgia, East and West Florida, The Cherokee Country....* Philadelphia: James and Johnson, 1791.

Basye, Arthur H. *The Lords Commissioners of Trade and Plantations, 1748–1782.* New Haven, Conn.: Yale University Press, 1925.

Bedini, Silvio A. *Early American Scientific Instruments and Their Makers.* Washington, D. C.: Museum of History and Technology, Smithsonian Institution, 1964.

Before the Indian Claims Commission. Docket No. 73, The Seminole Indians of the State of Florida, Petitioner; Docket No. 151, The Seminole Nation of Oklahoma, Petitioner, Versus United States of America, Defendant. ... Washington, D. C.: Government Printing Office, 1963.

Bell, Whitfield J. *Early American Science: Needs and Opportunities for Study.* Williamsburg, Va.: Institute of Early American History and Culture, 1955.

Bennet, Charles E. *Settlement of Florida.* Gainesville, Fla.: University of Florida Press, 1968.

Boyd, Julian P. (ed.). *The Papers of Thomas Jefferson.* 9 vols. Princeton, N. J.: Princeton University Press, 1955.

Brown, John P. *Old Frontiers: The Story of the Cherokee Indians from Earliest Times to the Date of Their Removal to the West, 1838.* Kingsport, Tenn.: Southern Publishers, Inc., 1938.

Brown, Ralph H. *Historical Geography of the United States.* New York: Harcourt Brace, 1948.

——— *Mirror for Americans: Likeness of the Eastern Seaboard, 1810.* American Geographical Society Special Publication No. 27. New York: American Geographical Society, 1943.

Callaway, James E. *The Early Settlement of Georgia*. Athens, Ga.: University of Georgia Press, 1948.

Candler, Allen D. (ed.). *The Colonial Records of the State of Georgia*. 19 vols. Atlanta, Ga.: Franklin Printing and Publishing Co., 1904–11.

Catesby, Mark. *The Natural History of Carolina, Florida and the Bahama Islands*. Rev. by Mr. Edwards. 2 vols. London, 1754.

Chalmers, Lionel. *An Account of the Weather and Diseases of South Carolina*. 2 vols. London: Edward and Charles Delly, 1776.

Church, A. H. (comp.). *The Royal Society, Some Account of the Letters and Papers of the Period 1741–1806, in the Archives*. Oxford, 1908.

Cohen, Hennig. *The South Carolina Gazette, 1732–1775*. Columbia, S. C.: University of South Carolina Press, 1953.

Corry, John P. *Indian Affairs in Georgia, 1732–1756*. Philadelphia: University of Pennsylvania Press, 1936.

Cotter, Charles H. *A History of Nautical Astronomy*. London: Hollis and Carter, 1968.

Coulter, E. Merton. *Georgia: A Short History*. Chapel Hill, N. C.: University of North Carolina Press, 1947.

———— *Wormsloe, Two Centuries of a Georgia Family*. Athens, Ga.: University of Georgia Press, 1955.

Cumming, William P. *The Southeast in Early Maps*. 2d ed. Chapel Hill, N. C.: University of North Carolina Press, 1962.

Davis, T. Frederick. *History of Jacksonville, Florida and Vicinity, 1513 to 1924*. Jacksonville, Fla.: The Florida Historical Society, 1925.

Day, Sir Archibald. *The Admiralty Hydrographic Service, 1795–1919*. London: Her Majesty's Stationery Office, 1967.

De Vorsey, Louis, Jr. *The Indian Boundary in the Southern Colonies, 1763–1775*. Chapel Hill, N. C.: University of North Carolina Press, 1966.

Doggett, Carita C. *Dr. Andrew Turnbull and the New Smyrna Colony of Florida*. Jacksonville, Fla.: Drew Press, 1919.

Douglas, Edward M. *Boundaries, Areas, Geographic Centers and Altitudes of the United States and the Several States*. Department of the Interior, Geological Survey, Bulletin 689. Washington, D. C.: Government Printing Office, 1923.

Ellicott, Andrew. *The Journal of Andrew Ellicott*. Philadelphia: Budd & Bartram, 1803.

Final Report of the United States De Soto Expedition Commission. 76th Congress, 1st Session, House Document No. 71. Washington, D. C.: Government Printing Office, 1939.

Forbes, James Grant. *Sketches, Historical and Topographical of the Floridas; More Particularly of East Florida*. New York: C. S. Van Winkle, 1821.

Force, Peter. *American Archives*. Vol. IV. Washington, D. C.: P. Force, 1843.

———— *Tracts and Other Papers*. 4 vols. Washington, D. C.: P. Force, 1836.

Forest Trees of Florida. 9th ed. rev. Tallahassee, Fla.: Florida Forest Service, 1967.

Fundaburk, Emma L. (ed.). *Southeastern Indians: Life Portraits, a Catalogue of Pictures, 1565–1860*. Laverne, Ala.: Emma L. Fundaburk, Publisher, 1957.

Gamble, Thomas, Jr. *A History of the City Government of Savannah, from 1790 to 1901*. Savannah, Ga.: Savannah City Council, 1900.

Gatschet, A. S. *Tchikilli's Kasi 'hta Legend in the Creek and Hitchiti Language*. St. Louis, Mo.: R. P. Studley & Co., 1888.

Gauld, George. *Observation on the Florida Kays, Reef and Gulf; with Directions for Sailing Along the Kays from Jamaica . . . : Also, A Description with Sailing Instructions, of the Coast of West Florida, Between the Bay of Spiritu Santo and Cape Sable*. London: W. Faden, 1796.

Glen, James. *A Description of South Carolina. . . .* London: R. & J. Dodsley, 1761.

Gray, Lewis C. *History of Agriculture in the Southern United States to 1860*. 2 vols. Washington, D. C.: The Carnegie Institution, 1933.

Hadley, John. *Concerning the Cause of the General Trade Winds. . . .* London, 1735.

Hamer, Philip M. (ed.). *The Papers of Henry Laurens*. Vol. I: Sept. 11, 1746–Oct. 31, 1755. Columbia, S. C.: University of South Carolina Press, 1968.

Harper, Francis (ed.). *The Travels of William Bartram: Naturalist's Edition*. New Haven, Conn.: Yale University Press, 1958.

Harrar, E. S. and Harrar, J. G. *The Guide to Southern Trees*. New York: Dover Publications, Inc., 1962.

Hewatt, Alexander. *An Historical Account of the Rise and Progress of the Colonies of South Carolina and Georgia*. 2 vols. London: Alexander Donaldson, 1779.

Hindle, Brooks. *The Pursuit of Science in Revolutionary America, 1735–1789*. Chapel Hill, N. C.: University of North Carolina Press, 1956.

Hinks, Arthur R. *Maps and Survey*. 3d ed. Cambridge, Eng.: Cambridge University Press, 1933.

Hirsch, Arthur Henry. *The Huguenots of Colonial South Carolina*. Durham, N. C.: Duke University Press, 1928.

Hotchkin, S. F. *Ancient and Modern Germantown, Mt. Airy and Chestnut Hill*. Philadelphia: Binder and Kelly, 1889.

———— *York Road, Old and New*. Philadelphia: Binder and Kelly, 1892.

Jacobs, Wilbur R. (ed.). *The Appalachian Indian Frontier: The Edmund Atkin Report and Plan of 1755*. Lincoln, Neb.: University of Nebraska Press, 1967.

Johnson, Cecil B. *British West Florida, 1763–1783*. New Haven, Conn.: Yale University Press, 1943.

Jones, Charles C. *The Dead Towns of Georgia*. Collections of the Georgia Historical Society, Vol. IV. Savannah, Ga.: For the Society, 1878.

———— *The History of Georgia*. 2 vols. Boston, Mass.: Houghton, Mifflin and Company, 1883.

Journal of the Commissioners for Trade and Plantations. Vol. XII. London: Her Majesty's Stationery Office, 1936.

Laforge, Lawrence et al. *Physical Geography of Georgia*. Geological Survey of Georgia, Bulletin No. 42. Atlanta, Ga.: Stein Printing Co. State Printers, 1925.

Lanning, John Tate. *The Spanish Missions of Georgia*. Chapel Hill, N. C.: University of N. C. Press, 1935.

Lowery, Woodbury. *The Spanish Settlements within the Present Limits of the United States, 1513–1561*. New York: G. P. Putnam's Sons, 1911.

McCall, Hugh. *The History of Georgia: Containing Brief Sketches of the Most Remarkable Events Up to the Present Day*. 2 vols. Savannah, Ga.: Seymour Williams, 1811.

McCrady, Edward. *The History of South Carolina Under the Royal Government, 1719–1776*. New York: Macmillan Co., 1901.

McDowell, William L., Jr. (ed.). *Documents Relating to Indian Affairs, 1754–1765*. Columbia, S. C.: University of South Carolina Press, 1970.

McLendon, Samuel G. *History of the Public Domain of Georgia*. Atlanta, Ga.: Foote & Davis Co., 1924.

Marschner, F. J. *Land Use and Its Patterns in the United States*. U. S. Department of Agriculture Handbook No. 153. Washington, D. C.: Government Printing Office, 1959.

Mears, Anne D. *The Old York Road and Its Early Association of History and Biography, 1670–1870*. Philadelphia: Harper, 1890.

Meriwether, Robert L. *The Expansion of South Carolina, 1729–1765*. Kingsport, Tenn.: Southern Publishers, Inc., 1940.

Merrens, Harry Roy. *Colonial North Carolina in the Eighteenth Century: A Study in Historical Geography*. Chapel Hill, N. C.: University of North Carolina Press, 1964.

Michel, Henri. *Scientific Instruments in Art and History*. Trans. by R. E. W. Maddison and F. R. Maddison. London: Barrie and Rockliff, 1967.

Milling, Chapman J. (ed.). *Colonial South Carolina: Two Contemporary Descriptions.* South Caroliniana Sesquicentennial Series, No. 1. Columbia, S. C.: University of South Carolina Press, 1951.

Mooney, James. *Myths of the Cherokees.* Nineteenth Annual Report of the Bureau of American Ethnology, to the Secretary of the Smithsonian Institution, 1897–1898, Pt. 1. Washington, D. C.: Government Printing Office, 1900.

Mowat, Charles Loch. *East Florida as a British Province, 1763–1784.* A Facsimile Reprint Series. Gainesville, Fla.: University of Florida Press, 1964.

Oglethorpe, James. *The Spanish Official Account of the Attack on the Colony of Georgia, In America, And of Its Defeat on St. Simon's Island.* Vol. VII, Pt. III of *Collections of the Georgia Historical Society.* Savannah, Ga.: *Savannah Morning News,* 1913.

Panagopoulos, E. P. *New Smyrna, An Eighteenth Century Greek Odyssey.* Gainesville, Fla.: University of Florida Press, 1966.

Paullin, Charles O. *Atlas of the Historical Geography of the United States.* Washington, D. C.: The Carnegie Institution, 1932.

Peckham, Howard H. *Pontiac and the Indian Uprising.* Princeton, N. J.: Princeton University Press, 1947.

Phillips, P. L. *Notes on the Life and Works of Bernard Romans.* Publication of the Florida State Historical Society No. 2. De Land, Fla.: The Florida State Historical Society, 1924.

Pownall, Thomas. *A Topographical Description of the Dominions of the United States of America.* . . . Ed. Lois Mulkearn. Pittsburgh, Pa.: University of Pittsburgh Press, 1949.

Prime, Alfred C. *The Arts and Crafts in Philadelphia, Maryland, and South Carolina, 1721–1785: Gleanings from Newspapers.* Toppsfield, Mass.: The Walpole Society, 1929.

Purry, Jean Pierre. *A Description of the Province of South Carolina Drawn Up At Charles Town In September, 1731.* Washington, D. C.: Peter Force, 1887.

———— *A Method for Determining the Best Climate of the Earth on a Principle.* . . . London, 1744.

Ramsey, J. G. M. *The Annals of Tennessee To the Eighteenth Century.* . . . Charleston, S. C.: John Russel, 1853.

Ravenel, Mrs. St. Julien. *Charleston, The Place and the People.* New York: Macmillan Company, 1929.

Read, William A. *Florida Place-Names of Indian Origin and Seminole Personal Names.* Baton Rouge, La.: Louisiana State University Press, 1934.

Richeson, A. W. *English Land Measuring to 1800: Instruments and Practices.* Cambridge, Mass.: The M. I. T. Press, 1966.

Roberts, R. A. *Calendar of Home Office Papers of the Reign of George III, 1760–1765.* 3 vols. London: Longman and Co., 1878.

Roberts, William. *An Account of the First Discovery and Natural History of Florida . . . Collected from the Best Authorities. . . .* London: T. Jefferys, 1763.

Rogers, George C., Jr. *Charleston in the Age of the Pinckneys.* Norman, Okla.: University of Oklahoma Press, 1969.

Romans, Bernard. *A Concise Natural History of East and West Florida.* A Facsimile Reproduction of the 1775 Edition with an Introduction by Rembert W. Patrick. Floridiana Facsimile Reprint Series. Gainesville, Fla.: University of Florida Press, 1962.

——— *A New and Enlarged Book of Sailing Directions for Capt. B. Romans . . . Also the Additions of Captains W. G. Debraham, Bishop, Hester, Archibald Dalzel, esq., George Gauld esq., Lieut. Woodriffe and other Experienced Navigators.* London: R. Laurie and J. Whittle, 1797.

Roselli, Bruno. *The Italians in Colonial Florida [1513–1821].* Jacksonville, Fla.: The Drew Press, 1940.

Royce, Charles C. *Indian Land Cessions in the United States.* Eighteenth Annual Report of the Bureau of American Ethnology to the Secretary of the Smithsonian Institution, 1896–97. Washington, D. C.: Government Printing Office, 1899.

——— *The Cherokee Nation of Indians.* Fifth Annual Report of the Bureau of American Ethnology to the Secretary of the Smithsonian Institution, 1883–84. Washington, D. C.: Government Printing Office, 1887.

Salley, A. S. *The Boundary Line between North Carolina and South Carolina.* Bulletin of the Historical Commission of South Carolina, No. 10. Columbia, S. C.: The State Company, 1929.

Seibert, Wilbur H. *Loyalists in East Florida, 1774 to 1785.* 2 vols. De Land, Fla., 1929.

Shyrock, Richard H. *Medicine and Society in America, 1660–1860.* New York: New York University Press, 1960.

Simpson, Clarence, and Boyd, Mark F. (eds.). *Florida Place-Names of Indian Derivation.* Tallahassee, Fla.: State Board of Conservation, 1956.

Singer, Charles, et al. *A History of Technology.* 4 vols. Oxford: Oxford University Press, 1965.

Sirmans, M. Eugene. *Colonial South Carolina: A Political History, 1663–1763.* Chapel Hill, N. C.: University of North Carolina Press, 1966.

Skaggs, Marvin L. *North Carolina Boundary Disputes Involving Her Southern Line.* Chapel Hill, N. C.: University of North Carolina Press, 1941.

Smith, W. Roy. *South Carolina as a Royal Province, 1719–1776.* New York: Macmillan Company, 1903.

Stewart, George R. *Names on the Land.* New York: Random House, 1945.

Swanton, John R. *Early History of the Creek Indians and Their Neighbors.* Bureau of American Ethnology, Smithsonian Institution, Bulletin 73. Washington, D. C.: Government Printing Office, 1922.

———— *Indian Tribes of the Lower Mississippi Valley and Adjacent Coast of the Gulf of Mexico.* Bureau of American Ethnology, Smithsonian Institution, Bulletin 43. Washington, D. C.: Government Printing Office, 1911.

———— *The Indian Tribes of North America.* Bureau of American Ethnology, Smithsonian Institution, Bulletin 145. Washington, D. C.: Government Printing Office, 1952.

Taylor, E. G. R. *The Haven Finding Art.* London: Hollis & Carter, 1956.

———— *The Mathematical Practitioners of Hanoverian England, 1714–1840.* Cambridge, Eng.: Cambridge University Press, 1966.

Timberlake, Henry. *Lieut. Henry Timberlake's Memoirs, 1756–1765.* With an Introduction and Annotations by Samuel Cole Williams. Marietta, Ga.: Continental Book Company, 1948.

Tinkcom, Harry M., and Tinkcom, Margaret B. *Historic Germantown from the Founding to the Early Part of the Nineteenth Century.* Philadelphia: The American Philosophical Society, 1955.

U. S. Department of Agriculture. *Sylvics of Forest Trees of the United States.* Agriculture Handbook No. 271. Washington, D. C.: Government Printing Office, 1965.

Varner, John G., and Varner, Jeannette J. *The Florida of the Inca.* Austin, Tex.: University of Texas Press, 1951.

Wallace, David D. *The History of South Carolina.* New York: The American Historical Society, Inc., 1934.

Weston, Plowden C. J. (ed.). *Documents Connected With the History of South Carolina.* London: Printed for Private Distribution, 1856.

Williams, Samuel C. (ed.). *Adair's History of the American Indians.* Johnson City, Tenn.: The Watauga Press, 1930.

———— *Dawn of Tennessee Valley and Tennessee History.* Johnson City, Tenn.: The Watauga Press, 1937.

———— *Early Travels in the Tennessee Country, 1540–1800.* Johnson City, Tenn.: The Watauga Press, 1928.

ARTICLES AND PAPERS

Anderson, J. Randolph. "The Spanish Era in Georgia, and the English Settlement in 1733," *The Georgia Historical Quarterly*, XVII (June 1933), 91–110.

"Articles of Capitulation Agreed Upon and Assented to by Captain Paul Demere, Commanding His Majesty's Forces at Fort Loudoun, and the Headmen and Warriors of the Overhill Cherokee Towns," *The Annual Register, Or A View of the History, Politics, and Literature for the Year 1760*, 7th ed. London: J. Dodsley, 1789, 219–20.

Bargar, B. D. "Charles Town Loyalism in 1775: The Secret Report of Alexander Innes," *The South Carolina Historical Magazine*, LXIII (Jan. 1962), 125–36.

Bartram, John. "Diary of a Journey Through the Carolinas, Georgia, and Florida from July 1, 1765, to April 10, 1766," ed. Francis Harper, *Transactions of the American Philosophical Society*, n.s., XXXIII, Pt. 1 (Dec. 1942).

Bartram, William. "Travels in Georgia and Florida, 1773–74: A Report to Dr. John Fothergill," annotated by Francis Harper, *Transactions of the American Philosophical Society*, n. s., XXXIII, Pt. 2 (Nov. 1943).

Boyd, Mark F. "A Map of the Road from Pensacola to St. Augustine, 1778," *The Florida Historical Quarterly*, XVII (July 1938), 15–24.

Brantley, R. L. "The Salzburgers in Georgia," *The Georgia Historical Quarterly*, XIV (Sept. 1930), 214–24.

Brown, Lloyd A. "The River in the Ocean," *Essays Honoring Lawrence C. Wroth*. Portland, Me., 1951, 69–84.

Brown, Ralph H. "The De Brahm Charts of the Atlantic Ocean, 1772–1776," *Geographical Review*, XXVIII (Jan. 1938), 124–32.

Chipman, Willis. "The Life and Times of Major Samuel Holland, Surveyor General, 1764–1801," *Ontario Historical Society Papers and Records*, XXI (1924), 11–90.

Corry, John P. "The Houses of Colonial Georgia," *The Georgia Historical Quarterly*, XIV (Sept. 1930), 181–201.

Corse, Carita D. "De Brahm's Report on East Florida, 1773," *The Florida Historical Quarterly*, XVII (Jan. 1939), 219–26.

Crane, Verner W. "Hints Relative to the Division and Government of the Conquered and Newly Acquired Countries in America," *The Mississippi Valley Historical Review*, XIII (Mar. 1922), 367–73.

———— "The Origin of Georgia," *The Georgia Historical Quarterly*, XIV (June 1930), 93–110.

Cumming, William P. "Geographic Misconceptions of the Southeast in the Cartography of the 17th and 18th Centuries," *Journal of Southern History*, IV (Nov. 1938), 476–92.

———— "Mapping of the Southeast: The First Two Centuries," *The Southeastern Geographer*, VI (1966), 3–19.

Davis, T. Frederick. "Juan Ponce De Leon's Voyages to Florida," *The Florida Historical Society Quarterly*, XIV (July 1935), the whole issue.

De Vorsey, Louis, Jr. "Early Maps as a Source in the Re-creation of Southern Indian Landscapes," Paper read before the 6th Annual Meeting of the Southern Anthropological Society, Athens, Ga., Apr. 9, 1970.

———— "Indian Boundaries in Colonial Georgia," *The Georgia Historical Quarterly*, LIV (spring 1970), 63–78.

———— "The Colonial Southeast on 'An Accurate General Map'," *The Southeastern Geographer*, VI (1966), 20–32.

———— "The Southern Indian Boundary Line in Colonial America—A Cartographic Reconstruction," Paper read before the 62d Annual Meeting of the Association of American Geographers, Toronto, Ontario, Aug. 31, 1966.

———— "William Gerard De Brahm: Eccentric Genius of Southeastern Geography," *The Southeastern Geographer*, X (Apr. 1970), 21–29.

Downes, Randolph C. "The Cherokee-American Relations in the Upper Tennessee Valley, 1776–1791," *East Tennessee Historical Society's Publications*, VIII (1936), 35–53.

Dunbar, Gary S. "Colonial Carolina Cowpens," *Agricultural History*, XXXV (July 1961), 125–30.

Farrand, Max. "The Indian Boundary Line," *The American Historical Review*, X (July 1905), 782–91.

Fillippin, Percy S. "The Royal Government in Georgia, 1752–1776," *The Georgia Historical Quarterly*, X (Mar. 1926), 1–25.

Floyd, Dolores B. "The Legend of Sir Walter Raleigh at Savannah," *The Georgia Historical Quarterly*, XXIII (June 1939), 103–21.

Ford, Worthington C. "Early Maps of Carolina," *Geographical Review*, XVI (Apr. 1926), 264–73.

Franklin, W. Neill. "Virginia and the Cherokee Indian Trade, 1673–1752," *East Tennessee Historical Society's Publications*, IV (1932), 3–21.

Gamble, Thomas. "Colonial William Bull—His Part in the Founding of Savannah," *The Georgia Historical Quarterly*, XVII (June 1933), 111–26.

Garth, R. E. "The Ecology of Spanish Moss (Tillandsia Usneoides): Its Growth and Distribution," *Ecology*, VL (summer 1964), 470–81.

Giuseppi, M. S. "Naturalizations of Foreign Protestants in the American Colonies Pursuant to Statute 13, George II, C. 7.," *The Publications of the Huguenot Society of London*, XXIV (1921).

Goff, John H. "Short Studies of Georgia Place Names," *Georgia Mineral News Letter*, XII (spring 1960), 35–42.

——— "Short Studies of Georgia Place Names," *Georgia Mineral News Letter*, VIII (spring 1955), 22–26.

Green, E. R. R. "Queensborough Township: Scotch-Irish Emigration and the Expansion of Georgia, 1763–1776," *William and Mary Quarterly*, 3d ser., XVII (Apr. 1960), 183–99.

Hamer, Marguerite B. "Edmund Gray and His Settlement at New Hanover," *The Georgia Historical Quarterly*, XIII (Mar. 1929), 1–12.

Hamer, Philip M. "Anglo-French Rivalry in the Cherokee Country, 1754–1757," *The North Carolina Historical Review*, II (July 1925), 303–22.

——— "Fort Loudoun in the Cherokee War, 1758–1761," *The North Carolina Historical Review*, II (Oct. 1925), 442–58.

Harley, J. B. "The Bankruptcy of Thomas Jefferys: An Episode in the Economic History of Eighteenth Century Map-Making," *Imago Mundi*, XX (1966), 27–48.

Hirsch, Arthur H. "French Influence in American Agriculture in the Colonial Period with Special Reference to Southern Provinces," *Agricultural History*, IV (Jan. 1930), 1–9.

Hitz, Alex M. "The Surveyor General of Georgia," *The Georgia Bar Journal*, LXX (Nov. 1956), 191–200.

——— "The Wrightsborough Quaker Town and Township in Georgia," *The Bulletin of Friends Historical Association*, XLVI (spring 1957), 10–22.

Hofer, J. M. "The Georgia Salzburgers," *The Georgia Historical Quarterly*, XVIII (June 1934), 99–117.

Howard, C. N. "The Military Occupation of British West Florida, 1763," *The Florida Historical Quarterly*, XVII (Jan. 1939), 181–99.

Jones, Charles C. "The English Colonization of Georgia, 1733–1752," in *Narrative and Critical History of America*, ed. Justin Winsor, 8 vols. (Boston and New York, 1889), V, 357–406.

Kelley, Paul. *Fort Loudoun: The After Years, 1760–1960*. Reprinted from *Tennessee Historical Quarterly*, XX (Dec. 1961).

——— *Historic Fort Loudoun*. Vonore, Tenn.: Fort Loudoun Association, 1961.

Leowald, Klaus G., Starika, Beverly, and Taylor, Paul S. (eds.). "Johann Martin Bolzius Answers a Questionnaire on Carolina and Georgia," *William and Mary Quarterly*, 3d ser., XIV (Apr. 1957), 218–61.

Macalpine, Ida, and Hunter, Richard. "Porphyria and King George III," *Scientific American*, CCXXI (July 1969), 38–46.

Mackall, Leonard L. "The Wymberly Jones De Renne Georgia Library," *The Georgia Historical Quarterly*, II (June 1918), 63–86.

McKintry, Mary T. "Silk Culture in the Colony of Georgia," *The Georgia Historical Quarterly*, XIV (Sept. 1930), 225–35.

Mallard, John B. "Liberty County, Georgia: An Address Delivered at Hinesville, July 4, 1876," *The Georgia Historical Quarterly*, II (Mar. 1918), 1–21.

Merrens, Harry R. "The Physical Environment of Early America: Images and Image Makers in Colonial South Carolina," *The Geographical Review*, LIX (Oct. 1969), 530–56.

Morrison, A. J. "John G. De Brahm," *South Atlantic Quarterly*, XXI (July 1922), 252–58.

Mowat, Charles L. "That 'Odd Being', De Brahm," *The Florida Historical Quarterly*, XX (Apr. 1942), 323–45.

Mustard, Harry S. "On the Building of Fort Johnson," *The South Carolina Historical and Genealogical Magazine*, LXIV (Jan. 1963), 129–35.

Nelson, Howard J. "Walled Cities of the United States," *Annals of the Association of American Geographers*, LI (Mar. 1961), 1–22.

Newton, Hester W. "The Agricultural Activities of the Salzburgers in Colonial Georgia," *The Georgia Historical Quarterly*, XVIII (Sept. 1934), 248–63.

———— "The Industrial and Social Influence of the Salzburgers in Colonial Georgia," *The Georgia Historical Quarterly*, XVIII (Dec. 1934), 335–53.

"Oglethorpe's Treaty with the Lower Creek Indians," *The Georgia Historical Quarterly*, IV (Mar. 1920), 3–16.

"Papers of the First Council of Safety of the Revolutionary Party in South Carolina, June–November 1775," *The South Carolina Historical and Genealogical Magazine*, III (Apr. 1902), 69–85.

"Petition to the Court of Chancery of the State of South Carolina . . . ," *The South Carolina Historical and Genealogical Magazine*, VIII (Oct. 1907).

"Queries and Answers," *The Georgia Historical Quarterly*, II (Mar. 1918), 58.

"Register Kept By The Rev. Wm. Hutson, Of Stoney Creek Independent Congregational Church and (Circular) Congregational Church in Charles Town, S. C., 1743–1760," *South Carolina Historical and Genealogical Magazine*, XXXVIII (Jan. 1937).

Reps, John W. "Town Planning in Colonial Georgia," *The Town Planning Review*, XXX (Jan. 1960), 273–85.

Rothrock, Mary W. "Carolina Traders among the Overhill Cherokees, 1690–1760," *East Tennessee Historical Society's Publications*, I (1929), 3–18.

Skelton, R. A. "King George III's Maritime Collection," *The British Museum Quarterly*, XVIII (July 1953), 63–64.

———— "The Hydrographic Collection of the British Museum," *Journal of the Institute for Navigation*, IX (July 1956), 323–34.

———— "The Royal Map Collections," *The British Museum Quarterly*, XXVI (Jan. 1963), 1–6.

Smith, Henry A. M. "Beaufort—The Original Plan and Earliest Settlers," *The South Carolina Historical and Genealogical Magazine*, IX (July 1908), 141–60.

"The Atlantic Pilot" (review). *The Monthly Review; Or Literary Journal*, XLVI (1772), 536–37.

"The Case of McIntosh," *The Georgia Historical Quarterly*, III (Sept. 1919), 131–45.

Webber, Mabel L. (comp.). "Death Notices From the South Carolina and American General Gazette, and its continuation The Royal Gazette, May 1766–June 1782," *South Carolina Historical and Genealogical Magazine*, XVII (Apr. 1916), 87–93.

White, J. E. "Topography of Savannah and Its Vicinity: A Report to the Georgia Medical Society, May 3, 1806," *The Georgia Historical Quarterly*, I (Sept. 1917), 236–42.

Williams, Samuel C. "Stephen Holston and Holston River," *East Tennessee Historical Society's Publications*, VIII (1936), 26–34.

Wroth, Lawrence. *Some American Contributions to the Art of Navigation, 1519–1802*. Providence, R. I.: John Carter Brown Library, 1947.

———— "Source Materials of Florida History in The John Carter Brown Library," *The Florida Historical Quarterly*, XX (Jan. 1940), 3–46.

———— "The Bibliographical Way," *The Colophon*, III, n. s. (spring, 1938), 225–37.

BIOGRAPHICAL AND BIBLIOGRAPHICAL GUIDES

Adams, Randolph G. *British Headquarters Maps and Sketches . . . A Descriptive List of the Original Manuscripts and Printed Documents in the William L. Clements Library. . . .* Ann Arbor, Mich.: The William L. Clements Library, 1926.

Andrews, Charles M. *Departmental and Miscellaneous Papers*. Vol. II of *Guide to the Materials for American History to 1783, in the Public Record Office of Great Britain*. Washington, D. C.: The Carnegie Institution, 1914.

———— *The State Papers*. Vol. I of *Guide to the Materials for American History to 1783, in the Public Record Office of Great Britain*. Washington, D. C.: The Carnegie Institution, 1912.

Andrews, Charles M., and Davenport, Frances G. *Guide to the Manuscript Materials for the History of the United States to 1783, in the British Museum, in Minor London Archives, and in the Libraries of Oxford and Cambridge.* Washington, D. C.: The Carnegie Institution, 1908.

Assiotti, Francis A. "List of Maps, Plans, etc., Belonging to the Right Hon:ble the Lords Commissioners for Trade and Plantations. Under the Care of Francis Aegidius Assiotti, Draughtsman, 1780." Ms. in Public Record Office, London.

Barker, Charles R. "A Register of the Burying Ground of Philadelphia." Ms. volume. Philadelphia, Historical Society of Pennsylvania, 1943.

Biddle, Clement. *The Philadelphia Directory.* Philadelphia: James and Johnson, 1791.

Bonacker, Wilhelm. *Kartenmacher Aller Länder and Zeiten.* Stuttgart: Anton Hiersemann, 1966.

Brun, Christian. *Guide to the Manuscript Maps in the William L. Clements Library.* Ann Arbor, Mich.: University of Michigan Press, 1959.

Catalogue of a Curious and Valuable Collection of Original Maps and Plans of Military Positions Held in the Old French and Revolutionary Wars. Boston, 1862.

Catalogue of the Manuscript Maps, Charts, and Plans, and of the Topographical Drawings in the British Museum. Vol. III. London: By the Trustees, 1861.

Clark, Thomas D. (ed.). *Travels in the Old South: A Bibliography.* Vol. I. Norman, Okla.: University of Oklahoma Press, 1956.

Easterby, J. H. *Guide to the Study and Reading of South Carolina History: A General Classified Bibliography.* Columbia, S. C.: Historical Commission of South Carolina, 1950.

Ewing, William S. (comp.). *Guide to the Manuscript Collections in the William L. Clements Library.* Ann Arbor, Mich.: Clements Library, 1953.

Field, Thomas W. *An Essay Towards An Indian Bibliography, Being A Catalogue of Books, Relating to the History, Antiquities, Languages, Customs, Religions, Wars, Literature, and Origin of the American Indians in the Library of Thomas W. Fields.* New York: Scribner, Armstrong, and Co., 1873.

Guthorn, Peter J. *American Maps and Map Makers of the Revolution.* Monmouth Beach, N. J.: Philip Freneau Press, 1966.

Heitman, F. B. *Historical Register of Officers of the Continental Army During the War of the Revolution, April 1775, to December 1783.* Washington, D. C., 1893.

Historical Manuscripts Commission. *The Manuscripts of the Earl of Dartmouth, American Papers.* 3 vols. London: Eyre and Spottswoode, 1887–96.

Hydrographic Department, Admiralty. *A Summary of Selected Manuscript Documents of Historic Importance Preserved in the Archives of the Department.* Hydrographic Department Professional Paper, No. 13. London: Hydrographic Department, 1950.

Index to the George Washington Papers. Washington, D. C.: Manuscript Division, Reference Department, Library of Congress, 1964.

Johnson, Allen, and Malone, Dumas (eds.). *Dictionary of American Biography.* New York: Charles Scribner's Sons, 1930.

List of Colonial Office Records Preserved in the Public Record Office. London: Public Record Office, 1911.

McManis, Douglas R. *Historical Geography of the United States: A Bibliography.* Ypsilanti, Mich.: Division of Field Services, Eastern Michigan University, 1965.

Maty, Paul H. *A General Index to the Philosophical Transactions From the First to the End of the Seventeenth Volume.* London: The Royal Society, 1787.

Murdock, George P. *Ethnographic Bibliography of North America.* 3d. ed. New Haven, Conn.: Human Relations Area Files, 1960.

Paullin, Charles O., and Paxson, F. L. *Guide to the Materials in London Archives for the History of the United States Since 1783.* Washington, D. C.: The Carnegie Institution, 1914.

Petty, Julian P. *A Bibliography of the Geography of the State of South Carolina.* University of South Carolina Publications, Series II, Physical Sciences, Bulletin No. 2. Columbia, S. C.: Research Committee, University of South Carolina, 1952.

Phillips, Philip L. *A List of Geographical Atlases in the Library of Congress.* 3 vols. Washington, D. C.: Government Printing Office, 1914.

——— *A List of Maps of America in the Library of Congress Preceded by a List of Works Relating to Cartography.* Washington, D. C.: Government Printing Office, 1901.

——— (ed.). *The Lowery Collection.* Washington, D. C.: Government Printing Office, 1912.

Pugh, R. B. *The Records of the Colonial and Dominions Offices.* London: Her Majesty's Stationery Office, 1964.

Reynolds, Emily B., and Faunt, Joan R. *Biographical Directory of the Senate of the State of South Carolina, 1776–1964.* Columbia, S. C.: South Carolina Archives Dept., 1964.

Salley, A. S. *Marriage Notices in the South Carolina and American Gazette, from May 30, 1766, to February 28, 1781.* . . . Columbia, S. C.: Historical Commission, 1914.

Smith, D. E. H. "An Account of the Tattnall and Fenwick Families in South Carolina," *The South Carolina Historical and Genealogical Magazine,* XIV (Jan. 1913), 3–19.

Stevens, Henry. *America: Catalogue of American Maps in the Library of the British Museum, 1856.* London: Henry Stevens, 1859.

Stevens, S. K., and Kend, Donald H. (eds.). *Bibliography of Pennsylvania History.* Harrisburg, Pa.: Pennsylvania Historical and Museum Commission, 1957.

The Catalogue of the Wymberly Jones De Renne Georgia Library at Wormsloe Isle of Hope, Near Savannah, Georgia. 3 vols. Wormsloe, Ga.: Privately printed, 1931.

The Dictionary of National Biography. Oxford: Oxford University Press, 1964.

The National Cyclopedia of American Biography, Being the History of the United States. Vol. XXIV. New York: James T. White & Co., 1935.

Webster's Biographical Dictionary. Springfield, Mass.: G. & C. Merriam Co., 1943.

Who Was Who in America. Vol. I. Chicago, Ill.: A. N. Marquis Co., 1963.

Index